Evaluation Practice in Review

David S. Cordray, *Editor*
U.S. General Accounting Office

Howard S. Bloom, *Editor*
New York University

Richard J. Light, *Editor*
Harvard University

NEW DIRECTIONS FOR PROGRAM EVALUATION

A Publication of the American Evaluation Association

*A joint organization of the Evaluation Research Society
and the Evaluation Network*

MARK W. LIPSEY, *Editor-in-Chief*
Claremont Graduate School

Number 34, Summer 1987

Paperback sourcebooks in
The Jossey-Bass Higher Education and
Social and Behavioral Sciences Series

Jossey-Bass Inc., Publishers
San Francisco • London

David S. Cordray, Howard S. Bloom, Richard J. Light (eds.).
Evaluation Practice in Review.
New Directions for Program Evaluation, no. 34.
San Francisco: Jossey-Bass, 1987.

New Directions for Program Evaluation Series
A publication of the American Evaluation Association
Mark W. Lipsey, *Editor-in-Chief*

New Directions for Program Evaluation is published quarterly by
Jossey-Bass Inc., Publishers (publication number USPS 449-050),
and is sponsored by the American Evaluation Association.
Second-class postage rates are paid at San Francisco, California,
and at additional mailing offices. POSTMASTER: Send address
changes to Jossey-Bass Inc., Publishers, 433 California Street,
San Francisco, California 94104.

Editorial correspondence should be sent to the Editor-in-Chief,
Mark Lipsey, Psychology Department, Claremont Graduate School,
Claremont, Calif. 91711.

Library of Congress Catalog Card Number LC 85-644749

International Standard Serial Number ISSN 0164-7989

International Standard Book Number ISBN 1-55542-969-6

Cover art by WILLI BAUM

Manufactured in the United States of America

Ordering Information

The paperback sourcebooks listed below are published quarterly and can be ordered either by subscription or single copy.

Subscriptions cost $52.00 per year for institutions, agencies, and libraries. Individuals can subscribe at the special rate of $39.00 per year *if payment is by personal check.* (Note that the full rate of $52.00 applies if payment is by institutional check, even if the subscription is designated for an individual.) Standing orders are accepted.

Single copies are available at $12.95 when payment accompanies order. (California, New Jersey, New York, and Washington, D.C., residents please include appropriate sales tax.) For billed orders, cost per copy is $12.95 plus postage and handling.

Substantial discounts are offered to organizations and individuals wishing to purchase bulk quantities of Jossey-Bass sourcebooks. Please inquire.

Please note that these prices are for the academic year 1986–1987 and are subject to change without prior notice. Also, some titles may be out of print and therefore not available for sale.

To ensure correct and prompt delivery, all orders must give either the *name of an individual* or an *official purchase order number.* Please submit your order as follows:

Subscriptions: specify series and year subscription is to begin.
Single Copies: specify sourcebook code (such as, PE1) and first two words of title.

Mail orders for United States and Possessions, Latin America, Canada, Japan, Australia, and New Zealand to:
Jossey-Bass Inc., Publishers
433 California Street
San Francisco, California 94104

Mail orders for all other parts of the world to:
Jossey-Bass Limited
28 Banner Street
London EC1Y 8QE

New Directions for Program Evaluation Series
Mark W. Lipsey, *Editor-in-Chief*

Contents

New Directions for Program Evaluation

A Quarterly Publication of the American Evaluation Association
(A Joint Organization of the Evaluation Research Society and the
Evaluation Network)

American Evaluation Association, 9555 Persimmon Tree Road, Potomac, MD 20854

Editors' Notes

In 1986 the American Evaluation Association (AEA) was formed when its predecessors, the Evaluation Research Society (ERS) and the Evaluation Network (ENet), were merged. In light of this union, it was appropriate to launch the AEA with a retrospective look at evaluation's short but exciting history. To this end, AEA President Richard Light chose "What Have We Learned?" as the organizing theme for the first annual AEA conference. Under this rubric, AEA members were asked to examine progress to date and consider such questions as What are we doing better now than ten years ago? Are there programs that evaluations determine to be especially successful? If so, what is the evidence? Participants were also asked to think more prescriptively about future directions for our field, gaps in knowledge, and recurrent methodological challenges.

To stimulate discussion, the AEA invited a variety of distinguished speakers to comment on past findings and future directions. Some were asked to focus on specific program areas such as mental health, education, and job training, while others were asked to examine the evaluation process itself. The chapters collected in this volume are representative comments on the practice of evaluation. They dramatically illustrate the many lessons learned over the last decade about how to organize, design, and interpret evaluation studies.

The practical and methodological issues facing the evaluation field are complex and challenging. The contents of this volume therefore represent a broad range of topics.

In Chapter One, Eleanor Chelimsky analyzes changes in our understanding of the politics of program evaluation and the implications for commonly held beliefs about how evaluation is accomplished. Chelimsky argues that working with the legislative and executive branches of government requires that evaluators engage in a continuous, five-part translation process.

In Chapter Two, Egon G. Guba systematically reviews the many ways in which our evaluation community defines naturalistic evaluation. He concludes that at least two kinds of naturalistic evaluation exist, and that answering the question "What have we learned?" depends on which kind we consider. Guba distinguishes between practices principally limited to the application of qualitative methods and those that are fundamentally different on ontological, epistemological, and methodological grounds, implying a radically different paradigm for the evaluation specialist. Here, little practical experience has accumulated.

Robert F. Boruch highlights lessons learned from planning and

1

executing randomized field tests of social programs in Chapter Three. Although evaluators know the scientific merits of experimentation, situational constraints continue to challenge those who attempt to mount this type of evaluation. Boruch details specific tactics that have been invented over the past decade to circumvent or accommodate such challenges.

Chapter Four, by William H. Yeaton and Lee Sechrest, is unique in that it pertains to a pervasive methodological issue—the interpretation of no-difference results—that has a long history but remarkably little formal literature. Most evaluators confront such findings often yet, contrary to common beliefs, Yeaton and Sechrest show that (1) it *is* possible to "prove" the null hypothesis, (2) good methodological practices hinge critically on being able to demonstrate no difference, and (3) the same levels of evidence we employ to demonstrate treatment effectiveness are needed to establish no-difference findings. They emphasize the need for theory and *a priori* specification of the expected patterns of data for strong, credible findings.

In Chapter Five, Henry M. Levin briskly summarizes cost-benefit and cost-effectiveness analyses. Using several indicators to assess the extent these analyses have been used to evaluate alternatives, he concludes that they are rarely a formal component of evaluation studies, they are rarely included as part of training programs, and they receive remarkably little serious attention in textbooks. Levin presents several compelling examples that we hope will correct this remarkable oversight.

What Have We Learned?

Several fascinating themes have emerged from our review of these chapters:

1. The role of the evaluation specialist has broadened over the past decade. No longer is the evaluator's role limited to technical issues of design, measurement, and analysis. Boruch identifies several new roles that are necessary to gain cooperation from agency personnel, clients, and other stakeholders. These are consistent with Chelimsky's description of the translation process required to be effective within the political arena. Chelimsky emphasizes the sociopolitical dimension, however. The most radical change in roles is embodied in Guba's naturalistic evaluation of the second kind. He characterizes evaluators as "subjective partners with stakeholders in the literal creation of evaluation data." Chelimsky, in contrast, recognizes the need to avoid partisanship as critical to maintain credibility with clients and other members of the policy-shaping community.

2. Historically, the evaluation community has focused its energy on assessing social programs. The past decade has seen a notable expansion in scope. This includes, for example, evaluation of policy options, such as lengthening the school day or year; management and personnel evaluation, such as teacher quality reviews; and forays into nonsocial programs and problems.

3. These chapters identify several areas that, when looked at in a broader, historical context, appear to have been overlooked or underutilized. Levin's chapter on cost-effectiveness and cost-benefit analyses is an illustration of such an area. The flurry of activity in naturalistic inquiry masks the fact that efforts following what Guba calls "naturalistic evaluation of the second kind" are relatively rare. Further, Yeaton and Sechrest show that there has been little formal attention directed at the interpretation of no-difference findings. Given the centrality of the topic within evaluation research, this is disconcerting.

4. With the exception of Guba's brief description of naturalistic inquiry of the second kind, these papers contain little formal discussion of evaluation's most distinctive feature—the rendering of a finding of merit or worth. However, the language of several authors suggests that future developments, especially in cost-benefit analyses, will correct this oversight.

The chapters in this volume represent a record of the state of the field as of 1986. Judging from the vigorous discussions in many of the AEA conference sessions, it is clear that these chapters represent some of the important lessons evaluators have learned over the past decade. This type of periodic summarizing is a means of acknowledging our collective progress, and a way of discovering where we might profitably build for the future.

David S. Cordray
Howard S. Bloom
Richard J. Light
Editors

David S. Cordray is group director for federal evaluation policy within the Program Evaluation and Methodology Division of the U.S. General Accounting Office, Washington, D.C. Prior to joining GAO, he was a professor at Northwestern University specializing in evaluation methodology.

Howard S. Bloom is an associate professor of public administration at New York University and co-principal investigator for the evaluation of the National Job Training Partnership Act being conducted at Abt Associates, Inc., Cambridge, Massachusetts. He has also been on the faculty at Harvard University.

Richard J. Light is a professor at the Graduate School of Education and the Kennedy School of Government at Harvard University. He is chairman of the Harvard Assessment Seminar, an interuniversity group of faculty and administrators organized to carry out evaluations in colleges and universities.

Evaluation must take into account both executive and legislative politics and their interactions. This implies an evaluation process that can be represented as a five-part continuum, and requires numerous departures from past thinking about evaluation. The evaluator must assume a major share of the responsibility for translating policy questions into knowledge that is credible, timely, responsive, and usable.

The Politics of Program Evaluation

Eleanor Chelimsky

What is meant by the phrase "politics of program evaluation"? Easton wrote that "the study of politics is concerned with understanding how authoritative decisions are made and executed for a society" (Easton, 1957, p. 383), and that "the output of a political system is a political decision or policy" (p. 395). Public policy, then, is the product of politics. Evaluation, with its purpose of providing high-quality information to decision makers, thus automatically claims a role for itself in the political process based on the idea that the best information, made available to decision makers, would certainly be useful to them in making and executing public policy. Unfortunately, in the early 1970s, rumors (confirmed later by studies) circulated that evaluations were in fact seldom used in decision making.

At first evaluators tried to come to grips with the problem in their best Kuhnian fashion by looking for solutions that would not require too many major changes in their paradigm or too many shifts in their methods. Evaluators concluded that their work was not used because some evaluations simply were not good enough (Bernstein and Freeman, 1975), forgetting—or not yet realizing—that policy makers typically use any data at hand (Stromsdorfer, 1981) and that mediocre evaluation work has been used well. Evaluators also theorized that evaluation was perhaps used, but

D. S. Cordray, H. S. Bloom, and R. J. Light (eds.). *Evaluation Practice in Review.*
New Directions for Program Evaluation, no. 34. San Francisco: Jossey-Bass, Summer 1987.

5

that its role was not easily traced because evaluation was just one of many factors influencing decision making (Chelimsky, 1985). Evaluation's use in decision making was too narrow a goal, and there were at least seven meanings attributable to the term *research utilization* (Chelimsky, 1985), and evaluators believed that there was a need to develop information supporting *negotiation* rather than information supporting *decision making* (Cronbach and Associates, 1980). The effect was to turn the question Why isn't evaluation used? into the question What, in fact, *is* reasonable use? This in turn led to the idea that expectations for the use of evaluations were perhaps unrealistically high (Cronbach and Associates, 1980).

However, Weiss (1973) made two crucial points: (1) "As a matter of record, relatively few evaluation studies have had a noticeable effect on the making and remaking of public policy" (p. 40), and (2) "only with sensitivity to the politics of evaluation research can the evaluator be as strategically useful as he should be" (p. 38). Thus the lack of evaluation was seen not so much as a problem that could be solved without major changes in the evaluation paradigm, but rather as the newly perceived and difficult problems of integrating the disparate worlds of politics and evaluation research.

Between about 1975 and 1980, many articles and studies that sought to relate evaluations generally to the larger political and policy context within which they operate were published. It is in looking back today at many of these studies that we can get the best sense not only of what we have learned about politics and evaluation, but also how we have changed in our outlook and practice. Although it was typical in those studies to read statements attesting to the importance of politics to evaluation—statements by Cronbach and Associates (1980) such as "a theory of evaluation must be as much a theory of political interaction as it is a theory of how to determine facts" or "the evaluators' professional conclusions cannot substitute for the political process"—there were not many cogent, action-oriented, systematic, and specific discussions of how the integration of evaluation and politics should or could take place. There were suggestions for the introduction of "research brokerage" (Sundquist, 1978), or of "a bridging function" (Chelimsky, 1977b), both of which sought to solve the integration problem by interposing a mediator between the evaluation and the political user. This suggestion, however, required a new breed of "interface analysts" and never bore fruit, as Sundquist predicted would happen when he broached the idea in 1978.

One reason for the scarcity of concrete suggestions may be that evaluators had little understanding of the political domain with which they had to interact. It was once considered unusual for evaluators from many different evaluative disciplines and from many different substantive program areas to meet with each other or with their policy-making and program-managing sponsors and users in different federal agencies. One symposium resulted in a set of concrete user dissatisfactions with evaluation's performance—many of which were political and unexpected.

Evaluators are often told that their evaluations cannot be used because of bureaucratic relationships and conflicts, that some program managers prefer to be ignorant, and that evaluations will only be used if management really wants them (Chelimsky, 1977b). Evaluation seemed to its users to be an ivory-tower process; and when it emerged from that tower it was too late to be useful, too full of jargon to be understood, too lengthy for the user reading time available, and too prone to be answering a question different than the policy question originally posed (Chelimsky, 1977a). These explanations were important not only because they served as a beginning excursion into the politics of evaluation, but also because the information had a chance of being assimilated or internalized by evaluators, given that most evaluations at that time had been developed for agencies of the executive branch.

Indeed, when Cronbach and Associates published their book on evaluation reform in 1980, many of the lessons of agency politics learned had clearly been integrated by at least some evaluators. However, a political framework comprehensive enough to use for planning evaluation remained elusive, because, for the most part, legislative politics had remained unexamined. This is not a criticism of Cronbach and Associates, but rather a reminder that time passes, experience broadens, and we learn new things.

John Kenneth Galbraith said that each step in a learning process builds on the one before and that critics of the earlier steps are not wiser, only later. However, although Cronbach and Associates (1980) reproached evaluators for taking a much too narrow view of the political arena in which agency decisions are made and evaluation use occurs, this view, in turn, seems narrow today because it failed to include legislative politics.

Considering what evaluators have learned after working with Congress, it seems clear that we need to rethink premises such as "a social agenda almost never calls for a choice between fixed alternatives," or "only rarely are 'go/no go' decisions made," or "timeliness is a much-overrated concern" (Cronbach and Associates, 1980, p. 63). Congress after all does continually make choices between fixed alternatives and does vote on "go/ no go" decisions, and an evaluator who does not understand the critical importance of the timing of congressional policy cycles involving program authorization, reauthorization, appropriations, and budget would be wasting time and money. The importance of timeliness with regard to legislative politics, at least, cannot be overstated (Florio, Behrmann, and Goltz, 1979). Also, without an understanding of legislative politics, we cannot understand—or worse, we actively misunderstand—the dynamics of cross-branch politics—the reciprocal process of legislative-executive agency interactions.

Another result of failing to include legislative politics in our thinking is the way in which we continue to restrict evaluation's application to social issues only. The literature repeatedly mentions evaluation's preoccupation with social programs, social reform, and social concerns. However, legislative politics means that evaluation must broaden its focus to be optimally useful. When working for Congress, evaluators are expected to exercise their skills in all policy areas, social or not.

The evaluator must assume a major share of responsibility for the politics of evaluation. This process is a five-part continuum that first involves the development of a policy question that is then translated into an evaluation question, which typically alters the policy question so that it becomes researchable. Then, in the third part of the continuum, the evaluation question is translated into the evaluation proper: its design, its performance, and the reporting of its findings. The fourth part is the translation back into policy language of the results of the evaluation; the policy answer responds to the original policy question. Finally, the fifth part comports the use of the evaluation findings somewhere in the cross-branch political process, and the return, completing the continuum, to the formulation of new policy questions.

What does such a framework imply in terms of changes from the old evaluation paradigm? I will examine the continuum and see what differences the parts and the whole may make for the way in which evaluators perform evaluation.

Development of the Policy Question

In this framework, the evaluation can no longer be seen as completely a creature of the evaluator's choosing (Weiss, 1973), nor can the evaluator alone determine the questions to be asked about the program (Cronbach and Associates, 1980). Instead, the framework, as applied to evaluation in political arenas means that the choice of the program to evaluate emerges in real terms from the political process, and that decision-makers, whether legislative, executive, or both, determine the types of policy questions to be asked.

As such, this framework empowers the decision-maker and shifts the role of the evaluators from the political role of seeking to reform society, or "to improve the way that society copes with social problems" (Weiss, 1973, p. 42), to the scientific role of bringing the best possible information to bear on a wide variety of policy questions.

This shift is consistent with definitions of evaluation as "the application of scientific research methods to the assessment of program concepts, implementation, and effectiveness" (U.S. General Accounting Office, 1986, p. i), or as the provision of "careful and unbiased data" (Weiss, 1973, p. 37) about programs, or as "a process by which society learns about itself" (Cronbach and Associates, 1980, p. 2). It is not consistent with the notion that "an evaluator should not undertake to serve an agency unless he is in sympathy with its general mission" (Cronbach and Associates, 1980, p. 211) or with program advocacy or partisanship definitions of evaluation in which evaluators seek to be a voice for the program, or a voice for the underdog or another special group. Similarly, it cannot accommodate precepts such as "It is unwise for evaluation to focus on whether a project has 'attained its goals'" (Cronbach and Associates, 1980, p. 5), because such a precept assumes that it is the evaluator who chooses the questions, and the politics of the legislative oversight function may require that evaluators focus on precisely that question.

The primary purpose of a policy question of major concern to politicians is to maximize the use of the findings. When the user generates the questions and when the purpose of the evaluation is to produce information of the best quality for policy or program use, this has the effect of eliminating any congressional suspicions that "the questions set for discovery (by the evaluators) have predetermined answers" or that "the assumed posture of objectivity among program evaluators masks subtle but important biases and hidden agendas" (Chelimsky, 1977b, p. 68).

In legislative politics, the most credible evaluations are those whose use will be maximized. This may seem paradoxical, considering that high methodological quality may not ensure use and that adversaries in the political process will often use any data that support their case (Stromsdorfer, 1981). Evaluators may believe, like Lindblom (1968), that the best way to achieve policy use is through partisan evaluation that supports either the policy makers' ideology or the evaluator's own. But credibility involves more than methodological quality: It involves responsiveness to the specific policy question and information need. Nor does partisan use support an evaluation's credibility. On the contrary, partisanship is at best a short-term strategy for use that is not well adapted to legislative politics. In Congress, partisan work that is well received by one committee may be quickly discredited by another, and worse, the reputation for partisanship would remain with the evaluator over time. Independent analysis that is methodologically strong and seeks to be as objective as is humanly possible serves a much wider legislative audience and can be the focus of debate between committees or even in sessions of Congress. This is not to say that the evaluation will not have a political influence; such an influence is inherent in the fundamental interaction of evaluation and politics. But evaluation's main long-term value to policy is not its capacity for political influence but its contribution of systematic, scholarly, and independent critical thinking to the decision-making process.

There is also a concern that decision makers may fail to ask certain kinds of questions because they do not want to, they do not think of them, or there is not time to obtain answers. I recently explored some of the questions decision makers at different levels and positions in both branches of government tend to ask, and determined that there are areas in which evaluators are not often asked questions despite the fact that they could probably contribute useful answers (Chelimsky, in press). For example, decision makers rarely pose relevant evaluative questions before the introduction of a new program. As a result, there is habitually a serious dearth of evaluative information entering the area of policy formulation in time to influence the proposal.

Many of us spend much time conducting retrospective studies, and these are and will continue to be the focus of evaluation. Congress requests them and asks the executive branch to conduct them; they are a necessary component of evaluation. However, these are not among those evaluations that are most easily entered into the political process, and they may well be the least propitious when practical use is considered. When evaluators at the U.S. General Accounting Office (GAO) conduct evaluations, they always try to focus on what can be accomplished uniquely through legislative means because they know how difficult change is in a long-established, well-entrenched agency program.

By contrast, before a program has started, evaluators can improve the reasoning behind program purposes or goals, identify the problems to be addressed, and select the best point of intervention and the type of intervention most likely to succeed. However, the timing of introducing new programs is critical. Senator Moynihan recently complained that the provisions of the Gramm-Rudman-Hollings bill were still being altered while he was being asked to vote on it. The pace often becomes so frantic that the lead-time necessary to prepare for evaluation is simply impossible to obtain.

The GAO is developing a method I call the Evaluation Planning Review, which is specifically intended to be useful in new program formulation. It is being tested in the evaluation of a proposed program focusing on teenage pregnancy (U.S. General Accounting Office, 1986). The method seeks to gather information about past, similar programs and apply it to the new program. Senator Chafee asked that we examine the bill he was introducing. We were given four months to conduct the evaluation, and it has succeeded from both the legislative and evaluative points of view.

From a more general, political perspective, providing prior understanding about a program's proposed effectiveness can render an invaluable public service either by helping to support a poorly conceived program or by validating the basic soundness of what is to be undertaken. There are useful questions that decision makers do not pose to evaluators; this poses a problem for the framework. However, even when evaluators have been free to choose the questions, this particular type of question has not often been asked. In addition, evaluators can always influence the next round of policy questions through their products.

Translation of the Policy Question into an Evaluation Question

Altering the question is one of the most sensitive and important political interactions in the entire process, and this stage marks the point at which the sponsor will be told whether the policy question is researchable or not. If it is not researchable, this may be because the issue or program is immature; it may be impossible to answer cause-and-effect questions if there has been little or no prior conceptual development in the field to guide the execution of such work. In this case, the question may be transformed from a cause-and-effect format to one that could be answered, if in fact such an answer would also be useful to the decision-maker. Instead of asking what factors cause high quality and productivity in an organization one might ask either what is known about high quality in an organization and how it is defined, or what characteristics of people and work processes exist in a number of selected organizations whose high quality and productivity are recognized. This eminently rational process of transforming a cause-and-effect question into a descriptive question based on evidence of researchability is fraught with risks.

Sponsors resist modification of their policy questions; they may believe that the researcher is substituting his or her wisdom for that of the policy maker. Changes need to be carefully and persuasively explained and negotiated. In addition, findings must be adaptable on a nationwide scale when Congress sponsors the evaluation, whether or not a national study is feasible in terms of time, costs, and the type or locus of the program. In programs heavily dependent on state variation, for example, there is a continuing problem of how to simultaneously obtain in-depth knowledge that can help illuminate that variation and develop more superficial but politically needed knowledge on a national scale—without going bankrupt.

In thinking forward to Part Four of the continuum—when evaluation findings will have to be translated back into policy findings—it is critical for both the evaluator and the sponsor to remember the importance that a powerful methodology will have at that time for being persuasive if the evaluation deals with a controversial policy area. The translation must be made with consideration given to the sponsor's time requirements, the cost, the relation of the type of findings expected to the particular policy need, the kind of program and its locus, the prior research done, and the likely controversiality of the issues.

The evaluator must also think beyond the sponsor to the entire federal context of the program. The question may have been raised by legislative policy actors, but the evaluator knows that executive branch policy actors must be convinced that the recommendations are right and must want to act on them. The evaluator will then have to consider such questions as Have we got the right problem from the agency viewpoint? If they don't think so, is that because it's unimportant or because they just don't want to think about it? Is the question perhaps symptomatic of a deeper problem that should be addressed? Who is in a position to do something about the problem? and What effect would a new administration or change in Senate majority have on the usefulness of the findings? The evaluator may have no control over these issues, but he or she and others may have a great impact on the eventual use of the findings. Legislative evaluators must maintain good relations with executive branch agency evaluators if it is those agencies that must implement the recommendations and ultimately resolve the problem.

A related consideration in conducting the negotiations on the change from policy to evaluation question involves considering the impatience of policy makers and their staffs with the typically equivocal nature of findings. Their political need to take unequivocal policy positions is uppermost. This emphasizes the necessity for evaluators to be aware of the type of political debate into which their finished evaluation will likely enter, and to structure the evaluation design not so as to deal with every conceivable issue, but to produce strong, well-focused, and practical information.

Translation of the Evaluation Question into the Evaluation Proper

The translation part of the continuum involves the actual evaluation. Although the evaluator now begins a phase of the work in which he or she is in at least relative control, both the evaluation design and the writing of the report need to be understood with the political context in mind. Decision makers look forward; evaluators look back. Although policy actors are genuinely interested in knowing what effects a program has had, their interest rarely stops there. The evaluator will be asked to interpret the evaluation findings in prescriptive terms: If it is a descriptive study, there will usually be a normative question posed and an invitation to express what the findings signify for future programs. GAO evaluators have finally grasped that they must expect these questions and, even in an exploratory study for the Congress, they will include a panel of experts, carefully chosen to reflect the widest possible spectrum of political opinion as well as both substantive and methodological expertise. These experts will be utilized to help develop the criteria to make use of in answering the normative questions. For example, in a descriptive management study, how will one decide what degree of communication in an organization is adequate and what degree is inadequate? In a medical study, what counts as "progress," and what counts as "lack of progress" in treatment or patient-management techniques? In a study of research utilization, how many omissions or distortions of the findings does it take to constitute misuse?

Cronbach and Associates (1980) wrote: "An evaluation of a particular project has its greatest implications for projects that will be put in place in the future" (p. 7). Evaluators have learned how to build features into a design that will allow them to more strongly express the significance of their findings for those future projects. This framework also implies the need for a wide range of approaches and methods, often used in combination so that the strengths of one can palliate the weaknesses of another. Responsiveness to a policy question does not allow the luxury of "chapels dedicated to the glorification of particular styles" (Cronbach and Associates, 1980, p. 1). However, the political environment has its exigencies even here. National data are nearly always wanted. There is again a similar kind of mystique surrounding heavily quantitative impact evaluations; congressional staff have more regard for them than any others. As a result, when the evaluation is situated within the confines of an emotional debate, a quantitative, generalizable impact study can protect the evaluator. However, such a study may be neither feasible nor appropriate to the question. Further, even when it is the right study to conduct, if legislative policy staff are given a choice between timeliness and the pervasive powerful methodology, staff will generally choose timeliness, so great are the political pressures of deadlines in Congress. Thus the translation from an evaluation question to a design that is appropriate (both methodologically and politically) is not always easy.

The evaluation design, once it is completed, must be approved. In the executive branch, this is straightforward, but discussion of evaluation designs with legislative staff has been much less frequent. This is a formal procedure in GAO-sponsored evaluations, and discussions about the design are used in several ways. First, the design will have come to some conclusions about the duration of evaluation, what methods will be used, how likely evaluators are to receive answers to the questions posed, how unequivocal these answers are likely to be, how credible the study will be (especially if it is on a controversial subject), and what types and numbers of reports will be produced. The design meeting with the sponsor involves a staff briefing, discussion of any changes the sponsor wants, and finally, agreement on how the evaluation will be conducted and reported. The reporting format—statement of fact, briefing report, testimony, or full-length report—will be based on the sponsor's timing needs.

Design discussions are also used to help familiarize legislative staff with technical aspects of evaluation. Congressional staff may misunderstand if they have not been carefully briefed on exactly what work is being pursued. Overestimations of what can be accomplished in a very short time and evaluation of a new type of program necessitate these discussions. In addition, design meetings typically allow congressional staff to explain how they expect to use the evaluation; this discussion may cause a modification in the design or the planned products. It also exposes evaluators to important cumulative insights into the legislative process and into congressional relationships with the executive branch. Achieving credibility during the conduct of the evaluation is another facet of this stage of the continuum. Although the GAO has a remarkable reputation for institutional objectivity, its evaluators ask independent researchers to periodically review its work. In addition to the previously mentioned panels, the GAO asks different expert reviewers to study its evaluation designs and draft reports.

A Cronbach and Associates thesis advised evaluators "to release findings piecemeal and informally to the audiences that need them" because "the impotence that comes with delay may be a greater risk than the possibility that early returns will be misread" (Cronbach and Associates, 1980, p. 6). This conflicts with former practices, but a worse and much more dangerous possibility is not that those early returns will be misread but that they will actually be wrong because they are early and have not been systematically checked. GAO indexing, referencing, and quality assurance regulations ensure safety in this regard. Staff not on the evaluation team do this work.

Despite the disagreeable nature of the quality control process, nearly everyone considers it indispensable. Evaluators tend not to release information until they are sure it has satisfied the quality control process, because they have learned that it is difficult to recover from a loss of credibility, and that it can prove irrevocable. In sum, while evaluators recognize the value Congress places on early information, credibility is even more important. Whether the issue is fairness, balance, methodological quality, or accuracy, no effort to establish credibility is ever wasted. The memory of poor quality lingers long after the relief after meeting a deadline has been forgotten.

Translation of Evaluation Findings into Responses to the Original Policy Question

At this stage, evaluation results are translated into policy answers to the original policy question. Here, evaluators communicate evaluation findings to a political audience in such a way that the findings will be both well understood and persuasive. In politics, priorities—not ideology, not even consistency or persistency, but putting first things first at the right time—are central. In evaluation, however, this achievement is difficult and in fact is rarely considered at all. Evaluators present their results in careful, neutral phrases, leaving it to the scientifically trained audience to perceive the areas of success, promise, no-result, and failure. They also document thoroughly, usually in the same neutral tone, with what has been described as "self-defeating thoroughness" (Cronbach and Associates, 1980, p. 6). The evaluation's entire set of findings seems important to its author, so it is difficult to order, edit, condense, rank, and select what is feasible.

It is important in a political context to be honest and admit that a conclusive answer is not available when it is not. The knowledge that no knowledge exists is important policy information that decision makers do not necessarily have. For example, an executive agency will inform Congress that there is no evidence of certain unfavorable results in some programs. However, this often means that the agency has not looked for such evidence. This is different from reporting that one has looked seriously and systematically and found no evidence one way or the other. If there is no evidence and this can be shown, then the way is cleared to obtain support for research that will, if possible, develop the needed information.

In trying to make findings clear, useful, and effectively available to policy makers, communication techniques need to be developed that may depart radically from typical evaluation practice. First, evaluation jargon must be banished, not merely for the sake of policy makers, but to avoid communicating that there is a special understanding, an incomprehensible ritual from which they are excluded. An elitist attitude may elicit an impatience and an irritation of the kind that Mencken expressed when he defined a metaphysician as one who, when you remark that twice two makes four, demands to know what you mean by the terms *twice, two, makes,* and *four.* The intelligibility of an evaluation report is critical for the use of the findings.

Second, the written products must be varied so that the information can be presented briefly and succinctly, but is supported by data needed by a variety of audiences. Third, reports must be delivered with as much oral communication as possible, as that style of reporting is most familiar to congressional policy makers. Congressional staff and members of Congress are accustomed to listening to constituents and lobbyists; they gather ideas and form judgments not only by reading but especially by talking with staff and colleagues, holding committee hearings, and interacting personally with a wide variety of people. In this environment, oral briefings are crucial; testimony can be more useful than a major report. Video is also helping to reconcile the tension between the need to document and the need for easy expression and understanding.

Another trend is toward anecdotal answers to policy questions. Evaluators seek the size, range, frequency, direction, and average characteristics of a problem. But evaluators find that one of the most effective ways to present findings is to rediscover the anecdote—to illustrate the general findings with specific cases and analogies that graphically focus attention on and explain the larger points. They do not stand alone as answers to policy questions, but are instead used as representatives of the broader evaluative evidence to explain the findings, increase political understanding and comfort levels, and above all improve the likelihood that the evaluation findings will be used.

Use of Evaluation Findings and Generation of New Policy Questions

In traditional agency-focused evaluation practice, it has often been difficult to trace the use of evaluation findings. This is less true with legislative evaluation. Evaluations have led to program reauthorization, and hearings are often organized around findings. Findings and recommendations are incorporated in legislative direction to the executive branch. Finally, findings used in legislative debates can directly affect congressional votes. In addition, the synthesis method brings together previous evaluations in a topic area and analyzes and compares them with the intent of developing a general finding about knowledge in that area.

Evaluators must influence successive rounds of policy questions that need to be asked but that for one reason or another may not be generated by policy actors. There are two types of questions: descriptive and impact. The first type, descriptive, is a challenging one in that it is difficult to persuade policy makers of the importance of descriptive information. Evaluation of hazardous waste programs found that no one knows how many million metric tons of waste is being generated every year in this country. Questions such as, What is the size of the problem? How many people are involved in the program? What characteristics do they have? What services do they receive and how do they feel about them? or How many messages are sent, who sends them, and who receives them? do not get asked in some agencies and, as a result, more sophisticated questions about program benefits or effects cannot be adequately answered when Congress needs them.

One political factor that contributes to the lack of strong program description is that "the more political support there is for a program, the more limited will be the available *systematic* information on that program" (Stromsdorfer, 1981, p. 6). Defense programs are a good example of this, and the classified nature of the information compounds the difficulty. Tests and evaluation findings are rarely archived even on a need-to-know basis, and every effort to evaluate every weapon system has to start from scratch, but fortunately Congress may reform this process.

However, relatively unpopular programs tend to produce more information and be evaluated more often. Leonard (1986) examines popular and unpopular programs and their ability to spend money without drawing attention to themselves. He documents the Social Security program's ability to commit over $100 billion annually for the last 40 years without much discussion, while political controversy surrounds AFDC's $10 billion annual budget. This is because much systematic descriptive information is available on AFDC, while a host of other more popular programs such as defense and Social Security have been largely able to avoid public scrutiny.

The second type of question that is infrequently asked in executive agencies—it is asked often in Congress—is the impact question. The impediment is twofold: the threat to decision-makers and the paucity of incentives for accountability (Chelimsky, 1977a). There has been a marked reduction in results-oriented evaluations sponsored by the executive branch. If these types of evaluations are to be conducted during the Reagan administration, Congress will have to mandate them, as has often happened in the past. The complication is that the administration has been phasing out much of the data system infrastructure needed to conduct these studies.

Although evaluators have sacrificed their traditional freedom to choose programs and questions in policy studies and have allowed them to emerge from the political arena, this does not mean that they would have been successful in prompting agency policy makers to ask many impact or descriptive questions. When sponsored policy studies are concerned, the evaluator's freedom to ask certain questions has always been nominal. However, by noting the absence of answers to these questions in findings and recommending that these questions be asked, it is possible to ensure that more attention is paid to their importance.

What Have We Learned?

I believe evaluators have learned a number of lessons related to the issues presented throughout this chapter.

1. Evaluators have learned that they must be useful to others, not just themselves. They must understand the political system in which evaluation operates and the information needs of those policy actors who utilize evaluation.

2. They have learned to more broadly conceptualize the political system and include all sectors that make the kinds of policy decisions into which evaluation feeds, including executive and legislative branch policymaking. Indeed, if the judicial branch should continue increasing its use of cost/benefit and risk analysis, evaluators will need to study and include the judiciary as well. Such study would certainly include evaluative and political ramifications of judicial use on decision making in the executive and legislative branches. This is important because evaluation's interactions with legislative and executive branch policy actors can be profoundly

modified by the inclusion of a new set of policy actors from a different branch of government. Policy is never made in isolation: Legislative policy affects executive branch policy integrally, and the converse is equally true. Evaluators need to understand political interactions no matter which branch they are working for.

3. Evaluators working for the legislative branch will be pressed to go beyond earlier social program horizons; congressional functions require evaluative skills in such areas as defense, the environment, energy, natural resources, health, education, and welfare.

4. Planning for use involves understanding the political conditions under which evaluation findings will be used. Two of these conditions are that the policy question posed must be of fundamental interest to the intended user and the eventual evaluation findings must answer that question. Both of these conditions empower the decision maker at the expense of a certain amount of evaluator discretion.

5. Credibility is a third political condition for use. If the evaluation is assailable on grounds of partisanship or poor methodological quality the use of its findings in Congress will be reduced. The high quality and acknowledged objectivity of a study cannot ensure use if the policy question is not of interest; but poor quality and subjectivity will weaken use regardless of the question.

6. Another condition for use is timeliness. Evaluators working for the legislative branch must concern themselves with the timing of the final product and how it coheres with congressional policy cycles and plans for use. An adequate design that will produce findings at the right time is often more important than producing the best design possible.

7. There is no perfect evaluation design; evaluators must try to achieve a balance involving timing, methodological strength, and cost. A methodology that doubles the time necessary for performing an evaluation may be unacceptable regardless of its advantages, but one that increases the time moderately while strengthening the conclusiveness of the information may be enthusiastically accepted under some political circumstances.

8. Planning for use always incorporates the question, Who will implement the study recommendations? Good relations with the implementing executive agency may be essential.

9. Evaluators have not conducted many prospective studies, but they have learned that one of the most felicitous times for the introduction of evaluative thinking into the policy forum is before a new bill is proposed. New techniques need to be developed to enable evaluators to accomplish this on a short time schedule.

10. Carefully chosen panels of experts can legitimize evaluation. They can strengthen the political credibility of an evaluation's findings, especially in a controversial area.

11. Evaluators must master a wide variety of evaluation approaches. No single design or method can be counted on to address the diversity of policy questions that political debates engender.

12. The transition from policy question to evaluative question to evaluation design is not straightforward, and it usually involves several iterations. It is wise to be sure the user agrees with the finished design and understands both how the study will be conducted and what kind of information will be available at its conclusion.

13. Indexing, referencing, and general checking of draft reports are essential steps; although time is important, and planning must take place, there is enormous risk in any weakening of credibility due to errors.

14. Prioritization of the evaluation findings is also a condition for use. It is essential to answer the policy question as clearly and simply as possible, emphasize a few critical and striking numbers, and highlight those findings that give rise to policy action. Much time needs to be devoted to determining how to present findings so that they can be intelligible to several audiences.

15. In the legislative branch, the use of evaluation findings is the rule, not the exception. In the past six years of working with Congress, the GAO's evaluators have learned that evaluations are a demonstrably important adjunct of policy making, they do figure in go/no go decisions, and they often set the agenda for national debates.

16. A further use of evaluations can be achieved via studies employing meta-analysis or evaluation synthesis. Such secondary evaluation is a major tool in helping decision makers make sense of conflicting findings and improve the quality of available information.

17. Policy makers typically do not raise descriptive questions, which means that systematic information about some programs is often missing. Emphasizing in an evaluation report that such information is both missing and needed can increase the possibility that it will be provided later.

18. Impact questions seem to be asked less frequently by executive branch agencies and more frequently by legislative policy makers. A legislative user can have very strong leverage on programs through the authorization and appropriations process or through oversight.

19. Taking political processes into account when conducting an evaluation transforms the way in which time is allocated. Evaluators have learned to devote much more time to negotiation, discussion, briefing, accuracy-checking, prioritizing, and presentation than before.

The use of evaluation congressional policy making is real, measurable, and growing dramatically. But if the profession is making progress, it is due largely to those who expressed failure in the past because they focused our attention on the political environment in which evaluators expected to be useful but knew very little about. This was important

20

because use does not happen by itself. It requires major modifications of traditional evaluation practice, such as those described earlier.

Victory is not yet achieved, and it will elude the profession as long as the Reagan administration continues to cut back its results-oriented evaluation work, although evaluators can hope that executive agencies may soon begin to realize there is growing risk in failing to evaluate their programs: If they do not, legislative agencies will.

However, evaluators have dispelled the notion that their practice is not useful in policy making. Evaluators can be optimistic about the future of evaluation research and practice, given the important role it is playing in improving the quality of information available to decision makers.

References

Bernstein, I. N., and Freeman, H. E. *Academic and Entrepreneurial Research: The Consequences of Diversity in Federal Evaluation Studies.* New York: Russell Sage Foundation, 1975.

Chelimsky, E. *An Analysis of the Proceedings of a Symposium on the Use of Evaluation by Federal Agencies.* Vol. 2. MITRE Corporation, 1977a.

Chelimsky, E. *Proceedings of a Symposium on the Use of Evaluation by Federal Agencies.* Vol. 1. MITRE Corporation, 1977b.

Chelimsky, E. *Program Evaluation: Patterns and Directions.* Washington, D.C.: American Society for Public Administration, 1985.

Chelimsky, E. "The Politics of Program Evaluation." In D. Palumbo (ed.), *Sage Yearbook in Politics and Public Policy.* Beverly Hills, Calif.: Sage, in press.

Cronbach, L., and Associates. *Toward Reform of Program Evaluation: Aims, Methods, and Institutional Arrangements.* San Francisco: Jossey-Bass, 1980.

Easton, D. "An Approach to the Analysis of Political Systems." In *World Politics,* Vol. 9. Princeton, N.J.: Princeton University Press, 1957.

Florio, D. H., Behrmann, M. M., and Goltz, D. L. "What Do Policy Makers Think of Educational Research and Evaluation? Or Do They?" *Educational Evaluation and Policy Analysis,* 1979, *1* (6).

Leonard, H. *Checks Unbalanced: The Quiet Side of Public Spending.* Cambridge, Mass.: Harvard University Press, 1986.

Lindblom, C. E. *The Policy Making Process.* Englewood Cliffs, N.J.: Prentice-Hall, 1968.

Stromsdorfer, E. W. *Social Science Analysis and the Formulation of Public Policy: What the President "Knows" and "How" He Comes to "Know" It.* Conference on Social Experimentation, National Bureau of Economic Research, Hilton Head, S.C., March 5-7, 1981.

Sundquist, J. L. "Research Brokerage: The Weak Link." In *Knowledge and Policy: The Uncertain Connection.* Washington, D.C.: National Research Council, 1978.

U.S. General Accounting Office. *Teenage Pregnancy: 500,000 Births a Year But Few Tested Programs.* (GAO/PEMD-86-16BR), Washington, D.C.: U.S. General Accounting Office, 1986.

Weiss, C. H. "Where Politics and Evaluation Research Meet." *Evaluation,* 1973, *1* (3).

Weiss, C. H. "The Many Meanings of Research Utilization." In E. Chelimsky, *Program Evaluation: Patterns and Directions.* Washington, D.C.: American Society for Public Administration, 1985.

Eleanor Chelimsky is director of the Program Evaluation and Methodology Division in the United States General Accounting Office, Washington, D.C. The views and opinions expressed are her own and should not be construed to be the policy or position of the U.S. General Accounting Office.

Two forms of naturalistic evaluation have appeared in the literature within the past decade. One form treats this perspective as a collection of usually qualitative techniques that are complementary with conventional quantitative methods. The second form represents an alternative paradigm for evaluation. It emphasizes the negotiation of multiple socially-constructed realities, interdependence of facts and values, and the emergent character of the evaluation process.

Naturalistic Evaluation

Egon G. Guba

The attempt to spell out what evaluators have learned about naturalistic evaluation requires a great deal of temerity. I am tempted to answer the question, "What have we learned?" with the curt reply, "Not much!" and let that suffice. But a combination of anxiety and pride impel me to pursue the issue. A difficulty that immediately presents itself can be stated as another question: "Just what *is* naturalistic evaluation anyway?" The terms *evaluation* and *naturalistic* have each been defined in many different ways, so that the number of meaningful combinations of *evaluation* and *naturalistic* must be very large. In addition, although I have my own definition of these terms and their combination, it would be parochial to fail to acknowledge other possibilities.

Thus I felt greatly relieved when a volume of New Directions for Program Evaluation focusing on naturalistic evaluation was published last year. "Surely," I thought, "the volume editor made it clear to the chapter authors what the title implied so that they wrote with a common concept in mind." But I was disappointed. In the Editor's Notes, David D. Williams declared naturalistic evaluation to be equatable with qualitative evaluation: ". . . the qualitative perspective, defensibly obtained, can radi-

Many of the ideas discussed in this chapter are the result of my fruitful collaboration with my colleague, Yvonna S. Lincoln, whose name could for all practical purposes have replaced mine above.

D. S. Cordray, H. S. Bloom, and R. J. Light (eds.). *Evaluation Practice in Review.*
New Directions for Program Evaluation, no. 34. San Francisco: Jossey-Bass, Summer 1987.

24

cally improve many evaluation efforts. More and more evaluators have begun to explore the naturalistic approach to see if and how it may be applied effectively in a variety of settings. Some have attempted evaluations that are exclusively naturalistic (including no quantitative methods) while others have combined naturalistic components (such as participant observations and repeated informal interviews) with more traditional tests, questionnaires, and structured interviews to create mixed-methods studies" (Williams, 1986a, p. 1). Thus, Williams defines naturalistic approaches as essentially acquiring their characteristics by virtue of the methods employed; he notes that it is possible (and perhaps desirable?) to devise mixed-methods studies and thereby achieve an effective accommodation.

Yvonne Hébert, author of the chapter entitled, "Naturalistic Evaluation in Practice: A Case Study," provides a different construction: "What is naturalistic evaluation in practice? Naturalistic evaluation is a process by which evaluators seek to know and understand an evaluand, then to present their knowledge and understanding to others. . . . It involves . . . the act of describing and judging as does any evaluation method. The difference lies in how the description and judgment are achieved and rendered. The generalizations that result from naturalistic evaluation are arrived at by 'recognizing the similarities of objects and issues in and out of context and by sensing the natural covariations of happenings' (Stake, 1978, p. 6). Hence naturalistic evaluation in practice aims at understanding, at extending experience, and at increasing the conviction in that which is known" (Hébert, 1986, p. 3). Hébert evidently believes that naturalistic evaluation is like any other kind of evaluation in purposes (to describe and to judge); it is the way in which one achieves those purposes that makes the difference. Hébert does not describe the method, unfortunately, although one may infer from her case example, which deals with Native American education in British Columbia, that the method is the case study. The product, the case report itself, putatively helps the reader to understand, gain vicarious experience, and build credibility.

In his chapter, "Conceptual Crossroads: Methods and Ethics in Ethnographic Evaluation," David Fetterman poses a third construction. Naturalistic evaluation, he asserts, cannot be understood as a "monolithic entity" (Fetterman, 1986). It is instead a "generic term for many different kinds of qualitative appraisals" (p. 23), among which he lists Lincoln and Guba's (1985) naturalistic inquiry, Eisner's (1979) educational connoisseurship and criticism, Patton's (1980) qualitative evaluation methods, and his own ethnographic educational evaluation. These are all forms of "qualitative and naturalistic evaluation. The tools and designs used in these approaches are very similar. They all require ethical and methodological introspection. Each approach, however, has its own set of standards. The appropriate criteria should be used to judge the success or failure of each approach" (Fetterman, 1986, p. 23). One is left to wonder why these various forms of essentially the same conceptual approach should each require its own set of goodness criteria.

In her chapter, "The Whole Is Greater: Combining Qualitative and Quantitative Approaches in Evaluation Studies," Mary Lee Smith offers a fourth construction specifically directed at the issue of terminology:

> A brief digression . . . is made necessary by the difference in terminology in the title of this chapter, which uses the term *qualitative,* and the title of this issue of New Directions for Program Evaluation, which uses the term *naturalistic.* For the purposes of this chapter, a qualitative approach involves the long-term and first-hand study of a case by the investigator for the purpose of understanding and describing human action in the context of that case. Field methods are used to collect data, including direct observation of action in its natural context, clinical interviews to elicit the multiple meanings of participants in that case, and collection of documents. A qualitative approach leads to reports primarily in the form of words, pictures, and displays rather than formal models or statistical findings.
>
> In my view, *qualitative* is a broader term than *naturalistic* or *ethnographic* and encompasses both inductive and hypothetico-deductive processes of inquiry as well as disciplines not limited to anthropology [Smith, 1986, p. 38].

For Smith, naturalistic evaluation is a subtype of qualitative evaluation. But the term *qualitative* as she uses it surely denotes a paradigm rather than merely a set of methods. Her introduction of the terms *natural setting* and *multiple meanings of participants* adds a dimension missing in the other formulations, and suggests a break from conventional thinking about inquiry.

In their chapter entitled, "On Your Own with Naturalistic Evaluation," Sari Knopp Biklen and Robert Bogdan pose a fifth construction, which makes the distinction implied by Mary Lee Smith overt and unmistakable: "Naturalistic methods can be used in two ways. First, and less forcefully, they can be used as techniques in a study that has not been framed from a naturalistic perspective. . . .

Second, the evaluator conceptualizes the study around what we call 'thinking naturalistically.' That is, the evaluator approaches reality as a multilayered, interactive, shared social experience that can be studied by first learning what participants consider important. In this case, the first days in the field are spent learning how participants think about and conceptualize issues" (Biklen and Bogdan, 1986, p. 95). Thus, Biklen and Bogdan identify two quite distinct modes of working with naturalistic approaches: as a collection of tools and techniques—the methods level—or as a wholly different way of viewing the world—the paradigm level. Nevertheless, they assert, these two apparently distinct approaches (naturalistic approaches of the first and second kind) "share some common threads when they are applied to naturalistic evaluation" (p. 95). These common threads include collecting descriptive data in the natural setting, with the evaluator serving as the inquiry instrument; focusing on "educational issues as they are perceived and experienced by people" (p. 95); and utilizing an inductive analytic process that focuses and narrows as the evaluation proceeds.

Even when naturalistic methods are used simply as techniques, they nevertheless have many properties that are also typical of the approach in which the evaluator thinks naturalistically. It is not surprising that there exists widespread confusion about whether the term *naturalistic* denotes technique or paradigm, although many more individuals adhere to the former than to the latter viewpoint. It is possible to use naturalistic techniques—alone or as part of a multimethods study—without stirring from the friendly confines of the traditional inquiry paradigm. Thinking naturalistically, however, requires a paradigm shift of revolutionary proportions that, once made, inevitably changes both the meaning and practice of evaluation in similarly revolutionary ways.

How Has Naturalistic Evaluation Been Used?

The five exemplar definitions I have cited provide ample evidence that there is no agreement on just what naturalistic evaluation is. Each author has his or her own construction, a state of affairs that comes as no surprise to a naturalist. Because the term *naturalistic evaluation* has so many different meanings, one expects that the ways in which naturalistic evaluation is reported to have been used should also be quite variable. Unfortunately, most reported uses exemplify Biklen and Bogdan's (1986) category of naturalistic methods rather than "thinking naturalistically." However, the vast majority of published reports of putative naturalistic evaluations can be classified into one or more of the following categories:

Exploration. Naturalistic approaches can be used to explore areas that are initially impossible to conceptualize, and so lay the basis for a more rigorous investigation later. The parallel distinction in research is often termed the *discovery/verification dualism.* Typically discovery is excluded from formal definitions of scientific method; the source of the theories, hypotheses, or questions that an inquirer aims to study is somewhat irrelevant to the scientific enterprise. It is important that a verification (falsification?) study be designed that tests hypotheses or answers questions in as rigorous a manner as possible. As John Kennedy (in Farley, 1986, p. 6) succinctly states: "Qualitative research . . . represents, for the most part, only one, albeit very exciting, stage of research. It is found, oftentimes, at the very beginning of the inquiry, the initial stage in the larger process of research. It is part of a larger drama where one becomes immersed in the data to generate insights. . . . The (qualitative methods) are great vehicles for the generation, for the positing of inferences that can eventually lead to research questions and hypotheses. But they constitute only one part, only one component, only one stage of the larger pursuit of trying to generate stable knowledge."

An interesting application of exploration is found in that subset of stakeholder-oriented evaluations that utilize qualitative methods to elicit audience inputs about the issues or questions which the evaluation should pursue, but that are otherwise conducted conventionally. An example is the evaluation of Push/Excel, sponsored by the National Institute of Education (NIE), as proposed by the Rev. Jesse Jackson (NIE, 1978). In their discussion of this case Farrar and House (1983, p. 35) point out that the Request for Proposal (RFP) for this evaluation "gave potential bidders considerable latitude. Since the evaluation would have several audiences—parents, teachers, community members, policy makers, and evaluators—the contractor was to consult with panels representing these groups during the design and implementation of the evaluation. Noting that this approach implied 'no technical compromises which will satisfy consumers but (lack) methodological rigor and clarity,' the request for proposals outlines seven questions that the contractor was to address" (NIE, 1978, pp. 8-9). The stakeholder surveys are regarded as explorations intended to yield questions with which the evaluation might deal in addition to those stipulated by NIE. But there were to be no compromises on the technical adequacy and rigor of the evaluation methodology; verification was the primary aim.

The concept of *exploration* should not be confused with that of *grounding* (Glaser and Strauss, 1967; Glaser, 1978; Lincoln and Guba, 1985), a matter of crucial importance to naturalistic evaluation. Exploration is seen by those such as Kennedy who advocate it as a beginning point, whereas the process of grounding is seen by its advocates as continuously evolving throughout an evaluation, not achieving fruition until the end point.

Description. Naturalistic approaches can be used in the service of description in two ways. First, in contrast to those approaches that, in the name of control, engage in context stripping (isolation from confounding variables), naturalistic evaluation emphasizes the crucial nature of context, arguing that context not only gives meaning to a phenomenon but is the very basis of its existence. Changing contexts distorts and may also eliminate a phenomenon. Thus, it might be argued, evaluations are incomplete unless they provide, in the language of Geertz (1973), "thick description" of the context so that the evaluand can be fully appreciated in respect to its situatedness.

As an example, consider the series of five case studies carried out by Skrtic, Guba, and Knowlton (1985) that assessed services provided to handicapped children by cooperatives in rural areas of the United States. Each of the five sites was studied in detail over two years, and qualitative and quantitative information was amassed about each. Each site was studied in relation to the requirements of PL 94-142 (The Education of All Handicapped Children Act), corresponding state legislation, state and local history and culture, characteristics of the served and unserved local handicapped populations, and so on. The case reports ranged in size from about 120 to 200 typewritten pages, with a large part of each devoted to detailed descriptions of the context in which the local cooperative was situated. The intent of the investigators was to provide the case study readers with a vicarious experience of what each site was like.

A second use of description in naturalistic evaluation is to support the ongoing monitoring of the processes involved in implementing an evaluand. There are very few quantitative indices that can assess ongoing process; indeed, it was the utter inability of physicists to deal with process within the atom that gave rise to the black box model of research: alter inputs and assess resulting outputs to infer process that cannot be observed directly. But direct observation of process *is* possible, at least to some extent, in virtually all human sciences. Qualitative methods can be used to elicit, record, and describe these processes, as constructed by the humans involved.

As an example we may consider the case study of a preschool art class carried out by Swann (1986). Her interest was to determine, by close observation over a year's time, the developmental patterns young children exhibited as they interacted with a number of teachers and a variety of materials in response to both open-ended and structured assignments. She documented developmental patterns as they related to peer and teacher interactions, particular activities, teaching strategies, and materials. She supplied detailed descriptions, including photographs, of the intervening processes. Events and outcomes could be understood as they occurred *in situ* rather than either being posited *a priori* and tested, or postulated *ex post facto*, both of which strategies are more common in conventional inquiry.

Illustration. Naturalistic approaches can be used to illustrate or exemplify what has been uncovered at a more general level through more rigorous forms of evaluation. An example may be found in the U.S. General Accounting Office (1982) study of the effects of block grant funds in selected cities. The case cited in this report, that of Dallas, was one of a series of four that was carried out. The hard data for the overall study, of which the case studies were a part, were derived from returns to a questionnaire sent to 650 cities. The case studies were "not intended to comprehensively evaluate program effectiveness" but to "provide insight on the kind and extent of housing activity under the Community Block Grant Development Program" (U.S. GAO, 1982). Files were reviewed, sites visited, and photographs taken, to illustrate the findings that the master study suggested.

Realization. Naturalistic approaches can be used to help audiences realize—in the sense of "make real"—both the particulars of a case and the construction of those particulars entertained by each of the separate audiences. In detailing particulars, cases are said to provide depth or realism to an evaluation. Cases can provide anecdotal materials. Cases can provide vicarious experience from which the reader can evolve "naturalistic generalizations" Stake (1978). Smith (1986, p. 37) states: "It happened during a post-mortem of a recent evaluation of the practices and effects of retaining children for a second year in kindergarten. I (the qualitative or naturalistic analyst) complained that no one remembered anything about the study except its statistical outcomes. My colleague, Lorrie Shepard (the quantitative analyst) confessed jealousy of my direct contact with the rich and meaningful evidence from interviews with teachers and observations of classrooms. I was 'close' to the data; she was quoted in the headlines of the newspaper." The electric effect of incisive cases on the White House is well known. Debate in Congress over authorizations or appropriations relating to handicapped children is punctuated by a steady procession of such children to testify; seeing is believing.

Some of the best examples of this use of naturalistic evaluation is found in the contributions of various students of Eisner, such as the excerpts reprinted in *The Educational Imagination* (Eisner, 1979). One begins with these gripping sentences: "This classroom is almost a caricature of the society. The curriculum is served up like Big Macs. Reading, math, language, even physical education and affective education are all precooked, prepackaged, artificially flavored" (p. 229).

Another example is the description of the Pine Springs School found in Cahan, Filby, McCutcheon, and Kyle (1983), one portion of which begins: "Until the December holidays, Mr. Jameson's classroom had been a bookroom. After class begins in the converted bookroom, the expelled books lean against one another, neglected in sagging cartons in the hall immediately outside his room" (p. 91). These brief quotations provide a sense of what it means to write a case in a way that will enable the reader to realize—make real—a situation.

The second sense of *realize*—to bring to life the varying constructions of different audiences, or even of different individuals—is more complex than the first. A good example can be found in Bogdan, Brown, and Foster's (1984) study of a critical care neonatal unit. In their summary the authors state:

> When we first asked the physicians what they told parents about their children's condition they said, "We are completely honest." Similarly during our first visits, when we

asked nurses what they told parents, they said, "Everything."
These phrases have a special and circumscribed meaning for
those who work on neonatal units. Further, in our interviews
with parents and through observations we began to see the
other side of staff/parent communication. What physicians
and other hospital staff thought they said to parents was
often not what parents heard. Our research was guided by
the questions: Who talks to parents? What do they say? What
do parents hear? Our presentation reveals that there are no
simple answers to these questions. Only through a description of salient aspects of the setting can we begin to grasp
the meaning, process, structure, and entangled communication in such a complex environment [p. 190].

Testing. Naturalistic approaches can be used to test hypotheses or
to answer questions that the investigator specifically targets ahead of time.
An interesting example is found in Pierce (1981). The author investigated
whether governmental bureaucracy was capable of implementing laws in
ways consistent with the intent of legislators. He developed a series of
cases, typically based on the data available from one or more completed
evaluations. Each case study was examined from the point of view of the
question, "Once a law is passed, under what conditions will the bureaucracy fail to give political leaders exactly what they ordered?" Conclusions
were reached by assimilating each case into a master table of conditions
that were themselves identified from one or more of the cases as contribut-
ing to failure. The individual cases served as the units of analysis in reach-
ing overall judgments. A similar approach is taken in the case survey
aggregation method proposed by Lucas (1974a, 1974b).

In another example, Roncek and Weinberger (1981) conducted an
evaluation in San Diego to test the hypothesis that certain federal funds
available to support public housing were used in ways that concentrated
such housing in less desirable portions of the city. The city itself was the
case unit; examination of characteristics of matched city blocks that did
and did not contain public housing led the evaluators to conclude that the
program was not "able to provide low-income households with 'suitable
living environments'" (p. 231).

So-called critical case sampling is often used when the purpose of a
case study is to test *a priori* hypotheses or answer *a priori* questions. The
logic of this approach, as succinctly put by Patton (1980), is this: "If it's
true of this one case, it's likely to be true of all other cases" (p. 105).

Two other observations are in order. First, although I have identified
five types of use—exploration, description, illustration, realization, and
testing—it should be clear that these types are not pure. Indeed, each of the
examples cited above exhibits the characteristics of one or more types other

than the type to which I arbitrarily assigned it. The typology is justified by its conceptual, analytic utility rather than by its pragmatic soundness.

Second, in most published studies naturalistic methods are not used independently but in tandem with more conventional methods in two ways. First, some studies can be characterized as side-by-side applications. These studies should not be confused with competitive studies; they do not represent horse races between naturalistic and conventional approaches. They are not a way of deciding which approach, quantitative or qualitative, yields better or truer or more complete information. They are, instead, a way of exploiting their putative complementarity. As Smith (1986) states:

> In designing the study, Shepard and I felt that the most persuasive study would be one with the strongest quantitative design but with a concrete and compelling narrative account as well. The quantitative portions of the study included an analysis of the costs of the process of identification, surveys of perceptions of the professional groups involved with identification, analysis of rates of prevalence of the learning disabled in Colorado, and a survey of pupils currently identified as learning disabled to document their characteristics. The qualitative portions of the evaluation included a linguistic analysis of definitions and diagnostic criteria of learning disabilities, a critique of tests used in identification, interviews with directors of special education, and a qualitative analysis of records of pupils so identified [p. 44].

More common than this side-by-side approach is the so-called multi-method or mixed-method approach. Naturalistic and conventional techniques have been mixed and matched in different ways, including by alternation, to facilitate the emergence of the evaluation or inquiry design (Sieber, 1973); by comparison, to provide a basis for triangulation (Denzin, 1978; Smith and Kleine, 1986); by offsetting obtrusiveness, to insert a qualitative unobtrusive nonreactive technique to augment data collected by more conventional—but also more reactive—means (Williams, 1986c); and by integration, to capitalize on the synergistic effects of multimethods (Smith and Kleine, 1986).

Accommodation Between Conventional and Naturalistic Paradigms

The possibility of the multimethod or mixed-method approach has led some evaluators to the conclusion that an accommodation is possible between the conventional and the naturalistic paradigms. But mixed-method designs are possible within either paradigm. One can use both quantitative and qualitative techniques in combination whether the paradigm of orientation is naturalistic or conventional. It would be patently absurd to suggest that evaluators whose paradigm of orientation is the conventional are limited to quantitative methods, or that evaluators whose paradigm of orientation is the naturalistic are limited to qualitative methods. But no possibility exists that there can be an accommodation at the paradigm level. What I call naturalistic evaluation of the first kind is possible within either paradigm, but naturalistic evaluation of the second kind ("thinking naturalistically," to return to Biklen and Bogdan's [1986] felicitous phrase) is necessarily bounded by the assumptions of the naturalistic paradigm. Naturalistic evaluation in this sense takes its meaning from the ontological, epistemological, and methodological assumptions of naturalism, and these are fundamentally at odds with those of positivism.

The Nature of the New Paradigm

It is useful to compare the development of a paradigm, and its implications, to the development of a geometry. In studying Euclidean geometry, one is told that one will learn how to prove a series of propositions about geometric spaces by referring them back to a basic set of axioms or assumptions. These axioms are self-evidently true; anything logically derivative from them must therefore also be true. The proof of theorems deriving from those axioms becomes a not always simple but always merely technical exercise in logical deduction.

Euclid had set himself the task of developing a proven set of theorems about geometry because of their importance for land surveying (note that the term *geometry* means "measurement of the land"), a highly arcane art in his time (the third century B.C.). Surveyors had many rules of thumb in which they believed implicitly, but had never been able to establish as undeniably true. Euclid aimed to rid these insights of their rootless condition. Beginning with four simple axioms (for example, given two points it is possible to connect them with a straight line) Euclid was able to demonstrate that many of the rules of thumb, now more reverently titled *theorems,* were rooted in the axioms; accept the axioms and the theorems were indubitably true. But one of the theorems he set out to prove turned out to be intractable. Finally, Euclid simply set this intractable theorem aside. But because he needed that theorem to prove certain others, he designated it as a fifth axiom, even if it was not quite so self-evidently true.

Euclid's fifth axiom has never been shown to be a logical consequence of the original four axioms; it retains its position as an axiom to this day. But in the many hundreds of attempts to derive a proof, mathematicians stumbled across entire new geometries (the so-called non-Euclidean geometries). Because the proposed theorem had not yielded to direct proofs, indirect proofs were tried. In one such approach the proposition to be proved is replaced by its opposite in the hope that this opposite

13. Change is a linear process that moves rationally from research through development and diffusion to adoption.

14. Evaluation is a form of scientific inquiry and hence has all the attributes of that genre.

15. Evaluation produces data untainted by values. Values are inexclusive to the evaluation process and distort scientific data by, for example, biasing them.

16. Accountability can always be assigned because it is determinable through the relevant cause-effect chain.

17. Evaluators can find a place to stand that will provide the leverage needed for the objective pursuit of evaluation activities.

18. Evaluators are the communication channels through which literally true data are passed to the audiences of evaluation reports.

19. Scientific evaluation data have special legitimacy and special status that confer on them priority over all other considerations.

13. Change is a nonlinear process that involves the infusion of new information and increased sophistication in its use into the constructions of the involved human constructors; the infusion derived from naturalistic inquiry is but one kind of information that will be (and probably should be) taken into account.

Theorems Applying Specifically to Evaluation

14. Evaluation is a form of naturalistic inquiry and hence has all the attributes of that genre.

15. Evaluation produces data in which facts and values are inextricably linked. Valuing is an intrinsic part of the evaluation process, providing the basis for attributing meaning.

16. Accountability is a characteristic of a conglomerate of mutual and simultaneous shapers, no one of which nor no one subset of which can be uniquely singled out for praise or blame.

17. Evaluators are subjective partners with stakeholders in the literal creation of evaluation data.

18. Evaluators are orchestrators of a negotiation process that attempts to culminate in consensus on better informed and more sophisticated constructions.

19. Evaluation data derived from naturalistic inquiry have neither special status nor legitimation; they represent simply another construction to be taken into account in the move toward consensus.

Several features of Table 2 are delineated here:

1. Many of the theorems hold for all forms of inquiry, by which I mean to include research and policy analysis as well as evaluation (Lincoln and Guba, 1986). Certain others have been included because of their special relevance for evaluation. Note the very different positions taken with respect to valuing and accountability, both of which are currently hotly debated issues.

2. The theorems are not listed in any priority order, although in a few cases selected theorems seem to be more encompassing than others, or logically prior.

3. There are no theorems dealing with criteria for judging the goodness of an inquiry. As has been shown (Morgan, 1983; Smircich, 1986), the criteria of goodness that are appropriate to an inquiry carried out within a particular paradigm are grounded in the identical assumptions that undergird the paradigm itself. Criteria appropriate to a scientific inquiry are not appropriate to a naturalistic one, and vice versa. Lincoln and Guba (1985) have treated the problem of goodness criteria and have proposed two sets of criteria for naturalistic studies: one that is parallel to conventional scientific criteria and another that is directly indigenous to (rooted in) naturalistic assumptions.

4. There are no theorems that deal with ethical considerations. On reflection, that should not be surprising; the table is meant to be contrastive, and scientific inquiry has no place in its formal structure for ethical considerations. Because of its claim that facts and values are independent

Table 3. The Ten Commandments of Evaluation:
Principles to Guide Fourth-Generation Evaluation Activities

1. Evaluation is a process whereby evaluators and stakeholding audiences jointly and collaboratively create (or move toward) a consensual valuing construction of some evaluand. It does not yield irrefutable, empirically confirmed information.

   Corollary 1A: Evaluation creates reality.

   Corollary 1B: The consensual valuing construction that is the product of evaluation is subject to continuous reconstruction (change) including refinement, revision, and replacement.

2. Evaluation is a process that subsumes both data collection and data valuing (interpreting) in an inseparable and simultaneous whole.

   Corollary 2A: No portion of the evalution process can be considered to be value-free.

3. Evaluation is a local process. Its outcomes depend on local contexts, local stakeholders, and local values, and cannot be generalized to other settings.

Table 3. *(continued)*

Corollary 3A: Evaluation data from other settings cannot be applied to local settings (although they may adapted).

4. Evaluation is a sociopolitical process. Social and political considerations, far from being distracting or distorting nuisances, are integral to the evaluation, and are at least as important as technical considerations.

5. Evaluation is a continuous, recursive, and divergent process, because its findings are created social constructions that are subject to reconstruction. Evaluations must be continuously recycled and updated.

   Corollary 5A: A good evaluation raises more questions than it answers.

   Corollary 5B: A good evaluation has no natural end point.

6. Evaluation is an emergent process. It cannot be fully designed in advance, for its focus (or foci) depends on inputs from stakeholders and its activities are serially contingent.

   Corollary 6A: Evaluation is a process with outcomes that are unpredictable in principle.

7. Evaluation is a process for sharing accountability rather than for fixing it.

8. Evaluation is a process that involves evaluators and stakeholders in a hermeneutic relationship.

   Corollary 8A: Evaluation is a joint process in that it integrates the constructions of stakeholder groups and the constructions that the evaluator(s) bring to the evaluation in an emergent etic-emic blend. It aims toward consensus but requires, at a minimum, the clarification of competing constructions. Evaluation thus implemented is an educative activity for all.

   Corollary 8B: Evaluation is a collaborative process in that the several stakeholder groups share control with the evaluators over the methodological and interpretive decisions that are made. Evaluation thus implemented is an empowering activity for all.

   Corollary 8C: Evaluation is a process that eliminates the distinction between basic and applied inquiry. Evaluation thus implemented simultaneously aids understanding and clarifies the nature of needed action.

   Corollary 8D: Evaluation is a process whose proper conduct requires the evaluator to engage in face-to-face interactions with individual stakeholders; effective evaluation cannot be accomplished at a distance.

9. Evaluators play many unconventional roles in orchestrating the evaluation process—collaborator, learner, teacher, reality shaper, mediator, and change agent—in addition to the more conventional but reinterpreted roles of technician (as a human instrument), describer (as an illuminator and historian), and judge (as orchestrator of the judgmental process).

10. Evaluators must possess not only technical expertise but also a variety of relevant interpersonal qualities. Perhaps chief among these are patience, humility, openness, and adaptability.

entities, and that science is value-free, the scientific paradigm can deal with ethics only as an external constraint, as evidenced by the existence of such entities as human subjects committees or statements of professional ethical standards. In contrast, the naturalistic paradigm demands ethical behavior as an essential part of its methodology; deceiving respondents (a term preferable to *subjects*) cannot lead to clarification of their emic constructions nor provide the basis for a hermeneutic dialectic.

Implications for Evaluation

My colleague Yvonna Lincoln and I believe that the implications of this discussion for the day-to-day practice of evaluation to be so strong that the kind of evaluation that takes proper account of them deserves a very different name from that of the past. We have referred to this new evaluation as *fourth-generation* evaluation (Guba and Lincoln, in press). We have chosen this term to reflect our construction that the new evaluation represents a distinct advance over each of the previous three generations: measurement, description, and judgment. The key concept of fourth-generation evaluation is negotiation, both in the sense that the process of evaluation is essentially one of negotiation with and among stakeholders, and that the product of evaluation is not construed as a series of conclusions and recommendations but as an agenda for further negotiation.

Thinking along these lines has led us to develop the ten commandments of evaluation, the principles that fourth-generation evaluators need to keep in mind while actually conducting an evaluation (Table 3). This list, like those preceding, is neither patent nor self-explanatory, but it is worth patient examination and contemplation.

Two Definitions of Naturalistic Evaluation

I began with the question that was posed to me: "What have we learned about naturalistic evaluation?" It is clear now that the answer to that question depends on how naturalistic evaluation is defined. There is no consensus on its definition, but, especially because of Biklen and Bogdan (1986), we discovered that there might be variations on two central themes. Theme one—naturalistic evaluation of the first kind—treats naturalistic evaluation as a collection of usually qualitative techniques. Theme two—naturalistic evaluation of the second kind—treats naturalistic evaluation as a new way of constructing the world, a wholly different paradigm.

Biklen and Bogdan's first theme demonstrates that naturalistic evaluation has achieved widespread use and general acceptance. We have learned how to use naturalistic (qualitative) methods for the purposes of exploration, description, illustration, realization, and testing. But these purposes are typically served within the confines of the conventional, scientific paradigm. In retrospect, it seems odd to me that there should have been so much heated debate between advocates of quantitative and qualitative approaches, because there should never have been any doubt that both kinds of methods were useful. That they can also be used in complementary ways (side-by-side or mixed-method) is a kind of added bonus. We can thus conclude that we have learned much about naturalistic evaluation of the first kind.

However, Biklen and Bogdan's second theme indicates that there exists very little systematic thinking about what a wholly new world view might mean or imply, and few illustrations in the literature on which we can draw. In relation to this definition of naturalistic evaluation we have learned little. However, this different paradigmatic approach may have more than a little utility for evaluation and evaluators. On their face naturalistic axioms and theorems look outrageously bizarre. Given the extensive and intensive socialization we all have had to bear in relation to the scientific paradigm, it is not surprising that our first reaction should be to want to reject them as nonsense. But suspend your disbelief and consider whether this approach may not mirror more faithfully your own experience. In the end, it may lead to a more productive way of doing evaluations, a way that is both educative and empowering for all.

References

Biklen, S. K., and Bogdan, R. "On Your Own with Naturalistic Evaluation." In D. D. Williams (ed.), *Naturalistic Evaluation.* New Directions for Program Evaluation, no. 30. San Francisco: Jossey-Bass, 1986.

Bogdan, R., Brown, M. A., and Foster, S. B. "Be Honest but Not Cruel: Staff-Parent Communication on a Neo-Natal Unit." S. J. Taylor and R. Bogdan (eds.), *Introduction to Qualitative Research Methods.* (2nd ed.) New York: Wiley, 1984.

Cahan, L., Filby, N., McCutcheon, G., and Kyle, D. *Class Size and Instruction.* New York: Longman, 1983.

Denzin, N. K. *Sociological Methods.* New York: McGraw-Hill, 1978.

Eisner, E. W. *The Educational Imagination.* New York: Macmillan, 1979.

Farley, F. (ed.). "The Debate." *Midwestern Educational Researcher,* 1986, 7, 5–33.

Farrar, E., and House, E. R. "The Evaluation of Push/Excel: A Case Study." In A. S. Bryk (ed.), *Stakeholder-Based Evaluation.* New Directions for Program Evaluation, no. 17. San Francisco: Jossey-Bass, 1983.

Fetterman, D. M. "Conceptual Crossroads: Methods and Ethics in Ethnographic Evaluation." In D. D. Williams (ed.), *Naturalistic Evaluation.* New Directions for Program Evaluation, no. 30. San Francisco: Jossey-Bass, 1986.

Geertz, C. *The Interpretation of Cultures: Selected Essays.* New York: Basic Books, 1973.

Glaser, B. G. *Theoretical Sensitivity: Advances in the Methodology of Grounded Theory.* Mill Valley, Calif.: Sociology Press, 1978.

Glaser, B. G., and Strauss, A. L. *The Discovery of Grounded Theory.* Chicago: Aldine, 1967.

Guba, E. G., and Lincoln, Y. S. "The Countenances of Fourth-Generation Evaluation: Description, Judgment, and Negotiation." In D. J. Palumbo (ed.), *The Politics of Program Evaluation.* Beverly Hills, Calif.: Sage, in press.

42

Hébert, Y. M. "Naturalistic Evaluation in Practice: A Case Study." In D. D. Williams (ed.), *Naturalistic Evaluation*. New Directions for Program Evaluation, no. 30. San Francisco: Jossey-Bass, 1986.

Lincoln, Y. S., and Guba, E. G. *Naturalistic Inquiry*. Beverly Hills, Calif.: Sage, 1985.

Lincoln, Y. S., and Guba, E. G. "Research, Evaluation, and Policy Analysis: Heuristics for Disciplined Inquiry." *Policy Studies Review*, 1986, *5*, 546–565.

Lucas, W. *The Case Survey and Alternative Methods for Research Aggregation*. Santa Monica, Calif.: Rand, 1974a.

Lucas, W. *The Case Survey Method: Aggregating Case Experience*. Santa Monica, Calif.: Rand, 1974b.

Morgan, G. *Beyond Method: Strategies for Social Research*. Beverly Hills, Calif.: Sage, 1983.

National Institute of Education. *Evaluation of Project Excel*. (FRP-NIE-R-78-0026) Washington, D.C.: The National Institute of Education, 1978.

Patton, M. Q. *Qualitative Evaluation Methods*. Beverly Hills, Calif.: Sage, 1980.

Pierce, W. S. *Bureaucratic Failure and Public Expenditure*. New York: Academic Press, 1981.

Roncek, D. W., and Weinberger, G. E. "Neighborhoods of Leased Public Housing." *Evaluation Review*, 1981, *5*, 231–244.

Sieber, S. D. "The Integration of Fieldwork and Survey Methods." *American Journal of Sociology*, 1973, *78*, 1335–1359.

Skrtic, T. M., Guba, E. G., and Knowlton, H. E. *Interorganizational Special Education Programming in Rural Areas: Technical Report on a Multi-Site Naturalistic Field Study*. Washington, D.C.: National Institute of Education, 1985.

Smircich, L. "Behind the Debate over the Validity of Alternative Paradigm Research." Paper presented at the annual meeting of the American Educational Research Association, San Francisco, April 16–20, 1986.

Smith, L. N., and Kleine, P. G. "Qualitative Research and Evaluation: Triangulation and Multimethods Reconsidered." In D. D. Williams (ed.), *Naturalistic Evaluation*. New Directions for Program Evaluation, no. 30. San Francisco: Jossey-Bass, 1986.

Smith, M. L. "The Whole Is Greater: Combining Qualitative and Quantitative Approaches in Evaluation Studies." In D. D. Williams (ed.), *Naturalistic Evaluation*. New Directions for Program Evaluation, no. 30. San Francisco: Jossey-Bass, 1986.

Stake, R. E. "Should Educational Evaluation Be More Objective or More Subjective? More Subjective!" Paper presented at the annual meeting of the American Educational Research Association, Toronto, Ontario, Canada, April 11–15, 1978.

Swann, A. C. "A Naturalistic Study of the Art-Making Process in a Pre-School Setting." Unpublished doctoral dissertation, Indiana University, 1986.

U.S. General Accounting Office. *Housing Block Grant Activity in Dallas: A Case Study*. CED-82-75. Washington, D.C.: U.S. General Accounting Office, 1982.

Williams, D. D. "Editor's Notes." In D. D. Williams (ed.), *Naturalistic Evaluation*. New Directions for Program Evaluation, no. 30. San Francisco: Jossey-Bass, 1986a.

Williams, D. D. (ed.). *Naturalistic Evaluation*. New Directions for Program Evaluation, no. 30. San Francisco: Jossey-Bass, 1986b.

Williams, D. D. "When Is Naturalistic Evaluation Appropriate?" In D. D. Williams (ed.), *Naturalistic Evaluation*. New Directions for Program Evaluation, no. 30. San Francisco: Jossey-Bass, 1986c.

Egon G. Guba is professor of education at Indiana University. His sustained interest in naturalistic evaluation has produced several books on the topic and numerous published articles.

Randomized field experiments have been regarded as a gold standard in producing good evidence about the effects of social programs. But they have not been easy to conduct. In the past decade, the use of alternative randomization plans and incentives has contributed to their operational feasibility; legal, ethical, and professional arguments for experimentation have matured; and expectations have become better aligned with practical constraints that are likely to be encountered.

Conducting Social Experiments

Robert F. Boruch

The concern among evaluators lies with an important means of discovering what is good, in a special sense, about a class of societal action. The focus is on randomized field tests of social programs, projects, or program elements. Such tests involve the random assignment of individuals or other entities to one of two or more regimens to permit a fair comparison.

One virtue of the random assignment is the guarantee of equivalence of the groups so assigned, at least in the long run, apart from the relative effects of the regimens. This virtue was recognized over a century ago by Jastrow and Peirce in psychophysical laboratory experiments (Stigler, 1978). The second virtue, actualized more recently by Kempthorne (1952), is that one can construct a statistically coherent statement of one's confidence in the randomized experiment's results. The ability to construct such a statement is important in medicine, education, engineering, and

Work on this topic has been supported at Northwestern University by the National Science Foundation and the Rockefeller Foundation and at the Center for Advanced Study in the Behavioral Sciences by the Spencer Foundation. Excerpts were presented at the annual meeting of the American Evaluation Association, October 31, 1986. I am indebted to Byron Brown, Shel Stryker, Lincoln Moses, Phoebe Cottingham, and Rob Hollister for recent conversation on the topic.

D. S. Cordray, H. S. Bloom, and R. J. Light (eds.). *Evaluation Practice in Review.*
New Directions for Program Evaluation, no. 34. San Francisco: Jossey-Bass, Summer 1987.

45

elsewhere. It is important here if the object is to produce interpretable evidence that informs decisions about what is good and to produce durable understanding.

Randomized experiments have not been easy to conduct, partly because of the political, ethical, and other difficulties they engender. The question posed for this chapter is: What have we learned about randomized field experiments? This question for the thoughtful inquirer provokes others:

- Who has learned about randomized experiments?
- What has been learned about their value?
- What has been learned about our capacity to conduct experiments?
- What has been learned about willingness to experiment?
- What has been learned about chronic issues?
- What are implications for the future?

Answers to such questions have been generated by a small but vigorous community of scholars, bureaucrat-scholars, practitioners, and even politicians. The benchmarks for progress here include the monograph by Riecken and Boruch (1974) for the Social Science Research Council and Campbell and Stanley's (1966) classic.

Randomized Field Experiments

Relying on the production of scholarly tracts on a new topic as an indicator of new understanding is dangerous. Despite, this, let me mark progress in randomized social experiments using this indicator, recognizing that learning proceeds well in advance of the printed word.

Textbooks that cover the mathematics of experimental design have been available for over forty years. In the 1960s, however, there were no major textbooks dedicated to the realities of randomized field experiments in the social and behavioral sciences. Campbell and Stanley's (1966) work is a remarkable exception, although they confined their ingenious attention to analytic realities. In 1977, Fairweather and Tornatsky (1977) demonstrated to mental health researchers how, when, and why randomized tests of rehabilitation programs can be run. Since then, the Federal Judicial Center (1983) produced an important monograph on the ethical propriety and desirability of experiments in the courts. The economists received Ferber and Hirsch's (1982) work on experiments to understand the effects of negative income tax plans on welfare reliance and work, of housing supports for the poor, and of peak load pricing in energy consumption. Updated reports on these experiments and thoughtful essays on the technical and policy issues they engender are given in Hausman and Wise (1985).

The thoughtful critic might object to this kind of evidence: Who aside from scholars, reads academic articles? Indeed, few are read even by scholars. In any case, real understanding in this area may be reflected better in contemporary events. There have in fact been major institutional changes in who appears to know about experiments. Whereas in 1976 few members of the U.S. General Accounting Office (GAO) were informed about the topic, in 1986 an entire division is acquainted with this and related technologies; for example, the Program Evaluation and Methodology Division directed by Eleanor Chelimsky (see Chapter One). Similarly, the Evaluation Division of the Food and Nutrition Service of the U.S. Department of Agriculture, directed by Michael Wargo and the Office of Research of the U.S. Internal Revenue Service, directed by Frank Malanga, have staff who employ experimental methods in the interest of improving cost control of government programs.

Randomized tests over the last decade have become part of the intellectual and administrative armament of the Division of Criminal Justice Research directed by Joel Garner at the National Institute of Justice. Intramural research at the National Institute of Mental Health has, with some courage, begun to mount trials to understand effects of therapies. Also, Manpower Research at the Department of Labor has had hard experience in mounting randomized trials to understand who benefits from employment and training programs.

The state-level and local institutional learning is no less important than that at the federal level. Learning in these arenas has indeed occurred, exemplified by the commitment of eight state governments to the experimental testing of work/welfare plans (Gueron, 1985). The learning is apparent in cleanly written requests for evaluation proposals issued, for example, by New York State's Department of Social Services (1986) for randomized tests of programs for welfare recipients with very young children. It is evident in the contribution of police departments in Charlotte, North Carolina; Atlanta, Georgia; Dade County, Florida; Colorado Springs, Colorado; Milwaukee, Wisconsin; and Omaha, Nebraska, to replicating the Minneapolis, Minnesota, department's experiments on police handling of domestic violence (Sherman and Berk, 1985). Those involved in tests of the Rockefeller Foundation's Minority Female Single Parent program have also learned and have often been models for evaluation researchers.

What of learning among public representatives? The indicators are weak. Part of what can be learned is reflected in information provided by the research arms of legislative bodies. The U.S. GAO's (1986) report to Congress on teenage pregnancy, for instance, is conscientious in differentiating more trustworthy from less trustworthy studies, and takes pains to identify the randomized tests. Testimony offered by Robert Hollister on behalf of the National Academy of Sciences Committee on Youth Employment Programs emphasizes how credibility of available evidence depends on the strengths of research designs (Betsey, Hollister, and Papagiordiou, 1985). Part of what is learned is reflected in legislative product. California's

GAIN legislation for example, is explicit in authorizing randomized controlled tests of employment and training approaches for the poor and badly educated.

What of private foundations? A few have been courageous in trying to discover the effects of the programs whose development they support. The Russell Sage Foundation, for instance, made distinctive early contributions in supporting experiments; Meyer and Borgotta's (1959) experiment on work-related rehabilitation of the mentally ill was the first of its kind. The Ford Foundation's recent contribution has led to remarkably good experiments on employment and training programs for the retarded (for example, Bangser, 1985). The Rockefeller Foundation, a recent entry to the field, has supported both program development and tests of programs for minority female single parents.

The Scientific Value of Experiments

Understanding the value of randomization did not come easily to Sir Ronald Fisher, the idea's developer, nor did he always find it easy to communicate the notion to his colleagues. In response to his opponents, who maintained that one should select and assign entities purposively to each regimen being compared, he said: "Systematic arrangements [for example, the purposive allocation tactics] are devised to deal with only a certain sort of devilish scheme. But the devil may choose any arrangement, even that for which the systematic design is least appropriate. . . ." (Box, 1978, p. 145). To avoid the devilish scheme, Fisher argued that one should rely on chance as well as on what is known, exploiting the theory of chance to accommodate the unknown influences.

More effective, perhaps, than a simple argument is an empirical comparison of the results of nonrandomized experiments against results achieved in randomized trials. This is an important idea, but it is not new. Fisher tried such a comparison in the 1930s, using research data on wheat and Charles Darwin's data on stock fertilization (Box, 1978). In the wheat case, the results of the experiment differed from those of the quasi-experimental tests, and results appear not to have differed in the reanalysis of Darwin's data.

Similarly, trials on the Salk vaccine gave estimates of the vaccine's effect based on randomized tests that differed from estimates based on non-randomized quasi-experiments (Meier, 1972). One of the best of recent texts on medical clinical trials takes pains to summarize differences between the results of randomized and nonrandomized trials of anticoagulant therapy for myocardial infarction cases, the use of the portocaval shunt, and other similar cases (Friedman, Furberg, and DeMets, 1981). In addition, Gordon and Morse (1975) found remarkably different estimates of social program effects when the evaluation design was taken into account, as did Glass and Smith with regard to the effect of class size on students' learning (see Light and Pillemer, 1984).

In this respect, recent comparisons of randomized and nonrandomized tests of manpower programs are important. The tradition of estimating program effects in manpower has customarily been based on econometric models. In the absence of a randomized trial, the econometrician posits an explicit statistical model on which to base estimates of program effect. Considerable progress has been made in assessing the errors in specification of these models in recent years, by Leamer (1983) among others. That sophisticated econometric models are at times inappropriate is clear from work by Fraker and Maynard (1985) and LaLonde (1986). In particular, a broad array of such models produced results that differed widely from well-run randomized field tests of programs on similar populations for youth. The experimental and quasi-experimental results, however, did not differ appreciably for samples of welfare-supported women with children.

The tension between modellers and randomizers, of course, is longstanding. It continues insofar as modellers are willing to trust their models and experimenters are unwilling to accept the assumptions those models require. It is fruitful insofar as the experimentalists take the time to discover the conditions under which their colleagues in the modelling camp are correct and incorrect.

The capacity to conduct randomized social experiments is important, and difficult to develop. It demands competent staff, money, and time. It means understanding, controlling, and tolerating or relaxing constraints on the randomization process, and requires developing special technical abilities. Riecken and Boruch (1974) dedicated considerable attention to the problem of how to randomize; the matter is fundamental to the integrity of the experiment after all. Their advice is still sound, judging from experience of the last decade. Much of this experience, however, is not reflected in the printed work. However fragile the latter may be, it is more durable than oral history. Werner Wothke and I, reckoning that able experimenters should write about their deeds, asked a variety of them to describe how they managed the randomization process (Boruch and Wothke, 1985). The contributors conclude that different, simultaneous randomization plans are essential. The most important of such plans involves constructing incentives and accommodating or removing disincentive to randomize. Because incentives bear more generally on willingness to experiment, it is discussed in the next section. Here, six other important types of randomization plans are summarized from recent work.

Pilot Tests of Randomization Procedures. Understanding how to field-test new programs in new contexts is complicated, and argues for pilot tests of experimental procedures such as those conducted in administrative justice research by Corsi and Hurley (1979). It argues for a grace period, or preexperiment running time or scouting (Riecken and Boruch, 1974), for any trials that cannot include formal pilot tests of research procedures. The cost engendered by this is obvious, but time is essential to ensure that supplied instructions actually work.

Control and Monitoring. Ensuring control over the randomization process is critical, judging from surveys by Conner (1977), for instance; and from such cases, such as those by Roos, Roos, and McKinley (1977) and Boruch and Wothke (1985). It is as easy to subvert randomization in social research as it is in medical trials. Who or what is to be excluded from random assignment should be specifiable beforehand, as it has been in the best of medical and social experiments. When exclusions are not foreseeable, pilot tests of the randomization process are warranted to discover which exclusions are critical. Moreover, regardless of the control that is thought to be exercised, surveillance of the actual randomization is essential.

The importance of control and monitoring of the randomization to the experiment's integrity is sufficient to justify description in final reports on experiments and conscientious checking of the ways in which groups that are purported to be randomly composed actually appear similar. The reports by Kerachsky and others (1985) on tests of training and employment programs are exemplary on both accounts, describing the control and the evidence on equivalence of groups that sustains the claim of good control relative to both number of individuals in each group who differ and percentage difference on variables such as age, secondary handicaps, living arrangements, and so on.

Negotiative Plans. No social experiment is approved without a good advocate who knows how to negotiate. Randomized experiments are not yet a natural, acceptable part of our environment; they must be sold. The greater part of selling in many settings is negotiation. This means understanding why experiments may be justified, judged legal, tailored so as to be ethical relative to local standards, and so on. It means being able to develop *quid pro quo*'s that meet a variety of stakeholders' objectives.

Contingency Plans. What can fail often will fail, so it seems sensible to design plans that recognize the fragility of randomized tests. The best of experimenters integrate contingency designs with randomized tests to ensure that if the randomization is subverted, then alternative (weaker but defensible) evidence is generated. (See Figure 1 in Lerman and others,' 1986, work on food stamp registration; it combines a time series with a randomized trial.)

Treatment and Control Plans. Certain features of program and control conditions may be flexible. This allows for negotiating in the interest of good evidence and a good program. For instance, delays in the delivery of services to some individuals, such as those randomly assigned to a control condition, is tolerable in some cases, but not in others. Similarly, developing a major program and a weak variation on the program is possible in some sites. In still other cases, one knows that extremes in need or merit will require limits on those randomized. One may rule that, for example, the worst criminal offenders, or the most needy poor, badly educated women with children may be automatically treated and excluded from randomization.

Manipulatable Features of the Experimental Design. Once said, it is obvious that units of randomization are manipulatable. One may, for instance, randomize schools or school districts rather than students in testing alternative regimens. One might randomize neighborhoods or groups or small geographic districts, as has been done in tests of fertility programs, court procedures, and nutrition-cultural enrichment programs, respectively. The units of randomization are one of a variety of important manipulatable features of design. (See Shadish, 1986, for new perspectives.) Balancing the need to produce evidence against local needs can be achieved at least partly though adjusting these features.

Similarly, the ratio of those assigned to treatment versus control is controllable. Ensuring that there are twice as many treated as untreated subjects in some settings, such as the Minority Female Single Parent Program, satisfies program staffers' needs to serve as many as possible without affecting the integrity of the experiment, although the tactic does affect statistical power.

Also, good statisticians know that blocked randomization can improve precision and informativeness of a research design. (See Riecken and Boruch, 1974, for nontechnical discussion and Cochran and Cox, 1950, or Kirk, 1982, or Winer, 1971, for technical discussion.) One of the lessons of the short history of field experiments is that blocked randomization is fundamental—at times critical—to the operational feasibility of an experiment. For instance, a field test that draws potential clients from numerous referral agencies must maintain good relations with those agencies to obtain the potential participants for the test. A completely random allocation scheme could yield disconcerting runs; for example, some referrals could be assigned to the control condition or all to the program condition. Blocked randomization such as allocation by pairs or quartets and so forth within an agency avoids the problem.

Society's Willingness to Conduct Randomized Experiments

Unwillingness to mount a randomized trial is not a new phenomenon. In the 1930s, Sir Ronald Fisher's superiors were experienced, well regarded, and informed about his work, but they failed to adapt his methods quickly to their own research, partly on account of the novelty of the idea of randomization (Box, 1978). Evaluators knew in the 1970s that they should have been able to explain a randomized experiment and why it is desirable, and to debate the whys in public forums. Evaluators did not realize that they had to explain the process better than Fisher could in order to do justice to the idea or to meet the demands of sophisticated audiences.

Scientific Incentives. The scientific justification for randomized assignment is generating a less equivocal, unbiased (or less biased) estimate of the relative effects of regimens or programs. It also represents a formal statistical statement about one's certainty in results. This reason is persuasive to scientists and some scholar-bureaucrats. It has at times also been persuasive to some judges asked to participate in court experiments (such as in Goldman, 1980), welfare program decision makers who must be able to justify their choices of welfare rules in public forums (such as in the case of Gueron, 1985), in tax administration (Perng, 1985), and in police departments concerned with how they can most effectively reduce domestic assaults (Sherman and Berk, 1985).

The rationale of better evidence is used, and is often useful, in arguing for randomized experiments across a variety of substansive areas. That this rationale is often not sufficient to generate support is also clear. Other incentives are worth considering for those whose responsibility lies in meeting other interests.

Monetary Incentives. If people are paid to participate in a randomized experiment, they will often agree to experiment. If they are not paid, prospects are much less promising. Further, the promise of future reward can be significant. For example, an important justification for the participation of certain community-based organizations in the Minority Female Single Parent program experiment was the hope that the experiment would demonstrate the worth of the program and support requests for the government or foundation or community sponsorship of future programs.

The fiscal vehicle for introducing such incentives is usually the Request for Proposal (RFP). A formal invitation is proffered by government or a private foundation to conduct the experiment. When an RFP prescribes randomization in medical tests, for instance, hospitals that are willing to collaborate respond. In the social sector, the Treatment of Depression trials mounted by the National Institute of Mental Health, described by Collins and Elkin (1985), are among the first to use this mechanism in the evaluation of treatments for mental illness.

The Work/Welfare Initiatives described by Gueron and Nathan (1985) took a different approach to employing fiscal incentives. Ford Foundation funds could be leveraged by a state to make additional funds available for mounting tests of new workfare programs. In the Rockefeller Foundation's Program for Minority Female Single Parents, community-based organizations are supported to develop a coherent array of services. They were further supported for their participation in randomized tests of the program. In a school system context Bickman (1985) took pains in his statewide education experiments to ensure that control schools received funds and technical assistance for their participation.

Monetary incentives have not been uniformly successful. Institutions have agreed to randomize and then have not, finding that they were unable or unwilling despite the money provided to implement the design. The National Congress of Neighbor Women in 1984–85, is an example of this kind of failure. Threats to withdraw funding for failure to deliver are, in principle, useable. It is difficult, however, to find illustrations of experiments sponsored by governments or private foundations that have been terminated on this account.

Debates About Propriety. Debates over social, individual, or professional propriety of randomized experiments can be complicated. But the occasional collision of different ethical systems seems no more complicated than it was in the eighteenth century. In Boston at that time, Cotton Mather introduced trial inoculation for smallpox and attempted to introduce it on a larger scale to stem the epidemic disease. To judge from able historians such as Cohen (1982), Mather and others believed that presenting good evidence based on limited-scale work would help inform a decision to adopt inoculation on a larger scale. Others regarded pilot evidence as irrelevant, arguing that any inoculation program interfered with God's wishes. There were also those who managed to obtain and interpret evidence purporting to show that inoculation was ineffective. It is interesting and perhaps a lesson that both empirical camps eventually exploited theological argument to make their cases.

Riecken and Boruch (1974) recognized the issue, dedicating considerable attention to ethical and legal problems engendered by randomized tests. Since then, what has been learned bears chiefly on the quick but often naive critic's complaints about a randomized allocation to a new program or to control conditions, namely: It is illegal, it is immoral, and it is no fun.

Considering law, for example, randomized field tests have been considered by the courts, legal counsel, advocacy groups, and constitutional scholars. The attention is limited but has been productive. Pertinent federal court decisions include *Aquayo* v. *Richardson* and *California Welfare Rights Organizations* v. *Richardson* (see the legal analyses given by Breger, 1983, and Teitelbaum, 1983). These cases, which were both dismissed, challenged the use of randomized experiments in assessing alternative approaches to health insurance and welfare. Bermant, Kelman, and Warwick (1978), the Federal Judicial Center (1983), and Rivlin and Timpane (1975) give more general treatments based less on case law than on broader ethical standards. Statutes that explicitly authorize randomized experiments are scarce, however, and that is one reason for being attentive to and encouraging explicit reference to randomized experiments in law. This does not mean randomized tests are always legal. It does mean that the equal protection clause is often immaterial and that evaluators understand something of the conditions under which it is immaterial (Breger, 1983).

As for immorality, Donald Campbell (Campbell and Stanley, 1966) appears to have been first in the social research arena to give life to a kind of fundamental ethical rule in deciding whether to randomize. The rule, simply put, is that when there is an oversupply of eligible recipients for scarce program services, randomized assignment of candidates for the resource is fair. Vancouver's Crisis Intervention Program for youthful offenders, for instance, offered equal opportunity to eligible recipients. (See Boruch and others, 1979.) Since all participants could not be accommodated well with available program resources, but were all equally eligible, they were randomly assigned to program or control conditions.

Exploiting the Campbell rule and others developed to meet good ethical standards, randomized experiments are most likely to be regarded as ethical when the services are in short supply, their effectiveness is not clear, and someone is interested in credible evidence about a regimen's effectiveness. This rationale coheres neatly with some administrative interests. Despite the aspirations of program advocates, for example, new programs cannot be emplaced all at once, but must be introduced in stages; as a result, services for some are delayed.

The argument that random assignment accords with good ethical standards with scarce resources is not pertinent when the program manager can simply spread resources more thinly, for example, by expanding the size of classes dedicated to special instruction in tests of training projects. Indeed, we have encountered managers of community-based organizations who maintain that they can always spread resources thinly. Others observe, however, that this ignores quality control.

We have also learned something of the negotiable features of this ethical problem. Being able to deliver a new program's services to two-thirds of a group seems to be more ethical to some human services program managers than delivering services to only one-half of them. The reverse may be true for criminal justice efforts. Why this should be the case is immaterial here. Altering the ratio of those involved in a new exercise relative to those provided service in a conventional way meets concerns about professional and social ethics, at least at times. It is a manipulatable feature of experiments that can make them more ethical, and represents something of what has been learned.

Operational Problems and Their Solutions

Once a commitment to experiment is made, other problems occur. Their nature, severity, and tractability vary depending on the context. The issues considered in what follows are illustrative and bear mainly on human resources experiments.

Target Groups. The target group is always smaller than anticipated. Even when individuals can be identified, they are difficult to entrain in the experiment. Program managers who promise to randomize sometimes merely presume the target population is large enough to supply both program and control conditions. This presumption has been wrong at times in medical research; for example, in the case of experiments in day-care for the chronically ill during the late 1970s. It has also been wrong in educational research, notably in attempts to conduct randomized field experiments on Head Start preschool programs in planned variations. And it has been wrong in manpower training programs before 1966, to judge from Rossi's (1969) description of the failure of the National Opinion Research Center (NORC) to recruit enough clients for early experimental tests of an employment training program. If there are too few individuals who are in need of the service and accessible and willing to participate, one will be unable to execute an experiment well.

The reasons for error in the presumption include ignorance: It is often difficult to estimate the number of those in need of special services, more difficult to identify them, and at times more difficult still to understand how to involve them in a program. The reasons include greed: The funds made available for an experiment can produce inflated counts of those in need.

Anticipating the problem is one of the lessons of the last decade. Consider, for instance, the randomized field tests reviewed by the Committee on Youth Employment Programs (Betsey, Hollister, and Papagiordiou, 1985). While many of these tests had sufficient participants, there have been notable exceptions.

In the CAVD program, for example, all CETA (Comprehensive Employment and Training Act) prime sponsors were to recruit a pool of at least 200 youths who met eligibility requirements and who desired and were available to be assigned to alternative treatments. Difficulty in recruitment was encountered in four of five sites. The difficulty was serious and said to have been caused by internal organizational problems such as a move to a different building or interinstitutional problems, as when one agency conducted the screening and another the program implementation. Similarly, the Project STEADY evaluation reported that "sufficient numbers of youth were difficult to recruit" (Grandy, 1981), while the SPICY project for Indochinese youths obtained only 70 to 80 of the 120 youths per site. Many other programs reported similar difficulties.

Obtaining good survey or record-based estimates of local target population size is fundamental to design and tests of programs. Relying on existing data is usually impossible, however. The targets are often special; for instance, minority female single parents or high school dropouts. Record systems are often inadequate and the time available for surveys and scouting is often short.

A second approach is to pilot test the experimental design itself. One might, for example, test in a city to estimate the number of those warranting attention, learn to recruit participants, control flow, and then mount a statewide test. Or one may design a five-year experiment, in which the first year is a pilot year, the data from which would not be considered reliable. Self-conscious pilot tests of the first kind have been run in administrative law experiments by Corsi and Hurley (1979), and a related strategy on experiments in postprison income support is represented in Rossi, Berk, and Lenihan (1980). The first year of randomization for the Rockefeller Foundation's Minority Female Single Parent Program experiments was a pilot year of the second kind.

A third option is the training and use of outreach specialists who are sophisticated in communicating about a program, generating interest among potential participants, and bringing them to the enrollment stage. The use of such specialists was significant in the Rockefeller trials to generate the sample sizes necessary to compensate for the lack of ability (or willingness) of referral agents to supply participants. The best of the outreach people know about marketing research and advertising, and learn how to inform and attract the special target population of interest.

Attrition. Attrition will occur at any stage in the experiment that it can occur: between recruitment and assignment, assignment and initial participation, initial participation and completion, completion and follow-up study. The problem is usually most severe for control group members.

Individuals who voluntarily participate in any social program are also free to abandon the program. Individuals who participate in a randomized control group or some alternative to which they have been randomly assigned are also free to withdraw. The loss of contact with individuals in either group is important insofar as it affects how easily and confidently one can interpret the results of an experiment. If contact is lost with individuals in either group, there is no clear way to determine the project's impact on participants.

If the program maintains good contact with the participants, for instance, but fails to track nonparticipants well, it may generate evidence that makes the program look damaging when it is ineffectual, or that makes the program appear effective when its impact is negligible or even negative. When the attrition rate in the program group differs appreciably from the rate in the control group, making inferences is more complicated. For instance, personnel experiments may indicate that all individuals who left the control group found jobs. Analysis that fails to recognize this would produce inflated estimates of the program's effect.

Problems in attrition in field experiments were sufficiently critical to warrant the Committee on Youth Employment Program's decision to reject over half of them for serious review (Betsey, Hollister, and Papagiordiou, 1985). This does not always imply that the work is unsalvageable;

merely that resources do not permit determining if the analytic problems engendered by attrition could be resolved. CAVD's differential in rate of interviewing, for instance, was substantial—80 percent for the participants and 50 percent for control subjects. There was no discussion of the potential problems, and no attempt was made to accommodate them in the report at hand. Tallmadge and Yuen's (1981) study of the Career Intern Project, however, is unusual in its attempt to accommodate the possible biases due to differential attrition by matching individuals first and then keeping only full pairs for analysis. They achieved rates of 50 to 70 percent for all four sites.

Evaluators knew that the problem of attrition was severe ten years ago; and they realize it better now. Improvements on the standard array of solutions to the problem are available: monitoring and controls in both the program and the research. None of the solutions for the research component of the experiment differ much from what is available in the survey research literature (Boruch and Dennis, 1986).

Experiment Stability. The stability of some experiments is influenced heavily by the involvement of program staff (practitioners) and referral agents that identify and screen candidates for random assignment. The experiment's stability is undermined to the extent that turnover among these is high or shifts in position are frequent, or that problems emerge that they cannot manage neatly.

Consider, for example, that staff members in the service organization will often be suspicious of random assignment and may misunderstand it and object to it on both irrelevant and legitimate grounds. One obvious option is to take the tasks of identifying, recruiting, and assigning individuals to the program entirely out of the hands of service staff. The subsequent problems turn around the fit between those referred and those who can actually be treated well through the service.

A second solution is to explain randomization in different ways to satisfy normal diversity of concerns among staff. Moreover, it must be explained repeatedly in the interest of compensating for staff turnover and the actual difficulty in understanding it. The repeated contacts are in addition essential to adjusting the randomization so as to satisfy local concerns that emerge during the test. A third solution is to train core individuals to explain and construct explanations—to sell the experiment. The group may consist entirely of insiders who learn through role-playing, trial runs, or focus groups. Their stability is important and so must be monitored.

Similarly, referral agents in human services projects will object when individuals whom they refer to service are deprived of that service on account of random assignment. Boards of directors for service agencies, potential sponsors, and donors may register similar objections. The strategies that apply to staff apply also to referral agents, donors, and so on. Three additional strategies are also likely to be helpful.

First, design experiments so that individuals are randomized within the agency. One of every pair of individuals provided by the agency is assigned to service and one to control. The paired assignment prevents the embarassment of a random string of control assignments and makes pipeline flow more predictable and manageable. Second, recognize that referral agents often cannot supply as many referrals as they believe they can. Further, train and use special outreach people to circumvent both referral agency incapacity to supply people and their occasional unwillingness to do so. Third, recognize that selection ratios in service programs vary appreciably and that no one knows them. The ratio of applicants to enrollees is typically unknown, as is the drop-out rate. In experiments, it is known. This leaves the questionable option of simply withholding information about specific ratios.

Treatment Delivery. Treatments may not be delivered as expected. Targeted recipients may receive less treatment than intended, different treatment, or no treatment. Controls may receive unintended treatment or unknown alternate treatment. Randomized tests are not especially informative unless one knows something about treatment and control conditions. This realization is far deeper now than in the 1960s and early 1970s. It is further understood that evaluators cannot treat social programs as unknown factors, treatment programs are rarely delivered as planned, and context is important.

Contemporary stress on what happens in the program under scrutiny has been influenced partly by colleagues of the naturalistic observation school, Guba and Lincoln (1981), House (1980), Stake (1975), and their colleagues. (See Cronbach, 1982, for a general discussion.) Contributions of those of the implementation analysis school have also been influential, especially those with an economic and policy slant such as Bardach (1977). At its crudest, measuring implementation may focus on structural features of the program's construction. So, for example, early research on food stamp recipients who were required to register for work found registration rates of 30 to 60 percent, depending on the site. In newer field experiments, procedures for failure to comply with requirements were created and used in 20 percent of cases, and registration rates were boosted substantially. Implementation study was integrated with the new food stamp-registration and job search experiments (Lerman and others, 1986).

It is also reasonable to expect local processes to influence implementation. Tallmadge and Yuen's (1981) report, for example, stresses staffing problems at all four experimental sites for employment and training programs, problems attributed to "extremely compressed time schedules and bad timing associated with start up operations" (p. 4). Related reports by the same authors cover the actual program composition and the qualitative features of client and program interaction.

The problems of ensuring that treatments are delivered as advertised, measuring the degree of implementation, and understanding how to couple implementation data and experimental data are not confined to the social arena, of course. Poorly planned and executed programs occur in the commercial sector, although information about this is sparse for obvious reasons. (See Hahn, 1984.) Despite good planning, meteorological experiments have been imperfect and admirably well-documented (Braham, 1979). Drug trials and other randomized clinical trials in medicine must often accommodate departures from protocol and noncompliance. (See Silverman, 1977.)

Steps to Progress

The communities involved in field experiments are diverse: police departments, private and public service organizations, schools, state governments, and so on. Institutional memory in these, and in academe, is often feeble. Turnover in staff or management, shifts in policy, and simple forgetting account for part of the problem. Academic, bureaucratic, and humanitarian provincialism exacerbates it. Impediments to communication are substantial, and this too degrades institutions' ability to learn and sustain learning about experimental evidence.

Improving Communication. How to transfer this technology called randomized experiments better and how to institutionalize it seem critical for the future. A variety of promising approaches to ameliorating communications components of the task are at hand. New journals such as *Evaluation Review, Program Planning and Evaluation,* and volumes of New Directions for Program Evaluation are an important base on which to build new options. One may reasonably consider, for instance, publishing excellent RFPs such as the National Institute of Justice's RFP on Replication of the Domestic Violence Experiments in the interest of ensuring that what is good is recognized as such. It seems reasonable to seriously consider videotaping productions for teaching what cannot be understood entirely from the printed work. Two examples of this are recordings of the Milwaukee, Wisconsin, city council's hearings on the legitimacy of experimental tests of their city's police procedures for handling domestic violence and the Atlanta Urban League's explanations to women about the Minority Female Single Parent Program. Workshops for practitioners and scholars, of the sort organized for the National Academy of Sciences for Criminal Justice Experiments by Richard Lempert, Jeff Roth, and Christy Visher are excellent devices for informing those who are interested in but not knowledgeable about promising new work.

Institutional arrangements that foster long-term resource building and institutional memory have not received sufficient attention. A policy and practice of joint ventures between police departments and academic researchers, regional nursing associations and evaluators, and so on seem desirable. The issues and options in their creation need to be better understood. Similarly, foundation policy that invites resource building, episodic and competitive joint ventures, and replication can help nicely to foster self-conscientious experimentation by institutions on large and small scales (Berk and others, 1985).

New Arenas. The use of randomized tests has advanced well beyond education to police, personnel training and employment, tax administration, and civil and criminal justice. Its use in these environments needs to be encouraged and made substantial. Other arenas for field experiments are less well explored but have great promise. Nursing research is a prime target, partly because of the growth in high-quality nursing research programs and their sensitivity to randomized trials. So too is the matter of testing alternative approaches to cost control such as those at the Department of Agriculture's Food and Nutrition Service. The international arena also badly needs attention. Efforts such as Parashar's (1984) to assure the high quality of research in India is not matched by many developing countries. Barbara Searle's (1985) efforts to ensure that one learns from failures of the experiment and, incidentally, the program, are worth emulating. State court systems seem not to have been vigorous in field tests, yet some are more than capable of doing a better job than the federal agencies. Small high-quality randomized field tests in the mental health arena exist; they are worth duplicating and the experience is worth capitalizing in larger scale efforts in deinstitutionalization work.

Policy and Law. Randomized experiments are infrequently explicitly authorized in law. Rather, authority is implicit in statutes that empower government to improve programs. Explicitness is justified partly on grounds of clarity—making plain that experiments are an option— and partly because it encourages more serious consideration of evaluation design that produces better evidence.

There is a need for developing model statutes on evaluation generally and on experiments in particular. There is an opportunity to better recognize, document, and encourage regulations, requests for proposals, and similar vehicles for creating good field tests. No archive or other device to permit emulation and criticism of the best of these exists; this should be remedied.

The production of better law, policy, regulations, and so on can build on earlier work. Betsey, Hollister, and Papagiordiou (1985) have assessed the remarkable Knowledge Development Plan initiated by the U.S. Department of Labor; the assessment led to changes in policy. The Omnibus Budget Reconciliation Act warrants attention partly because it seems to have opened opportunity for better field testing (Gueron, 1985). Replication policy, represented in criminal justice field tests and in scholarly tracts on experimentation policy (such as that in Berk and others, 1985), demand serious intellectual and bureaucratic attention.

Finally, experimentation policy needs to be linked to policy bearing on other kinds of research. So, for instance, one may envision developing policy that fosters periodically adding experiments to ongoing longitudinal research in the interest of refreshing the latter, addressing impact questions far better than possible with the longitudinal study alone (Boruch and Pearson, 1985). One can envision policy that fosters routine comparisons between randomized and nonrandomized tests to assay conditions under which the latter produce results that accord well with those produced in the randomized test.

Theory. The theories underlying programs are often fragile at best and fragmented and poorly articulated at worst. They need to be strengthened and coupled to evaluation design. Resources must be dedicated to the effort. Even in the engineering sciences, elements of theory can be weak. The conflation of several complex theories or laws operating in a complex environment may lead to intractable analytic problems. It is therefore common to design randomized experiments to assess changes in chemical production processes, acoustics, and other areas (Hahn, 1984).

In the social sector, the science is young and there are few good theories. Indeed, the absence of well-explicated theory is a justification for randomized trials in the social sector, just as experiments are sometimes invoked to achieve understanding in the engineering arena. Commonsense notions of how a program is supposed to produce an effect is theory of sorts, but examples of inadequate commonsense theory and well-articulated theory are easy to find. There is room for improving both varieties in different ways (Chen and Rossi, 1980).

The need for enlarging the supply of good theory seems obvious. To take a simple variable such as time, for instance, few formal social or behavioral theories have been laid out (partly because experience is sparse) to explain the time required for a new project's stabilization, time required on tasks to produce effects on skills, time required to benefit through skills in the marketplace, or time involved in the decay of benefits. Yet theory that incorporates time variables seems essential to designing, executing, and evaluating programs well.

Microlevel examples are not hard to develop. For example, so-called selection models have been developed by Heckman and Robb (1985), among others, to described analytically how program applicants are placed in one program regimen rather than another. This is amateur theory despite its mathematical elegance. The approach seems sensible insofar as it leads to a substitute for experiments and better analyses of nonrandomized trials. The shortcomings of such models lie in their parochialism: Each is a notion developed by a mathematically oriented analyst who is unlikely to have conducted empirical studies of the enrollment process or taken the trouble to exploit theory from disciplines outside economics. Far more integration of theory and practical program development and evaluation is warranted. Without integration, it is doubtful that one will learn much that is durable.

Technical Design and Analysis. The recent stress on meta-analysis has promise for improving our understanding of the distribution of program effect sizes. This will help to make power analyses more realistic. More important, it will help illuminate conditions under which randomized trials and alternative nonrandomized approaches produce comparable or disparate results. Still, more important, the more ecumenical varieties of meta-analysis should help to better understand attrition rates and reasons and target population sizes and participant flow. Meta-analysis in the interest of improving designs, begun by Cordray (1985) and Orwin (1985), among others, needs to be exploited more vigorously and made easier in the sense of incorporating results into machine-readable form.

Recent improvements in analysis of self-selection, missing data, and other pertinent areas have been substantial (Morris, 1983), but those improvements are not well-coupled to design. A recent Social Science Research Council Conference on the topic, for instance, involving some of the brightest statistical analysts, failed to produce much of interest to the designer. But it did succeed in bringing designers and analysts together and demonstrating that better coupling is not easy and has promise.

Evaluators know enough to pay careful attention to program implementation and process in an experiment. But they do not know how to analyze the resulting observations well and in conjunction with the conventional techniques for analyzing randomized data. One would expect multiple analyses or comparisons to be warranted, but this expectation is vague. The problem of linking these two kinds of information is related to missing data issues: Self-selection into or out of a program is part of implementation. Yet the relation seems unrecognized. The technical work by Rosenbaum and Rubin (1983) on observational studies seems promising on this account to the extent that an imperfectly implemented experiment becomes more like an observational study. Both Morris (1983) and Rubin (1978) believe Bayesian approaches are sufficiently interesting to justify serious attention. Despite remarkable mathematical-statistical contributions, applications of these and related approaches to real data generated by methodological experiments are infrequent; they deserve much more testing by the field experimenter.

A General View of the Future. While others are content with supposition and anecdote, the experimenter is unusual in trying to affix numerical evidence to a purported solution to a problem. Stranger still is the belief that random assignment will produce less equivocal evidence. With time, the randomized experiment will become more the norm. To achieve this will require further work of an unusual sort. Reality demands that the gratuitous distinction between qualitative evaluation and quantitative evaluation be abandoned, and that it be supplanted by an enriched methodology. It demands that the distance between politician and experimenter be diminished to a point where researchers add to the ranks of not only the civil service but the legislature. It demands a government research policy that self-consciously builds on earlier work instead of shifting it dramatically with a new political regime.

The tension is between finding out and doing what is purported to be good. The world often deals with this by resorting to the idea that whatever is done is good, that the appearance and intent to do good is sufficient. This is unconvincing. It prevents variation, diagnosis, and understanding. Still, it appears often. Experimenters must take this into account and doubt only that which is worth doubting. This is a wise course, but it is not always safe. It is also an endeavor whose target justifies that risk: building durable understanding in the interest of doing durable good.

References

Bangser, M. R. *Lessons from Transitional Employment: The STETS Demonstration for Mentally Retarded Workers.* New York: Manpower Demonstration Research Corporation, 1985.

Bardach, E. *The Implementation Game: What Happens After a Bill Becomes Law.* Cambridge, Mass.: MIT Press, 1977.

Berk, R. A., Boruch, R. F., Chambers, D. L., Rossi, P. H., and Witte, A. D. "Social Policy Experimentation: A Position Paper." *Evaluation Review,* 1985, *9* (4), 387–429.

Bermant, G., Kelman, H. C., and Warwick, D. P. *The Ethics of Social Experimentation.* New York: Wiley, 1978.

Betsey, C., Hollister, R., and Papagiordiou, M. (eds.). *Youth Employment and Training Programs: The YEDPA Years.* Washington, D.C.: National Academy of Sciences Press, 1985.

Bickman, L. "Randomized Field Experiments in Education: Implementation Lessons." In R. F. Boruch and W. Wothke (eds.), *Randomization and Field Experimentation.* New Directions for Program Evaluation, no. 28. San Francisco: Jossey-Bass, 1985.

Boruch, R. F., Anderson, P. S., Rindskopf, D. M., Amidjaya, I. A., and Jansson, D. "Randomized Experiments for Evaluating and Planning Local Programs: A Summary on Appropriateness and Feasibility." *Public Administration Review,* 1979, *39* (1), 36–40.

Boruch, R. F., and Dennis, M. "Cooperation in Field Experiments Versus Observational Surveys." In *Proceedings of the Second Annual Census Research Conference.* Washington, D.C.: U.S. Census Bureau, 1986.

Boruch, R. F., and Pearson, R. W. *The Comparative Evaluation of Longitudinal Surveys.* New York: Social Science Research Council, 1985.

Boruch, R. F., and Wothke, W. "Seven Kinds of Randomization Plans for Designing Field Experiments." In R. F. Boruch and W. Wothke (eds.), *Randomization and Field Experimentation.* New Directions for Program Evaluation, no. 28. San Francisco: Jossey-Bass, 1985.

Box, J. F. *R. A. Fisher: The Life of a Scientist.* New York: Wiley, 1978.

Braham, R. E. "Field Experimentation in Weather Modification." *Journal of the American Statistical Association,* 1979, *74* (365), 57–104.

64

Breger, M. "Randomized Social Experiments and the Law." In R. F. Boruch and J. S. Cecil (eds.), *Solutions to Legal and Ethical Problems in Applied Social Research*. New York: Academic Press, 1983.

Campbell, D. T., and Stanley, J. C. *Experimental and Quasi-Experimental Designs for Research*. Chicago: Rand McNally, 1966.

Chen, H.-T., and Rossi, P. H. "The Multi-Goal, Theory Driven Approach to Evaluation: A Model Linking Basic and Applied Social Science." *Social Forces*, 1980, *59* (1), 106–122.

Cochran, W. G., and Cox, G. M. *Experimental Designs*. New York: Wiley, 1950.

Cohen, P. C. *Numeracy in Early America*. Chicago: University of Chicago Press, 1982.

Collins, J. F., and Elkin, I. "Randomization in the NIMH Treatment of Depression Collaborative Research Program." In R. F. Boruch and W. Wothke (eds.), *Randomization and Field Experimentation*. New Directions for Program Evaluation, no. 28. San Francisco: Jossey-Bass, 1985.

Conner, R. F. "Selecting a Control Group: An Analysis of the Randomization Process in Twelve Social Reform Programs." *Evaluation Quarterly*, 1977, *1* (2), 195–243.

Cordray, D. S. (ed.). *Utilizing Prior Research in Evaluation Planning*. New Directions for Program Evaluation, no. 27. San Francisco: Jossey-Bass, 1985.

Corsi, J. R., and Hurley, T. L. "Pilot Study Report on the Use of the Telephone in Administrative Fair Hearings." *Administrative Law Review*, 1979, *31* (4), 484–524.

Cronbach, L. J. *Designing Evaluation of Educational and Social Programs*. San Francisco: Jossey-Bass, 1982.

Fairweather, G. W., and Tornatsky, L. G. *Experimental Methods for Social Policy Research*. New York: Pergamon, 1977.

Federal Judicial Center. *Social Experimentation and the Law*. Washington, D.C.: Federal Judicial Center, 1983.

Ferber, R., and Hirsch, W. A. *Social Experimentation and Economic Policy*. Cambridge, Mass.: Cambridge University Press, 1982.

Fraker, T., and Maynard, R. *The Use of Comparison Group Designs in Evaluations of Employment-Related Programs*. Princeton, N.J.: Mathematica Policy Research, 1985.

Friedman, L. M., Furberg, C. D., and DeMets, D. L. *Fundamentals of Clinical Trials*. Boston: John Wright-PSG, 1981.

Goldman, J. *Ineffective Justice: Evaluating the Pretrial Conference*. Beverly Hills, Calif.: Sage, 1980.

Gordon, G., and Morse, E. V. "Evaluation Research." *Annual Review of Sociology*, 1975, *1*, 339–361.

Grandy, J. *Assessment of the U.S. Employment Service Project STEADY*. Technical Report No. 9, prepared under contract to the U.S. Department of Labor, Office of Youth Programs. Princeton, N.J.: Educational Testing Service, 1981.

Guba, D. G., and Lincoln, Y. S. *Effective Evaluation: Improving the Usefulness of Evaluation Results Through Responsive and Naturalistic Approaches*. San Francisco: Jossey-Bass, 1981.

Gueron, J. M. "The Demonstration of State Work/Welfare Initiatives." In R. F. Boruch and W. Wothke (eds.), *Randomization and Field Experimentation*. New Directions for Program Evaluation, no. 28. San Francisco: Jossey-Bass, 1985.

Gueron, J. M., and Nathan, R. "The MDRC Work/Welfare Project: Objectives, Status, Significance." *Policy Studies Review*, 1985, *4* (3).

Hahn, G. J. "Experimental Design in the Complex World." *Technometrics*, 1984, *26* (1), 19–31.

Hausman, J. A., and Wise, D. A. (eds.). *Social Experimentation*. Chicago: University of Chicago Press, 1985.

Heckman, J., and Robb, R. "Alternative Methods for Evaluating the Impact of Interventions: An Overview." Presented at the Social Science Research Council Workshops on Backtranslation, Committee on Comparative Evaluation of Longitudinal Surveys, New York, 1985.

House, E. R. *Evaluating with Validity*. Beverly Hills, Calif.: Sage, 1980.

Kempthorne, O. *The Design and Analysis of Experiments*. New York: Wiley, 1952.

Kerachsky, S., Thornton, C., Bloomenthal, A., Maynard, R., Stephens, S., Good, T., and Fox, D. *Impacts of Transitional Employment on Mentally Retarded Young Adults: Results of the STETS Demonstration*. Princeton, N.J.: Mathematica Policy Research, 1985.

Kirk, R. E. *Experimental Design: Procedures for the Behavioral Sciences*. (2nd ed.) Monterey, Calif.: Brooks/Cole, 1982.

LaLonde, R. J. "Evaluating the Econometric Evaluations of Training Programs with Experimental Data." *American Economic Review*, 1986, *76* (4), 604–619.

Leamer, E. E., "Model Choice and Specification Analysis." In Z. Griliches and M. Intriligator (eds.). *Handbook of Econometrics*, Vol. A. Amsterdam: North-Holland, 1983.

Lerman, R., Friedman, B., and others. *Food Stamp Registration and Job Search Demonstration: Final Report*. (Contract No. 53–33198-0-85). Waltham, Mass., and Cambridge, Mass.: Brandeis University and Abt Associates, 1986.

Light, R. J., and Pillemer, D. B. *Summing Up: The Science of Reviewing Research*. Cambridge, Mass.: Harvard University Press, 1984.

Meier, P. "The Biggest Public Health Experiment Ever: The 1954 Field Trial of the Salk Poliomyelitis Vaccine." In J. M. Tanur, F. Mosteller, W. H. Kruskal, R. F., Link, R. S. Pieters, and G. Rising (eds.), *Statistics: A Guide to the Unknown*. San Francisco: Holden–Day, 1972.

Meyer, H. J., and Borgotta, E. F. *An Experiment in Mental Patient Rehabilitation*. New York: Russell Sage Foundation, 1959.

Morris, C. "Nonresponse Issues in Public Policy Experiments, with Emphasis on the Health Insurance Study." In W. G. Madow and I. Olkin (eds.), *Incomplete Data in Sample Surveys: Proceedings of the Symposium*, Vol. 3. New York: Academic Press, 1983.

New York State Department of Social Services. *Request for Proposal: Evaluation of the Comprehensive Employment Opportunity Support Centers (CEOSC)*. Albany, N.Y.: New York State Department of Social Services, 1986.

Orwin, R. "Obstacles to Using Prior Research and Evaluations." In D. S. Cordray (ed.), *Utilizing Prior Research in Evaluation Planning*. New Directions for Program Evaluation, no. 27. San Francisco: Jossey-Bass, 1985.

Parashar, R. K. "Evaluating Social Action Projects in India." In R. F. Boruch (ed.), *Project Evaluation: Problems of Methodology*. Paris: UNESCO, 1984.

Perng, S. S. "The Accounts Receivable Treatments Study." In R. F. Boruch and W. Wothke (eds.), *Randomization and Field Experimentation*. New Directions for Program Evaluation, no. 28. San Francisco: Jossey-Bass, 1985.

Riecken, H. W., and Boruch, R. F. (eds.). *Social Experimentation: A Method for Planning and Evaluating Social Programs*. New York: Academic Press, 1974.

Rivlin, A. M., and Timpane, P. M. (eds.). *Ethical and Legal Issues of Social Experimentation*. Washington, D.C.: Brookings Institution, 1975.

Roos, L. L., Roos, N., and McKinley, B. "Implementing Randomization." *Policy Analysis*, 1977, *3* (4), 547–559.

66

Rosenbaum, P. R., and Rubin, D. B. "The Central Role of the Propensity Score in Observational Studies for Causal Effects." *Biometrika*, 1983, *70* (1), 41–55.

Rossi, P. H. "Practice, Method, and Theory in Evaluating Social Action Programs." In D. P. Moynihan (ed.), *On Understanding Poverty*. New York: Basic Books, 1969.

Rossi, P. H., Berk, R. A., and Lenihan, K. J. *Money, Work, and Crime: Experimental Evidence*. New York: Academic Press, 1980.

Rubin, D. B. "Bayesian Interference for Causal Effects: The Role of Randomization." *Annals of Statistics*, 1978, *6*, 34–58.

Searle, B. (ed.). *Evaluation in World Bank Education Projects*. Washington, D.C.: World Bank, 1985.

Shadish, W. "Units of Analysis." Paper presented at the annual meeting of the American Evaluation Association, Oct. 29–Nov. 1, 1986.

Sherman, L. W., and Berk, R. "The Randomization of Arrest." In R. F. Boruch and W. Wothke (eds.), *Randomization and Field Experimentation*. New Directions for Program Evaluation, no. 28. San Francisco: Jossey-Bass, 1985.

Silverman, W. A. "The Lesson of Retrolental Fibroplasia." *Scientfic American*, 1977, *236* (6), 100–107.

Stake, R. *Evaluating the Arts in Education*. Columbus, Ohio: Merrill, 1975.

Stigler, S. M. "Mathematical Statistics in the Early States." *Annals of Statistics*, 1978, *6*, 239–265.

Tallmadge, G. K., and Yuen, S. D. *Study of the Career Intern Program. Final Report—Task B: Assessment of Intern Outcomes*. Mountain View, Calif.: RMC Research Corporation, 1981.

Teitelbaum, L. E. "Spurious Tractable and Intractable Legal Problems: A Positivist Approach to Law and Social Science Research." In R. F. Boruch and J. S. Cecil (eds.), *Solutions to Ethical and Legal Problems in Social Research*. New York: Academic Press, 1983.

U.S. General Accounting Office. *Teenage Pregnancy: 500,000 Births a Year But Few Tested Programs*. (GAO/PEMD-86-16BR). Washington, D.C.: U.S. General Accounting Office, 1986.

Winer, B. J. *Statistical Principles in Experimental Design*. New York: McGraw-Hill, 1971.

Robert F. Boruch is professor of psychology, education, and statistics at Northwestern University. He is currently at the Center for Advanced Study in the Behavioral Sciences, Stanford, California.

Because no-difference research has been relatively unexplored by evaluators, a series of empirical studies was conducted. In this chapter distinguishing characteristics of no-difference research are examined, its acceptance by the research community is probed, and possible strategies for conducting no-difference studies are discussed. The centrality of no-difference findings within the experimental and non-experimental paradigms is also discussed.

No-Difference Research

William H. Yeaton, Lee Sechrest

In a recent volume of New Directions for Program Evaluation, Trochim (1985) edited six chapters on recent advances in quasi-experimental design and analysis. No such volume could be written about no-difference research (studies in which no differences among groups or conditions are found) because the very notion of advances implies that there is an existing, definable, coherent approach that can be modified and reconceptualized in the future. No-difference research deserves such a past because, although it has largely escaped the view of evaluators, it offers the promise of generating lessons likely to improve research practice and making a significant contribution to evaluation theory. Additionally, the approaches we have taken in studying no-difference research are consistent with the conceptualization of research as an effort to convince a particular audience, a thrust that necessarily forces one to confront the role of judgment and decision making in forming inferences from both no-difference and difference studies (Einhorn and Hogarth, 1986).

Our first goal in this chapter is to briefly summarize the existing commentary on no-difference research. We then introduce our no-differ-

The authors wish to thank Ellen Whipple, William Silagi, and Kim Orchen for their assistance in coding characteristics of studies and for compiling much of the data for Tables 1 and 2. This work was supported by grant HS 04825 from the National Center for Health Services Research.

D. S. Cordray, H. S. Bloom, and R. J. Light (eds.). *Evaluation Practice in Review.*
New Directions for Program Evaluation, no. 34. San Francisco: Jossey-Bass, Summer 1987.

67

ence research that examines conditions under which no-difference conclusions are viable and illustrates patterns of evidence that have been used to make the no-difference case. Next, we outline a series of studies we have conducted that have several purposes: to compare characteristics in no-difference and difference studies; to estimate the acceptability of existing no-difference research by using both citation analysis and a controlled, empirical study; and to develop and test a set of strategies that might be used in the planning, analysis, and interpretation of no-difference research. We conclude with a discussion of the role of no-difference findings in establishing study quality from the perspective of the evaluation paradigm of Donald Campbell and his colleagues.

Existing Critiques of No-Difference Roles

Most if not all of the existing literature treats no-difference research as an undesirable result to be avoided, perhaps because of the bias against publishing no-difference studies (Greenwald, 1975). We review only briefly several of the more common suggestions for improving no-difference research, but wish to make it clear that the thrust of our efforts has been in a different vein.

Surveys of the no-difference research (for example, Freiman and others, 1978) have shown that statistical power has been inadequate in most cases, and blame is most often placed on small sample size (Cohen, 1977). Other researchers have suggested that insensitive and unreliable measures may be part of the problem (Lipsey, 1983; Sutcliffe, 1980). We have called attention to the negative contribution of weak treatments delivered with low integrity (Yeaton and Sechrest, 1981). Other methodologists have argued that research designs that minimize variability (Kirk, 1968) have considerable potential in avoiding no-difference results. Still others have focused on statistical analysis, pointing out the preference for parametric rather than nonparametric tests of statistical significance where feasible (Hollander and Wolfe, 1973). Finally philosophers of science have discussed the futility in making no-difference claims given the lack of a firm, logical structure for such claims (for example, Bakan, 1966). In the next section, we examine a philosophical forefather of no-difference research, attempts to prove the null hypothesis.

An Epistemological Trek

In 1772, Captain James Cook, intrepid in so many ways, set out to do what so many contemporary research methodologists say cannot be done: prove the null hypothesis. Specifically, Captain Cook undertook a global circumnavigation in the lower southern latitudes to determine whether a southern continent, thought since Aristotle's time to be necessary to balance the northern continent(s), actually existed (Boorstin, 1983). Disregarding Antarctica, which did not meet the requirements of the theory, Captain Cook proved conclusively that no southern continent existed. He did, in fact, prove the null hypothesis.

More recently, another group has embarked, figuratively, on an attempt to prove that there is no extraterrestrial intelligence (Crease and Mann, 1984). Similarly, cryptozoologists are attempting to show that there are no examples on earth of such mythical animals as the Ri (a sort of mermaid), the Loch Ness monster, Bigfoot, and so on. Captain Cook succeeded in proving the null hypothesis, but we can expect that disproof of the extraterrestrial intelligence will fail and that evidence against the existence of cryptozooforms will be unpersuasive to the cryptozoologists.

These examples illustrate that the null hypothesis is sometimes tested, but that acquiring adequate proof may be difficult or impossible under most circumstances. What made disproof of the existence of the southern continent—proof of the null hypothesis—possible was the specification of finite space and time for observation of its existence, with a reasonable consensus, if only implicit, of what a positive sign of its existence would look like. The southern continent, if it did exist, had to exist in the space crossed by Cook's circumnavigation, and it had to exist in 1772-73. The hypothesis did not admit the possibility that it might once have existed (like Atlantis) or that it might appear at some future time. One knew when and where the southern continent was supposed to be—one looked there and then—and, not finding it, accepted the fact of its nonexistence.

The case for extraterrestrial intelligence is different. Cook had a good idea of what a continent should look like. He could easily reject as evidence any islands, icebergs, or other (relatively) small land masses that he encountered. What are the searchers for extraterrestrial intelligence looking for? They do not really know. How, then, will they know they have not found it? They also do not know where in space they should be looking nor with what precision. Nor does the failure to find something within any particular time frame rule out the possibility that extraterrestrial intelligence once existed but has expired or that it exists but is not yet detectable because of the vast reaches of space across which communication must travel.

The cryptozoologists have similar but not identical problems in arriving at the null hypothesis. One problem is that they do not know exactly what they are looking for. Are the unicorns of recent circus fame for real? How much like a mermaid must a Ri be or how monstrous need we find the Loch Ness monster? A second problem is that the space to be searched is only seemingly finite. Loch Ness can be searched with excruciating care, but the monster may only be moving with matching precision. An intensive search for the Abominable Snowman may only drive the creature further into the vastnesses of the Himalayas. And we may so pester these cryptocreatures that they expire before we can locate and identify them.

The moral here is that, contrary to the usual assumptions of the philosophy of science, the null hypothesis is provable, but only if we are willing to state with some exactness the conditions of its acceptance. The null hypothesis will be provable only within a closed system that has definitional, spatial, and temporal limits.

The Patterns of Evidence Approach

The notion that a research study can be conceptualized as an argument (Campbell, 1982) is a metaphor of considerable utility in our view of no-difference research. We believe that instances of acceptance of no-difference (and difference) studies form patterns that are related to features of the problem, the manner in which the research was conducted, and the particular results obtained. Some patterns and conditions are likely to be more believable than others, based on their similarity to patterns that a research consumer has previously encountered in the literature and judged to be acceptable. We illustrate several of these patterns to determine what they might tell us about the likely acceptability of no-difference research in varying circumstances both within and across studies (see questions in items 16 and 17 in Table 1 for the relative occurrence of these patterns in both difference and no-difference research). We refer the interested reader to a related article that discusses the patterns of evidence approach at greater length (Sechrest and Yeaton, 1986).

A particularly convincing case may be made for the noneffect of a given intervention in the face of an abysmal failure. For example, the rates of cancer and leukemia in children whose mothers had and had not received ultrasound were so nearly identical (risk ratios .98 and 1.00, respectively) that even the staunchest critic of ultrasound is unlikely to claim that it has a detrimental effect during pregnancy. *"Coup de grace"* characterizes a set of circumstances in which a single, well-conducted experiment destroys any lingering doubt about treatment effectiveness. This was the case with gastric freezing, because one randomized, double-blind trial demonstrated that the procedure was not more effective than a sham operation (Ruffin and others, 1969). *Preponderance of evidence* is a pattern in which the sheer weight of the evidence makes the no-difference case. To illustrate, Nelson and others (1980) reported that there were only two significant differences between a Leboyer group and a group receiving conventional childbirth from a lengthy list of maternal and infant behaviors.

A pattern we have termed *gross inconsistency* refers to a situation in which differences are found about as often in one direction as another. Smith (1980) concluded that there was no sex bias in counseling and psychotherapy due to the fact that her meta-analysis indicated that there were just as many studies showing bias for males as for females. *Context* refers to the possibility that a given no-difference finding would most likely be accepted in a context of previous no-difference findings. Another study that fails to find a cure for the common cold would be readily assimilated into the literature. Finally, *contrast effect* refers to an instance in which a no-difference result occurs within a study along with a difference outcome. Alexander, Cropp, and Chai's (1979) conclusion that relaxation training had no effect on respiratory functioning of young children was strengthened by the fact that a standard bronchodilator did produce beneficial change, thus allaying any criticism that treatment failure was attributable to measurement insensitivity or small sample size.

Characteristics of No-Difference Research

Certainly, one could imagine many viable ways of investigating no-difference research. However, we were immediately drawn to the question of whether no-difference studies differ from their perceived complement, difference studies. Rather than try to identify a particular universe of no-difference articles, we preferred instead to choose a set of studies collected for their policy relevance and their judged importance. The large majority of studies were from the health or medical area, but several were chosen from psychology and education. Nearly all of the 47 no-difference studies in this data set were published in the last five years, and all were taken from peer-reviewed journals.

Although it was a relatively straightforward matter to identify a modestly sized group of no-difference studies, it was not nearly as simple to choose an appropriate comparison group of difference studies. We considered choosing a random sample of difference studies from the same journals over the same period. This alternative was not attractive because it required an enumeration of a list of all difference studies with particular specifications. Instead, a difference study was chosen for each no-difference study by identifying the next difference study published in the same or next issue of the journal in which the no-difference study had been published. We judged this matching process to be preferable because it controlled for general content (same journal) and quality (same journal and year of publication), and seem likely to be essentially random. We did not consider it plausible that journal editors arranged difference and no-difference articles within issues of a particular journal in any systematic fashion.

Given this set of procedures, we identified a list of characteristics that focused on research methodology, data analysis, outcome measures, and study interpretation. We were guided in this choice of characteristics by published checklists of aspects considered intrinsic to high-quality research (Chalmers and others, 1981), more general discussions of methods of conducting research (Sackett, 1981), and our own previous thinking about important dimensions of no-difference research. A coding sheet was developed to incorporate these characteristics (see Table 1), and a graduate

Table 1. Percentages of Various Characteristics in 47 Difference and 47 No-Difference Studies

ND	D	Methods
18	10	1. Participants selected randomly (39, 39)
		2. Type of design employed: (45, 43)
56	77	case study, correlation, quasi-experimental
44	23	true experiments
34	31	3. Groups tested for equivalence of baseline measures (41, 39)
37	35	4. Patients blind to treatment condition (38, 34)
31	32	5. Provider blind to treatment condition (29, 34)
65	70	6. Delivery of treatment described in detail (43, 43)

ND	D	Analyses
38	28	7. *A posteriori* comparisons conducted to support authors' conclusion
11	0	8. Power analysis conducted prior to results (47, 47)
22	2	9. Power analysis conducted after results obtained (45, 47)

ND	D	Measures
		10. Number of outcome variables reported: (46, 47)
35	23	1–2
30	21	3–4
11	13	5–6
7	17	7–8
0	11	9–10
17	15	greater than 10
79	85	11. Multiple measures reported (47, 47)
		12. Percent objective measures reported: (47, 47)
9	13	0–25
13	6	26–50
4	13	51–75
74	68	76–100
52	41	13. Consistency of findings across measures (46, 46)
28	20	14. Consistency of findings across subject types (46, 46)
11	9	15. Consistency of findings across settings (47, 47)

ND	D	Interpretation
3	2	16. Patterns of evidence: How is the argument cast within this study? (32, 42)
3	2	abysmal failure
3	2	coup de grâce
78	31	preponderance of evidence
6	2	gross inconsistency

Table 1. *(continued)*

ND	D	Interpretation
3	2	16. Patterns of evidence: How is the argument cast within this study? (32, 42)
3	2	abysmal failure
3	2	coup de grâce
78	31	preponderance of evidence
6	2	gross inconsistency
3	31	context
6	33	contrast effect
		(10 ND studies provided multiple arguments, as did 3 D studies)
		17. Pattern of evidence: How is argument cast across studies? (19, 18)
0	0	abysmal failure
32	0	coup de grâce
16	6	preponderance of evidence
5	11	gross inconsistency
26	72	context
21	11	contrast effect
		(1 ND study provided a multiple argument, as did 4 D studies)
57		18. Authors indicate the possibility that they may have failed to detect an existing difference (46)
		19. Shortcomings cited to explain no-difference finding related to: (16)
19		treatment
6		experimental group
0		control group
0		sample size
50		methods
0		results
25		analysis
		(12 ND studies listed multiple shortcomings)
0		20. The difference is described as (34)
0		absolutely small
24		comparatively small compared to other study differences
0		uniformly small (small standard deviation)
0		small and symmetric about the mean
62		statistically insignificant
15		none of the above
		(9 ND studies proved multiple answers)
9		21. A no-difference conclusion is made by arguing that difference results occasionally occur by chance (46)
43		22. A no-difference conclusion is made by arguing that the results are consistent with other data in the literature (46)

Notes: ND = No-difference; D = Difference. Parentheses indicate the total number of no-difference and difference studies on which percents are based. "Not Applicable," "Not Discernable," and "Multiple" responses were not included in these totals. Percents within some questions do not equal 100 percent due to rounding errors.

student and two advanced undergraduate students read and coded the 47 no-difference and 47 difference studies. Several lengthy training sessions were conducted and numerous practice articles were coded to ensure the high quality of coded articles.

Percentages of no-difference and difference studies with various methodological, analytic, measurement, and interpretive characteristics are displayed in Table 1. One is first struck by the remarkable similarity of characteristics shown in these two study types. Only 12 of 39 contrasts (31 percent) between no-difference and difference studies yielded a difference greater than 10 percent. In fact, only 5 of 39 contrasts were greater than 25 percent, and each of these five were in items 17 and 18, which had six options. Thus we would conclude that there are few large and consistent differences between no-difference and difference studies, at least for the particular subset of no-difference and difference studies chosen and for these specific study characteristics.

Although differences were in most instances absolutely small, it is interesting to note that in the first 15 items, the percentage of no-difference studies including desirable methodological, analytic, and measurement characteristics was greater in 10 of the 15 cases. No-difference studies tended to use a higher percent of randomized designs (44 percent versus 23 percent). They also tended to utilize power analyses more frequently both before (11 percent versus 0 percent) and after (22 percent versus 2 percent) results were calculated, although these levels were low in absolute terms. In more than one third of the instances, no-difference studies do not provide detailed descriptions of treatment delivery (item 6), and this deficiency is even greater in difference studies. However, consistent no-difference results are reported more frequently across measures, subject type, and settings than consistent difference results, as indicated by items 13 through 15.

Authors of no-difference studies are not particularly adept in utilizing convincing interpretive strategies in making the no-difference case. The majority of studies simply pointed to the statistical nonsignificance of the results in making the no-difference case (item 20), and less than half (43 percent) of the no-difference studies argued that the results were consistent with other data from the published literature (item 22). In making the no-difference case within a given study (item 16), most authors utilized a single strategy—they argued that the preponderance of evidence favored a no-difference conclusion. In contrast, when arguing for the no-difference case across studies, several other strategies were also utilized frequently, including coup de grace, context, and contrast effect.

Acceptance of No-Difference Studies

Several authors have noted the relative infrequency of no-difference articles in the published literature both in the biological sciences (for example, Freiman and others, 1978) and in the social sciences (for example, Fagley, 1985). The similarity of characteristics in difference and no-difference articles illustrated in Table 1 prompts one to ask whether there is a difference in the tendency of authors to accept these two kinds of studies independent of study quality.

To investigate this question, we utilized the Science Citation Index as an objective indicator of acceptance. Each of the 47 no-difference and difference articles was located in the Science Citation Index. Two citations were sought for each of the 94 published studies. Citations included research studies, editorial commentaries, and literature reviews. If there were exactly two citations during the year in which a given article was published, these two citations were used to establish acceptance. If there was only one citation, or if there was no citation, the next year of the index was consulted (or the previous year if the next year's index was not yet published). If there were more than two citations available, a table of random digits was used to determine which two citations would be chosen. All citations by any of the authors of the cited article were omitted. Using this procedure, 22 of the no-difference articles were identified for which there were two citations, 7 no-difference articles had one citation, and no citations were found for 18 of the no-difference articles (see Table 2). Similarly, 29 of the difference articles had been cited two times, 3 difference articles had been cited once, and 25 difference articles had not been cited (see Table 2).

An article was classified as accepted if the author had incorporated it into his or her study or had not in any way refuted the findings. The original article was rejected if the author(s) disputed the findings or questioned in any way the methods utilized or the results found.

Based on 32 of the 47 articles for which it was possible to find at least one citation, no-difference articles were more likely to be accepted than rejected (see Table 2). In fact, 41 of the 51 instances in which a no-difference article was cited, it had been accepted into the literature in 30 instances from the subset in which both citations accepted the article, plus 5 articles from a subset termed *mixed* in which one article accepted and one article rejected the original article, plus 6 articles in which only one citation was found.

Similarly, difference articles were more likely to be accepted than rejected (Table 2) based on analogous calculations. These findings were tested for their statistical significance and chi-square values were significant at the .05 level. Interestingly, although the acceptance rate of the difference studies was slightly higher than that of the no-difference studies (85 percent versus 80 percent), this difference was not statistically significant (note the use of the contrast argument in this case). Thus, at least for this subset of difference and no-difference studies using this definition of acceptance, published no-difference studies are accepted as often as difference studies.

76

Table 2. Acceptance of No-Difference and Difference Articles

	Accepted	Mixed	Rejected	Chi-square[1]
	No-Difference Articles (N = 47)			
Two citations N = 22	15/22	5/22	2/22	12.64, p < .05, df = 2
One citation N = 7	6/7	—	1/7	—
No citations N = 8	—	—	—	—
Total	41/51	—	10/51	18.84, p < .05, df = 1
	Difference Articles (N = 47)			
Two citations N = 29	23/29	5/29	1/29	26.63, p < .05, df = 2
One citation N = 3	1/3	—	2/3	—
No citations N = 15	—	—	—	—
Total	52/61	—	9/61	30.32, p < .05, df = 1

[1]Accepted = Citation(s) accept no-difference article; Rejected = Citation(s) reject no-difference article; Mixed = One citation accepts, one citation rejects no-difference article; Total = Total number citations accepting (rejecting).

In the above approach to studying acceptance, existing no-difference studies and a matched cohort of difference studies were found to differ little in their acceptance rates, a finding strengthened by the fact that most important study characteristics occurred with similar frequencies. Unfortunately, although the use of intact studies enhances the face validity and generality of the results, one is not able to control the particular combination of important characteristics that appears in each study. Moreover, these factors in their uncontrolled combinations are likely to alter judgments of acceptance.

To remedy these circumstances, 160 members of the American Evaluation Association (AEA) were asked to judge the degree of acceptability and accept or reject a simulated no-difference study (Yeaton and Sechrest, 1987). Each judge was also asked to gauge the acceptability of an otherwise equivalent difference study so that results could be compared for the two study types. Four characteristics were chosen to be systematically varied in a $2 \times 2 \times 2 \times 2$ factorial design for each simulated difference and no-difference study: randomization/no-randomization, one/three outcomes, power = .88/.60, and equivalence in all eight/all but two of eight baseline measures. Thus, 16 subgroups of 10 different members of AEA responded to one of 16 different combinations of two simulated studies, one that reported no-difference results and a second that reported difference results, and judged the degree of acceptability and either accepted or rejected the findings.

The most consistent result in this research was that random allocation is an important factor in judgments of the acceptability of both no-difference and difference research irrespective of the outcome measure (a dichotomous accept or reject choice or a 1–10 point scale reflecting the degree of acceptance). Including multiple measures had some impact, although its influence was not consistent across study type. Enhancing statistical power, despite its widely cited importance in no-difference research (for example, Reed and Slaichert, 1981) was not associated with greater acceptability. Surprisingly, baseline equivalence, the primary purpose of randomization, was not judged an importance factor in either the no-difference or difference case for either kind of outcome measure. Further, if one assumes that use of multiple measures and enhanced statistical power should be important in making the no-difference case, then it is obvious that consumers of research will need to be better educated about the likely importance of these factors.

Developing a Strategy for Conducting and Interpreting No-Difference Research

Although there are numerous sources of information on the design, interpretation, and analysis of research, they typically offer suggestions by prominent members of a given field based on their experience and what seems most appropriate. Unfortunately, these sources are seldom tailored to the specific research context. Nor are they tailored to the specific nature of the question being asked, despite the probable utility of this information for those who conduct research or interpret its findings.

The above deficiency is particularly apparent with studies that either are constructed to make the no-difference case or those whose results are informative should they be of the no-difference variety. As noted above, research tactics that include using random allocation, providing multiple outcome measures, enhancing statistical power, and ensuring equivalence of baseline measures have varying influence on the acceptability of no-difference research. Thus, we (Yeaton and Sechrest, 1985) recently set out to develop and assess a set of tactics for planning, analyzing, and interpreting no-difference research within the context of several important research scenarios.

In particular, 14 methodological experts responded to a questionnaire that included one of two sets of four different scenarios (for example, "The problem to which the intervention is aimed is critical, and it is important that no premature conclusions about the effectiveness of an intervention be reached") for which ten methodological tactics (for example, maximize sample size) and seven analytic or interpretation stage tactics (for example, emphasize the non-significance of statistical tests) were to be rated. The tactics were chosen to reflect important charcteristics of research found in Table 1, and included factors judged to be critical to acceptance of no-difference research as well as strategies judged to be fundamental to the believability of research by prominent experts (for example, Campbell, 1982).

Based on these ratings, the use of a randomized experiment was viewed as the most important methodological element to support the no-difference argument irrespective of the set of scenarios reported. Maximizing the strength and precision of the intervention and maximizing sample size were also chosen as relatively important tactics. In the analysis and interpretation stage, there was far less consensus regarding judged importance of tactics. However, raters believed it was relatively critical to establish the theoretical link between intervention and outcome, emphasize the small mean difference(s) attained, and discuss the consistency of the findings with previously reported literature. Although we did not attempt to test the significance of the differences between these tactics due to the relatively small sample size, it appeared that raters have initial preferences for tactics that will make the no-difference argument more convincing.

Role of No-Difference Findings in Establishing Paradigmatic Quality

In each of the preceding sections, we have treated no-difference research as a neglected study type, first contrasting characteristics of no-difference and difference research to gather possible leads that might be pursued to make this class of research more persuasive. We noted that no-difference research studies are readily accepted by the research community, at least to the same relative degree as comparable difference studies. In the context of a simulated research study, we have investigated more closely a small set of characteristics with varying potential to influence acceptability by an audience of likely evaluation consumers. And we have asked methodological experts to assess tactics that might be useful in planning and evaluating no-difference studies.

In the final portion of this chapter, we wish to focus on a different, although still related, topic. Here, we discuss individual no-difference findings as a viable unit of exploration. This perspective has proven to be exciting for a number of reasons. First, it has broadened the range of applicability of no-difference inquiry, since no-difference findings occur in both difference and no-difference studies. More fundamental, however, is the fact that no-difference findings are intrinsic to the way in which inference is drawn in science.

To illustrate, Holland (1986, p. 946) notes: ". . . the effect of a cause is *always* relative to another cause. For example, the phrase 'A causes B' always means that A causes B relative to some other cause that includes the condition 'not A.' The terminology becomes rather tortured if we try to stick with the usual causal language, but it is straightforward if we use the language of experiments—treatment (i.e., one cause) versus control (i.e., another cause)." Thus, the very notion of causal inference is based on demonstrating that one variable produces some effect (results in a difference) and that some other variable does not produce the same effect (results in no-difference). No-difference and difference findings are inextricably intertwined in the logic of causality, a highly specific duality necessary for establishing cause.

We have explored this role of no-difference findings (Yeaton and Sechrest, 1986) from the point of view of establishing internal validity in the threats to validity framework of Campbell and his colleagues (Campbell and Stanley, 1966; Cook and Campbell, 1979). To ascertain that some intervention or independent variable is causally related to some effect or dependent variable, one must not only demonstrate the relationship between the intervention and its effect but also eliminate other plausible causes—the so-called threats to internal validity. This process of elimination involves a no-difference argument, either implicitly without the use of empirical data or explicitly when a specific no-difference finding indicates that some other variable did not produce the effect in question.

For example, selection is a strong threat to validity in attempts to establish a causal link between attitudes such as stoicism, denial, and fighting spirit and cancer survival rates (Levy, 1985). One must eliminate initial physiological differences such as the intactness of the immunological system or the initial severity of disease; that is, show that there are no group differences on these variables in groups displaying different attitudes as a prerequisite to attributing benefit to certain attitude constellations. One must show that there is no difference between groups in these other two variables that may account for the attitude—survival rate difference.

We have expanded the role of no-difference findings in eliminating threats to validity to three other kinds of validity: external, construct, and statistical conclusion in the threats to validity approach of Campbell and his colleagues. In fact, we have argued that no-difference findings are central to eliminating validity threats in each of these three other validity types, and have systematically noted their use as well as their misuse in each of these three cases (Yeaton and Sechrest, 1986).

No-difference findings are also central to the notion of replication, a feature that several authors deem necessary for establishing cause (Campbell, 1984; Cook and Campbell, 1979). Here, replication is not taken to mean the exact reproduction of a set of findings (Sidman, 1960), but rather the conduct of a study that yields a similar pattern of results. Such pattern matching (Trochim, 1985) is also imbedded in the critical multiplist view of Cook and Shadish (Shadish, Cook, and Houts, 1986; Cook and Shadish, 1986) in which different outcome measures, different designs, different analyses, and different sets of assumptions produce results that are similar.

Determining if replication has been achieved, much like the decision whether to accept the results of a no-difference study or whether a threat to validity has been eliminated by a particular no-difference finding, is fundamentally a judgment made by a research consumer. In fact, the contribution of the decision-making literature to these judgments is only beginning to be made explicit (for example, Einhorn and Hogarth, 1986), and its applicability to an evaluation audience only recently articulated (Cordray, 1986). Perhaps the probes we have made into the no-difference arena will provide some guidance as we begin to learn more about the factors influencing these judgments.

References

Alexander, A. B., Cropp, G.J.A., and Chai, H. "Effects of Relaxation Training on Pulmonary Mechanics in Children with Asthma." *Journal of Applied Behavior Analysis*, 1979, *12*, 27–35.

Bakan, D. "The Test of Significance in Psychological Research." *Psychological Bulletin*, 1966, *66*, 423–467.

Boorstin, D. J. *The Discoverers*. New York: Random House, 1983.

Campbell, D. T. "Experiments as Arguments." *Knowledge: Creation, Diffusion, Utilization*, 1982, *3*, 327–337.

Campbell, D. T. "Can We Be Scientific in Applied Social Research?" In R. F. Conner, D. G. Altman, and C. Jackson (eds.), *Evaluation Studies Review Annual*. Vol. 9. Beverly Hills, Calif.: Sage, 1984.

Campbell, D. T., and Stanley, J. C. *Experimental and Quasi-Experimental Designs for Research*. Chicago: Rand McNally, 1966.

Carpenter, W. T., Sadler, J. H., Light, P. D., Hanlon, T. E., Kurland, A. A., Penna, M. W., Reed, W. P., Wilkinson, E. H., and Bartko, J. J. "The Therapeutic Efficacy of Hemodialysis in Schizophrenia." *The New England Journal of Medicine*, 1983, *308*, 669–675.

Chalmers, T. C., Smith, H., Blackburn, B., Silverman, B., Biruta, S., Reitman, D., and Ambroz, A. "A Method for Assessing the Quality of a Randomized Control Trial." *Controlled Clinical Trials*, 1981, *2*, 31–49.

Cohen, J. *Statistical Power Analysis for the Behavioral Sciences*. New York: Academic Press, 1977.

Cook, T. D., and Campbell, D. T. *Quasi-Experimentation: Design and Analysis Issues for Field Settings*. Chicago: Rand McNally, 1979.

Cook, T. D., and Shadish, W. R. "Program Evaluation: The Worldly Science." *Annual Review of Psychology*, 1986, *37*, 193–232.

Cordray, D. S. "Quasi-Experimental Analysis: A Mixture of Methods and Judgment." In W. Trochim (ed.), *Advances in Quasi-Experimental Design and Analysis*. New Directions for Program Evaluation, no. 31. San Francisco: Jossey-Bass, 1986.

Coronary Artery Surgery Study Principal Investigators and Their Associates. "Coronary Artery Surgery Study: A Randomized Trial of Coronary Artery Bypass Graft Surgery." *Circulation*, 1983, *68*, 939–950.

Crease, R. P., and Mann, C. C. "The Search for Life on Other Planets." *Atlantic Monthly*, 1984, *245*, 122-127.

Einhorn, H. J., and Hogarth, R. M. "Judging Probable Cause." *Psychological Bulletin*, 1986, *99*, 3-19.

Fagley, N. S. "Applied Statistical Power Analysis and the Interpretation of Nonsignificant Results by Research Consumers." *Journal of Counseling Psychology*, 1985, *32*, 391-396.

Freiman, J. A., Chalmers, T. C., Smith, H., and Kuebler, R. R. "The Importance of Beta, the Type II Error, and Sample Size in the Design and Interpretation of the Randomized Control Trial." *New England Journal of Medicine*, 1978, *299*, 690-694.

Gaw, A. C., Chang, L. W., and Shaw, L.-C. "Efficacy of Acupuncture on Osteoarthritic Pain." *The New England Journal of Medicine*, 1975, *293*, 375-378.

Greenwald, A. G. "Consequences of Prejudice Against the Null Hypothesis." *Psychological Bulletin*, 1975, *82*, 1-20.

Holland, P. W. "Statistics and Causal Inference." *Journal of the American Statistical Association*, 1986, *81*, 945-960.

Hollander, M., and Wolfe, D. A. *Nonparametric Statistical Methods*. New York: Wiley, 1973.

Kagan, J., Kearsley, R. B., and Zelazo, P. R. "The Effects of Infant Day Care on Psychological Development," *Evaluation Quarterly*, 1977, *1*, 109-142.

Kirk, R. E. *Experimental Design: Procedures for the Behavioral Sciences*. Monterey, Calif.: Brooks/Cole, 1968.

Levy, S. M. *Behavior and Cancer: Life-Style and Psychosocial Factors in the Initiation and Progression of Cancer*. San Francisco: Jossey-Bass, 1985.

Lipsey, M. W. "A Scheme for Assessing Measurement Sensitivity in Program Evaluation and Other Applied Research." *Psychological Bulletin*, 1983, *94*, 152-165.

Multiple Risk Factor Intervention Trial Research Group Trial. "Multiple Risk Factor Intervention Trial." *The Journal of the American Medical Association*, 1982, *248*, 1465-1477.

Nelson, N. M., Enkin, M. W., Saigal, S., Bennett, K. J., Milner, R., and Sackett, D. L. "A Randomized Clinical Trial of the Leboyer Approach to Childbirth." *New England Journal of Medicine*, 1980, *302*, 655-660.

Reed, J. F., and Slaichert, W. "Statistical Proof in Inconclusive 'Negative' Trials." *Archives of Internal Medicine*, 1981, *141*, 1307-1310.

Ruffin, J. M., Frizzle, J. E., Hightower, N. C., McHardy, G., Shull, H., and Kisner, J. B. "A Co-operative Double-Blind Evaluation of Gastric 'Freezing' in the Treatment of Duodenal Ulcers." *New England Journal of Medicine*, 1969, *281*, 16-19.

Sackett, D. L. "How to Read Clinical Journals: V: To Distinguish Useful from Useless or Even Harmful Therapy." *CMA Journal*, 1981, *241*, 1156-1162.

Sechrest, L., and Yeaton, W. H. *Role of No-Difference Findings in Medical Research*, 1986, Institute for Social Research, University of Michigan, unpublished manuscript.

Shadish, W. R., Cook, T. D., and Houts, A. C. "Quasi-Experimentation in a Critical Multiplist Mode." In W. Trochim (ed.), *Advances in Quasi-Experimental Design and Analysis*, New Directions for Program Evaluation, no. 31. San Francisco: Jossey-Bass, 1986.

Sidman, M. *Tactics of Scientific Research*. New York: Basic Books, 1960.

Smith, M. L. "Sex Bias in Counseling and Psychotherapy." *Psychological Bulletin*, 1980, *87*, 392-407.

Sutcliffe, J. P. "On the Relationship of Reliability to Statistical Power." *Psychological Bulletin*, 1980, *88*, 509-515.

Trochim, W. "Pattern Matching, Validity, and Conceptualization in Program Evaluation." *Evaluation Review*, 1985, *9*, 575–604.

Yeaton, W. H., and Sechrest, L. "Critical Dimensions in the Choice and Maintenance of Successful Treatments: Strength, Integrity, and Effectiveness." *Journal of Consulting and Clinical Psychology*, 1981, *49*, 156–167.

Yeaton, W. H., and Sechrest, L. *Assessing Tactics in Planning No-Difference Research*, 1985, Institute for Social Research, University of Michigan, unpublished manuscript.

Yeaton, W. H., and Sechrest, L. "Use and Misuse of No-Difference Findings in Eliminating Validity Threats." *Evaluation Review*, 1986, *10*, 836–852.

Yeaton, W. H., and Sechrest, L. "Assessing Factors Influencing Acceptance of No-Difference Research." *Evaluation Review*, 1987, *11*, 131–142.

William H. Yeaton is assistant research scientist at the Institute for Social Research at the University of Michigan. His current interests include medical research methodology and research synthesis.

Lee Sechrest is professor of psychology and head of the psychology department at the University of Arizona in Tucson. His primary research interest concerns the development of tactics for improving the quality of social science research.

Cost-benefit and cost-effectiveness analyses have not been used extensively in program evaluation, despite their obvious value when public and private resources are limited and several courses of action are feasible. Future developments in this area will require consideration of multiple objectives, limited information, and lack of proficiency of decision makers in the use of these techniques.

Cost-Benefit and Cost-Effectiveness Analyses

Henry M. Levin

Cost-benefit analysis and cost-effectiveness analysis are two tools that are often mentioned but rarely used in evaluation. The last decade has seen a slow accumulation of such studies in the evaluation literature. The purpose of this chapter is to consider what evaluators have learned about these tools as they obtain more experience in using them in evaluation activities.

Because many readers will only have a casual familiarity with cost-benefit and cost-effectiveness analysis, I will first provide a brief summary of the two types of analysis and their potential importance for decision making. Second, I will comment on the extent to which these tools are actually used in evaluation studies and the quality of such studies. Third, I will address the possible connections between meta-analysis and cost-effectiveness analysis, and whether cooperation is possible. Fourth, I will explore the connection between effect sizes and benefit-cost ratios. Finally, I will address the shape of future developments on the basis of what we have learned.

Cost-Benefit and Cost-Effectiveness Analyses

Two closely related techniques—cost-benefit and cost-effectiveness analyses—are used to inform decisions regarding alternative uses of

D. S. Cordray, H. S. Bloom, and R. J. Light (eds.). *Evaluation Practice in Review.*
New Directions for Program Evaluation, no. 34. San Francisco: Jossey-Bass, Summer 1987.

resources (Levin, 1983). Both assume that the decision maker faces a set of alternatives from which choices must be made. Both also assume that the criteria for making the choice must include not only what will be gained— the benefits or effects—but the value of resources that will be sacrificed to achieve these gains—the costs. Both tools are decision-oriented in taking account of the fact that decision-making units are always faced with finite resources. Allocating resources to those alternatives with the largest benefits relative to costs (excluding those whose benefits are less than costs) or those with the largest effectiveness relative to costs provides the largest contribution of those resources to achieving the decision unit's goals.

Both cost-benefit and cost-effectiveness analyses measure costs in the same way. The resources or ingredients that are needed for each alternative are specified and assessed according to their market values or another technique that simulates their market values. But benefits and effectiveness represent different approaches to the measurement of outcomes. Benefit-cost analysis compares the benefits and costs of alternatives when the outcomes can be assessed in monetary terms. It lends itself especially well to those alternatives or interventions in which the outcomes are market-oriented. For example, educational and training programs that are designed to improve employment and earnings or reduce poverty can be evaluated with a cost-benefit approach when the benefits are the additional earnings associated with the interventions.

In these cases, both benefits and costs can be assessed in monetary units and compared to each other for each alternative. In general, decision makers would choose only among alternatives whose benefits exceeded costs. The most attractive alternatives would be those with the lowest cost-benefit ratios (or highest benefit-cost ratios) or that maximize net benefits (the difference between benefits and costs). The use of a cost-benefit guideline has two major advantages to decision makers. First, one can ascertain if the benefits exceed costs, the necessary criterion for considering an alternative. In addition, one can compare the attractiveness of alternatives both within programs and among programs with different goals. For example, the fact that costs and benefits are both evaluated in monetary terms means that cost-benefit ratios or net benefits of a given investment can be compared among programs with similar goals or among ones with different goals. Thus, cost-benefit analysis can be used to compare the efficiency of using resources among programs as diverse as health, education, criminal justice, and public assistance.

Many social interventions, however, are characterized by outcomes that cannot be easily converted to market outcomes. As illustrations, juvenile justice programs may be concerned with reductions in delinquency, school reading programs may be concerned with rises in reading proficiency, and mental health programs may address the attainment of functional competencies. In each of these cases the outcomes of programs addressing a common goal can be evaluated in terms of effectiveness with relation to that goal, but they cannot be readily translated into monetary values. This is the typical situation for most program evaluations.

In these cases a cost-effectiveness approach is taken. Effectiveness is assessed by standard evaluation techniques for a common set of goals among the interventions that are considered as alternatives. For example, the effectiveness of educational programs may be evaluated by using tests of achievement in the subjects that are being considered, health programs may use measures of morbidity or improvement in mental and physical functioning, criminal justice interventions may use measures of recidivism, and so on. In these cases, alternatives with the same goals can be compared according to their costs and effectiveness. Those alternatives with the lowest cost-effectiveness ratios would be considered to be the most promising with respect to the use of an agency's or society's resources. Such interventions would use the least resources to achieve a particular program objective.

In some cases, attempts have been made to convert effects into economic measures of outcome (Nagel, 1983), and in other cases utility scores have been used to place values on outcomes (Edwards and Newman, 1982). These approaches generally require the decision maker to make a range of subjective judgments about outcomes and their values (Keeney and Raiffa, 1976). The heavy reliance on subjective judgments makes them less attractive to evaluation experts who seek evidence that is publicly replicable when comparing alternatives. But they do address two of the major obstacles to more traditional cost-effectiveness and cost-benefit studies—multiple objectives and imperfect information. These issues will be discussed later.

Importance for Decision Making

The importance of cost-benefit and cost-effectiveness tools for evaluation is linked to the challenge that decision makers face in trying to maximize the effectiveness of the limited resources that are available to them. By choosing those interventions that are most cost-effective or that have the lowest cost-benefit ratios, it is possible to provide a greater impact with available resources than by choosing less cost-effective approaches. For example, in the quest to raise student achievement, there are many alternatives, including better teacher selection, smaller classes, longer school days, peer tutoring, and computer-assisted instruction. A cost-effectiveness study has suggested that it is five to ten times more cost-effective to select teachers with higher verbal ability at the same level of experience than to select teachers with greater experience at the same level of verbal ability (Levin, 1970). Another study has shown that peer tutoring is about four times as cost-effective in raising student achievement at the elementary level as extending the school day (Levin, Glass, and Meister, in press).

Differences in cost-effectiveness of this magnitude suggest that resources can be used far more efficiently when allocated to some alternatives than to others. This is an important message at a time when most public services are facing stringent budgets and rising demands for services. It is also an important consideration for both profit-making and nonprofit firms that are seeking to operate more efficiently. In short, evaluations that only produce information on the effectiveness of alternatives are not adequate for decision making in an environment of limited resources. In many cases, the most effective alternatives are not the most cost-effective ones. Clearly, it is effectiveness relative to resource requirements that must be considered rather than effectiveness alone.

Extent of Use

How extensively are cost-effectiveness or cost-benefit approaches used to evaluate alternatives? Virtually all indicators of use produce the same answer. Cost-effectiveness and cost-benefit analyses are only rarely used in evaluation studies, and they are hardly found in the training programs of professional evaluators. Evidence for this assessment follows:

- Of the 500 presentations listed in the program of the 1986 Annual Meeting of the American Evaluation Association in Kansas City, only two indicated a focus on cost-effectiveness and none addressed cost-benefit analysis
- A review of the major texts on evaluation showed only one text (Rossi and Freeman, 1985) with as much as a chapter on cost analysis in evaluation, and other texts varied from no mention of the tools to brief references with no substance
- Few than 1,000 of the tens of thousands of Educational Resources Information Center (ERIC) documents had any reference to costs (on the basis of key words), less than 100 had attempted any serious cost analysis, and only 40 met even minimal quality standards
- The Citation Index for health books and periodicals published in 1984 found about 100 studies that used cost-effectiveness or cost-benefit analysis—in a year in which the health sector accounted for over $300 billion, or a ratio of one study for over $3 billion in expenditure in the sector.

By any standard, very little cost-effectiveness or cost-benefit analysis is carried out in the evaluation arena. This is the inevitable conclusion whether examining representation of such studies at professional meetings of evaluators, evaluation studies, textbooks used for evaluation training, or the scarcity of such studies relative to the magnitude of resources that might be affected by the results. It is also confirmed by systematic studies of the education evaluation literature and a survey of the program evaluation units of the 50 state departments of education (Smith and Smith, 1985).

As I have pointed out (Levin, 1978), there are several reasons for this. First, few evaluation programs provide training in cost analysis. Persons who are trained in cost-effectiveness and cost-benefit analysis are most likely to obtain their education in economics, although some business schools and public policy schools provide at least some familiarity with the tools. Second, the area of cost analysis is not one with which most evaluators feel comfortable. It does not build on their substantive knowledge of fields, such as criminal justice, education, health, and training or the various methodologies associated with mainstream evaluation, such as statistics, ethnography, psychological measurement, social experimentation, and implementation.

The cost of adding cost information to an evaluation design is not a serious obstacle. For example, the Educational Testing Service's four-year evaluation of computer-assisted instruction had a cost of over $1.5 million, including the cost of the experiment itself (Ragosta, Holland, and Jamison, 1982). However, the cost analysis component of the evaluation was less than $10,000 (Levin and Woo, 1981). In general, the data requirements for a component cost analysis represent only a small portion of the overall costs of a systematic evaluation. Accordingly, the cost of providing cost information in evaluation studies is not likely to be a serious obstacle, although the cost of evaluations may not always be warranted (Alkin and Solmon, 1983).

Cost-effectiveness and cost-benefit analyses have become slightly more prominent in evaluation studies in the last decade through the efforts of such evaluation periodicals as *Evaluation Review* and as reflected in the publication of a recent volume of New Directions for Program Evaluation on cost-effectiveness analysis (Catterall, 1985). The past decade has also produced surveys of applications of these tools to education (Levin, 1981), psychotherapy (Yates and Newman, 1980), and health (Shepard and Thompson, 1979; Thompson, 1980), as well as more general works on the use of cost-benefit and cost-effectiveness techniques (Gramlich, 1981; Levin, 1983; Mishan, 1976). But there must be more progress before they are a standard tool in the evaluator's kit.

A reasonable conclusion is that more and better training is needed among evaluators in cost-effectiveness and cost-benefit analyses. This could be accomplished by expanding the scope of such training in the major evaluation training programs through adding required courses, improving existing ones, and creating joint training programs with other units of the university that provide exposure to cost-effectiveness and cost-benefit tools. It would also seem wise to consider the provision of intensive programs of training for professional evaluators under the aegis of the American Evaluation Association and other professional associations. These might go beyond the standard one- or two-day regimen that usually characterizes such programs.

Meta-Analysis and Cost-Effectiveness Analysis

Clearly, one of the major developments in evaluation over the last decade has been that of meta-analysis. Meta-analysis represents the attempt to use various analytic techniques to generalize about a specific phenomenon from a wide variety of independent and disparate studies (Glass, McGaw, and Smith, 1981). Typically, a meta-analysis will collect all of the available studies on a particular phenomenon and estimate an effect size. The effect size will be a standard score such as a z-score on the criterion variable. Meta-analyses have been carried out on a wide variety of topics, including the effects of reducing class size (Glass, Cohen, Smith, and Filby, 1982), psychotherapy (Glass, McGaw, and Smith, 1981), computer-assisted instruction (Bangert-Drowns, Kulik, and Kulik, 1985; Kulik, Kulik, and Bangert-Drowns, 1985), tutoring (Cohen, Kulik, and Kulik, 1982), a range of educational interventions (Walberg, 1984), and predictive validity of devices for personnel selection (Schmitt, Gooding, Noe, and Kirsch, 1984).

A representative meta-analysis study will provide two types of outcomes. First, it will provide an average effect size for a particular type of intervention. Usually this will be expressed in terms of an average effect of an intervention among a set of studies as some standard score relative to what would be expected in the absence of the intervention. The second type of outcome represents an attempt to assess the sources of differences in outcomes among a set of studies. For this purpose, studies are coded according to their features to determine if such classifications are associated with different effect sizes.

Although meta-analysis has been widely accepted in the evaluation literature, it is also the subject of criticism. Among these concerns are the issues of inclusion of studies that are based upon poor design and procedures, issues of how to average results among different studies, coding and classification aspects of the studies, and appropriate interpretation of results (Hedges and Olkin, 1985; Slavin, 1984; 1986). But a different issue is the question of whether the result of meta-analytic summaries—even ones of high quality—should be used for cost-effectiveness analysis.

The attraction of using meta-analysis results for cost-effectiveness is straightforward. Assume that good meta-analyses exist to summarize the effects of two alternative interventions. Why not obtain the costs of the two interventions and combine them with their respective effect sizes to compare the cost-effectiveness of the two alternatives? The basic problem is that meta-analyses deal with averages rather than actual programs, while decision-makers are concerned with choosing among concrete alternatives. This can be seen more clearly when examining a specific meta-analytic result.

As mentioned above, Cohen, Kulik, and Kulik (1982) conducted a meta-analysis of peer tutoring in which they obtained an effect size of .4 in student achievement. Accordingly, one might estimate the costs of the program that produced this effect size and compare the costs and effects with other alternatives such as computer-assisted instruction which has shown an effect size of about .47 (Kulik, Kulik, and Bangert-Drowns, 1985). The problem is that there is no program to cost out, because the effect size is based on an average of many programs: those that failed and those that succeeded, those that provide training for tutors and those that do not, those that monitor tutors and that provide instructional materials, and those that simply tell some students to tutor others.

From a cost-effectiveness perspective for decision making, this type of result is not helpful for several reasons. First, there is no specific program intervention that is associated with the effect size of .4. Decision makers are concerned with what results they will be able to obtain with a specific intervention, not what are the average effects from many different versions of that intervention—some that were poorly designed and executed and others that were well-designed and executed. Thus the average effect size makes no sense to the decision maker who must consider the impacts of concrete interventions that can be clearly specified and considered for implementation.

Nor is it possible to provide a cost for a program that provides the average effect size. The costing of programs requires that there be a specific set of processes and resource ingredients. The fact that the effect size is not based on a single program, but on a mixture of many different programs, means that there is no conceptual or practical way to identify costs. The effect size simply does not refer to a program alternative with specific resource requirements.

Third, decision makers are primarily concerned with a specification of alternative interventions that have the following properties. They can be readily implemented and do not depend on special circumstances beyond the capabilities of the decision unit. Unfortunately, many of the studies that are reflected in the meta-analysis literature violate this standard because they were initiated and implemented by researchers rather than practitioners. Indeed, many were doctoral dissertations or laboratory studies carried out by university researchers under conditions for the intervention that are not easily generalizable to nonexperimental settings. For example, one can hardly assume that effect sizes for an experimental intervention of a few weeks are extrapolatable to a year of instruction. Kulik, Bangert-Drowns, and Williams (1983) found an effect size of .56 for computer-assisted instruction in projects lasting less than four weeks, but an average effect size of .20 for projects lasting more than eight weeks. Such results are not useful to the decision maker unless it can be shown that the interventions can be readily implemented into nonexperimental situations and replicated beyond the original site.

It is also important that the results be based on evaluations that are of an acceptable design and quality. Again, many of the studies captured by the meta-analyses are extremely poor in quality. One evaluation found that three-fourths of the evaluations that were summarized in a specific meta-analysis had serious flaws (Clark, 1985).

Finally, the types of interventions that should be considered for policy must not only meet the criteria of replicability with information from sound evaluations; they should also be those that show success. Decision makers are not interested in considering an average of good and poor interventions. They want information on how to replicate those specific alternatives that have shown good results. The conflicts between what meta-analysis has to offer now and what decision makers need is reflected in a debate comparing the cost-effectiveness of peer tutoring with computer-assisted instruction between Levin and Meister (1986); Niemiec, Blackwell, and Walberg (1986); and Levin, Glass, and Meister (1986).

The most general conclusion that can be drawn on what has been learned about the potential link between cost-effectiveness analysis and meta-analysis is probably that it is tenuous at best. The two techniques were developed to address different purposes. Meta-analysis was developed to summarize the results of a large number of disparate studies on a single general subject. In doing so, it was never designed to identify exemplary practices that have been found to be replicable and that meet the other standards that are appropriate for policy consideration. It combines the good and the bad in terms of both successful and unsuccessful interventions and low-quality and high-quality evaluations. Its very value derives from its claims to summarize very diverse types of approaches and evaluations within a general rubric.

Cost-effectiveness analysis was designed to assist decision makers in choosing among successful practices on the basis of which ones would maximize the impact of available resources. In this vein the quality of existing evaluations and replication experience are crucial as well as ruling out those practices or interventions that have failed. An average effect for all evaluations of a particular class of interventions is not useful for this purpose, because the average is not embodied in any specific program. And the lack of a specific program means that what is embedded in the average effect size cannot be costed or implemented.

Usefulness of Interventions with Small Effects

It is common in evaluation studies to find that interventions have statistically significant effects that are small in terms of their apparent consequences. It seems reasonable to suggest that programs with small effects should not be important candidates for policy consideration. Of course, what is large and what is small remain somewhat arbitrary as seen in the debate over whether an effect size of .1 of a standard deviation in achievement is important or unimportant (Alexander and Pallas, 1985; Hoffer, Greeley, and Coleman, 1985; Willms, 1985).

One criterion for addressing this issue is to use a cost-benefit approach whenever possible. In some cases, an apparently large effect size may show low benefits relative to costs. In other cases, apparently small effects may be justified on cost-benefit criteria because the benefits exceed the costs for obtaining those effects. The latter possibility is especially important in programs based on behavior modification with regard to the reduction of obesity, alcohol or drug abuse, and smoking. Most short-range interventions of low intensity (a few hours a week for a few weeks) have a limited effect, if one assesses that effect according to the numbers of participants who change their behavior substantially for at least one year (for example, giving up smoking). But what is not considered is that even small effects may have relatively large benefits in relation to costs.

A recent study of a smoking cessation program is a case in point (Weiss, Jurs, Lesage, and Iverson, 1984). The specific program was based on two sessions of 1½ hours a week for four weeks. The goals of the program were to make the participants aware of the reasons that they smoked, provide techniques of behavior modification to assist them in quitting, and provide techniques to reinforce their nonsmoking. Obviously, this was a modest intervention. On the basis of follow-up data, the authors concluded that the percentage of participants who quit smoking may have been as low as 16 percent, although it appeared that three-fourths of the others had reduced their smoking. Unfortunately, they had no control group, and the participants were self-selected.

The conversion of the results into a cost-benefit analysis revealed that the benefits in relation to costs were so high for the employer, that even if only one participant out of 20 quit smoking, the cost-benefit ratio could be favorable. Costs consisted of the direct costs of the program, which amounted to about $30 per participant, and the lost wages of the participant during the program, which amounted to a value from about $46 to $117 depending on the gender and age of the participant. The total costs per participant varied from about $76 to $147 per participant.

Benefits included the savings to the firm in reduced costs of fire, life, health, and workman's compensation insurance, as well as the savings from excess absenteeism and reduced productivity that are associated with smoking. The total value of these benefits depended on the age and gender of the worker (because of differences in wages and cost savings from each source by gender and the expected length of employment in the firm). Depending on the gender and age composition of workers as well as assumptions regarding success rates in stopping smoking, the benefits exceeded cost by from $2,700 (a cost-benefit ratio of about .72) to over $30,000 (a cost-benefit of .08) on the investment of the firm in the intervention. The investment return is positive in the first year for females and early in the second year for males, meaning that the cost-benefit ratio is favorable even if there is a relatively high rate of employee turnover.

As this illustration shows, cost-benefit analysis represents one method of ascertaining whether small effects are valuable by assessing whether the benefits of such effects exceed the costs of obtaining them. As the illustrative study on smoking cessation showed, even programs that show small effects might show benefits that exceed costs if costs are relatively modest and the benefits for even small successes are relatively large. This finding suggests that, if possible, an attempt should be made to view results within some type of cost-benefit framework before assuming that the effects are small or inconsequential.

Further, at least some classes of studies such as those using inexpensive techniques of behavioral modification might have favorable cost-benefit ratios, even when the overall changes in behavior appear to be modest. This is certainly a possibility that should be explored in future studies. At the very least, no program should be automatically dismissed from consideration for policy because it has what appear to be small effects. Those effects should be subjected to further scrutiny to explore the possibility that they might show high benefits relative to costs.

Future Developments

Most decision frameworks in both the public and private sectors are characterized by multiple objectives and imperfect information. If cost-effectiveness techniques are to become useful in these settings, they must accommodate both challenges. Further, most decision makers do not have the training or experience to apply cost-effectiveness approaches to decision making. Future developments must build on the decision maker's substantive expertise and experience, while providing assistance in using cost-effectiveness tools for decision making. In this section, I review these criteria and suggest a path for future developments.

Multiple Objectives. Although most evaluations focus on a single outcome, the evaluative context is often characterized by alternatives in which many outcomes should be considered. For example, interventions to reduce the discomfort of arthritis might alleviate inflammation and pain and increase range of motion to joints. To the degree that medications are used, there might also be side effects. An evaluation of alternative approaches to treating arthritis may consider the impact of interventions on inflammation, pain, range of motion, and side effects. Educational interventions are often designed to raise student achievement and improve student motivation. In some cases, such as reduction of class size or extension of the school day, the interventions might be expected to influence achievement in a number of subject areas.

In these cases, the assumption of a single objective and measure of outcome is inappropriate. Cost-benefit studies address this problem by converting all outcomes into dollar values. Thus, the study that was cited on smoking cessation estimated the benefits of reduced smoking in terms of gains to the employer from savings on insurance, lower absenteeism, and reductions in lost productivity on the job from respiratory illness. But, as noted in the introduction, not all of the outcomes of many types of interventions can be converted into monetary values for a cost-benefit analysis.

The challenge is how to convert multiple outcomes into a single index that can be compared among alternative interventions. This challenge is one for the field of evaluation generally, not just cost-effectiveness evaluations. The most common response to the challenge is to convert the various outcomes to ratings on utility scales that share common measurement properties, although other techniques have also been suggested (Nagel, 1983). The separate utility scales can be aggregated into a total utility index through a variety of procedures (Keeney and Raiffa, 1976; Bell, Keeney, and Raiffa, 1977). The utility scores can be combined with costs for each alternative intervention to derive cost-utility ratios.

Imperfect Information. A related challenge that faces most decision makers is the lack of information on effectiveness of alternatives. The estimation of cost-benefit or cost-effectiveness ratios requires considerable information and analysis that is derived from an appropriate experimental or statistical design. Often a decision maker does not have time, resources, or expertise to carry out such studies. Rather, the decision must be based on existing information, and the information that is available will have many gaps. At best the information might be based on systematic studies of the alternatives in other sites, while much of what is called information will be based on anecdotes, observations, and conventional wisdom.

A combination of multiple objectives and a lack of systematic evaluative information is characteristic of most decision-making contexts. As an example of this type of situation, the training division of a major international organization provides training for economic development projects around the world. The training programs are extremely diverse, ranging in duration from a few days to a few months and from such narrow focuses as water resource or transportation development to broader agricultural and industrial development to national economic management.

As one of its functions in supporting this activity, the training division allocates about $1 million a year to instructional materials ranging from workbooks, textbooks, and other printed materials to audio-visual aids, videocassettes, and computer software. Individual training projects make requests for funds, and a panel of the training division must decide among the different requests.

Clearly, traditional cost-benefit or cost-effectiveness approaches are inappropriate. The training materials attend to such a wide range of objectives that they cannot be easily compared in terms of effectiveness, and the outcomes cannot be easily converted into monetary values. Moreover, it would not be economic to conduct experimental or quasi-experimental studies of each alternative to obtain information on outcomes (Cook and Campbell, 1979). Satisfying the standard evaluation requirements would take considerable time and require greater resources than the value of the instructional material requests themselves. Yet the agency must make choices among proposals for instructional materials, because requests for funding far outstrip available resources.

Decision-Makers' Proficiencies. Finally, most decision makers have little knowledge of or familiarity with cost-effectiveness techniques or applications. This requires little elaboration. If evaluators have such slight familiarity with the tool, decision makers are even less likely to have had exposure to it, with the possible exception of those who have received training at the graduate level in certain business schools or schools of public policy. Even among business school and public administration graduates, only a small number will have proficiencies in cost-effectiveness analysis.

What Needs to Be Done. In order to expand the use of cost-effectiveness tools by decision makers, it will be necessary to take account of multiple outcomes, imperfect information, and a lack of decision maker proficiency in the use of the tool. What follows is a sketch of a solution that can take account of these obstacles.

The basic goal is to develop a computer-based approach for carrying out the cost-effectiveness or cost-utility analysis. The procedures would be based on the development of interacting processes with decision-makers with stages for assisting in problem definition and establishment of alternatives, measuring effectiveness, conducting the cost analysis, and making cost-utility comparisons and evaluating their consequences. Most of the knowledge base and software requirements already exist in some form (Keeney and Raiffa, 1976; Bell, Keeney, and Raiffa, 1977; and Schoemaker, 1982). The challenge will be to link them into an integrated package in an interactive way.

Typically, the decision maker would begin with a problem that has important ramifications for resource allocation. The decision maker would state the problem as clearly as possible. The computer program would assist the decision maker to define clearly the nature of the problem and the alternatives for solving it. A tutorial would present definitions, criteria, and illustrations for making the problem tractable in a cost-utility framework with prompts or suggestions to test the appropriateness of the stated problem.

This first phase would be based on the development of an expert system for analyzing the nature of problems and alternative solutions. Problem definition and development would be based on the establishment of a dialogue between the decision maker and the computer in which the administrator will be given queries and guidelines to determine if the question is properly formulated. A similar strategy would be used to develop alternatives. The decision maker would be asked to solicit opinion from others on alternatives and produce his or her own. It may be possible to provide certain suggestions that will increase the creativity of the administrator in developing alternatives.

Measuring Effectiveness. Specification of dimensions for measuring effectiveness begins with the decision-maker's criteria for considering alternatives. This process would be assisted through a dialogue between the computer and the user in which the decision maker is asked to list the issues and attributes of alternatives that are central to the decision. These would be further refined and formalized with the assistance of prompts and examples or illustrations.

Each dimension must be converted into a measurement scale that the decision maker can understand. In the case in which formal evaluations have been carried out among the alternatives, the measures will be taken from the evaluations. However, in other cases the measurement scales will have to be constructed in order to provide assessments. The user will be assisted in this process by computer-based definitions, criteria, and alternative constructs for measurement scales.

In the case in which formal evaluation results will not be available, the decision maker will need to collect evidence and set out the probable effects of each alternative on the outcome measures. One way of doing this is to divide all possible outcomes on a particular dimension into a small number of mutually exclusive subcategories and instruct the user to indicate the probability that the event in any particular category is likely to occur when the sum of the probabilities is equal to 1. The user would be given instructions for categorization and construction of a probability distribution.

The probability assessments would be based on the various sources of information on each alternative, such as previous experiences, the experiences of others, intuition, and so on. A subroutine could be used to incorporate a Bayesian procedure for using evidence to estimate probabilities (Schlaifer, 1969; Pollard, 1986). Finally, a calculation routine would be used to transform the probability distribution for each outcome dimension into an expected value for that dimension for each alternative.

At this point there would be effectiveness scores from evaluations for each outcome dimension or expected values based on subjective rating procedures. These subscores for each dimension must be combined into a grand measure of effectiveness or utility to compare them among alternatives. In order to accomplish this result, the decision maker must develop a value function that allows the outcome to be translated into utilities. Essentially, the value function sets ranking or priorities among the different outcomes. Procedures for doing this are suggested in Keeney and Raiffa (1976); Bell, Keeney, and Raiffa (1977); and Edwards and Newman (1982); and are summarized in Schoemaker (1982).

In order to make this process user-friendly, it is necessary to establish simple techniques that will be accessible to the nonexpert. One method is to establish utilities through paired comparisons of different outcomes. Utility scales could be constructed through these exercises and algorithms that were internal to the computer software. Results could be tested for rationality in terms of transitivity of preferences and other criteria. Different computing rules could be selected to aggregate the revealed utilities among outcomes into overall utility ratings for each alternative.

Subroutines could also be established to construct the ratings by different audiences or to follow iterative ranking procedures such as delphi techniques. In the latter case, the process might involve a panel that would interact through a local area network. Ratings and measurement of the various outcome dimensions would build on the use of graphics to display scales and show how different assumptions change the overall patterns of results. For many users, graphic representations are more palpable than numeric ones. Finally, the program would enable a sensitivity analysis to see how the results might change under different assumptions.

Cost Estimates. The cost analysis would be based on the techniques described above and in Levin (1983). These can be developed in a simplified form by incorporating a standard type of financial spreadsheet analysis. The decision maker would be provided with guidance in developing the ingredients list and in finding sources of information for identifying and specifying ingredients. A data base program would be used to store the costs of most of the standard inputs, such as the costs of different types of personnel, facilities, and equipment. The user could update this cost matrix on a periodic basis and could add costs as they were needed. Assistance would be provided on determining the cost of each ingredient through a help menu. Calculation procedures for annualizing costs and carrying out other types of cost analysis would also be included.

Cost-Effectiveness Estimates. The final stage would entail combining costs and effectiveness or utility scores to produce cost-effectiveness or cost-utility ratios. These would be used to rank the different alternatives. Sensitivity analysis would also be used at this stage to see if rankings of alternatives are robust under different cost and effectiveness assumptions. This computer-based approach would provide advice to users on the interpretation of the findings and on the conditions under which estimated ratios might differ enough to be considered as a basis for policy.

Cost Analysis: What We Have Learned

What have we learned about the use of cost-benefit and cost-effectiveness? First, we have learned that despite their great potential for providing useful information in situations in which choices will affect resource allocation, few evaluations utilize these techniques. Moreover, few evaluators are familiar with the approaches and virtually no evaluation training programs provide or require systematic training in the application of cost-benefit and cost-effectiveness approaches. These findings suggest that major efforts must be made in encouraging the incorporation of the methods into evaluation and training.

Second, we have learned that there is not likely to be a happy marriage between meta-analysis and cost-benefit or cost-effectiveness analysis. The two approaches address different issues and have many incompatible characteristics. Third, we have learned that sometimes small effects of interventions might have important policy implications. When such effects are associated with relatively low costs and large benefits, the cost-benefit ratio may be highly favorable. Accordingly, an attempt should be made to apply cost-benefit techniques to evaluation results in order to see how consequential the benefits are relative to costs.

Finally, we have learned that the future expansion of cost-benefit and cost-effectiveness applications will depend on success in addressing three challenges: multiple objectives, limited information, and lack of proficiency of decision-makers in the use of these techniques. A computer-based approach to addressing these problems was proposed that would enable decision-makers to conduct their own analysis. This will represent an important agenda for the next decade.

References

Alexander, K. L., and Pallas, A. M. "School Sector and Cognitive Performance: When Is a Little a Little?" *Sociology of Education*, 1985,, *58*, 115–128.

Alkin, M. C., and Solmon, L. C. (eds.). *The Costs of Evaluation*. Beverly Hills, Calif.: Sage, 1983.

Bangert-Drowns, R. L., Kulik, J. A., and Kulik, C. C. "Effectiveness of Computer-Based Education in Secondary Schools." *Journal of Computer-Based Education*, 1985, *12*, 59–68.

Bell, D. E., Keeney, R. L., and Raiffa, H. *Conflicting Objectives in Decisions*. New York: Wiley, 1977.

Catterall, J. S. (ed.). *Economic Evaluation of Public Programs*. New Directions for Program Evaluation, no. 26. San Francisco: Jossey-Bass, 1985.

Clark, R. E. "Evidence for Confounding in Computer-Based Instruction Studies: Analyzing the Meta-Analyses." *Educational Technology and Communication Journal*, 1985, *33*, 249–262.

Cohen, P. A., Kulik, J. A., and Kulik, C. C. "Educational Outcomes of Tutoring: A Meta-Analysis of Findings." *American Educational Research Journal*, 1982, *19*, 237–248.

Cook, T. D., and Campbell, D. T. *Quasi-Experimentation*. Chicago: Rand McNally, 1979.

Edwards, W., and Newman, J. R. *Multiattribute Evaluation*, Quantitative Applications in the Social Sciences, No. 26. Beverly Hills, Calif.: Sage, 1982.

Glass, G., Cohen, L., Smith, M. L., and Filby, N. *School Class Size*. Beverly Hills, Calif.: Sage, 1982.

Glass, G. V., McGaw, B., and Smith, M. L. *Meta-Analysis in Social Research*. Beverly Hills, Calif.: Sage, 1981.

98

Gramlich, E. *Benefit-Cost Analysis of Government Programs.* Englewood Cliffs, N.J.: Prentice-Hall, 1981.

Hedges, L. V., and Olkin, I. *Statistical Methods for Meta-Analysis.* Orlando, Fla.: Academic Press, 1985.

Hoffer, T., Greeley, A., and Coleman, J. S. "Achievement Growth in Public and Catholic Schools." *Sociology of Education,* 1985, *58,* 74–97.

Keeney, R., and Raiffa, H. *Decisions with Multiple Objectives: Preferences and Value Tradeoffs.* New York: Wiley, 1976.

Kulik, J. A., Bangert-Drowns, R. L., and Williams, G. W. "Effects of Computer-Based Teaching on Secondary School Students." *Journal of Educational Psychology,* 1983, *75,* 19–26.

Kulik, J. A., Kulik, C. C., and Bangert-Drowns, R. L. "Effectiveness of Computer-Based Education in Elementary Schools." *Computers in Human Behavior,* 1985, *1,* 59–74.

Levin, H. M. "A Cost-Effectiveness Analysis of Teacher Selection." *Journal of Human Resources,* 1970, *5,* 24–33.

Levin, H. M. "Cost and Economic Aspects of Evaluation: A Grand Illusion." Paper presented at annual meeting of the Evaluation Network, Aspen, Colorado, August 1978.

Levin, H. M. "Cost Analysis." In N. L. Smith (ed.), *New Techniques for Evaluation.* Beverly Hills, Calif.: Sage, 1981.

Levin, H. M. *Cost-Effectiveness: A Primer.* Beverly Hills, Calif.: Sage, 1983.

Levin, H. M., Glass, G. V., and Meister, G. R. "The Political Arithmetic of Cost-Effectiveness Analysis." *Phi Delta Kappan,* 1986, *68,* 69–72.

Levin, H. M., Glass, G. V., and Meister, G. R., "A Cost-Effectiveness Analysis of Computer-Assisted Instruction." *Evaluation Review,* in press.

Levin, H. M., and Meister, G. R. "Is CAI Cost-Effective?" *Phi Delta Kappan,* 1986, *67,* 745–749.

Levin, H. M., and Woo, L. "An Evaluation of the Costs of Computer-Assisted Instruction." *Economics of Education Review,* 1981, *1,* 1–26.

Mishan, E. J. *Cost-Benefit Analysis.* New York: Praeger, 1976.

Nagel, S. "Nonmonetary Variables in Benefit-Cost Analyses." *Evaluation Review,* 1983, *7,* 37–64.

Niemiec, R. P., Blackwell, M. C., and Walberg, H. J. "CAI Can Be Doubly Effective." *Phi Delta Kappan,* 1986, *67,* 750–751.

Pollard, W. E. *Bayesian Statistics for Evaluation Research.* Beverly Hills, Calif.: Sage, 1986.

Ragosta, M., Holland, P. W., and Jamison, D. T. *Computer-Assisted Instruction and Compensatory Education: The ETS/LAUSD Study,* Final Report, Project Report No. 19. Princeton, N.J.: Educational Testing Service, 1982.

Rossi, P. H., and Freeman, H. E. *Evaluation: A Systematic Approach.* (3rd Ed.) Beverly Hills, Calif.: Sage, 1985.

Schlaifer, R. *Analysis of Decisions Under Uncertainty.* New York: McGraw-Hill, 1969.

Schmitt, N., Gooding, R. Z., Noe, R. A., and Kirsch, M. "Meta-Analyses of Validity Studies Published Between 1964 and 1982 and the Investigation of Study Characteristics." *Personnel Psychology,* 1984, *37,* 407–422.

Schoemaker, P.J.H. "The Expected Utility Model: Its Variants, Purposes, Evidence, and Limitations." *Journal of Economic Literature,* 1982, *20,* 529–563.

Shepard, D. S., and Thompson, M. S. "First Principles of Cost-Effectiveness in Health." *Public Health Reports,* 1979, *94,* 535–543.

Slavin, R. E. "Meta-Analysis in Education: How Has It Been Used?" *Educational Researcher,* 1984, *13,* 6–15, 24–27.

Slavin, R. E. "Best-Evidence Synthesis: An Alternative to Meta-Analytic and Traditional Reviews." *Educational Researcher,* 1986, *15,* 5-11.

Smith, N. L., and Smith, J. K. "State-Level Evaluation Uses of Cost Analysis: A National Descriptive Survey." In J. S. Catterall (ed.), *Economic Evaluation of Public Programs.* New Directions for Program Evaluation, No. 26. San Francisco: Jossey-Bass, 1985.

Thompson, M. S. *Benefit-Cost Analysis for Program Evaluation.* Beverly Hills, Calif.: Sage, 1980.

Walberg, H. J. "Improving the Productivity of America's Schools." *Educational Leadership,* 1984, *41,* 19-27.

Weiss, S. J., Jurs, S., Lesage, J. P., and Iverson, D. C. "A Cost-Benefit Analysis of a Smoking Cessation Program." *Evaluation and Program Planning,* 1984, 7, 337-346.

Willms, J. D. "Catholic School Effects on Academic Achievement: New Evidence from the High School and Beyond Follow-Up Study." *Sociology of Education,* 1985, *58,* 98-114.

Yates, B. T., and Newman, F. L. "Approaches to Cost-Effectiveness Analysis and Cost-Benefit Analyses of Psychotherapy." In G. R. Vanden Bos (ed.), *Psychotherapy: Practice, Research, Policy.* Beverly Hills, Calif.: Sage, 1980.

Henry M. Levin is professor of education and affiliated professor of economics at Stanford University.

Index

Radio Engineering for Wireless Communication and Sensor Applications

For a listing of recent titles in the *Artech House Mobile Communications Series,*
turn to the back of this book.

Radio Engineering for Wireless Communication and Sensor Applications

Antti V. Räisänen
Arto Lehto

Artech House
Boston • London
www.artechhouse.com

Library of Congress Cataloging-in-Publication Data
Räisänen, Antti V.
   Radio engineering for wireless communication and sensor applications /
   Antti V. Räisänen, Arto Lehto.
      p. cm. — (Artech House mobile communications series)
   Includes bibliographical references and index.
   ISBN 1-58053-542-9 (alk. paper)
   1. Radio circuits.   2. Wireless communication systems—Equipment and supplies.
   3. Detectors.   I. Lehto, Arto.   II. Title.   II. Series.

   TK6560.R35   2003
   621.384—dc21   2003048098

British Library Cataloguing in Publication Data
Räisänen, Antti V.
   Radio engineering for wireless communication and sensor applications. — (Artech
   House mobile communications series)
   1. Radio   2. Wireless communication systems
   I. Title   II. Lehto, Arto
   621.3'84

   ISBN 1-58053-542-9

Cover design by Igor Valdman

© **2003 ARTECH HOUSE, INC.**
685 Canton Street
Norwood, MA 02062

International Standard Book Number: 1-58053-542-9
Library of Congress Catalog Card Number: 2003048098

10 9 8 7 6 5 4 3 2 1

To our respective spouses, Hannele and Pirjo

Contents

Preface

The word *radio* means techniques that are used in transmitting and receiving information or power in the atmosphere or free space, or in transmission lines utilizing electromagnetic waves—so-called radio waves—but also the equipment needed therein.

This book provides the reader with the basics in radio engineering, the techniques needed to generate, control, detect, and use radio waves. The text approaches the relevant problems both from the electromagnetic theory based on Maxwell's equations and from the circuit theory based on Kirchoff and Ohm's laws. Brief introductions to the electromagnetic theory as well as to the circuit theory are provided. Besides passive transmission lines and components, active RF circuits are also addressed. The treatment of the fundamentals of antennas and radio wave propagation in this book leads the reader to radio systems with noise and modulation considerations. Finally, a broad range of applications are described in addition to various wireless communication applications: radionavigation, radar, radiometry, remote sensing, radio astronomy, RF sensors, power and medical applications, and electronic warfare. The book ends with a short review of biological effects and safety standards. While numerous books specializing in various topics of radio engineering are available, this book gives a well-balanced, general overview of the whole topic. To the authors' knowledge, there are no similar books available.

This book got its origin from course lectures on the same topic at the Helsinki University of Technology. When we found that the Finnish text of our book (which was first published in 1992) written for our students became very popular in the well-known Finnish wireless industry, we decided to write a similar book in English in order to provide an overview of this important technology to engineers, managers, sales representatives, and administrators globally.

In order to take full advantage from the contents of this book, one needs a solid background in physics and mathematics. The text can be used also without this background to obtain a general understanding of radio engineering, especially in Chapters 1, 12, and 13, and partly in Chapters 9, 10, and 11.

Acknowledgments

We authors would like to thank our many colleagues and students, former and current, at the Helsinki University of Technology for their encouragement and many useful comments. We especially want to mention the help of Professors Sergei Tretyakov, Pertti Vainikainen, and Pekka Eskelinen. We would also like to express our appreciation of the professional drawings made by Harri Frestadius.

Dr. Räisänen is grateful to the Observatoire de Paris (LERMA) and Université de Paris 6, and especially to Professor Pierre Encrenaz for providing excellent conditions and good atmosphere for this writing task during his sabbatical leave.

Finally, we would like to thank our family members for their very important emotional support during the writing of this book.

1

Introduction to Radio Waves and Radio Engineering

Electromagnetic waves propagate in a vacuum with the speed of light, $c = 299{,}792{,}458$ m/s or about 3×10^8 m/s. The electric and magnetic fields of a plane wave oscillate in phase and are perpendicular to each other and to the direction of propagation. The frequency of oscillation is f, and the wavelength is $\lambda = c/f$. Electromagnetic waves also may be considered to behave like particles of zero rest mass. The radiation consists of quanta, photons that have an energy of $W = hf$ where $h = 6.6256 \times 10^{-34}$ Js is Planck's constant.

There are many sources of electromagnetic radiation. Accelerating charges produce electromagnetic radiation, as when charges decelerating in an electric field produce bremsstrahlung and charges orbiting in a magnetic field produce synchrotron radiation. The random thermal motion of charged particles in matter produces thermal radiation. Atoms and molecules emit spectral line radiation as their energy level changes. The radiation generated by oscillators and emitted by antennas is based on high-frequency alternating currents.

1.1 Radio Waves as a Part of the Electromagnetic Spectrum

Electromagnetic waves cover a wide range of frequencies or wavelengths, as shown in Figure 1.1. The classification is based mainly on the sources of

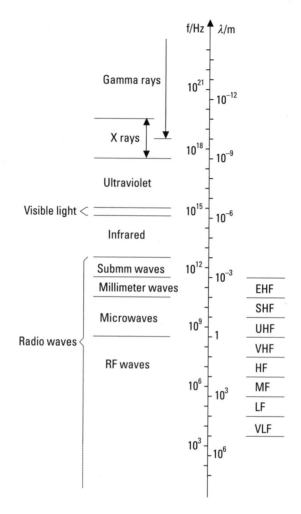

Figure 1.1 Electromagnetic spectrum.

radiation. Boundaries of the ranges are not sharp, since different sources may produce waves in overlapping ranges of frequencies. The wavelengths of radio waves range from thousands of kilometers down to 0.1 mm. The frequency range is from a few hertz up to 3 THz. The waves having shorter wavelengths or higher frequencies than radio waves are classified as infrared, visible light, ultraviolet, x-rays, and gamma rays. Infrared waves are produced by molecules and hot bodies, light and ultraviolet waves by atoms and molecules, and x-rays by the inner electrons in atoms. Commercial x-ray tubes emit bremsstrahlung. Gamma rays originate in the nuclei of atoms and overlap the upper part of the x-ray spectrum.

The spectrum of radio waves is divided into ranges having a width of one decade, as indicated in Table 1.1 and Figure 1.1. Waves below 300 MHz are often called *radio frequency* (RF) waves. *Ultrahigh frequency* (UHF) and *superhigh frequency* (SHF) waves (300 MHz to 30 GHz) are called microwaves. Often the boundary between RF waves and microwaves is set to 1 GHz. The microwave range is further subdivided into bands according to waveguide bands, as shown in Table 1.2. *Extremely high frequency* (EHF) range is called the millimeter-wave range and the frequency range from 300 GHz to 3,000 GHz the submillimeter-wave range.

The interaction of electromagnetic waves with matter depends on the energy of photons. In general, shorter waves corresponding to energetic photons interact more strongly than longer waves. The photons of radio waves have low energies; for example, at 1,000 GHz the energy is only 4×10^{-3} eV (1 eV = 1.6×10^{-19} Ws = 1.6×10^{-19} J). The energy needed to ionize molecules in biological tissue is at least 12 eV. Thus, ultraviolet

Table 1.1
Ranges of Radio Waves

Name of Frequency Range and Abbreviation	Frequencies
Very low frequency (VLF)	3–30 kHz
Low frequency (LF)	30–300 kHz
Medium frequency (MF)	300–3,000 kHz
High frequency (HF)	3–30 MHz
Very high frequency (VHF)	30–300 MHz
Ultrahigh frequency (UHF)	300–3,000 MHz
Superhigh frequency (SHF)	3–30 GHz
Extremely high frequency (EHF)	30–300 GHz

Table 1.2
Frequency Bands of Microwaves

Band	Frequencies
L	1–2 GHz
S	2–4 GHz
C	4–8 GHz
X	8–12 GHz
Ku	12–18 GHz
K	18–26 GHz
Ka	26–40 GHz

and radiation having even shorter wavelengths can ionize and dissociate molecules of biological tissues. Radio waves can only heat these materials. For example, water molecules are polar, and an electric field turns them back and forth, thus warming the food in a microwave oven.

Human beings gather a lot of information through electromagnetic waves. The retina of our eyes is sensitive to visible light, that is, wavelengths from 380 nm to 780 nm. The human skin can sense infrared or thermal radiation. Other parts of the spectrum cannot be sensed directly; they require their own specialized techniques to make the information carried by electromagnetic waves detectable. This book deals with the basic physics of radio waves and the techniques, which are needed to generate, transmit, and detect radio waves.

1.2 What Is Radio Engineering?

Radio engineering covers activities that use the possibilities offered by radio waves to serve the various goals of people. Some of these useful activities are:

- Broadcasting;
- Fixed communication (e.g., fixed radio links);
- Mobile communication;
- Radionavigation;
- Radiolocation (e.g., many radar applications);
- Amateur radio;
- Radio astronomy.

Radio engineering also covers the techniques needed to produce, process, investigate, measure, and use radio waves that make these services possible.

Electrical circuits and devices, in which the finite propagation speed of electric fields has to be taken into account or whose dimensions are of the same order as a wavelength, often are considered to belong to the field of radio engineering.

1.3 Allocation of Radio Frequencies

Radio waves have many applications and many users. However, the radio-frequency spectrum is a limited natural resource. Harmful interference between users would take place if everybody sent signals at will. Therefore, the use of radio frequencies for different applications has been coordinated internationally.

The International Telecommunication Union (ITU) was reorganized in 1993. The *ITU Radiocommunication Sector* (ITU-R) comprises the former Comité Consultatif International des Radiocommunications (CCIR) and International Frequency Registration Board (IFRB), and is responsible for all of the ITU's work in the field of radiocommunication. The mission of ITU-R is to ensure rational, equitable, efficient, and economical use of the radio-frequency spectrum by all radiocommunication services, and to carry out studies and adopt recommendations on radiocommunication matters. Technical matters are drafted in ITU-R study groups and confirmed in *World Radiocommunication Conferences* (WRCs) every second or third year. The use of the radio-frequency spectrum is regulated in the Radio Regulations [1], which are updated according to the decisions made by WRCs.

In most applications, the use of radio frequencies cannot cause interference worldwide. For example, microwaves cannot propagate far beyond the horizon. For the allocation of frequencies, the world has been divided into three regions, as shown in Figure 1.2. For example, Region 1 includes Europe, Russia, Africa, the Middle East, and parts of Asia.

The radio-frequency spectrum is allocated for about 40 radio services in the Radio Regulations. Table 1.3 is an extract of the table of frequency allocation [1] and shows the use of frequency band 10 to 10.7 GHz for

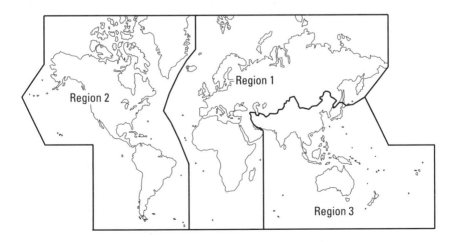

Figure 1.2 Division of world in three regions for frequency allocation. (*After:* [1].)

Table 1.3
Frequency Allocation for the Frequency Band 10–10.7 GHz

10–10.45 GHz	Fixed (Region 1 and 3)
	Mobile (Region 1 and 3)
	Radiolocation
	(Amateur)
10.45–10.5 GHz	Radiolocation
	(Amateur, amateur satellite)
10.5–10.55 GHz	Fixed
	Mobile
	Radiolocation (Region 2
	and 3; secondary in Region 1)
10.55–10.6 GHz	Fixed
	Mobile, except aeronautical mobile
	(Radiolocation)
10.6–10.68 GHz	Earth exploration satellite, passive
	Fixed
	Mobile, except aeronautical mobile
	Radio astronomy
	Space research, passive
	(Radiolocation)
10.68–10.7 GHz	Earth exploration satellite, passive
	Radio astronomy
	Space research, passive

Source: [1].

primary and secondary services (regional limitations and secondary services are shown in parentheses).

In addition to the frequency allocation, all radio and other electrical equipment must comply with the *electromagnetic compatibility* (EMC) requirements and standards to assure interference-free operation [2]. Standards set limits to the emission of equipment and give requirements for their immunity against interference.

1.4 History of Radio Engineering from Maxwell to the Present

The Scottish physicist and mathematician James Clerk Maxwell (1831–1879) predicted the existence of electromagnetic waves. He combined Gauss' law for electric and magnetic fields, Ampère's law for magnetic fields, and the Faraday-Henry law of electromagnetic induction, and added displacement current to Ampère's law. He formulated a set of equations, which he published in 1864. These equations showed the interrelation of electric and magnetic fields. Maxwell proposed that visible light is formed of electromagnetic vibrations and that electromagnetic waves of other wavelengths propagating with the speed of light were possible.

The German physicist Heinrich Hertz (1857–1894) was the first to prove experimentally the existence of radio waves, thus verifying Maxwell's equations [3]. In 1888, he released the results of his first experiments. The transmitter was an end-loaded dipole antenna with a spark gap. A current oscillating back and forth was produced as the charged antenna was discharged across the spark gap. The receiver consisted of a loop antenna and a spark gap. With this apparatus operating at about 50 MHz, Hertz was able to show that there are radio waves. Later he showed the reflection, diffraction, and polarization of radio waves, and he measured the wavelength from an interference pattern of radio waves.

The first person to use radio waves for communication was the Italian inventor Guglielmo Marconi (1874–1937). He made experiments in 1895 and submitted his patent application "Improvements in transmitting electrical impulses and signals and in apparatus therefor" in England in 1896. In 1901, Marconi, using his wireless telegraph, succeeded in sending the letter S in Morse code from Poldhu in Cornwall across the Atlantic to St. Johns in Newfoundland. Because the distance was over 3,000 km, this experiment demonstrated that radio waves could be sent beyond the horizon, contrary to the common belief of that time. The Russian physicist Alexander Popov (1859–1906) made experiments nearly simultaneously with Marconi. He demonstrated his apparatus in 1896 to a scientific audience in St. Petersburg.

Hertz used a spark gap between antenna terminals as a receiver. In 1891, the French physicist Edouard Branly (1846–1940) published a better detector, a coherer. It was based on the properties of small metal particles between two electrodes in an evacuated glass tube. Both Marconi and Popov used coherers in their early experiments. The invention of vacuum tubes was a great step forward toward better transmitters and receivers. In 1904, the British physicist John Ambrose Fleming (1849–1945) invented the rectifying vacuum tube, the diode. In 1906 the American inventor Lee De Forest (1873–1961) added a third electrode, called a grid, and thereby invented the triode. The grid controlled the current and made amplification possible. The efficiency of the electron tubes was greatly improved by using concentric cylinders as electrodes. One of the first inventors was the Finnish engineer Eric Tigerstedt (1886–1925), who filed his patent application for such a triode in 1914.

De Forest and the American engineer and inventor Edwin Armstrong (1890–1954) independently discovered regenerative feedback in 1912. This phenomenon was used to produce a continuous carrier wave, which could be modulated by a voice signal. Armstrong invented also the superheterodyne receiver. These techniques made broadcasting possible. AM stations began broadcasting in 1919 and 1920. Regular TV transmissions started in Germany in 1935. Armstrong's third great broadcasting invention was FM radio, but FM broadcasting was accepted not until after World War II.

Communication was not the only application of radio waves. Karl Jansky (1905–1950), while studying radio noise at Bell Labs in 1932, detected a steady hiss from our own galaxy, the Milky Way. This was the beginning of radio astronomy. The invention of microwave tubes, of klystron in 1939, and of magnetron in 1940 was essential for the development of microwave radar during World War II. The principle of radar had been introduced much earlier by the German engineer Christian Hülsmeyer (1881–1957), who made experiments in 1903. Due to the lack of financing, the idea was abandoned until 1922, when Marconi proposed using radar for detecting ships in fog.

The Radiation Laboratory, which was established at the Massachusetts Institute of Technology during World War II, had a great impact on the development of radio engineering. Many leading American physicists were gathered there to develop radar, radionavigation, microwave components, microwave theory, electronics, and education in the field, and gave written 27 books on the research conducted there.

The rectifying properties of semiconductors were noted in the late nineteenth century. However, the development of semiconductor devices was slow because vacuum tubes could do all the necessary operations, such as amplification and detection. A serious study of semiconductors began in the 1940s. The high-frequency capabilities of the point-contact semiconductor diode had already been observed. The invention of the transistor by Bardeen, Brattain, and Shockley started a new era in electronics. Their point-contact transistor worked for the first time in 1947. The principle of the bipolar junction transistor was proposed the next year.

The subsequent development of semiconductor devices is a prerequisite for the radio engineering of today. The continuous development of components and integrated circuits has made it possible to pack more complex functions to an ever-smaller space, which in turn has made possible many modern systems, such as mobile communication, satellite communication, and satellite navigation systems.

References

[1] *Radio Regulations,* Vol. I, Geneva, Switzerland: International Telecommunication Union, 2001.

[2] Paul, C. R., *Introduction to Electromagnetic Compatibility,* New York: John Wiley & Sons, 1992.

[3] Levy, R., (ed.), "Special Issue Commemorating the Centennial of Heinrich Hertz," *IEEE Trans. on Microwave Theory and Techniques,* Vol. 36, No. 5, 1988, pp. 801–858.

2

Fundamentals of Electromagnetic Fields

In this chapter, we outline the fundamentals of electromagnetic theory that we will need in the analysis of waveguides, antennas, and other devices. Here we use the following electric and magnetic quantities:

$\mathbf{E}$, electric field strength [V/m];
$\mathbf{D}$, electric flux density [C/m^2 = As/m^2];
$\mathbf{H}$, magnetic field strength [A/m];
$\mathbf{B}$, magnetic flux density [Wb/m^2 = Vs/m^2];
$\mathbf{J}$, electric current density [A/m^2];
$\mathbf{J_s}$, electric surface current density [A/m];
ρ, electric charge density [C/m^3 = As/m^3].

2.1 Maxwell's Equations

Maxwell's equations relate the fields ($\mathbf{E}$ and $\mathbf{H}$) and their sources (ρ and $\mathbf{J}$) to each other. The electric field strength $\mathbf{E}$ and the magnetic flux density $\mathbf{B}$ may be considered the basic quantities, because they allow calculation of a force $\mathbf{F}$, applied to a charge, q, moving at a velocity, $\mathbf{v}$, in an electromagnetic field; this is obtained using Lorentz's force law:

$$\mathbf{F} = q(\mathbf{E} + \mathbf{v} \times \mathbf{B}) \tag{2.1}$$

11

The electric flux density **D** and the magnetic field strength **H** take into account the presence of materials. The electric and magnetic properties of media bind the field strengths and flux densities; the constitutive relations are

$$\mathbf{D} = \epsilon \mathbf{E} \tag{2.2}$$

$$\mathbf{B} = \mu \mathbf{H} \tag{2.3}$$

where ϵ is the permittivity [F/m = As/Vm] and μ is the permeability [H/m = Vs/Am] of the medium.

Maxwell's equations in differential form are

I $\nabla \cdot \mathbf{D} = \rho$ Gauss' law   (2.4)

II $\nabla \cdot \mathbf{B} = 0$ (2.5)

III $\nabla \times \mathbf{E} = -\dfrac{\partial \mathbf{B}}{\partial t}$ Faraday's law   (2.6)

IV $\nabla \times \mathbf{H} = \mathbf{J} + \dfrac{\partial \mathbf{D}}{\partial t}$ Ampère's law and Maxwell's addition   (2.7)

As also mentioned in the above equations, a lot of the knowledge of electromagnetic theory was already developed before Maxwell by Gauss, Faraday, Ampère, and others. Maxwell's contribution was to put the existing knowledge together and to add the hypothetical displacement current, which then led to Hertz and Marconi's discoveries and to modern radio engineering.

How did Maxwell discover the displacement current? We may speculate and simplify this process of invention as follows (see [1], Chapter 18): Maxwell studied the known laws and expressed them as differential equations for each vector component, because the nabla notation (curl and divergence of a vector quantity) was not yet known. Nevertheless, we use the nabla notation here. He found that while Gauss' and Faraday's laws are true in general, there is a problem in Ampère's law:

$$\nabla \times \mathbf{H} = \mathbf{J} \tag{2.8}$$

If one takes the divergence of this equation, the left-hand side is zero, because the divergence of a curl is always zero. However, if the divergence of **J** is zero, then the total flux of current through any closed surface is zero. Maxwell correctly understood the law of charge conservation: The flux of current through a closed surface must be equal to the change of charge inside the surface (in the volume), that is,

$$\nabla \cdot \mathbf{J} = -\frac{\partial \rho}{\partial t} \qquad (2.9)$$

In order to avoid the controversy, Maxwell added the displacement current term, $\partial \mathbf{D}/\partial t$, to the right-hand side of Ampère's law in a general case and got

$$\nabla \times \mathbf{H} = \mathbf{J} + \frac{\partial \mathbf{D}}{\partial t} \qquad (2.10)$$

With this addition the principle of charge conservation holds, because by using Gauss' law we obtain

$$\nabla \cdot \nabla \times \mathbf{H} = \nabla \cdot \mathbf{J} + \frac{\partial}{\partial t} \nabla \cdot \mathbf{D} = \nabla \cdot \mathbf{J} + \frac{\partial \rho}{\partial t} = 0$$

The differential equations, (2.4) through (2.7), describe the fields locally or at a given point. In other words, they allow us to obtain the change of field versus space or time. Maxwell's equations in integral form describe how the field integrals over a closed surface S ($\oint_S$) or along a closed loop Γ ($\oint_\Gamma$) depend on the sources and changes of the fields versus time. Maxwell's equations in integral form are:

$$\text{I} \quad \oint_S \mathbf{D} \cdot d\mathbf{S} = \int_V \rho dV \qquad (2.11)$$

$$\text{II} \quad \oint_S \mathbf{B} \cdot d\mathbf{S} = 0 \qquad (2.12)$$

$$\text{III} \quad \oint_\Gamma \mathbf{E} \cdot d\mathbf{l} = -\frac{\partial}{\partial t} \int_S \mathbf{B} \cdot d\mathbf{S} \qquad (2.13)$$

$$\text{IV} \quad \oint_\Gamma \mathbf{H} \cdot d\mathbf{l} = \int_S \left(\mathbf{J} + \frac{\partial \mathbf{D}}{\partial t} \right) \cdot d\mathbf{S} \qquad (2.14)$$

where $d\mathbf{S}$ is an element vector perpendicular to surface S having a magnitude equal to the surface element area, $d\mathbf{l}$ is a length element parallel to the loop, and dV is a volume element. The volume, V, is enclosed by the closed surface S. Equations (2.11) and (2.12) are obtained by applying Gauss' theorem, according to which for any vector quantity $\mathbf{A}$ it holds

$$\oint_S \mathbf{A} \cdot d\mathbf{S} = \int_V \nabla \cdot \mathbf{A} \, dV \qquad (2.15)$$

and (2.13) and (2.14) are obtained by applying Stokes' theorem

$$\oint_\Gamma \mathbf{A} \cdot d\mathbf{l} = \int_S (\nabla \times \mathbf{A}) \cdot d\mathbf{S} \qquad (2.16)$$

Maxwell's equations would be symmetric in relation to electric and magnetic quantities if magnetic charge density ρ_M [Wb/m^3 = Vs/m^3] and magnetic current density $\mathbf{M}$ [V/m^2] were also introduced into them. However, there is no experimental evidence of their existence.

2.1.1 Maxwell's Equations in Case of Harmonic Time Dependence

Time harmonic fields, that is, fields having a sinusoidal time dependence at angular frequency of $\omega = 2\pi f$, may be presented as

$$\mathbf{A}(x, y, z, t) = \text{Re}\,[\mathbf{A}(x, y, z)\,e^{j\omega t}] \qquad (2.17)$$

At a given point (x, y, z), the field may be thought to be a vector rotating on the complex plane and having a constant amplitude, the real part of which is the field value at a given instant. Most phenomena in radio engineering are time harmonic or can be thought to be superpositions of several time harmonics. Therefore, in this book we will confine ourselves to the time harmonic cases. Assuming the $e^{j\omega t}$ time dependence, the time derivatives can be replaced by multiplications by $j\omega$. For such sinusoidal fields and sources, Maxwell's equations in differential form are

$$\text{I} \qquad \nabla \cdot \mathbf{D} = \rho \qquad (2.18)$$

$$\text{II} \qquad \nabla \cdot \mathbf{B} = 0 \qquad (2.19)$$

$$\text{III} \qquad \nabla \times \mathbf{E} = -j\omega\mathbf{B} = -j\omega\mu\mathbf{H} \qquad (2.20)$$

$$\text{IV} \qquad \nabla \times \mathbf{H} = \mathbf{J} + j\omega\mathbf{D} = (\sigma + j\omega\epsilon)\mathbf{E} \qquad (2.21)$$

and in integral form

$$\text{I} \quad \oint_S \mathbf{D} \cdot d\mathbf{S} = \int_V \rho dV \qquad (2.22)$$

$$\text{II} \quad \oint_S \mathbf{B} \cdot d\mathbf{S} = 0 \qquad (2.23)$$

$$\text{III} \quad \oint_\Gamma \mathbf{E} \cdot d\mathbf{l} = -j\omega \int_S \mathbf{B} \cdot d\mathbf{S} = -j\omega\mu \int_S \mathbf{H} \cdot d\mathbf{S} \qquad (2.24)$$

$$\text{IV} \quad \oint_\Gamma \mathbf{H} \cdot d\mathbf{l} = \int_S (\mathbf{J} + j\omega\mathbf{D}) \cdot d\mathbf{S} = (\sigma + j\omega\epsilon) \int_S \mathbf{E} \cdot d\mathbf{S} \qquad (2.25)$$

In (2.21) and (2.25) we have taken into account that

$$\mathbf{J} = \sigma\mathbf{E} \qquad (2.26)$$

where σ is the conductivity [S/m = A/Vm] of the medium.

2.1.2 Interpretations of Maxwell's Equations

Maxwell's equations may be presented in words as follows:

I The electric flux (surface integral of the electric flux) through a closed surface is equal to the total charge within the volume confined by the surface.

II The magnetic flux (surface integral of the magnetic flux) through any closed surface is zero.

III The line integral of the electric field along a closed contour is equal to the negative time derivative of the magnetic flux through the closed contour.

IV The line integral of the magnetic field along a closed contour is equal to the sum of the total current through the closed contour and the time derivative of the electric flux.

Figure 2.1 illustrates Maxwell's equations in integral form. These qualitative interpretations are as follows:

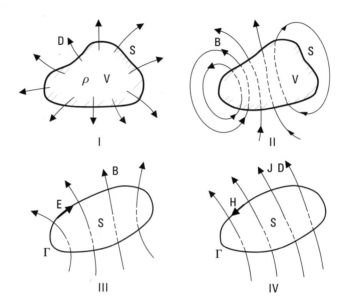

Figure 2.1 Maxwell's equations (in integral form).

I   The distribution of the electric charge determines the electric field.

II The magnetic flux lines are closed; in other words, there are no magnetic charges.

III A changing magnetic flux creates an electric field.

IV Both a moving charge (current) and a changing electric flux create a magnetic field.

The creation of an electromagnetic field is easy to understand qualitatively with the aid of Maxwell's equations. Let us consider a current loop with a changing current. The changing current creates a changing magnetic field (IV); the changing magnetic field creates a changing electric field (III); the changing electric field creates a changing magnetic field (IV); and so on. Figure 2.2 illustrates the creation of a propagating wave.

Maxwell's equations form the basis of radio engineering and, in fact, of the whole of electrical engineering. These equations cannot be derived from other laws; they are based on empirical research. Their validity comes from their capability to predict the electromagnetic phenomena correctly. Many books deal with fundamentals of the electromagnetic fields, such as those listed in [1–8].

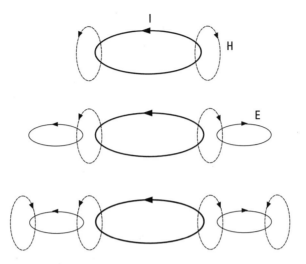

Figure 2.2 Electromagnetic wave produced by a current loop.

2.2 Fields in Media

In the above equations, the permittivity ϵ and permeability μ represent the properties of the medium. A medium is homogeneous if its properties are constant, independent of location. An isotropic medium has the same properties in all directions. The properties of a linear medium are independent on field strength.

In a vacuum, $\epsilon = \epsilon_0 \approx 8.8542 \times 10^{-12}$ F/m and $\mu = \mu_0 = 4\pi \times 10^{-7}$ H/m. In other homogeneous media, $\epsilon = \epsilon_r \epsilon_0$ and $\mu = \mu_r \mu_0$, where the dielectric constant ϵ_r, that is, the relative permittivity, and the relative permeability, μ_r, depend on the structure of the material. For air we can take $\epsilon_r = \mu_r = 1$ for most applications. In general, in a lossy medium, ϵ_r or μ_r are complex, and in an anisotropic medium ϵ_r or μ_r are tensors.

Let us consider a dielectric that has no freely moving charges. The electric field, however, causes polarization of the material, that is, the electric dipole moments tend to align along the field. The field induces a dipole moment into the atoms by disturbing the movement of electrons. The so-called polar molecules, such as the water molecule, have a stationary dipole moment, because the charge is distributed unevenly in the molecule.

Electric polarization may be illustrated with a plate capacitor, the plates of which have an area of A and charges of $+Q$ and $-Q$. If the fringing field lines are negligible, the electric flux density is $D = Q/A$. If there is vacuum (or air) between the plates, the electric field strength is $E_0 = D/\epsilon_0$; see

Figure 2.3(a). When a dielectric material is introduced between the plates, the dipole moments align along the field lines; see Figure 2.3(b). The flux density does not change if Q does not change, because the charge density in the dielectric is zero. However, the field strength decreases, because the field caused by the dipole moments cancels part of the original field. Therefore, the electric flux density may be written as

$$\mathbf{D} = \epsilon_0 \mathbf{E} + \mathbf{P_e} \tag{2.27}$$

where $\mathbf{P_e}$ is a dipole moment per unit volume due to polarization. If a constant voltage is applied between the plates, the electric field strength stays constant, and the electric flux density and the charge of the plates increase when dielectric material is introduced between the plates. In a linear medium, the electric polarization depends linearly on the field strength

$$\mathbf{P_e} = \epsilon_0 \chi_e \mathbf{E} \tag{2.28}$$

where χ_e is the electric susceptibility, which may be complex. Now

$$\mathbf{D} = \epsilon_0 (1 + \chi_e)\mathbf{E} = \epsilon \mathbf{E} \tag{2.29}$$

where

$$\epsilon = \epsilon_0 (1 + \chi_e) = \epsilon_0 \epsilon_r = \epsilon_0 (\epsilon_r' - j\epsilon_r'') \tag{2.30}$$

is the complex permittivity. The imaginary part is due to loss in the medium; damping of the vibrating dipole moments causes heat, because the polar molecules cannot follow the changing electric flux due to friction.

The loss in a medium may also be due to conductivity of the material. In this case there are free charges in the material that are moved by the

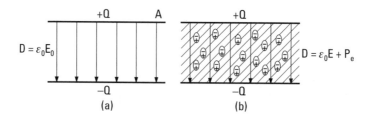

Figure 2.3 Plate capacitor, which has as its insulator (a) vacuum, and (b) dielectric material that has electric dipole moments.

electric field. When the conduction current density $\mathbf{J} = \sigma\mathbf{E}$ is introduced in Maxwell's IV equation, one obtains

$$\nabla \times \mathbf{H} = [\sigma + j\omega\epsilon_0(\epsilon_r' - j\epsilon_r'')]\mathbf{E} = j\omega\epsilon_0\left(\epsilon_r' - j\epsilon_r'' - j\frac{\sigma}{\omega\epsilon_0}\right)\mathbf{E}$$

(2.31)

which shows that damping due to polarization and damping due to conduction are indistinguishable without a measurement at several frequencies. Often $\sigma/(\omega\epsilon_0)$ is included in ϵ_r''. Loss of a medium is often characterized by the loss tangent

$$\tan\delta = \frac{\epsilon_r'' + \sigma/(\omega\epsilon_0)}{\epsilon_r'}$$

(2.32)

which allows us to write (2.31) in form

$$\nabla \times \mathbf{H} = j\omega\epsilon_0\epsilon_r'(1 - j\tan\delta)\mathbf{E}$$

(2.33)

In case of magnetic materials, the situation is analogous: The magnetic field aligns magnetic dipole moments, that is, polarizes the material magnetically. The permeability can be divided into a real part μ_r' and an imaginary part μ_r''; the latter causes magnetic loss.

The same medium may be considered as a dielectric at a very high frequency but a conductor at a low frequency. One may argue that a material is a dielectric if $\sigma/(\omega\epsilon_r'\epsilon_0) < 1/100$ and a conductor if $\sigma/(\omega\epsilon_r'\epsilon_0) > 100$. Table 2.1 shows conductivity, the real part of the dielectric constant, and the frequency at which the conduction current is equal to the displacement current for some media common in nature.

Table 2.1
Conductivity, Real Part of Dielectric Constant, and Frequency f_T at Which the Conduction Current Is Equal to the Displacement Current of Some Materials

Material	σ [S/m]	ϵ_r'	f_T [MHz]
Sea water	5	70	1300
Fresh water	3×10^{-3}	80	0.7
Moist soil	10^{-2}	30	6
Dry soil	10^{-4}	3	0.6
Ice	$10^{-5} \ldots 10^{-4}$	3	0.06–0.6

2.3 Boundary Conditions

In electronics and radio engineering we often have electromagnetic problems where the properties of the medium change abruptly. We have to know the behavior of fields at such interfaces, that is, we have to know the boundary conditions. They can be deduced from Maxwell's equations in integral form.

Let us consider a general interface between the two media presented in Figure 2.4. Medium 1 is characterized by ϵ_1 and μ_1, and medium 2 by ϵ_2 and μ_2. In the following, fields normal to the surface (of the interface) are denoted with subscript n and fields tangential to the surface with subscript t.

Let us consider a closed contour with dimensions Δl and h as shown in Figure 2.4. If h approaches 0, we obtain from Maxwell's III equation, (2.24):

$$\oint_\Gamma \mathbf{E} \cdot d\mathbf{l} = E_{1t}\Delta l - E_{2t}\Delta l = -j\omega \int_S \mathbf{B} \cdot d\mathbf{S}$$

which approaches zero because as the area $\Delta l h$ vanishes, the magnetic flux through the contour must also vanish. Therefore $E_{1t} = E_{2t}$, or

$$\mathbf{n} \times (\mathbf{E}_1 - \mathbf{E}_2) = 0 \tag{2.34}$$

Next we utilize Maxwell's IV equation, (2.25)

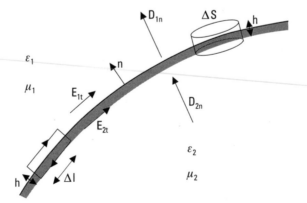

Figure 2.4 Boundary between two media.

$$\oint_{\Gamma} \mathbf{H} \cdot d\mathbf{l} = H_{1t}\Delta l - H_{2t}\Delta l = \int_{S} (\mathbf{J} + j\omega\mathbf{D}) \cdot d\mathbf{S}$$

which approaches a value of $J_s \Delta l$ as h approaches zero, because when the area $\Delta l h$ vanishes the electric flux through the contour must vanish, but a current remains due to the surface current density J_s at the interface. Now we obtain

$$\mathbf{n} \times (\mathbf{H}_1 - \mathbf{H}_2) = \mathbf{J_s} \qquad (2.35)$$

Next we consider a "pillbox," a cylinder also shown in Figure 2.4. Its dimensions are height h and end surface area ΔS. Utilizing Maxwell's I equation, (2.22), in the case where h approaches 0, we obtain

$$\oint_{S} \mathbf{D} \cdot d\mathbf{S} = D_{2n}\Delta S - D_{1n}\Delta S = \int_{V} \rho dV = \rho_s \Delta S$$

where ρ_s is the surface charge density at the interface. Now we obtain the following boundary condition:

$$\mathbf{n} \cdot (\mathbf{D}_1 - \mathbf{D}_2) = \mathbf{n} \cdot (\epsilon_1 \mathbf{E}_1 - \epsilon_2 \mathbf{E}_2) = \rho_s \qquad (2.36)$$

Similarly we can derive the following result for the magnetic flux density $\mathbf{B}$ (Maxwell's II equation):

$$\mathbf{n} \cdot (\mathbf{B}_1 - \mathbf{B}_2) = \mathbf{n} \cdot (\mu_1 \mathbf{H}_1 - \mu_2 \mathbf{H}_2) = 0 \qquad (2.37)$$

In case of an interface between two media, we obtain the following boundary conditions:

$$\mathbf{n} \times (\mathbf{E}_1 - \mathbf{E}_2) = 0 \qquad (2.38)$$

$$\mathbf{n} \times (\mathbf{H}_1 - \mathbf{H}_2) = 0 \qquad (2.39)$$

$$\mathbf{n} \cdot (\mathbf{D}_1 - \mathbf{D}_2) = 0 \qquad (2.40)$$

$$\mathbf{n} \cdot (\mathbf{B}_1 - \mathbf{B}_2) = 0 \qquad (2.41)$$

These equations state that the tangential components of $\mathbf{E}$ and $\mathbf{H}$ as well as the normal components of $\mathbf{D}$ and $\mathbf{B}$ are equal on both sides of the interface, that is, they are continuous across the interface.

In radio engineering we often consider a case where we have an interface with a good conductor. Fields penetrate only a short distance into a good conductor such as metal and not at all into a perfect conductor ($\sigma = \infty$). We often approximate a good conductor with a perfect conductor, which is lossless. The boundary conditions at the interface of a dielectric and a perfect conductor are:

$$\mathbf{n} \times \mathbf{E} = 0 \tag{2.42}$$

$$\mathbf{n} \times \mathbf{H} = \mathbf{J_s} \tag{2.43}$$

$$\mathbf{n} \cdot \mathbf{D} = \rho_s \tag{2.44}$$

$$\mathbf{n} \cdot \mathbf{B} = 0 \tag{2.45}$$

Such a boundary is also called an *electric wall.* Dual to the electric wall is the *magnetic wall,* where the tangential component of **H** vanishes.

2.4 Helmholtz Equation and Its Plane Wave Solution

In a source-free ($\rho = 0$, $\mathbf{J} = 0$), linear, and isotropic medium, Maxwell's equations are simplified into the following forms:

$$\nabla \cdot \mathbf{E} = 0 \tag{2.46}$$

$$\nabla \cdot \mathbf{H} = 0 \tag{2.47}$$

$$\nabla \times \mathbf{E} = -j\omega\mu\mathbf{H} \tag{2.48}$$

$$\nabla \times \mathbf{H} = j\omega\epsilon\mathbf{E} \tag{2.49}$$

When the $\nabla \times$ operator is applied on both sides of (2.48), we obtain in a homogeneous medium

$$\nabla \times \nabla \times \mathbf{E} = -j\omega\mu\nabla \times \mathbf{H} \tag{2.50}$$

which leads, after utilizing vector identity

$$\nabla \times \nabla \times \mathbf{A} = \nabla(\nabla \cdot \mathbf{A}) - \nabla^2\mathbf{A} \tag{2.51}$$

and (2.46), to

$$\nabla^2\mathbf{E} = -\omega^2\mu\epsilon\mathbf{E} = -k^2\mathbf{E} \tag{2.52}$$

This equation is called the Helmholtz equation, which is a special case of the wave equation

$$\nabla^2 \mathbf{E} - \mu\epsilon \frac{\partial^2 \mathbf{E}}{\partial t^2} = 0 \qquad (2.53)$$

The constant $k = \omega\sqrt{\mu\epsilon}$ is called the wave number [1/m].

Let us first consider propagation of a wave in a lossless medium, where ϵ_r and μ_r are real. Then k is also real. Let us assume that the electric field has only the x component, that the field is uniform in the x and y directions, and that the wave propagates in the z direction. The Helmholtz equation reduces to

$$\frac{\partial^2 E_x}{\partial z^2} + k^2 E_x = 0 \qquad (2.54)$$

The solution of this equation is

$$E_x(z) = E^+ e^{-jkz} + E^- e^{jkz} \qquad (2.55)$$

where E^+ and E^- are arbitrary amplitudes of waves propagating into the $+z$ and $-z$ directions, respectively. The exact values of E^+ and E^- are determined by the sources and the boundary conditions. In the time domain, (2.55) can be rewritten as

$$E_x(z, t) = E^+ \cos(\omega t - kz) + E^- \cos(\omega t + kz) \qquad (2.56)$$

where E^+ and E^- are now real constants.

The magnetic field of a plane wave can be solved from (2.49). The result is

$$H_y = \frac{1}{\eta}(E^+ e^{-jkz} - E^- e^{jkz}) \qquad (2.57)$$

that is, the magnetic field has a component that is perpendicular to the electric field and to the direction of propagation. The ratio of the electric and magnetic fields is called the wave impedance, and it is $\eta = \sqrt{\mu/\epsilon}$. In vacuum $\eta_0 = \sqrt{\mu_0/\epsilon_0} \approx 120\pi\,\Omega \approx 377\,\Omega$. Figure 2.5 illustrates a plane

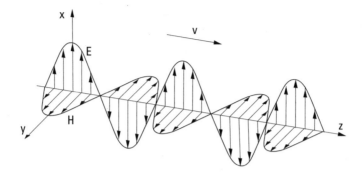

Figure 2.5 Plane wave propagating into the +z direction.

wave propagating into the +z direction. The fields of a plane wave repeat themselves periodically in the z direction; the wavelength is

$$\lambda = \frac{2\pi}{k} = \frac{2\pi}{\omega\sqrt{\mu\epsilon}} = \frac{1}{f\sqrt{\mu\epsilon}} \qquad (2.58)$$

The propagation velocity of the wave is

$$v = f\lambda = \frac{1}{\sqrt{\mu\epsilon}} \qquad (2.59)$$

In a vacuum, the propagation velocity is the speed of light:

$$v = c = \frac{1}{\sqrt{\mu_0\epsilon_0}} \approx 2.998 \times 10^8 \text{ m/s} \qquad (2.60)$$

In a lossy medium having conductivity σ, Maxwell's III and IV equations (the curl equations) are

$$\nabla \times \mathbf{E} = -j\omega\mu\mathbf{H} \qquad (2.61)$$

$$\nabla \times \mathbf{H} = \sigma\mathbf{E} + j\omega\epsilon\mathbf{E} \qquad (2.62)$$

Now the Helmholtz equation gets the following form:

$$\nabla^2\mathbf{E} + \omega^2\mu\epsilon\left(1 - j\frac{\sigma}{\omega\epsilon}\right)\mathbf{E} = 0 \qquad (2.63)$$

Compared to (2.52), here jk is replaced by a complex propagation constant,

$$\gamma = \alpha + j\beta = j\omega\sqrt{\mu\epsilon}\sqrt{1 - j\frac{\sigma}{\omega\epsilon}} \tag{2.64}$$

where α is the attenuation constant and β is the phase constant. In the case of a plane wave propagating into the z direction, we have

$$\frac{\partial^2 E_x}{\partial z^2} - \gamma^2 E_x = 0 \tag{2.65}$$

leading to

$$E_x(z) = E^+ e^{-\gamma z} + E^- e^{\gamma z} \tag{2.66}$$

In the time domain

$$E_x(z, t) = E^+ e^{-\alpha z}\cos(\omega t - \beta z) + E^- e^{\alpha z}\cos(\omega t + \beta z) \tag{2.67}$$

In the case of a good conductor, that is, when $\sigma \gg \omega\epsilon$, we obtain the propagation constant as

$$\gamma = \alpha + j\beta \approx j\omega\sqrt{\mu\epsilon}\sqrt{\frac{\sigma}{j\omega\epsilon}} = (1 + j)\sqrt{\frac{\omega\mu\sigma}{2}} \tag{2.68}$$

When a plane wave meets a surface of a lossy medium in the perpendicular direction and penetrates into it, its field is damped into $1/e$ part over a distance called the skin depth:

$$\delta_s = \frac{1}{\alpha} = \sqrt{\frac{2}{\omega\mu\sigma}} \tag{2.69}$$

Example 2.1

Find the attenuation of a 4 μm-thick copper layer at 10 GHz.

Solution

At a frequency of 10 GHz the skin depth in pure copper ($\sigma = 5.8 \times 10^7$ S/m, $\mu = \mu_0$) is only 6.6×10^{-7} m. Therefore, at this frequency a uniform electromagnetic shield made of pure copper of thickness of 4 μm (= 6 skin depths) provides an attenuation of about $-20 \log (1/e)^6 \approx 6 \times 8.68$ dB $\approx$ 50 dB.

In a general case, each field component can be solved from the general Helmholtz equation:

$$\frac{\partial^2 E_i}{\partial x^2} + \frac{\partial^2 E_i}{\partial y^2} + \frac{\partial^2 E_i}{\partial z^2} - \gamma^2 E_i = 0, \ i = x, y, z \qquad (2.70)$$

The solution is found by using the separation of variables. By assuming that $E_i = f(x)g(y)h(z)$,

$$\frac{f''}{f} + \frac{g''}{g} + \frac{h''}{h} - \gamma^2 = 0 \qquad (2.71)$$

where the double prime denotes the second derivative. The first three terms of this equation are each a function of one independent variable. As the sum of these terms is constant (γ^2), each term must also be constant. Therefore, (2.71) can be divided into three independent equations of form $f''/f - \gamma_x^2 = 0$, which have solutions as shown previously.

2.5 Polarization of a Plane Wave

Electromagnetic fields are vector quantities, which have a direction in space. The polarization of a plane wave refers to this orientation of the electric field vector, which may be a fixed orientation (a linear polarization) or may change with time (a circular or elliptical polarization).

The electric field of a plane wave can be presented as a sum of two orthogonal components

$$\mathbf{E} = (E_1 \mathbf{u_x} + E_2 \mathbf{u_y}) e^{-jkz} \qquad (2.72)$$

where $\mathbf{u_x}$ and $\mathbf{u_y}$ are the unit vectors in the x and y direction, respectively. In a general case this represents an elliptically polarized wave. The polarization ellipse shown in Figure 2.6(a) is characterized by the axial ratio E_{max}/E_{min}, tilt angle τ, and direction of rotation. The direction of rotation, as seen in

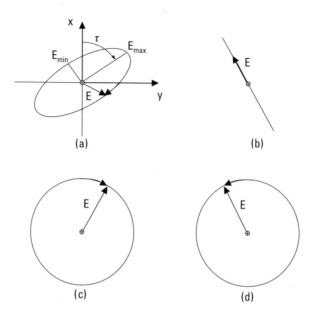

Figure 2.6 Polarization of a plane wave: (a) elliptic; (b) linear; (c) clockwise circular; and
(d) counterclockwise circular.

the direction of propagation and observed in a plane perpendicular to the
direction of propagation, is either clockwise (right-handed) or counterclockwise (left-handed).

Special cases of an elliptic polarization are the linear polarization, Figure
2.6(b), and circular polarization, Figure 2.6(c, d). If $E_1 \neq 0$ and $E_2 = 0$, we
have a wave polarized linearly in the x direction. If both E_1 and E_2 are
nonzero but real and the components are in the same phase, we have a
linearly polarized wave, the polarization direction of which is in angle

$$\tau = \arctan (E_2/E_1) \tag{2.73}$$

In the case of circular polarization, the components have equal amplitudes and a 90° phase difference, that is, $E_1 = \pm jE_2 = E_0$ (E_0 real), and the
electric field is

$$\mathbf{E} = E_0 (\mathbf{u_x} - j\mathbf{u_y}) e^{-jkz} \tag{2.74}$$

or

$$\mathbf{E} = E_0 (\mathbf{u_x} + j\mathbf{u_y}) e^{-jkz} \tag{2.75}$$

The former represents a clockwise, circularly polarized wave, and the latter a counterclockwise, circularly polarized wave. In the time domain the circularly polarized wave can be presented as (clockwise)

$$\mathbf{E}(z,\, t) = E_0[\mathbf{u_x} \cos(\omega t - kz) + \mathbf{u_y} \cos(\omega t - kz - \pi/2)] \quad (2.76)$$

and (counterclockwise)

$$\mathbf{E}(z,\, t) = E_0[\mathbf{u_x} \cos(\omega t - kz) - \mathbf{u_y} \cos(\omega t - kz - \pi/2)] \quad (2.77)$$

At $z = 0$, (2.76) and (2.77) are reduced to

$$\mathbf{E}(t) = E_0[\mathbf{u_x} \cos \omega t \pm \mathbf{u_y} \cos(\omega t - \pi/2)] \quad (2.78)$$

2.6 Reflection and Transmission at a Dielectric Interface

Let us consider a plane wave that is incident at a planar interface of two lossless media, as illustrated in Figure 2.7. The wave comes from medium 1, which is characterized by ϵ_1 and μ_1, to medium 2 with ϵ_2 and μ_2. The planar interface is at $z = 0$. The angle of incidence is θ_1 and the propagation vector $\mathbf{k}_1$ is in the xz-plane. Part $E_1{}'$ from the incident field is reflected at an angle $\theta_1{}'$ and part E_2 is transmitted through the interface and leaves at an angle of θ_2.

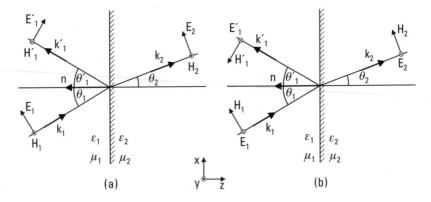

Figure 2.7 Reflection and transmission of a plane wave in case of an oblique incidence at an interface of two lossless media: (a) parallel polarization, and (b) perpendicular polarization.

According to the boundary conditions, the tangential components of the electric and magnetic field are equal on both sides of the interface in each point of plane $z = 0$. This is possible only if the phase of the incident, reflected, and transmitted waves change equally in the x direction, in other words, the phase velocities in the x direction are the same, or

$$\frac{v_1}{\sin \theta_1} = \frac{v_1}{\sin \theta_1'} = \frac{v_2}{\sin \theta_2} \tag{2.79}$$

where v_1 and v_2 ($v_i = \omega/k_i$) are the wave velocities in medium 1 and 2, respectively. From (2.79) it follows

$$\theta_1' = \theta_1 \tag{2.80}$$

which means the angle of incidence and angle of reflection are equal, and the angle of propagation of the transmitted wave is obtained from

$$\frac{\sin \theta_2}{\sin \theta_1} = \sqrt{\frac{\mu_1 \epsilon_1}{\mu_2 \epsilon_2}} \tag{2.81}$$

Let us assume in the following that $\mu_1 = \mu_2 = \mu_0$, which is valid in most cases of interest in practice. Then (2.81), which is called Snell's law, can be rewritten as

$$\frac{\sin \theta_2}{\sin \theta_1} = \sqrt{\frac{\epsilon_1}{\epsilon_2}} = \sqrt{\frac{\epsilon_{r1}}{\epsilon_{r2}}} = \frac{n_1}{n_2} \tag{2.82}$$

where $n_1 = \sqrt{\epsilon_{r1}}$ and $n_2 = \sqrt{\epsilon_{r2}}$ are the refraction indices of the materials.

The reflection and transmission coefficients depend on the polarization of the incident wave. Important special cases are the so-called parallel and perpendicular polarizations; see Figure 2.7. The parallel polarization means that the electric field vector is in the same plane with $\mathbf{k}_1$ and the normal $\mathbf{n}$ of the plane, that is, the field vector is in the xz-plane. The perpendicular polarization means that the electric field vector is perpendicular to the plane described previously, that is, it is parallel to the y-axis. The polarization of an arbitrary incident plane wave can be thought to be a superposition of the parallel and perpendicular polarizations.

In the case of the parallel polarization, the condition of continuity of the tangential electric field is

$$E_1 \cos \theta_1 + E_1' \cos \theta_1' = E_2 \cos \theta_2 \tag{2.83}$$

which leads, with the aid of (2.80) and (2.82), to

$$(E_1 + E_1') \cos \theta_1 = E_2 \sqrt{1 - \frac{\epsilon_1}{\epsilon_2} \sin^2 \theta_1} \tag{2.84}$$

The magnetic field has only a component in the y direction. The continuity of the tangential magnetic field leads to

$$(E_1 - E_1') \sqrt{\epsilon_1} = E_2 \sqrt{\epsilon_2} \tag{2.85}$$

From (2.84) and (2.85) we can solve for the parallel polarization the reflection and transmission coefficients, $\rho_\parallel$ and $\tau_\parallel$, respectively:

$$\rho_\parallel = \frac{E_1'}{E_1} = \frac{\sqrt{\dfrac{\epsilon_2}{\epsilon_1} - \sin^2 \theta_1} - \dfrac{\epsilon_2}{\epsilon_1} \cos \theta_1}{\sqrt{\dfrac{\epsilon_2}{\epsilon_1} - \sin^2 \theta_1} + \dfrac{\epsilon_2}{\epsilon_1} \cos \theta_1} \tag{2.86}$$

$$\tau_\parallel = \frac{E_2}{E_1} = \frac{2\sqrt{\dfrac{\epsilon_2}{\epsilon_1}} \cos \theta_1}{\sqrt{\dfrac{\epsilon_2}{\epsilon_1} - \sin^2 \theta_1} + \dfrac{\epsilon_2}{\epsilon_1} \cos \theta_1} \tag{2.87}$$

When the angle of incidence is 90°, that is, when the incident wave approaches perpendicularly to the surface, it holds for ρ and τ that

$$1 + \rho = \tau \tag{2.88}$$

In case of the perpendicular polarization, the boundary conditions lead to

$$E_1 + E_1' = E_2 \tag{2.89}$$

$$(E_1 - E_1') \sqrt{\epsilon_1} \cos \theta_1 = E_2 \sqrt{\epsilon_2} \cos \theta_2 \tag{2.90}$$

from which we can solve for the perpendicular polarization

$$\rho_\perp = \frac{\cos\,\theta_1 - \sqrt{\dfrac{\epsilon_2}{\epsilon_1} - \sin^2\,\theta_1}}{\sqrt{\dfrac{\epsilon_2}{\epsilon_1} - \sin^2\,\theta_1} + \cos\,\theta_1} \tag{2.91}$$

$$\tau_\perp = \frac{2\,\cos\,\theta_1}{\sqrt{\dfrac{\epsilon_2}{\epsilon_1} - \sin^2\,\theta_1} + \cos\,\theta_1} \tag{2.92}$$

Figure 2.8 shows the behavior of the reflection coefficient as a function of the angle of incidence for both polarizations, when $n_1 < n_2$, that is, $\epsilon_1 < \epsilon_2$. In case of the parallel polarization, the reflection coefficient is equal to zero at Brewster's angle

$$\theta_B = \arcsin\sqrt{\frac{\epsilon_2}{\epsilon_2 + \epsilon_1}} \tag{2.93}$$

If $\epsilon_1 > \epsilon_2$, a total reflection occurs at angles of incidence

$$\theta_1 \geq \arcsin\sqrt{\frac{\epsilon_2}{\epsilon_1}} \tag{2.94}$$

2.7 Energy and Power

Let us consider the principle of energy conservation in volume V, which is enclosed by a surface S. The medium filling the volume V is characterized

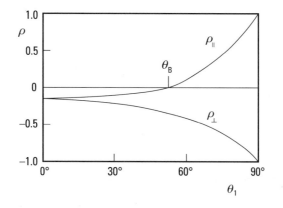

Figure 2.8 The reflection coefficient for the parallel ($\rho_\parallel$) and perpendicular ($\rho_\perp$) polarization as a function of the angle of incidence θ_1, when $\epsilon_1 < \epsilon_2$.

by ϵ_r, μ_r, and σ. Let us assume that in the volume V there are the electromagnetic sources $\mathbf{J}$ and $\mathbf{M}$ ($\mathbf{M}$ is the magnetic current density; see Section 2.1), which cause fields $\mathbf{E}$ and $\mathbf{H}$. The complex power that these sources produce is

$$P_s = -\frac{1}{2} \int_V (\mathbf{E} \cdot \mathbf{J}^* + \mathbf{H}^* \cdot \mathbf{M}) \, dV \qquad (2.95)$$

In a sinusoidal steady-state case, the time-averaged stored electric energy in the volume V is

$$W_e = \frac{\epsilon_0}{4} \int_V \epsilon_r' \mathbf{E} \cdot \mathbf{E}^* \, dV = \frac{\epsilon_0}{4} \int_V \epsilon_r' |\mathbf{E}|^2 \, dV \qquad (2.96)$$

Accordingly, the time-averaged stored magnetic energy in the volume V is

$$W_m = \frac{\mu_0}{4} \int_V \mu_r' \mathbf{H} \cdot \mathbf{H}^* \, dV = \frac{\mu_0}{4} \int_V \mu_r' |\mathbf{H}|^2 \, dV \qquad (2.97)$$

Using Poynting's vector we can calculate the power flow out of the closed surface S

$$P_o = \frac{1}{2} \mathrm{Re} \oint_S \mathbf{E} \times \mathbf{H}^* \cdot d\mathbf{S} \qquad (2.98)$$

Power dissipated in the volume V due to conduction, dielectric, and magnetic losses is

$$P_l = \frac{1}{2} \int_V \sigma |\mathbf{E}|^2 \, dV + \frac{\omega}{2} \int_V \left(\epsilon_0 \epsilon_r'' |\mathbf{E}|^2 + \mu_0 \mu_r'' |\mathbf{H}|^2 \right) dV \quad (2.99)$$

According to the energy conservation principle, the power delivered by the sources in the volume V is equal to the sum of the power transmitted through the surface S and power dissipated in the volume, plus 2ω times the net reactive energy stored in the volume. This principle is called Poynting's theorem, which can be written as

$$P_s = P_o + P_l + 2j\omega(W_m - W_e) \tag{2.100}$$

Equation (2.100) combines the powers and energies presented in (2.95)–(2.99).

References

[1]   Feynman, R. P., R. B. Leighton, and M. Sands, *The Feynman Lectures on Physics, Vol. II,* Reading, MA: Addison-Wesley, 1964.

[2]   Collin, R. E., *Foundations for Microwave Engineering,* 2nd ed., New York: IEEE Press, 2001.

[3]   Gardiol, F. E., *Introduction to Microwaves,* Dedham, MA: Artech House, 1984.

[4]   Kong, J. A., *Electromagnetic Wave Theory,* New York: John Wiley & Sons, 1986.

[5]   Kraus, J., and D. Fleisch, *Electromagnetics with Applications,* 5th ed., Boston, MA: McGraw-Hill, 1998.

[6]   Pozar, D. M., *Microwave Engineering,* 2nd ed., New York: John Wiley & Sons, 1998.

[7]   Ramo, S., J. Whinnery, and T. van Duzer, *Fields and Waves in Communication Electronics,* New York: John Wiley & Sons, 1965.

[8]   Van Bladel, J., *Electromagnetic Fields,* Washington, D.C.: Hemisphere Publishing, 1985.

3

Transmission Lines and Waveguides

Transmission lines and waveguides carry signals and power between different devices and within them. We can form many kinds of components, such as directional couplers and filters, by connecting sections of transmission lines or waveguides (see Chapters 6 and 7). Usually, lines consisting of two or more conductors are called transmission lines, and lines or wave-guiding structures having a single metal tube or no conductors at all are called waveguides. However, the use of these terms is not always consistent, and often in analysis a transmission line model is used for a waveguide (see Section 3.10).

Several types of transmission lines and waveguides have been developed for various applications. They are characterized by their attenuation, bandwidth, dispersion, purity of wave mode, power-handling capability, physical size, and applicability for integration. Dispersion means the frequency dependence of wave propagation.

Figure 3.1 shows some types of transmission lines and waveguides, which are briefly described later. The electrical properties of the lines in Figure 3.1(a–d, f) are explained more detailed later in this chapter; see also [1–6]. A comparison of the lines in Figure 3.1(a, d, f) is given in Table 3.1.

A rectangular metal waveguide is a hollow metal pipe having a rectangular cross section. It has low losses and a high power-handling capability. Due to its closed structure, the fields are well isolated from the outside world. A large physical size and difficulty in integrating its components within the waveguide are the main disadvantages. The usable bandwidth for

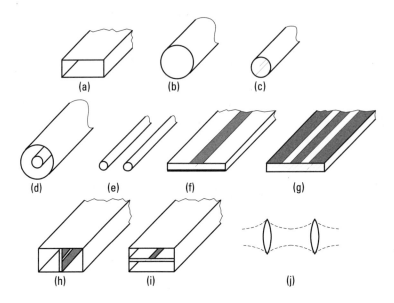

Figure 3.1 Transmission lines and waveguides: (a) rectangular metal waveguide; (b) circular metal waveguide; (c) circular dielectric waveguide; (d) coaxial line; (e) parallel-wire line; (f) microstrip line; (g) coplanar waveguide; (h) fin line; (i) suspended stripline; and (j) quasioptical waveguide.

Table 3.1
Comparison of Some Common Lines

Characteristic	Rectangular Waveguide	Coaxial Line	Microstrip Line
Mode	TE_{10}	TEM	Quasi-TEM
Bandwidth	Medium	Broad	Broad
Dispersion	Medium	None	Low
Losses	Low	Medium	High
Power capability	High	Medium	Low
Size	Large	Medium	Small
Ease of fabrication	Medium	Medium	Easy
Integration	Difficult	Difficult	Easy

the pure fundamental mode TE_{10} is less than 1 octave. Rectangular metal waveguides are used for various applications from below 1 GHz up to 1,000 GHz and even higher frequencies.

The properties of a circular metal waveguide are generally the same as those of the rectangular metal waveguide. However, the usable bandwidth for single-mode operation is even narrower, only about 25%. In an oversized circular metal waveguide, a very low-loss TE_{01} mode can propagate if the excitation of other modes can be prevented. (Later in this book we use the terms "rectangular waveguide" and "circular waveguide" omitting the word "metal," as is often the practice in the literature.)

A circular dielectric waveguide is made of a dielectric low-loss material. Bends and other discontinuities in the line radiate easily. For example, an optical fiber is a dielectric waveguide.

A coaxial line consists of an outer and an inner conductor with circular cross sections. The space between the conductors is filled with a low-loss insulating material, such as air or Teflon. The coaxial line has a broad, single-mode bandwidth from 0 Hz to an upper limit, which depends on the dimensions of the conductors and may be as high as 60 GHz.

A parallel-wire line consists of two parallel conductors. It cannot be used at higher frequencies than in the VHF range because it has a high radiation loss at higher frequencies.

A microstrip line is made on an insulating substrate. The metal layer on the opposite side of the strip operates as a ground plane. The advantages of the microstrip line are a broad bandwidth, small size, and a good applicability for integration and mass production. The disadvantages are fairly high losses, radiation due to the open structure, and low power capability. Microstrip lines are used up to 100 GHz and even higher frequencies.

A coplanar waveguide has ground-plane conductors on both sides of a metal strip. All conductors are on the same side of the substrate. Both series and parallel components can easily be integrated with this line. Coplanar waveguides are used, for example, in monolithic integrated circuits operating at millimeter wavelengths.

A fin line is composed of a substrate in the E-plane of a rectangular (metal) waveguide. The field concentrates in a slot on the metallization of the substrate. The fin line has a low radiation loss, and components can be integrated quite easily with this line. Fin lines are used up to 200 GHz.

A suspended stripline has a substrate in the H-plane of a rectangular waveguide. There is a metal strip on the substrate.

A quasioptical waveguide is made of focusing lenses or mirrors, which maintain the energy in a beam in free space. Quasioptical waveguides are used from about 100 GHz up to infrared waves. Other lines become lossy and difficult to fabricate at such high frequencies.

3.1 Basic Equations for Transmission Lines and Waveguides

The Helmholtz equation (2.52) is valid in the sourceless medium of a transmission line or a waveguide. Let us assume that a wave is propagating in a uniform line along the z direction. Now, the Helmholtz equation is separable so that a solution having a form of $f(z)g(x, y)$ can be found. The z-dependence of the field has a form of $e^{-\gamma z}$. Thus, the electric field may be written as

$$\mathbf{E} = \mathbf{E}(x, y, z) = \mathbf{g}(x, y)\, e^{-\gamma z} \tag{3.1}$$

where $\mathbf{g}(x, y)$ is the field distribution in the transverse plane. By setting this to the Helmholtz equation, we get

$$\nabla^2 \mathbf{E} = \nabla_{xy}^2 \mathbf{E} + \frac{\partial^2 \mathbf{E}}{\partial z^2} = \nabla_{xy}^2 \mathbf{E} + \gamma^2 \mathbf{E} = -\omega^2 \mu \epsilon \mathbf{E} \tag{3.2}$$

where ∇_{xy}^2 includes the partial derivatives of ∇^2 with respect to x and y. Because similar equations can be derived for the magnetic field, the partial differential equations applicable for all uniform lines are

$$\nabla_{xy}^2 \mathbf{E} = -(\gamma^2 + \omega^2 \mu \epsilon)\, \mathbf{E} \tag{3.3}$$

$$\nabla_{xy}^2 \mathbf{H} = -(\gamma^2 + \omega^2 \mu \epsilon)\, \mathbf{H} \tag{3.4}$$

At first, the longitudinal or z-component of the electric or magnetic field is solved using the boundary conditions set by the structure of the line. When E_z or H_z is known, the x- and y-components of the fields may be solved from Maxwell's III and IV equations. Equation $\nabla \times \mathbf{E} = -j\omega\mu\mathbf{H}$ may be divided into three parts:

$$\partial E_z / \partial y + \gamma E_y = -j\omega\mu H_x$$

$$-\gamma E_x - \partial E_z / \partial x = -j\omega\mu H_y$$

$$\partial E_y / \partial x - \partial E_x / \partial y = -j\omega\mu H_z$$

Correspondingly, $\nabla \times \mathbf{H} = j\omega\epsilon\mathbf{E}$ is divided into three parts:

$$\partial H_z / \partial y + \gamma H_y = j\omega\epsilon E_x$$

$$-\gamma H_x - \partial H_z / \partial x = j\omega\epsilon E_y$$

$$\partial H_y / \partial x - \partial H_x / \partial y = j\omega\epsilon E_z$$

From these, the transverse components E_x, E_y, H_x, and H_y are solved as functions of the longitudinal components E_z and H_z:

$$E_x = \frac{-1}{\gamma^2 + \omega^2 \mu\epsilon} \left(\gamma \frac{\partial E_z}{\partial x} + j\omega\mu \frac{\partial H_z}{\partial y} \right) \qquad (3.5)$$

$$E_y = \frac{1}{\gamma^2 + \omega^2 \mu\epsilon} \left(-\gamma \frac{\partial E_z}{\partial y} + j\omega\mu \frac{\partial H_z}{\partial x} \right) \qquad (3.6)$$

$$H_x = \frac{1}{\gamma^2 + \omega^2 \mu\epsilon} \left(j\omega\epsilon \frac{\partial E_z}{\partial y} - \gamma \frac{\partial H_z}{\partial x} \right) \qquad (3.7)$$

$$H_y = \frac{-1}{\gamma^2 + \omega^2 \mu\epsilon} \left(j\omega\epsilon \frac{\partial E_z}{\partial x} + \gamma \frac{\partial H_z}{\partial y} \right) \qquad (3.8)$$

In a cylindrical coordinate system, the solution of the Helmholtz equation has the form of $f(z)g(r, \phi)$. As above, the transverse r- and ϕ-components are calculated from the longitudinal components:

$$E_r = \frac{-1}{\gamma^2 + \omega^2 \mu\epsilon} \left(\gamma \frac{\partial E_z}{\partial r} + \frac{j\omega\mu}{r} \frac{\partial H_z}{\partial \phi} \right) \qquad (3.9)$$

$$E_\phi = \frac{1}{\gamma^2 + \omega^2 \mu\epsilon} \left(-\frac{\gamma}{r} \frac{\partial E_z}{\partial \phi} + j\omega\mu \frac{\partial H_z}{\partial r} \right) \qquad (3.10)$$

$$H_r = \frac{1}{\gamma^2 + \omega^2 \mu\epsilon} \left(\frac{j\omega\epsilon}{r} \frac{\partial E_z}{\partial \phi} - \gamma \frac{\partial H_z}{\partial r} \right) \qquad (3.11)$$

$$H_\phi = \frac{-1}{\gamma^2 + \omega^2 \mu\epsilon} \left(j\omega\epsilon \frac{\partial E_z}{\partial r} + \frac{\gamma}{r} \frac{\partial H_z}{\partial \phi} \right) \qquad (3.12)$$

In a given waveguide at a given frequency, several field configurations may satisfy Maxwell's equations. These field configurations are called wave modes. Every mode has its own propagation characteristics: velocity, attenuation, and cutoff frequency. Because different modes propagate at different velocities, signals may be distorted due to the multimode propagation. Using the waveguide at low enough frequencies, so that only one mode—the dominant or fundamental mode—can propagate along the waveguide, prevents this multimode distortion.

3.2 Transverse Electromagnetic Wave Modes

In lossless and, with a good approximation, in low-loss two-conductor transmission lines, as in coaxial lines, fields can propagate as *transverse electromagnetic* (TEM) waves. TEM waves have no longitudinal field components. TEM waves may propagate at all frequencies, so the TEM mode has no cutoff frequency.

When $E_z = 0$ and $H_z = 0$, it follows from (3.5) through (3.8) that the x- and y-components of the fields are also zero, unless

$$\gamma^2 + \omega^2 \mu\epsilon = 0 \tag{3.13}$$

Therefore, the propagation constant of a TEM wave is

$$\gamma = \pm j\omega\sqrt{\mu\epsilon} = \pm j\frac{2\pi}{\lambda} = \pm j\beta \tag{3.14}$$

The velocity v_p is independent of frequency, assuming that the material parameters ϵ and μ are independent of frequency:

$$v_p = \frac{\omega}{\beta} = \frac{1}{\sqrt{\mu\epsilon}} \tag{3.15}$$

Thus, there is no dispersion, and the TEM wave in a transmission line propagates at the same velocity as a wave in free space having the same ϵ and μ as the insulator of the transmission line. The wave equations for a TEM wave are

$$\nabla_{xy}^2 \mathbf{E} = 0 \tag{3.16}$$

$$\nabla_{xy}^2 \mathbf{H} = 0 \tag{3.17}$$

The fields of a wave propagating along the z direction satisfy the equation

$$\frac{E_x}{H_y} = -\frac{E_y}{H_x} = \eta \tag{3.18}$$

where $\eta = \sqrt{\mu/\epsilon}$ is the wave impedance.

Laplace's equations, (3.16) and (3.17), are valid also for static fields. In electrostatics, the electric field may be presented as the gradient of the scalar transverse potential:

$$\mathbf{E}(x, y) = -\nabla_{xy}\Phi(x, y) \tag{3.19}$$

Because $\nabla \times \nabla f = 0$, the transverse curl of the electric field must vanish in order for (3.19) to be valid. Here this is the case, because

$$\nabla_{xy} \times \mathbf{E} = -j\omega\mu H_z \mathbf{u_z} = 0 \tag{3.20}$$

where $\mathbf{u_z}$ is a unit vector pointing in the direction of the positive z-axis. Gauss' law in a sourceless space states that $\nabla \cdot \mathbf{D} = \epsilon\nabla_{xy} \cdot \mathbf{E} = 0$. From this and (3.19) it follows that $\Phi(x, y)$ is also a solution of Laplace's equation, or

$$\nabla_{xy}^2 \Phi(x, y) = 0 \tag{3.21}$$

The voltage of a two-conductor line is

$$V_{12} = \int_1^2 \mathbf{E} \cdot d\mathbf{l} = \Phi_1 - \Phi_2 \tag{3.22}$$

where Φ_1 and Φ_2 are the potentials of the conductors. From Ampère's law, the current of the line is

$$I = \oint_\Gamma \mathbf{H} \cdot d\mathbf{l} \tag{3.23}$$

where Γ is a closed line surrounding the conductor.

3.3 Transverse Electric and Transverse Magnetic Wave Modes

A wave mode may have also longitudinal field components in addition to the transverse components. *Transverse electric* (TE) modes have $E_z = 0$ but a nonzero longitudinal magnetic field H_z. *Transverse magnetic* (TM) modes have $H_z = 0$ and a nonzero E_z:

From (3.4) it follows for a TE mode

$$\nabla^2_{xy} H_z = -(\gamma^2 + \omega^2 \mu\epsilon) H_z = -k_c^2 H_z \tag{3.24}$$

Correspondingly, for a TM mode

$$\nabla^2_{xy} E_z = -(\gamma^2 + \omega^2 \mu\epsilon) E_z = -k_c^2 E_z \tag{3.25}$$

The coefficient k_c is solved from (3.24) or (3.25) using the boundary conditions set by the waveguide. For a given waveguide, an infinite number of k_c values can usually be found. Each k_c corresponds to a propagating wave mode. We can prove that in the case of a waveguide such as a rectangular or circular waveguide, in which a conductor surrounds an insulator, k_c is always a positive real number.

The propagation constant is

$$\gamma = \sqrt{k_c^2 - \omega^2 \mu\epsilon} \tag{3.26}$$

If the insulating material is lossless, $\omega^2 \mu\epsilon$ is real. The frequency at which $\omega^2 \mu\epsilon = k_c^2$ is called the cutoff frequency:

$$f_c = \frac{k_c}{2\pi\sqrt{\mu\epsilon}} \tag{3.27}$$

The corresponding cutoff wavelength is

$$\lambda_c = \frac{2\pi}{k_c} \tag{3.28}$$

At frequencies below the cutoff frequency, $f < f_c$, no wave can propagate. The field attenuates rapidly and has an attenuation constant

$$\gamma = \alpha = \frac{2\pi}{\lambda_c} \sqrt{1 - \left(\frac{f}{f_c}\right)^2} \qquad (3.29)$$

At frequencies much below the cutoff frequency, $f \ll f_c$, the attenuation constant is $\alpha = 2\pi/\lambda_c$ or 2π nepers (54.6 dB) per cutoff wavelength. Figure 3.2 shows the attenuation at frequencies below the cutoff frequency.

At frequencies higher than the cutoff frequency, $f > f_c$, waves can propagate and the propagation constant γ is complex. In a lossless line, γ is imaginary:

$$\gamma = j\beta_g = j\frac{2\pi}{\lambda} \sqrt{1 - \left(\frac{f_c}{f}\right)^2} \qquad (3.30)$$

where λ is the wavelength in free space composed of the same material as the insulator of the line. The wavelength in the line is

$$\lambda_g = \frac{2\pi}{\beta_g} = \frac{\lambda}{\sqrt{1 - (f_c/f)^2}} \qquad (3.31)$$

Figure 3.3 shows how the wavelength λ_g depends on frequency. The phase velocity (see Section 3.9) is

$$v_p = \frac{v}{\sqrt{1 - (f_c/f)^2}} \qquad (3.32)$$

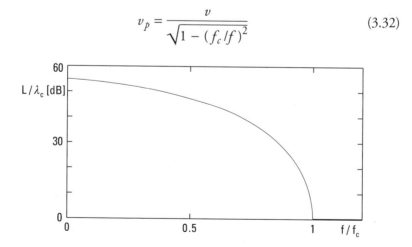

Figure 3.2 Attenuation of TE and TM waves below the cutoff frequency in a lossless waveguide.

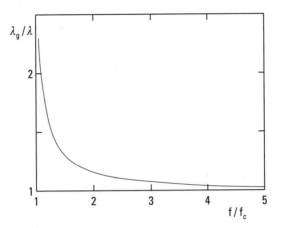

Figure 3.3 Wavelength of TE and TM waves above the cutoff frequency.

which is larger than the speed v of a plane wave in the same material as the insulator of the line. The propagation velocity of energy or the group velocity

$$v_g = v \sqrt{1 - (f_c / f)^2} \tag{3.33}$$

is smaller than the speed of the plane wave in this material. Thus, the propagation velocity of TE and TM waves depends on frequency, and waveguides carrying these modes are dispersive.

3.4 Rectangular Waveguide

Both TE and TM wave modes may propagate in the rectangular waveguide shown in Figure 3.4. The longitudinal electric field of a TE mode is zero, $E_z = 0$, while for a TM mode the longitudinal magnetic field is zero, $H_z = 0$.

3.4.1 TE Wave Modes in Rectangular Waveguide

Let us assume that the solution of the longitudinal magnetic field has a form of

$$H_z(x, y) = A \cos(k_1 x) \cos(k_2 y) \tag{3.34}$$

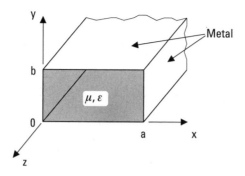

Figure 3.4 Rectangular waveguide.

where A is an arbitrary amplitude constant. By introducing the field of (3.34) to the equation of the TE wave mode, (3.24), we note that the differential equation is fulfilled if

$$k_1^2 + k_2^2 = \gamma^2 + \omega^2 \mu \epsilon = k_c^2 \tag{3.35}$$

The transverse field components can be solved from (3.5) through (3.8):

$$E_x = j \frac{\omega \mu k_2}{k_c^2} A \cos(k_1 x) \sin(k_2 y) \tag{3.36}$$

$$E_y = -j \frac{\omega \mu k_1}{k_c^2} A \sin(k_1 x) \cos(k_2 y) \tag{3.37}$$

$$H_x = -\frac{E_y}{Z_{TE}} \tag{3.38}$$

$$H_y = \frac{E_x}{Z_{TE}} \tag{3.39}$$

The wave impedance of the TE wave mode is

$$Z_{TE} = \frac{\eta}{\sqrt{1 - (f_c/f)^2}} \tag{3.40}$$

From the boundary conditions for the fields in a metal waveguide it follows that the transverse magnetic field cannot have a normal component at the boundary, that is, $\mathbf{n} \cdot \mathbf{H} = 0$. It follows from (3.7) and (3.8) that $\partial H_z / \partial x = 0$, when $x = 0$ or a, and $\partial H_z / \partial y = 0$, when $y = 0$ or b.

Also, the tangential component of the electric field must vanish at the boundary or $\mathbf{n} \times \mathbf{E} = 0$: $E_x(x, 0) = 0$, $E_x(x, b) = 0$, $E_y(0, y) = 0$, $E_y(a, y) = 0$.

It results from these boundary conditions that $k_1 a = n\pi$ and $k_2 b = m\pi$, where $n = 0, 1, 2, \ldots$ and $m = 0, 1, 2, \ldots$, and therefore,

$$k_c^2 = \left(\frac{n\pi}{a}\right)^2 + \left(\frac{m\pi}{b}\right)^2 \tag{3.41}$$

The cutoff wavelength and cutoff frequency are:

$$\lambda_{cnm} = \frac{2\pi}{k_c} = \frac{2}{\sqrt{(n/a)^2 + (m/b)^2}} \tag{3.42}$$

$$f_{cnm} = \frac{1}{2\sqrt{\mu\epsilon}} \sqrt{\left(\frac{n}{a}\right)^2 + \left(\frac{m}{b}\right)^2} \tag{3.43}$$

The subscripts n and m refer to the number of field maxima in the x and y directions, respectively.

In most applications, we use the fundamental mode TE_{10} having the lowest cutoff frequency:

$$f_{cTE10} = \frac{1}{2a\sqrt{\mu\epsilon}} \tag{3.44}$$

In the case of an air-filled waveguide, we obtain $f_{cTE10} = c/(2a)$. The cutoff wavelength is $\lambda_c = 2a$. If the waveguide width a is twice the height b, $a = 2b$, the TE_{20} and TE_{01} wave modes have a cutoff frequency of $2f_{cTE10}$.

The fields of the TE_{10} wave mode are solved from the Helmholtz equation and boundary conditions as follows:

$$E_x = 0 \tag{3.45}$$

$$E_y = E_0 \sin \frac{\pi x}{a} \qquad (3.46)$$

$$H_z = j \frac{E_0}{\eta} \frac{\lambda}{2a} \cos \frac{\pi x}{a} \qquad (3.47)$$

$$H_x = -\frac{E_0}{\eta} \sqrt{1 - \left(\frac{\lambda}{2a}\right)^2} \sin \frac{\pi x}{a} \qquad (3.48)$$

$$H_y = 0 \qquad (3.49)$$

E_0 is the maximum value of the electric field, which has only a y-component. All field components depend on time and the z-coordinate as $\exp(j\omega t - \gamma z)$. Figure 3.5 illustrates the fields and the surface currents of the TE_{10} wave mode.

The wave impedance of the TE_{10} mode is

$$Z_{TE10} = \left|\frac{E_y}{H_x}\right| = \frac{\eta}{\sqrt{1 - [\lambda/(2a)]^2}} \qquad (3.50)$$

For example, at a frequency of $1.5f_c$, the wave impedance of an air-filled waveguide is 506Ω. The wave impedance depends on frequency and is characteristic for each wave mode.

The characteristic impedance Z_0 of a transmission line is the ratio of voltage and current in an infinitely long line or in a line terminated with a

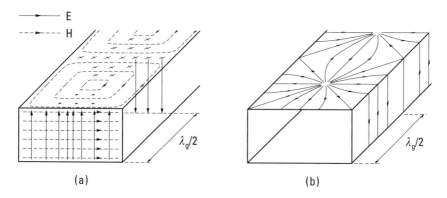

Figure 3.5 (a) Fields and (b) surface currents of the TE_{10} wave mode in a rectangular waveguide at a given instant of time.

matched load having a wave propagating only in one direction. However, we cannot uniquely define the voltage and current of a waveguide as we can do for a two-conductor transmission line. Therefore, we may have many definitions for the characteristic impedance of a waveguide using any two of the following three quantities: power, voltage, current. The characteristic impedance can be calculated from the power propagating in the waveguide, P_p given in (3.53), and the voltage U, which is obtained by integrating the electric field in the middle of the waveguide from the upper wall to the lower wall, as

$$Z_{0TE10} = \frac{U^2}{P_p} = \frac{(E_0 b)^2 / 2}{P_p} = \frac{2b}{a} Z_{TE10} \tag{3.51}$$

Note that the characteristic impedance of the TE_{10} wave mode depends on the height b, whereas the wave impedance of (3.50) does not. The characteristic impedance in (3.51) has been found to be the best definition in practice when problems concerning impedance matching to various loads are being solved.

The power propagating in a waveguide is obtained by integrating Poynting's vector over the area of the cross section S:

$$P_p = \frac{1}{2} \text{Re} \int_S \mathbf{E} \times \mathbf{H}^* \cdot d\mathbf{S} \tag{3.52}$$

The power propagating at the TE_{10} wave mode is

$$P_p = \frac{1}{2} \text{Re} \int_S E_y H_x^* \, dS = \frac{E_0^2}{Z_{TE10}} \frac{ab}{4} \tag{3.53}$$

The finite conductivity of the metal, σ_m, causes loss in the walls of the waveguide. Also, the insulating material may have dielectric loss due to ϵ_r'' and conduction loss due to σ_d. The attenuation constant can be given as

$$\alpha = \frac{P_l}{2P_p} \tag{3.54}$$

where P_l is the power loss per unit length.

The power loss of conductors is calculated from the surface current density $\mathbf{J_s} = \mathbf{n} \times \mathbf{H}$ ($\mathbf{n}$ is a unit vector perpendicular to the surface) by integrating $|\mathbf{J_s}|^2 R_s / 2$ over the surface of the conductor. Although in the preceding analysis the fields of the waveguide are derived assuming the conductors to be ideal, this method is accurate enough if the losses are low. The surface resistance of a conductor is $R_s = \sqrt{\omega \mu_0 / (2\sigma_m)}$. The attenuation constant of conductor loss for the TE_{10} wave mode is obtained as

$$\alpha_{cTE10} = \frac{R_s}{\eta\sqrt{1 - [\lambda/(2a)]^2}} \left(\frac{1}{b} + \frac{\lambda^2}{2a^3} \right) \tag{3.55}$$

Close to the cutoff frequency, the attenuation is high, approaching infinite. If the dielectric material filling the waveguide has loss, the attenuation constant of dielectric loss is for all wave modes

$$\alpha_d = \frac{\pi}{\lambda} \frac{\tan \delta}{\sqrt{1 - (f_c/f)^2}} \tag{3.56}$$

The total attenuation constant is $\alpha = \alpha_c + \alpha_d$.

The recommended frequency range for waveguides operating at the TE_{10} wave mode is about from 1.2 to 1.9 times the cutoff frequency f_{cTE10}. The increase of attenuation sets the lower limit, whereas the excitation of higher-order modes sets the higher limit. Hence, we need a large number of waveguides to cover the whole microwave and millimeter-wave range. Standard waveguides that cover the 10 GHz to 100 GHz range are listed in Table 3.2. In most cases $a = 2b$. Figure 3.6 shows the theoretical attenuation of some standard waveguides made of copper. In practice, the attenuation is higher due to the surface roughness.

Example 3.1

Find the maximum power that can be fed to a WR-90 waveguide at 10 GHz. The maximum electric field that air can withstand without breakdown—the dielectric strength of air—is about 3 kV/mm.

Solution

The dimensions of the waveguide are $a = 22.86$ mm and $b = 10.16$ mm. From (3.50), the wave impedance of the TE_{10} wave mode at 10 GHz ($\lambda = 30$ mm) is $Z_{TE10} = 500\Omega$. By setting $E_0 = 3$ kV/mm into (3.53), we find the maximum power to be 1.05 MW. Because the attenuation is about

Table 3.2
Standard Waveguides

Abbreviation	a [mm]	b [mm]	f_c [GHz]	Range [GHz]
WR-90	22.86	10.16	6.56	8.2–12.4
WR-75	19.05	9.53	7.87	10–15
WR-62	15.80	7.90	9.49	12.4–18
WR-51	12.95	6.48	11.6	15–22
WR-42	10.67	4.32	14.1	18–26.5
WR-34	8.64	4.32	17.4	22–33
WR-28	7.11	3.56	21.1	26.5–40
WR-22	5.69	2.84	26.3	33–50
WR-19	4.78	2.39	31.4	40–60
WR-15	3.76	1.88	39.9	50–75
WR-12	3.10	1.55	48.4	60–90
WR-10	2.54	1.27	59.0	75–110
WR-8	2.03	1.02	73.8	90–140

0.1 dB/cm, the power absorbed into the walls of the waveguide is about 240 W/cm at the maximum power. If the load reflects some of the power, the maximum field strength is due to the standing wave higher than in the matched case. Then, the maximum power is lower than that calculated above.

3.4.2 TM Wave Modes in Rectangular Waveguide

TM wave modes have no longitudinal magnetic field component, $H_z = 0$. The solution of the longitudinal electric field has a form of

$$E_z = B \sin(k_1 x) \sin(k_2 y) \qquad (3.57)$$

The other field components are

$$H_x = j \frac{\omega \epsilon k_2}{k_c^2} B \sin(k_1 x) \cos(k_2 y) \qquad (3.58)$$

$$H_y = -j \frac{\omega \epsilon k_1}{k_c^2} B \cos(k_1 x) \sin(k_2 y) \qquad (3.59)$$

$$E_x = Z_{TM} H_y \qquad (3.60)$$

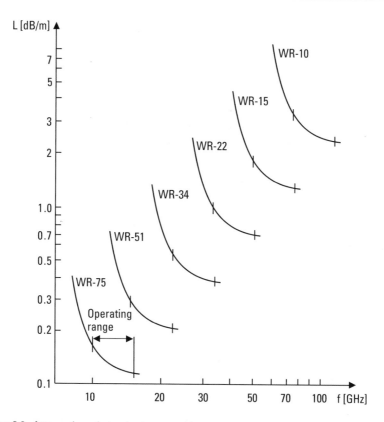

Figure 3.6 Attenuation of standard waveguides.

$$E_y = -Z_{TM} H_x \qquad (3.61)$$

The wave impedance of TM modes is

$$Z_{TM} = \eta \sqrt{1 - (f_c/f)^2} \qquad (3.62)$$

From boundary conditions it follows that the equations for the cutoff wavelength and cutoff frequency are the same as those for the TE wave modes. Now, both indices n and m have to be nonzero. The TM wave mode having the lowest cutoff frequency is TM_{11}. Although TM_{11} and TE_{11} wave modes have equal cutoff frequencies, their field distributions are different. Figure 3.7 shows transverse field distributions of some TE and TM wave modes.

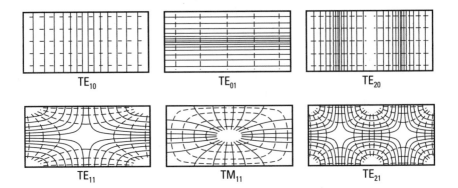

Figure 3.7 Transverse field distributions of some TE and TM wave modes of a rectangular waveguide. Solid lines represent electric field lines, dashed lines magnetic field lines.

3.5 Circular Waveguide

The analysis of a circular waveguide shown in Figure 3.8 is best carried out using the cylindrical coordinate system. The principle of analysis is similar to that of the rectangular waveguide.

The solutions of the longitudinal magnetic fields of the TE wave modes are

$$H_z = A J_n (k_c r) \cos (n\phi) \tag{3.63}$$

where J_n is the Bessel function of the order n. From the boundary condition $H_r(r = a) = 0$, it follows that $\partial H_r / \partial r (r = a) = 0$, and further that $J_n'(k_c a) = 0$, in which the apostrophe stands for derivative. From this we get

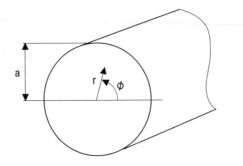

Figure 3.8 Circular waveguide.

$$k_{cnm} = \frac{p'_{nm}}{a} \tag{3.64}$$

where p'_{nm} is the mth zero of J'_n. The corresponding cutoff wavelength is

$$\lambda_{cTEnm} = \frac{2\pi a}{p'_{nm}} \tag{3.65}$$

The solutions of the longitudinal electric fields of the TM wave modes are

$$E_z = BJ_n(k_c r) \cos(n\phi) \tag{3.66}$$

From the boundary condition $E_z(r = a) = 0$ it follows that $J_n(k_c a) = 0$, or

$$k_{cnm} = \frac{p_{nm}}{a} \tag{3.67}$$

where p_{nm} is the mth zero of J_n. The cutoff wavelength is

$$\lambda_{cTMnm} = \frac{2\pi a}{p_{nm}} \tag{3.68}$$

The subscript n denotes the number of periods in the field distribution along the ϕ angle. The subscript m gives the number of axial field minima in the radial direction. Figure 3.9 shows the transverse field distributions of some wave modes. Table 3.3 gives the cutoff wavelengths of the wave modes having the lowest cutoff frequencies.

The relative bandwidth of the circular waveguide operating at the fundamental mode TE_{11} is smaller than that of the rectangular waveguide operating at the TE_{10} mode, as shown in Figure 3.10. Therefore, many standard waveguide sizes are needed to cover a broad frequency range.

The conductor losses of the circular waveguide are calculated from the surface currents and surface resistance the same way as in the case of the rectangular waveguide. A special feature of the TE_{01} wave mode is that its attenuation decreases monotonously as the frequency increases. The attenuation constant of the TE_{01} wave mode is

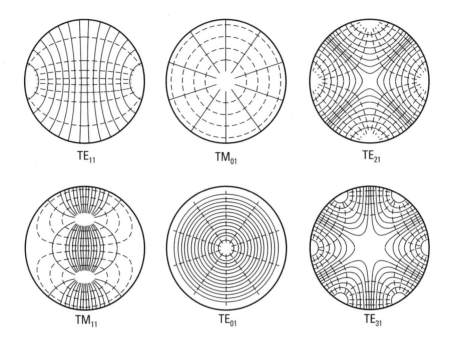

Figure 3.9 Transverse field distributions of some TE and TM wave modes in a circular waveguide. Solid lines represent electric field lines, dashed lines magnetic field lines.

Table 3.3

Cutoff Wavelengths of Wave Modes in a Circular Waveguide with Radius a

Wave Mode	p_{nm} or p'_{nm}	λ_c
TE_{11}	$p'_{11} = 1.841$	$3.41a$
TM_{01}	$p_{01} = 2.405$	$2.61a$
TE_{21}	$p'_{21} = 3.054$	$2.06a$
TE_{01}	$p'_{01} = 3.832$	$1.64a$
TM_{11}	$p_{11} = 3.832$	$1.64a$

$$\alpha_{cTE01} = \frac{R_s}{a\eta} \frac{(f_c/f)^2}{\sqrt{1 - (f_c/f)^2}} \tag{3.69}$$

The attenuation of the TE_{01} wave mode is very low if the operating frequency is much higher than the cutoff frequency f_c. However, many other modes

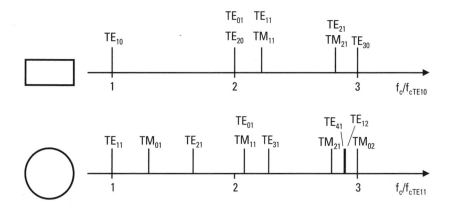

Figure 3.10 Cutoff frequencies of the lowest wave modes of rectangular and circular waveguides.

can propagate in such an oversized waveguide. A low attenuation is achieved only if the excitation of unwanted modes is prevented.

Example 3.2

Calculate the conductor losses at 60 GHz for the TE_{01} wave mode in a circular waveguide made of copper. The radius of the waveguide is (a) 3.5 mm, and (b) 20 mm.

Solution

The surface resistance is

$$R_s = \sqrt{\pi f \mu_0 / \sigma}$$

$$= \sqrt{\pi \times 60 \times 10^9 \times 4\pi \times 10^{-7}/58 \times 10^6} \ \Omega/m$$

$$= 0.064 \ \Omega/m.$$

The cutoff frequency of the TE_{01} wave mode is $f_c = c/\lambda_c = c/(1.64a)$. (a) When $a = 3.5$ mm, $f_c = 52.3$ GHz. From (3.69) we solve the attenuation constant $\alpha_{cTE01} = 0.0753$ 1/m. The attenuation of a waveguide having a length l is in decibels $20 \log e^{\alpha l}$, from which we obtain an attenuation of 0.65 dB/m. (b) When $a = 20$ mm, $f_c = 9.15$ GHz and $\alpha_{cTE01} = 1.14 \times 10^{-3}$ 1/m. The attenuation is now only 0.010 dB/m or 1.0 dB/100m.

3.6 Optical Fiber

TE and TM wave modes may propagate, not only in hollow metal waveguides, but also in dielectric waveguides. An optical fiber is actually a dielectric waveguide with a circular cross section, in which total internal reflection confines light in the fiber. Optical fibers are used in many kinds of communication networks, usually at wavelengths of 0.8 to 1.6 μm at infrared. The optical carrier is modulated with data rates up to several gigabits per second.

Optical fibers are made of quartz, glass, or plastic. An optical fiber consists of a core and a cladding. The index of refraction $n = \sqrt{\epsilon_r}$ of the core is larger than that of the cladding. The refractive index of the cladding is adjusted to a proper value by doping quartz with metal oxides as TiO_2, Al_2O_3, GeO_2, or P_2O_3. Optical fibers can be divided into three types, as shown in Figure 3.11:

1. Single-mode fiber: core radius 1–16 μm, cladding radius 50–100 μm.
2. Multimode fiber with a step in the index of refraction: core radius 25–60 μm, cladding radius 50–150 μm.
3. Multimode fiber with a continuous change in the index of refraction: core radius 10–35 μm, cladding radius 50–80 μm.

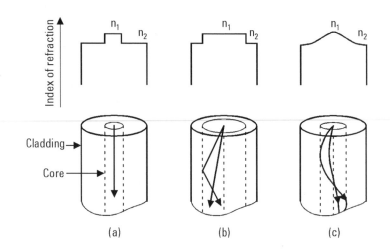

Figure 3.11 Structures of optical fibers: (a) a single-mode fiber; (b) a multimode fiber with a step in the refractive index; (c) a multimode fiber with a continuous change in the refractive index.

An optical cable is usually made of several optical fibers. Steel wires and textile fibers as nylon give strength to the cable and support the fibers. Copper wires carry current for the repeater amplifiers if needed.

The solutions of the longitudinal field components in the core are

$$E_z = AJ_n(kr) \cos(n\phi) \tag{3.70}$$

$$H_z = BJ_n(kr) \sin(n\phi) \tag{3.71}$$

The solutions in the cladding are

$$E_z = CH_n(\chi r) \cos(n\phi) \tag{3.72}$$

$$H_z = DH_n(\chi r) \sin(n\phi) \tag{3.73}$$

In these equations, $J_n(kr)$ is the Bessel function of the first kind of order n; $H_n(\chi_r)$ is the Hankel function of the first kind of order n; k is the transverse propagation constant in the core; and χ is the transverse propagation constant in the cladding. Other field components are solved from these longitudinal fields, as in the case of metal waveguides, except now the boundary conditions are different, that is, the tangential components of E and H are continuous at the boundary of two dielectric materials.

From the expressions of longitudinal fields we can see that only cylindrically symmetric ($n = 0$) wave modes are either TE or TM wave modes. Other wave modes are hybrid modes, denoted as EH or HE wave modes, for which both electric and magnetic fields have nonzero longitudinal components.

In a multimode fiber the number of propagating wave modes may be very large. The number of modes is approximately [7]

$$N = \frac{16}{\lambda_0^2}(n_1^2 - n_2^2)a^2 \tag{3.74}$$

where λ_0 is the wavelength in free vacuum, n_1 and n_2 are the refractive indices of core and cladding, respectively, and a is the radius of the core.

Example 3.3

Find the number of wave modes at a wavelength of 1.55 μm in a quartz fiber having a core radius of 40 μm. The refractive index of the cladding is 1% lower than that of the core.

Solution

The dielectric constant of quartz is $\epsilon_r = 3.8$. Hence $n_1 = \sqrt{3.8} = 1.95$ and $n_2 = 0.99 \times 1.95 = 1.93$. From (3.74) we obtain the number of wave modes, $N = 800$.

The loss mechanisms of an optical fiber are:

- Dielectric absorption loss;
- Scattering loss due to the imperfections of the fiber;
- Radiation loss due to the bending of the fiber.

Properties making the optical fiber an excellent transmission medium for many applications are

- Small size and weight;
- Low attenuation—only 0.2 dB/km at 1.55 μm—allowing cables hundreds of kilometers long without any repeater amplifiers;
- Immunity to interference and difficulty of interception;
- Reliability;
- Broad bandwidth;
- Low price compared to copper cable.

3.7 Coaxial Line

A coaxial line consists of two concentric conductors with circular cross sections and insulating material between them, as shown in Figure 3.12.

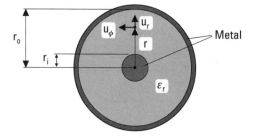

Figure 3.12 Cross section of a coaxial line.

The inner radius of the outer conductor is r_o and the radius of the inner conductor is r_i; the relative permittivity of the insulator is ϵ_r. The fields are confined to the space between the conductors.

The fields of the TEM wave mode of the coaxial line can be derived from Laplace's equation (3.21) using the scalar potential $\Phi(r, \phi)$. In the cylindrical coordinate system, Laplace's equation is written as

$$\frac{1}{r}\frac{\partial}{\partial r}\left(r\frac{\partial\Phi(r, \phi)}{\partial r}\right) + \frac{1}{r^2}\frac{\partial^2\Phi(r, \phi)}{\partial\phi^2} = 0 \qquad (3.75)$$

Applying the boundary conditions $\Phi(r_o, \phi) = 0$ and $\Phi(r_i, \phi) = V$, the potential is solved to be

$$\Phi(r, \phi) = V\frac{\ln(r_o/r)}{\ln(r_o/r_i)} \qquad (3.76)$$

The electric field is the negative gradient of the potential:

$$\mathbf{E}(r, \phi) = -\nabla\Phi(r, \phi) = \mathbf{u_r}\frac{V}{\ln(r_o/r_i)}\frac{1}{r} \qquad (3.77)$$

where $\mathbf{u_r}$ is the unit vector in the radial direction. This is also the electric field of a cylindrical capacitor. The magnetic field of the coaxial line is

$$\mathbf{H}(r, \phi) = \frac{1}{\eta}\mathbf{u_z} \times \mathbf{E}(r, \phi) = \mathbf{u}_\phi\frac{V}{\eta r\ln(r_o/r_i)} = \mathbf{u}_\phi\frac{I}{2\pi r} \qquad (3.78)$$

where $\eta = \sqrt{\mu/\epsilon}$ is the wave impedance, I is the current in the inner conductor, and $\mathbf{u}_\phi$ is the unit vector perpendicular to the radial direction. A current I flows also in the outer conductor but to the opposite direction.

The characteristic impedance of the coaxial line is

$$Z_0 = \frac{V}{I} = \frac{\eta}{2\pi}\ln(r_o/r_i) \qquad (3.79)$$

The 50-Ω characteristic impedance has become a standard value. Most measurement instruments and thus also most devices have 50-Ω input and output connectors.

The attenuation constant due to conductor loss is

$$\alpha_c = \frac{R_s}{4\pi Z_0}\left(\frac{1}{r_o} + \frac{1}{r_i}\right) \tag{3.80}$$

For an air-filled coaxial line with a given outer conductor dimension, the minimum of the attenuation constant is obtained when the characteristic impedance is $Z_0 = 77\Omega$. The attenuation constant due to dielectric loss is

$$\alpha_d = \frac{\pi}{\lambda}\tan \delta \tag{3.81}$$

Also TE and TM wave modes may propagate in a coaxial line, if the operating frequency is larger than the cutoff frequency of these wave modes. To avoid losses and unanticipated phenomena due to these modes, the operating frequency should be chosen to be low enough. An approximate rule is that the circumference corresponding to the average radius should be smaller than the operating wavelength:

$$\lambda > \pi(r_o + r_i) \tag{3.82}$$

Consequently, the coaxial lines used at high frequencies should be thin enough to make sure that only the TEM wave mode may propagate.

Example 3.4

Show that the attenuation constant of an air-filled coaxial line having a fixed diameter is at minimum when the characteristic impedance is $Z_0 = 77\Omega$.

Solution

According to (3.79) and (3.80) the attenuation constant is proportional to the quantity

$$\frac{1}{r_o}\left(1 + \frac{r_o}{r_i}\right)\frac{1}{\ln(r_o/r_i)}$$

Now r_o is constant. Let us denote $r_o/r_i = x$ and derivate with respect of x:

$$D\left[\frac{1}{r_o}\frac{1+x}{\ln x}\right] = \frac{1}{r_o}\frac{\ln x - (1+x)(1/x)}{\ln^2 x}$$

By setting this derivative equal to zero, we obtain

$$\ln x = \frac{1}{x} + 1$$

The solution of this equation is $x = r_o/r_i = 3.591$. By substituting this in (3.79), we obtain $Z_0 = 76.7\,\Omega$.

3.8 Microstrip Line

A microstrip line consists of a metal strip on one side and a ground plane on the other side of a substrate, as shown in Figure 3.13. The substrate is made of a low-loss dielectric material such as polytetrafluoroethylene (Teflon), aluminum oxide (alumina), or quartz.

A pure TEM wave mode can propagate in a microstrip line only if all fields are in the same medium. Then the solution for the field can be derived from Laplace's equation. In a case where the nonstatic fields are in two different media, the field has also longitudinal components. At low frequencies, or more precisely when $\lambda \gg h$, the fields are nearly the same as those in a static case, and we call them quasi-TEM. However, the analytical solution

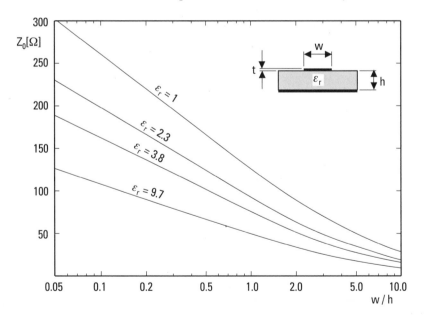

Figure 3.13 The cross section of a microstrip line and the characteristic impedance Z_0 as a function of the ratio of strip width to substrate height w/h for different substrate materials.

of the quasi-TEM wave mode is complicated and therefore a practical design of microstrip lines is based on graphs or approximate equations.

The phase constant of a quasi-TEM wave can be expressed as

$$\beta = \frac{2\pi}{\lambda} = \omega\sqrt{\mu\epsilon_0\,\epsilon_{reff}} \qquad (3.83)$$

where ϵ_{reff} is the effective relative permittivity. This is obtained by measuring or calculating the capacitance of the line per unit length C_{eff} and the capacitance of an air-filled but otherwise similar line per unit length C_0:

$$\epsilon_{reff} = \frac{C_{eff}}{C_0} \qquad (3.84)$$

The designer often knows the required characteristic impedance Z_0 and the required length of the line in wavelengths l/λ. Then the width of the strip w and the physical length l have to be determined. Z_0 and ϵ_{reff} depend mainly on the width of the strip w and on the height h and the relative permittivity ϵ_r of the substrate. The velocity of the wave and the wavelength depend on ϵ_{reff}, as given by (3.83). Sometimes the problem is inverse: The characteristic impedance has to be calculated from the dimensions and permittivity. Approximate design of a microstrip line can be carried out by using Figure 3.13 or the following equations [8]. These equations are valid when $0.05 \leq w/h \leq 20$ and $\epsilon_r \leq 16$.

When $w/h \leq 1$, the effective relative permittivity and characteristic impedance are

$$\epsilon_{reff} \approx \frac{\epsilon_r + 1}{2} + \frac{\epsilon_r - 1}{2}\left[\frac{1}{\sqrt{1 + 12h/w}} + 0.04\left(1 - \frac{w}{h}\right)^2\right] \qquad (3.85)$$

$$Z_0 \approx \frac{60}{\sqrt{\epsilon_{reff}}}\ln\left(\frac{8h}{w} + \frac{w}{4h}\right)\ \Omega \qquad (3.86)$$

When $w/h \geq 1$,

$$\epsilon_{reff} \approx \frac{\epsilon_r + 1}{2} + \frac{\epsilon_r - 1}{2}\frac{1}{\sqrt{1 + 12h/w}} \qquad (3.87)$$

$$Z_0 \approx \frac{377}{\sqrt{\epsilon_{reff}}\,[w/h + 1.393 + 0.667\,\ln(w/h + 1.444)]}\ \Omega \quad (3.88)$$

The width of the strip corresponding to a known Z_0 is obtained for $w/h \le 2$ from

$$\frac{w}{h} \approx \frac{8e^A}{e^{2A} - 2} \quad (3.89)$$

where

$$A = \frac{Z_0}{60\Omega}\sqrt{\frac{\epsilon_r + 1}{2}} + \frac{\epsilon_r - 1}{\epsilon_r + 1}\left(0.23 + \frac{0.11}{\epsilon_r}\right) \quad (3.90)$$

When $w/h \ge 2$,

$$\frac{w}{h} \approx \frac{2}{\pi}\left\{B - 1 - \ln(2B - 1) + \frac{\epsilon_r - 1}{2\epsilon_r}\left[\ln(B - 1) + 0.39 - \frac{0.61}{\epsilon_r}\right]\right\}$$
$$(3.91)$$

where

$$B = \frac{377\pi\Omega}{2Z_0\sqrt{\epsilon_r}} \quad (3.92)$$

In the preceding equations, it has been assumed that the thickness t of the strip is very small. In practice, the capacitance of the line per unit length will be slightly larger due to the finite thickness t compared to the case $t = 0$. This will lower the characteristic impedance. Due to the extra capacitance, the width of the strip seems to increase by

$$\Delta w_e = \frac{t}{\pi}(1 + \ln D) \quad (3.93)$$

where $D = 2h/t$, when $w/h \ge 1/(2\pi)$, and $D = 4\pi w/t$, when $w/h \le 1/(2\pi)$. Equation (3.93) is valid for $t < h$ and $t < w/2$. Equations (3.86), (3.88), (3.89), and (3.91) can be used for a strip having a finite thickness by replacing w by $w_e = w + \Delta w_e$.

The sources of losses in a microstrip line are:

- Conductor loss in the strip and ground plane;
- Dielectric and conduction losses in the substrate;
- Radiation loss;
- Surface wave loss.

Assuming a constant current distribution over the strip width, the attenuation constant due to metal loss is

$$\alpha_c = \frac{R_s}{Z_0 w} \tag{3.94}$$

The accuracy of this equation is best for a wide strip. In practice, the value of the surface resistance R_s is larger than the theoretical one. For example, the surface roughness of the substrate increases R_s. The thickness of the conductors should be at least four times the skin depth $\delta_s = \sqrt{2/(\omega\mu\sigma_m)}$. A metallization thinner than twice the skin depth would yield excessive attenuation.

Dielectric loss is usually much lower than conductor loss. The attenuation constant due to dielectric loss is

$$\alpha_d = \pi \frac{\epsilon_r(\epsilon_{reff} - 1)}{\sqrt{\epsilon_{reff}}(\epsilon_r - 1)} \frac{\tan\delta}{\lambda_0} \tag{3.95}$$

where λ_0 is the wavelength in free vacuum.

Discontinuities of the microstrip line produce radiation to free space. For a given line, radiation loss increases rapidly as the frequency increases. To avoid leakage and interference, microstrip circuits are usually shielded within a metal case. In microstrip antennas, leaking radiation is harnessed into use.

Surface waves are waves that are trapped by total reflection within the substrate. They may produce unwanted radiation from the edges of the substrate and spurious coupling between circuit elements.

Example 3.5

Find the width of the strip for a 50-Ω microstrip line. The substrate has a thickness of $h = 0.254$ mm and a relative permittivity of $\epsilon_r = 9.7$. The thickness of the strip is $t = 5$ μm. Find the wavelength in the line at a frequency of 10 GHz.

Solution

From Figure 3.13 we see that w/h is about 1. Equation (3.90) gives $A = 2.124$. From (3.89) we solve $w/h = 0.985$ or $w = 0.250$ mm. To account for the effect of the strip thickness, we calculate $D = 2h/t = 101.6$ and solve from (3.93) to get $\Delta w_e = 0.009$ mm. Therefore, the strip width should be 0.250 mm − 0.009 mm = 0.241 mm. A 5 μm thick and 0.241 mm wide strip corresponds to a 0.250 mm wide strip with $t = 0$. From (3.85) we obtain $\epsilon_{reff} = 6.548$. The wavelength at $f = 10$ GHz is $\lambda = c/(f\sqrt{\epsilon_{reff}}) = 11.72$ mm. (In practice, microstrip lines are dispersive and ϵ_{reff} increases as the frequency increases. Therefore, λ is slightly shorter.)

3.9 Wave and Signal Velocities

In a vacuum, radio waves propagate at the speed of light, $c = 299,792,458$ m/s. In a medium with parameters ϵ_r and μ_r the velocity of propagation is

$$v = \frac{1}{\sqrt{\mu\epsilon}} = \frac{1}{\sqrt{\mu_r\epsilon_r}}c \qquad (3.96)$$

The phase velocity

$$v_p = \frac{\omega}{\beta} \qquad (3.97)$$

is that velocity with which the constant-phase points of a wave propagate. In case of a plane wave or a TEM wave propagating in a transmission line, the phase velocity is equal to the velocity of propagation in free space filled with the same medium, $v_p = v$. Generally, the phase velocity of a wave propagating in a waveguide may be smaller or larger than v.

If the phase velocity and attenuation of a propagating wave do not depend on frequency, the waveform of a broadband signal does not distort as it propagates. However, if the phase velocity is frequency-dependent, the waveform will distort. This phenomenon is called dispersion (see Section 3.3).

The group velocity, v_g, is that velocity with which the energy of a narrow-band signal (or signal experiencing no significant dispersion) propagates. The group velocity of a plane wave or a TEM wave is equal to the velocity of propagation in free space filled with the same medium. For other wave modes, the group velocity is smaller than v. The group velocity can never exceed the speed of light. The group velocity is given by [2, 5]

$$v_g = \left(\frac{d\beta}{d\omega}\right)^{-1} \tag{3.98}$$

3.10 Transmission Line Model

A transmission line exhibits properties of capacitance, inductance, resistance, and conductance: The electric field between the conductors contains electric energy in the same way as a capacitor; the magnetic field produced by the currents contains magnetic energy as an inductor; the conductors have losses as a resistor; the leakage currents in the insulator produce losses as a resistor or a conductor. These properties cannot be separated because they are distributed along the line. Figure 3.14 shows the transmission line model, a short section of a transmission line with a length Δz having a series inductance L, a parallel capacitance C, a series resistance R, and a parallel conductance G, all being values per unit length.

In the transmission line model, voltages and currents are used instead of electric and magnetic fields to represent the propagating wave. This model best suits transmission lines carrying TEM wave modes. However, the transmission line model may also be applied for other transmission lines and waveguides by defining the voltage and current properly and by restricting the analysis for such a narrow band that dispersion may be neglected.

The voltage and current on a transmission line depend on the position and time, $V(z, t)$ and $I(z, t)$. We can derive for voltage and current the so-called telegrapher equations:

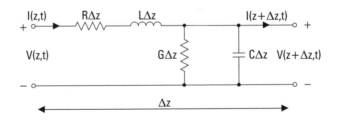

Figure 3.14 Transmission line model.

$$\frac{\partial^2 V(z, t)}{\partial z^2} = LC \frac{\partial^2 V(z, t)}{\partial t^2} + (RC + LG) \frac{\partial V(z, t)}{\partial t} + RGV(z, t)$$

$$(3.99)$$

$$\frac{\partial^2 I(z, t)}{\partial z^2} = LC \frac{\partial^2 I(z, t)}{\partial t^2} + (RC + LG) \frac{\partial I(z, t)}{\partial t} + RGI(z, t)$$

$$(3.100)$$

The voltage and current of a sinusoidal signal are

$$V(z, t) = V(z) e^{j\omega t} \qquad (3.101)$$

$$I(z, t) = I(z) e^{j\omega t} \qquad (3.102)$$

For sinusoidal signals, the telegrapher equations simplify to

$$\frac{d^2 V(z)}{dz^2} - \gamma^2 V(z) = 0 \qquad (3.103)$$

$$\frac{d^2 I(z)}{dz^2} - \gamma^2 I(z) = 0 \qquad (3.104)$$

where

$$\gamma = \sqrt{(R + j\omega L)(G + j\omega C)} = \alpha + j\beta \qquad (3.105)$$

The solutions of the telegrapher equations are of the form

$$V(z) = V^+ e^{-\gamma z} + V^- e^{+\gamma z} \qquad (3.106)$$

$$I(z) = \frac{V^+}{Z_0} e^{-\gamma z} - \frac{V^-}{Z_0} e^{+\gamma z} = I^+ e^{-\gamma z} - I^- e^{+\gamma z} \qquad (3.107)$$

where

$$Z_0 = \sqrt{\frac{R + j\omega L}{G + j\omega C}} \qquad (3.108)$$

is the complex characteristic impedance of the transmission line. In (3.106) and (3.107) V^+ and I^+ are the complex amplitudes for a wave propagating into the positive z direction and V^- and I^- are those for a wave propagating into the negative z direction.

References

[1]   Chatterjee, R., *Elements of Microwave Engineering,* Chichester, England: Ellis Horwood, 1986.

[2]   Collin, R. E., *Foundations for Microwave Engineering,* 2nd ed., New York: IEEE Press, 2001.

[3]   Collin, R. E., *Field Theory of Guided Waves,* New York: IEEE Press, 1991.

[4]   Gardiol, F. E., *Introduction to Microwaves,* Dedham, MA: Artech House, 1984.

[5]   Pozar, D. M., *Microwave Engineering,* 2nd ed., New York: John Wiley & Sons, 1998.

[6]   Ramo, S., J. Whinnery, and T. van Duzer, *Fields and Waves in Communication Electronics,* New York: John Wiley & Sons, 1965.

[7]   Liao, S. Y., *Microwave Circuit Analysis and Amplifier Design,* Englewood Cliffs, NJ: Prentice Hall, 1987.

[8]   Bahl, I. J., and D. K. Trivedi, "A Designer's Guide to Microstrip Line," *Microwaves,* May 1977, pp. 174–182.

4

Impedance Matching

In Chapter 3 we considered homogeneous transmission lines and waveguides in which a wave propagates only in the z direction. In a homogeneous line the characteristic impedance is independent of z, and accordingly the ratio of the electric and magnetic field as well as the ratio of the voltage and current (in a TEM line) is constant.

If there is a discontinuity in the line disturbing the fields, the impedance changes and a reflection occurs. The discontinuity may be a change in the line dimensions or a terminating load, the impedance of which is different from that of the line. This mismatch of impedances may cause serious problems. Elimination of the reflection—that is, matching the load to the line—is a frequent and important task in radio engineering.

In this chapter we first consider the fundamental concepts needed in impedance matching: the reflection coefficient, input impedance, standing wave, and the Smith chart. Then we consider different methods of impedance matching, such as matching with lumped elements, with tuning stubs, with quarter-wave transformers, and with a resistive circuit.

4.1 Reflection from a Mismatched Load

In the following analysis we will use the transmission line model and use voltages and currents. In principle we could, of course, use electric and magnetic fields, but the advantage of using voltages and currents is that the characteristic impedance of a line is always (by definition) the ratio of the voltage and current, but not always directly the ratio of the electric and magnetic field [see (3.51)]. In impedance matching it is the characteristic impedance of the line that matters, not the wave impedance.

Let us consider a situation shown in Figure 4.1 in which the line is terminated at $z = 0$ with a load. The characteristic impedance of the line is Z_0 and the impedance of the load is Z_L. Let us assume that there is a voltage wave propagating toward the load, $V^+ e^{-\gamma z}$, and the corresponding current wave is $I^+ e^{-\gamma z}$ ($Z_0 = V^+/I^+$). Then at the input of the load, normally one part of the propagating wave power is reflected while the other part is absorbed to the load. The reflected voltage wave is $V^- e^{+\gamma z}$, and the corresponding reflected current wave is $I^- e^{+\gamma z}$ ($Z_0 = V^-/I^-$). V^+, I^+, V^-, and I^- are complex amplitudes. At $z = 0$ the voltages of the line and those of the load must be equal, and the same applies of course to the currents:

$$V^+ + V^- = V_L \tag{4.1}$$

$$I^+ - I^- = I_L \tag{4.2}$$

Note that the directions of positive I^+ and I^- are defined to be opposites. As $Z_L = V_L/I_L$, we can present (4.2) as

$$\frac{V^+}{Z_0} - \frac{V^-}{Z_0} = \frac{V_L}{Z_L} \tag{4.3}$$

The voltage reflection coefficient of the load is defined as

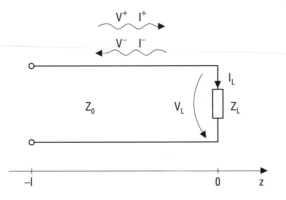

Figure 4.1 A line terminated with a load.

$$\rho_L = \frac{V^-}{V^+} \tag{4.4}$$

If we eliminate V^- from (4.1) and (4.3), and then solve for ρ_L, we obtain

$$\rho_L = \frac{Z_L - Z_0}{Z_L + Z_0} = \frac{z_L - 1}{z_L + 1} \tag{4.5}$$

where $z_L = Z_L/Z_0$ is the normalized load impedance (do not confuse the normalized impedances with the z coordinate). The voltage transmission coefficient is

$$\tau_L = \frac{V_L}{V^+} = 1 + \rho_L = \frac{2Z_L}{Z_L + Z_0} \tag{4.6}$$

If the load impedance and the characteristic impedance of the line are equal, there will be no reflected wave but all power will be absorbed into the load. In such a case the load is matched to the line.

If the load is mismatched or $Z_L \neq Z_0$, there will be a wave propagating in both directions, that is, the voltage and current as a function of z are

$$V(z) = V^+ e^{-\gamma z} + V^- e^{+\gamma z} \tag{4.7}$$

$$I(z) = I^+ e^{-\gamma z} - I^- e^{+\gamma z} = \frac{V^+}{Z_0} e^{-\gamma z} - \frac{V^-}{Z_0} e^{+\gamma z} \tag{4.8}$$

Let us assume that the length of the line is l. In the following we consider the load impedance seen through this line. At $z = -l$ the voltage reflection coefficient is

$$\rho(-l) = \frac{V^- e^{-\gamma l}}{V^+ e^{+\gamma l}} = \rho_L e^{-2\gamma l} \tag{4.9}$$

Now the input impedance at $z = -l$ is

$$Z(-l) = \frac{V(-l)}{I(-l)} = Z_0 \frac{V^+ e^{+\gamma l} + V^- e^{-\gamma l}}{V^+ e^{+\gamma l} - V^- e^{-\gamma l}} = Z_0 \frac{1 + \rho_L e^{-2\gamma l}}{1 - \rho_L e^{-2\gamma l}} = Z_0 \frac{1 + \rho(-l)}{1 - \rho(-l)} \tag{4.10}$$

When substituting (4.5) into (4.10) and taking into account that $e^x = \sinh x + \cosh x$, we obtain

$$Z(-l) = Z_0 \frac{Z_L + Z_0 \tanh \gamma l}{Z_0 + Z_L \tanh \gamma l} \qquad (4.11)$$

In practice we use low-loss lines, which means that the attenuation (or damping) constant is small, often negligible, and then we can assume that $\gamma = j\beta$. In such a case the input impedance is

$$Z(-l) = Z_0 \frac{Z_L + jZ_0 \tan \beta l}{Z_0 + jZ_L \tan \beta l} \qquad (4.12)$$

In a lossless case the line voltage as a function of z is

$$V(z) = V^+ e^{-j\beta z}(1 + \rho_L e^{2j\beta z}) \qquad (4.13)$$

The voltage (or the field strength) repeats itself periodically at every half-wavelength, so there is a standing wave in the line, as shown in Figure 4.2. At the maximum, the voltages of the forward and reflected waves are in the same phase, and therefore the total amplitude is $V_{max} = |V^+| + |V^-|$. At the minimum, the voltages are in an opposite phase, and therefore the total amplitude V_{min} is the difference $|V^+| - |V^-|$. On the other hand, the current has a minimum where the voltage has a maximum, and vice versa. The voltage standing wave ratio is defined as

$$VSWR = \frac{V_{max}}{V_{min}} = \frac{|V^+| + |V^-|}{|V^+| - |V^-|} = \frac{1 + |\rho_L|}{1 - |\rho_L|} \qquad (4.14)$$

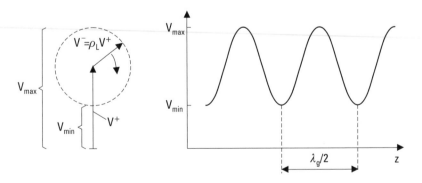

Figure 4.2 Standing wave pattern (rhs) and its phasor presentation (lhs).

VSWR is equal to 1 when the load is matched, and $1 < VSWR \leq \infty$ when the load is mismatched. The input impedance of the line is $Z_0 \times VSWR$ at the maximum and $Z_0/VSWR$ at the minimum, that is, it is real in both cases.

There are many problems caused by the load mismatch:

- Part of the power is not absorbed by the load. Power is proportional to the square of the voltage (or field strength); therefore the power reflection coefficient is $|\rho_L|^2$. If the forward propagating power is P, then the reflected power is $|\rho_L|^2 \times P$ and the power absorbed by the load is $(1 - |\rho_L|^2) \times P$. The power loss due to reflection or the reflection loss L_{refl} is (in decibels)

$$L_{refl} = 10 \log \frac{1}{1 - |\rho_L|^2} \qquad (4.15)$$

The return loss L_{retn} describes how much smaller the reflected power is compared to the incident power P, and is defined (in decibels) as

$$L_{retn} = 10 \log \frac{1}{|\rho_L|^2} \qquad (4.16)$$

- Due to reflection, the field strength may be doubled at the standing wave maximum, and therefore danger of electrical breakdown increases in high-power applications such as radar.
- The standing wave increases the conductor loss in the line. The loss is proportional to the square of the current. At the current maximum the loss increase is higher than the decrease at the current minimum compared to a matched case.
- A mismatch at the input of a sensitive receiver deteriorates the signal-to-noise ratio of the receiver.
- If the line is long, the input impedance fluctuates rapidly versus frequency. This is a disadvantage for active devices such as amplifiers because their performance depends on the feeding impedance. For example, the gain of an amplifier may change greatly if its input load impedance (feed impedance) changes.
- In digital radio systems the reflected pulses may cause symbol errors.

- In an antenna array a mismatched element causes deterioration of the overall antenna performance due to phase and amplitude errors.

A standing wave in a line can be measured and displayed using a slotted line, which is usually made of a rectangular metal waveguide or a coaxial line. In the case of a rectangular waveguide, there is a narrow slot in the middle of the wide wall, as shown in Figure 4.3; this slot does not disturb the fields of the waveguide because the surface currents of the TE_{10} mode do not cross the centerline of the wide wall. In the slot there is a movable probe, into which a voltage proportional to the electric field is induced. This voltage is then measured with a square-law diode detector and displayed with a proper device. By moving the probe, the maximum and minimum are found and their ratio gives the *VSWR*. The impedance at the standing wave minimum is $Z_0/VSWR$. Then the impedance at any position z can be calculated using (4.12). In practice, nowadays the impedance is measured using a network analyzer. For more information concerning measurement techniques, see [1].

4.2 Smith Chart

The Smith chart is a useful tool for displaying impedances measured versus frequency or for solving a matching problem in a circuit design. The Smith chart clearly shows the connection between the reflection coefficient and

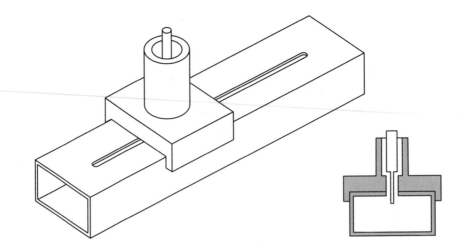

Figure 4.3 A slotted line made of a rectangular waveguide.

impedance, and also displays readily how the input impedance changes when moving along the line.

If the load is passive, the absolute value of the voltage reflection coefficient is never more than 1. Then any complex reflection coefficient of a passive load can be presented in the polar form within a unity circle. All possible normalized impedances of passive loads can be presented within this unity circle. This is the great idea of the Smith chart, presented by P. Smith in 1939 [2].

The normalized input impedance at $z = -l$ can be presented as

$$z(-l) = \frac{Z(-l)}{Z_0} = r + jx \tag{4.17}$$

The corresponding voltage reflection coefficient is

$$\rho(-l) = \rho_L e^{-2j\beta l} = u + jv \tag{4.18}$$

According to (4.10) we have

$$z(-l) = \frac{1 + \rho_L e^{-2j\beta l}}{1 - \rho_L e^{-2j\beta l}} \tag{4.19}$$

and after substituting (4.17) and (4.18) into this we obtain

$$r + jx = \frac{1 + (u + jv)}{1 - (u + jv)} \tag{4.20}$$

We can form the two following equations by separating (4.20) into real and imaginary parts:

$$r = \frac{1 - (u^2 + v^2)}{(1 - u)^2 + v^2} \tag{4.21}$$

$$x = \frac{2v}{(1 - u)^2 + v^2} \tag{4.22}$$

These can be solved for two equations of circles as

$$\left(u - \frac{r}{1+r}\right)^2 + v^2 = \frac{1}{(1+r)^2} \tag{4.23}$$

$$(u-1)^2 + \left(v - \frac{1}{x}\right)^2 = \frac{1}{x^2} \tag{4.24}$$

Graphically presented, these equations form the Smith chart shown in Figure 4.4.

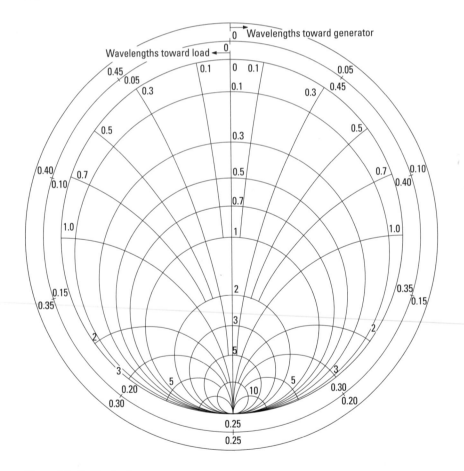

Figure 4.4 Smith chart.

At the center of the Smith chart the normalized impedance is $z = 1$; that is, the load is matched to the line ($\rho = 0$). At the top of the Smith chart there is a point representing a short circuit, $z = 0$ or $\rho = -1$, and at the bottom there is a point representing an open circuit, $z = \infty$ or $\rho = 1$. Points elsewhere on the unity circle perimeter represent pure imaginary impedances $(|\rho| = 1)$. All pure real impedances are on the vertical diameter, and from that to the left there are the capacitive impedances and to the right the inductive impedances.

Figure 4.5 shows how an impedance is related to the corresponding voltage reflection coefficient. Point A represents a normalized load impedance, $z_L = 0.5 + j0.5$. The magnitude of the reflection coefficient is the distance of point A from the center of the chart, point O, or $|\rho| = 0.45$ (remember that the radius of the chart is 1). The phase of the reflection coefficient is the angle between the directions from point O to the point $z = \infty$ and to point A measured counterclockwise, in this case $\angle\rho = 117°$.

When moving along a lossless line, the absolute value of the reflection coefficient is constant and the phase changes 360° per one half-wavelength. Therefore the impedance locus following this move is along a circle, the

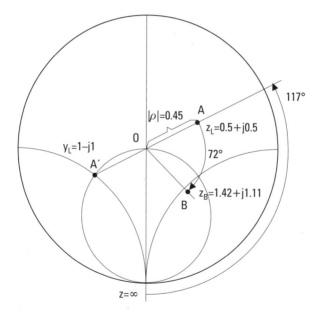

Figure 4.5 Using the Smith chart: The relation between an impedance and the corresponding voltage reflection coefficient, movement along a lossless transmission line (A → B), and the relation between an impedance (point A) and the corresponding admittance (point A′).

radius of which is equal to the absolute value of the load reflection coefficient. If the movement is toward the load, the direction on the Smith chart is counterclockwise. If the movement is away from the load, that is, toward the generator, the direction is clockwise. The impedance of the load, $z_L = 0.5 + j0.5$, seen through a line of $0.1\lambda_g$ long, is obtained by moving from point A clockwise $360°/5 = 72°$ to point B, where the impedance is $z_B = 1.42 + j1.11$.

One of the great features of the Smith chart is that the admittance y_L corresponding to the impedance z_L is obtained as the mirror image A′ of point A. When $z_L = 0.5 + j0.5$, we can read from the Smith chart that $y_L = 1.0 - j1.0$. This can be easily checked using the definition of admittance

$$y(-l) = \frac{1}{z(-l)} = \frac{Z_0}{Z_{in}(-l)} = g + jb \qquad (4.25)$$

4.3 Matching Methods

The purpose of matching is to eliminate the wave reflected from a load. From the matching point of view, a load may be not only a circuit or device into which the power is absorbed from the line, but also a generator feeding the line. This is why we have to consider cautiously the directions "toward generator—clockwise" and "toward load—counterclockwise" on the Smith chart. In most cases we measure the reflection coefficient of the "load" first. In the measurement we use an auxiliary generator, and accordingly we can always use the direction "clockwise—toward generator" when designing a matching circuit. Figure 4.6 illustrates this in the case of an amplifier with both an input and output matching circuit in order to maximize gain. When designing the input matching circuit, we measure first the transistor reflection coefficient, ρ_{in}, from the input side, but when designing the output matching circuit we measure the reflection coefficient, ρ_{out}, from the output side.

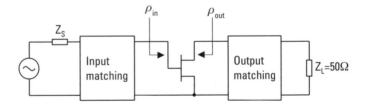

Figure 4.6 A transistor amplifier with both input and output matching, illustrating the direction of measurement of the reflection coefficients.

Note that impedance tuners are needed in place of matching circuits to optimize the transistor performance before and during measurement. In the case of a bilateral transistor, ρ_{in} depends on the output load impedance and ρ_{out} depends on the input load impedance. Therefore, some iteration is needed to find the reflection coefficients providing the maximum gain. After these measurements, in both cases, we use the Smith chart in a clockwise manner when designing the matching circuits.

Usually the load is matched to the line with a matching circuit in front of the load. The matching circuit contains reactive elements such as inductors (coils), capacitors, transformers, tuning stubs, or special elements such as a tuning screw or an iris in a metal waveguide. The reactive elements represent discontinuities that cause reflections, which cancel the reflection from the load, so that ideally all power is absorbed into the load although there are multiple reflections between the load and the matching circuit (see Section 4.3.3). In case of a quarter-wave transformer these discontinuities are the abrupt changes in the characteristic impedance of the line. In some cases the load is matched resistively, but then the reflected wave is absorbed into the matching circuit and therefore lost.

Furthermore, in some cases the load impedance can be tuned actively. For example, the impedance of a diode detector depends on the diode bias current. By introducing a proper bias current, the matching of the detector can be optimized.

In Section 4.3 we assume that the load impedance will be matched to the real impedance of the line feeding the load. Generally, matching is realized between circuits having complex impedances—for example, between a source with an output impedance Z_S and a load with an input impedance Z_{in}. Then conjugate matching

$$Z_{in} = Z_S^* \qquad (4.26)$$

results in maximum power transfer to the load for a fixed source impedance. In fact, in the following we realize the same because the matching circuit transforms the real line impedance to the complex conjugate of the load impedance.

4.3.1 Matching with Lumped Reactive Elements

In the megahertz range, a coil may perform as an ideal inductance and a capacitor as an ideal capacitance. In the microwave region, coils and capacitors may still be useful elements for realizing reactive matching circuits, but care must be taken with the size of these elements. The size of the lumped element must be much smaller than a wavelength. In hybrid integrated circuits, chip capacitors or interdigital gap capacitors and wire coils are successfully used at least to several gigahertz, and in monolithic integrated circuits *metal–insulator–metal* (MIM) capacitors as well as loop and spiral inductors are used successfully at millimeter wavelengths. However, parasitic elements of such capacitors and inductors must also be taken into account in the circuit design, meaning that a careful modeling of these elements is necessary. Figure 4.7 illustrates some lumped elements used in integrated circuits.

Matching with a lumped reactive element is realized by placing a single element at a proper distance from the load in series or in parallel as shown in Figure 4.8. It is possible to move from any load impedance z_L toward the generator such a distance $l_1 < \lambda_g/2$, so that the load is seen as an impedance $1 + jx_0$. If we add at this point a series reactance of $-x_0$, the

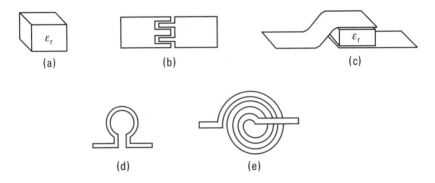

Figure 4.7 Reactive lumped elements for integrated circuits: (a) chip capacitor; (b) interdigital gap capacitor; (c) metal–insulator–metal capacitor; (d) loop inductor; and (e) spiral inductor (with an airbridge).

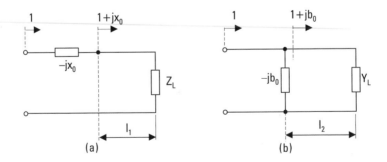

Figure 4.8 Matching with a single reactive element placed at a proper distance from the load: (a) with a series element; and (b) with a shunt element.

input impedance is $1 + jx_0 - jx_0 = 1$, and the load is matched to the line; see Figure 4.8(a). On the other hand, from any load admittance it is possible to move toward the generator a distance $l_2 < \lambda_g/2$, so that the load admittance is seen as $1 + jb_0$. By adding in this point a shunt susceptance $-b_0$, we get a match, as in Figure 4.8(b).

Example 4.1

Match a load impedance of $Z_L = R_L + jX_L = (150 + j100)\Omega$ to $Z_0 = 50\Omega$ at 100 MHz according to Figure 4.8.

Solution

Let us first place the normalized load impedance $z_L = Z_L/Z_0 = 3 + j2$ on the Smith chart in Figure 4.9; we are at point A. If we then move along a circle (radius OA) clockwise on the Smith chart (corresponding to moving along a lossless 50-Ω line away from the load), we first come to the unity circle after $0.096\lambda_g$ at point B, where the impedance is $1 - j1.62$. By adding a series inductance with a normalized reactance of $x = +1.62$ ($L = xZ_0/\omega = 128$ nH) in this point, we match the load. Another possibility is to move further away (a distance of $0.206\lambda_g$ from load) to point B′, which is on the mirror image circle of circle $r = 1$. The corresponding admittance at point C′ is $1 + j1.62$. By adding a shunt inductance with susceptance of $b = -1.62$ ($L = -Z_0/(\omega b) = 49$ nH) at this point we also match the load. A further possibility is to move to point B″ (distance from load $0.346\lambda_g$) and add a shunt capacitance with susceptance of $b = +1.62$ ($C = b/(\omega Z_0)$

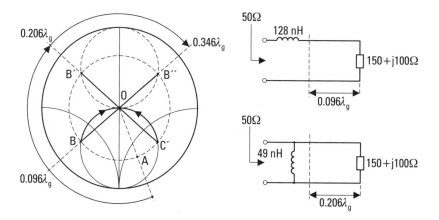

Figure 4.9 Matching the load impedance of $Z_L = R_L + jX_L = (150 + j100)\Omega$ to $Z_0 = 50\Omega$ using a single lumped reactive element.

= 52 pF). However, the widest matching bandwidth is obtained when the reactive (susceptive) element is placed as close to the load as possible.

Another possibility in realizing a reactive match is to use an *LC* (or *LL* or *CC*) circuit in front of the load, as shown in Figure 4.10. The series or shunt element next to the load now replaces the line section needed above, and the matching circuit is more compact.

If $z_L = r_L + jx_L$ is inside the $1 + jx$ circle, there are two distinct possibilities to match the load with two reactive elements: first either a capacitor or an inductor in parallel to the load and then in series an inductor or a capacitor, respectively, toward the line. If $z_L = r_L + jx_L$ is inside the mirror image circle of the $1 + jx$ circle, there are again two distinct possibilities: first either an inductor or a capacitor in series with the load and then a

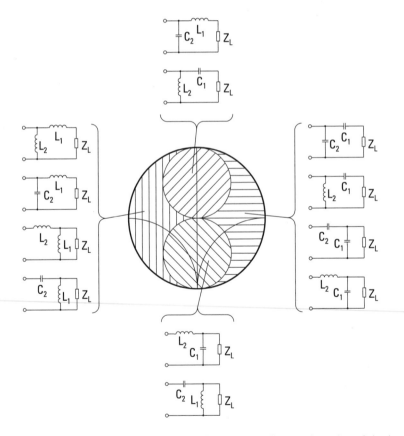

Figure 4.10 Matching with two reactive elements: Depending on the value of the load impedance $z_L = r_L + jx_L$, the Smith chart is divided into four regions, each of which leads to different possibilities in matching with two reactive elements.

shunting capacitor or inductor, respectively, toward the line. If the load impedance is outside of both of the regions, in the vertically or horizontally shaded area of the Smith chart in Figure 4.10, there are more matching possibilities. If the load impedance $z_L = r_L + jx_L$ is in the vertically shaded area, that is, if z_L is capacitive, there are four distinct possibilities to construct the matching circuit with two reactive elements, but we must start with an inductor next to the load. This inductor may be either in series or in parallel; the other component (respectively in parallel or in series) may be an inductor or a capacitor. Similarly, when z_L is in the horizontally shaded region— when the load impedance is inductive—there are again four different possibilities, but now we must start with a capacitor next to the load. Again, this capacitor may be either in series or in parallel; the other component (respectively in parallel or in series) may be an inductor or a capacitor. Let us study these in more detail through some examples, which also serve the reader for getting more confidence in using the Smith chart.

Example 4.2

Match a load impedance of $Z_L = R_L + jX_L = (20 - j30)\Omega$ to $Z_0 = 50\Omega$ at 100 MHz starting with a series inductor next to the load.

Solution

Let us first mark the normalized impedance $z_L = Z_L/Z_0 = 0.4 - j0.6$ on the Smith chart as shown in Figure 4.11; we are at point A. If we add at this point a series reactance of $x = 1.09$, we get to the mirror image circle of the circle $r = 1$ to point B, where the impedance is $0.4 + j0.49$. The

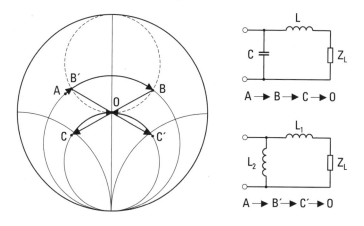

Figure 4.11 Matching of a load $Z_L = R_L + jX_L = (20 - j30)\Omega$ to $Z_0 = 50\Omega$ using lumped reactive elements.

corresponding admittance is $1.0 - j1.22$ (point C), so that by adding a parallel susceptance of $b = 1.22$, we match the load. The inductance corresponding to the normalized series reactance x is $L = xZ_0/\omega$, and the capacitance corresponding to the normalized parallel susceptance is $C = b/(\omega Z_0)$. The component values at 100 MHz are $L = 87$ nH and $C = 39$ pF. Another possibility is first to add a small series reactance of $x = 0.11$ to get to point B′ where the impedance is $0.4 - j0.49$. Then the corresponding admittance is $1.0 + j1.22$ (point C′). After adding a parallel susceptance of $b = -1.22$, we also have obtained a match. Now both of the reactive components are inductances; the series component is $L_1 = Z_0x/\omega = 8.8$ nH and the parallel component is $L_2 = -Z_0/(b\omega) = 65$ nH. (*Note:* This load impedance can also be matched starting with a shunt inductance next to the load; in order to realize this, start from the load admittance.)

Example 4.3

Match a load impedance of $Z_L = R_L + jX_L = (150 + j100)\Omega$ to $Z_0 = 50\Omega$ at 100 MHz with two reactive elements.

Solution

Let us first mark the normalized impedance $z_L = Z_L/Z_0 = 3 + j2$ on the Smith chart as shown in Figure 4.12; we are at point A. We first transform to the corresponding admittance, $y_L = 0.23 - j0.15$. From there we move along circle $g = 0.23$ to the mirror image circle of $g = 1$ either to point B′ or point B″. Moving to B′ corresponds to adding a shunt susceptance of $b = -0.26$ (i.e., $L_1 = -Z_0/(b\omega) = 306$ nH), and moving to B″ corresponds

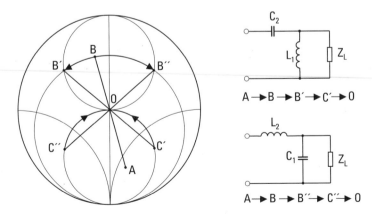

Figure 4.12 Matching of a load $Z_L = R_L + jX_L = (150 + j100)\Omega$ to $Z_0 = 50\Omega$ using lumped reactive elements.

to adding a shunt susceptance of $b = 0.56$ (i.e., $C_1 = b/(\omega Z_0) = 18$ pF). Then we transform back to the impedance and get to either point C′ or C″, respectively. In order to get to the center of the Smith chart, we now have to add a series component. In the case of point C′ we add a series capacitor with a reactance of $x = -1.8$ ($C_2 = -1/(Z_0 x \omega) = 18$ pF), and in the case of point C″ we add a series inductor with a reactance of 1.8 ($L_2 = x Z_0/\omega = 143$ nH).

Example 4.4

Match a load impedance of $Z_L = R_L + j X_L = (15 - j15)\Omega$ to $Z_0 = 50\Omega$ at 100 MHz with two lumped reactive elements.

Solution

Let us first mark the normalized impedance $z_L = Z_L/Z_0 = 0.3 - j0.3$ on the Smith chart as shown in Figure 4.13; we are at point A. If we now add a series reactance of $x = 0.758$, we move along the circle $r = 0.3$ and get to the mirror image circle of the circle $r = 1$ to point B, where the impedance is $0.3 + j0.458$. The corresponding admittance is $1.0 - j1.528$ (point C), so that by adding a parallel susceptance of $b = 1.528$ we match the load. The inductance corresponding to the normalized series reactance x is $L_1 = x Z_0/\omega = 60$ nH, and the capacitance corresponding to the normalized parallel susceptance is $C_1 = b/(\omega Z_0) = 49$ pF at 100 MHz. Another possibility is to add first a series reactance of $x = -0.158$ to get to point B′ where the impedance is $0.3 - j0.458$. Then the corresponding admittance

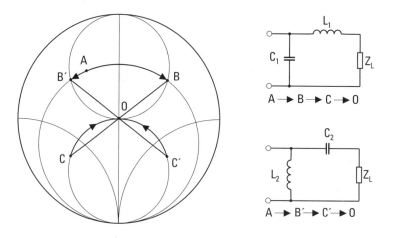

Figure 4.13 Matching of a load $Z_L = R_L + j X_L = (15 - j15)\Omega$ to $Z_0 = 50\Omega$ using lumped reactive elements.

is $1.0 + j1.528$ (point C'). After adding a parallel susceptance of -1.528, we have obtained a match. Now the component values are for the series capacitance $C_2 = -1/(Z_0 x \omega) = 201$ pF and for the parallel inductance $L_2 = -Z_0/(b\omega) = 52$ nH.

4.3.2 Matching with Tuning Stubs (with Short Sections of Line)

In the microwave region, the inductors and capacitors do not represent ideal inductances and capacitances but often behave as resonant circuits. At such high frequencies the desired reactance may often be more easily realizable by using a tuning stub, which is a short section of a line terminated with either a short circuit or an open circuit. As we can easily calculate using (4.12), a short-circuited tuning stub is inductive when its length is from 0 to $\lambda_g/4$ and capacitive when its length is from $\lambda_g/4$ to $\lambda_g/2$. An open-circuited tuning stub is capacitive when its length is from 0 to $\lambda_g/4$ and inductive when its length is from $\lambda_g/4$ to $\lambda_g/2$. Depending on the line type used, there may be only one choice: In a metal waveguide only a short-circuited stub is possible because an open end acts as an antenna. On the other hand, in microstrip circuits a short circuit is difficult to realize and therefore open-circuited stubs are used.

Matching with one tuning stub is realized according to Figure 4.8. In theory, we can use either a series stub or a parallel stub. In practice the choice is more limited. For example, in a microstrip circuit only a parallel stub is possible.

If the characteristic impedance of the tuning stub is the same as that of the line to which the load is to be matched, the length of a short-circuited stub is obtained from the following [see also (4.12)]

$$j \tan \beta l = -jx_0 = \frac{1}{-jb_0} \tag{4.27}$$

Accordingly, the length of an open-circuited stub is obtained from

$$\frac{1}{j \tan \beta l} = -jx_0 = \frac{1}{-jb_0} \tag{4.28}$$

The characteristic impedance of the stub may also differ from that of the line; then the proper length is calculated using (4.12). Since the impedance of a stub is periodic with a period of $\lambda_g/2$, the stub length can also be $l + n\lambda_g/2$, but a short stub is preferred because it provides a wider matching bandwidth.

Example 4.5

Match the normalized admittance of $y_L = 0.3 + j0.3$ to a 50-Ω line using a short-circuited tuning stub.

Solution

Figures 4.14 and 4.15 show how this problem is solved on the Smith chart. First we place the normalized admittance on the Smith chart, point A. Then we move along a circle (along a 50-Ω line) a distance of $0.123\lambda_g$ and come to the unity circle $g = 1$ to point B, where the admittance is $1 + j1.4$. If we now add at this point a parallel susceptance of -1.4, we obtain a match. Another possibility is to move along the 50-Ω line to point B′, where the admittance is $1 - j1.4$, and add at this point a parallel susceptance of $+j1.4$ in order to get a match. The required length of the parallel stub is either obtained from (4.27) or by using the Smith chart. Figure 4.15 shows how the length of a short-circuited stub with a normalized admittance of $-j1.4$ is obtained. We start from $y = \infty$ and move along the outer circle of the

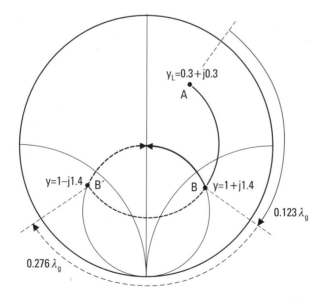

Figure 4.14 Matching of a load with a shunt susceptance according to Figure 4.8(b) presented on the Smith chart.

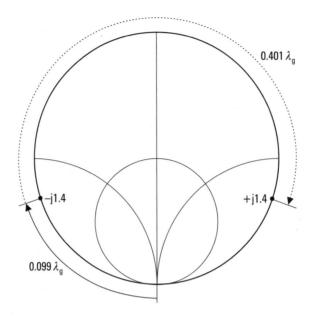

Figure 4.15 Using the Smith chart to obtain the lengths of short-circuited tuning stubs corresponding to normalized admittances of $-j1.4$ and $+j1.4$.

Smith chart to the point where the normalized admittance is $-j1.4$: The length $l = 0.099\lambda_g$ can be read from the Smith chart. Accordingly, the admittance $+j1.4$ can be realized with a short-circuited stub of length $l = 0.401\lambda_g$, as also shown in Figure 4.15. The obtained matching circuits are presented in Figure 4.16.

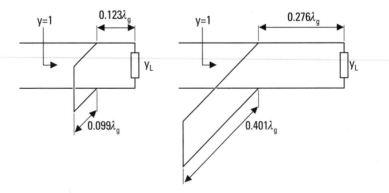

Figure 4.16 Tuning-stub matching of a load with a normalized admittance of $y_L = 0.3 + j0.3$.

The above matching with a single tuning stub is simple but requires placing the stub in a new position when the frequency is changed, even if the stub length is adjustable. The tuning stubs can be placed in a fixed position when two or three stubs are used [3]. The remaining task is to find correct lengths of the stubs. Two tuning stubs allow matching of almost all possible load impedances. In practice, a limiting factor is the attenuation in the line; it limits the range of the obtainable stub susceptances. A wide matching bandwidth also requires that the distance between the stubs be close to either 0 or $\lambda_g/2$. In practice the tuning stubs are placed at a distance of $\lambda_g/8$ or $3\lambda_g/8$ from each other. For measurement setups, tuners are available with three adjustable stubs. Such a tuner can match any load impedance to the line.

4.3.3 Quarter-Wave Transformer

Let us consider the situation presented in Figure 4.17. A real load impedance R_L must be matched into a line with a characteristic impedance of Z_0. Matching is realized by using a line section of length $\lambda_g/4$ and characteristic impedance Z_t. Because $\tan(\beta\lambda_g/4) = \infty$, we obtain from (4.12) that the impedance loading the original line is

$$R_L' = \frac{Z_t^2}{R_L} \tag{4.29}$$

If we choose $Z_t = \sqrt{Z_0 R_L}$, the load is matched to the line. The quarter-wavelength-long line section acts as a transformer, with a number-of-turns ratio equal to $\sqrt{Z_0/R_L}$. If the load impedance is not real, we use a line section with a proper length and characteristic impedance between the load and the transformer so that the load impedance seen through this section is real.

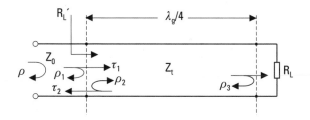

Figure 4.17 Quarter-wave transformer.

Example 4.6

Match a load impedance of $Z_L = (20 + j40)\Omega$ to a line with $Z_0 = 50\Omega$ using a quarter-wave transformer.

Solution

Figure 4.18 shows, on the Smith chart, how the problem is solved. First we need to make the load impedance real: We place a line section having a characteristic impedance of Z_0 between the load and the transformer. The load impedance normalized to Z_0 is $z_L = 0.4 + j0.8$. We need a line section of $0.135\lambda_g$ to make the load impedance real. When we move from $z_L = 0.4 + j0.8$ toward the generator a distance of $0.135\lambda_g$, we come to a real impedance (normalized) of $r = 4.27$, that is, $R = rZ_0 = 214\Omega$. According to (4.29) the required transformer impedance is $\sqrt{Z_0 R} = \sqrt{rZ_0} = 103\Omega$. Then we normalize the impedance R to Z_t and obtain $R/Z_t = \sqrt{r}$. We move on the Smith chart to $\sqrt{r} = 2.07$, and then move a distance of $\lambda_g/4$ toward the generator and get impedance $1/\sqrt{r}$. When we normalize this back to Z_0, we get an impedance of $Z_t/(\sqrt{r}Z_0) = 1$; in other words, the load is matched.

Let us now consider what actually happens in the quarter-wave transformer of Figure 4.17 to the wave approaching the load. The wave is reflected

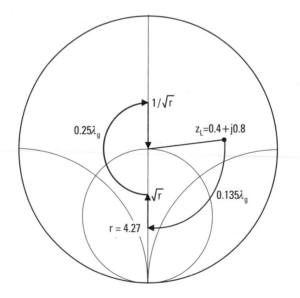

Figure 4.18 Matching of a load $Z_L = (20 + j40)\Omega$ to a 50-Ω line using a quarter-wave transformer, presented on the Smith chart.

and transmitted multiple times at the two boundaries, as shown in Figure 4.19. Let us first define the reflection and transmission coefficients as follows:

ρ = total reflection coefficient of the incident wave on the $\lambda/4$ transformer

ρ_1 = reflection coefficient of a wave incident on a load Z_t from a Z_0 line

ρ_2 = reflection coefficient of a wave incident on a load Z_0 from a Z_t line

ρ_3 = reflection coefficient of a wave incident on a load R_L from a Z_t line

τ_1 = transmission coefficient of a wave from a Z_0 line into a Z_t line

τ_2 = transmission coefficient of a wave from a Z_t line into a Z_0 line.

According to (4.5) and (4.6), these coefficients can be expressed as

$$\rho_1 = (Z_t - Z_0)/(Z_t + Z_0)$$
$$\rho_2 = (Z_0 - Z_t)/(Z_0 + Z_t) = -\rho_1$$
$$\rho_3 = (R_L - Z_t)/(R_L + Z_t)$$
$$\tau_1 = 2Z_t/(Z_t + Z_0)$$
$$\tau_2 = 2Z_0/(Z_t + Z_0)$$

The total reflection coefficient is obtained as an infinite series of individual reflections and, taking into account that there is a phase shift of $e^{-2j\theta}$ for each round-trip in the transformer, can be expressed as

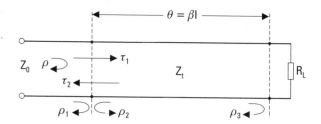

Figure 4.19 Multiple-reflection analysis of the $\lambda/4$ transformer.

$$\rho = \rho_1 + \tau_1 \tau_2 \rho_3 e^{-2j\theta} + \tau_1 \tau_2 \rho_2 \rho_3^2 e^{-4j\theta} + \tau_1 \tau_2 \rho_2^2 \rho_3^3 e^{-6j\theta} + \dots$$

$$= \rho_1 + \tau_1 \tau_2 \rho_3 e^{-2j\theta} \sum_{n=0}^{\infty} \left(\rho_2 \rho_3 e^{-2j\theta} \right)^n$$

$$= \rho_1 + \frac{\tau_1 \tau_2 \rho_3 e^{-2j\theta}}{1 - \rho_2 \rho_3 e^{-2j\theta}} \qquad (4.30)$$

The last result is obtained using the sum rule of an infinite geometric series, since $|\rho_2| < 1$ and $|\rho_3| < 1$. If we furthermore take into account that $\rho_2 = -\rho_1$, and $\tau_1 = 1 + \rho_1$ and $\tau_2 = 1 - \rho_1$, we get

$$\rho = \frac{\rho_1 + \rho_3 e^{-2j\theta}}{1 + \rho_1 \rho_3 e^{-2j\theta}} \qquad (4.31)$$

From this we see, because the transformer characteristic impedance is $Z_t = \sqrt{Z_0 R_L}$ and therefore $\rho_1 = \rho_3$, and at the center frequency $e^{-2j\theta} = -1$, that the total reflected wave fully disappears at the center frequency. If the discontinuities between the impedances Z_0 and Z_t as well as between Z_t and R_L are small, then $|\rho_1 \rho_3| \ll 1$, and we can approximate $\rho \approx \rho_1 + \rho_3 e^{-2j\theta}$.

The problem with the quarter-wave transformer is its narrow matching bandwidth. The transformer offers a match only at the frequency where the transformer length is exactly $\lambda_g/4$ (or $\lambda_g/4 + n\lambda_g/2$). The bandwidth, over which the reflection coefficient is small, is narrow. Sometimes this is sufficient, but in many applications we need a wider bandwidth.

A wider bandwidth can be obtained by using several consecutive transformer sections, the characteristic impedances of which change with small steps between R_L and Z_0. Depending on how the impedance steps are chosen, different frequency responses of the reflection coefficient are obtained. A binomial transformer provides a maximally flat response. A Chebyshev transformer provides a frequency response where the reflection coefficient fluctuates between certain limits over the matching bandwidth. Figure 4.20 shows the frequency response of a single $\lambda/4$ transformer, a two-section binomial transformer, and a three-section Chebyshev transformer. The design procedures of the binomial and Chebyshev transformers can be found in many books [3, 4].

Often a $\lambda/4$ transformer is used to match two lines with different characteristic impedances. Figure 4.21(a) shows how a low- and high-imped-

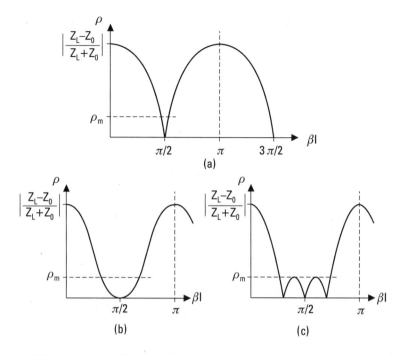

Figure 4.20 Reflection coefficient of matching transformers as a function of the transformer section electrical length $\beta l = 2\pi l / \lambda_g$: (a) a single $\lambda/4$ transformer; (b) a two-section binomial transformer; and (c) a three-section Chebyshev transformer.

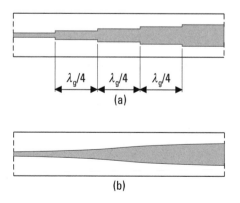

Figure 4.21 Matching of a low- and high-impedance coaxial line using (a) a multisection $\lambda/4$ transformer and (b) a tapered section.

ance coaxial line are matched to each other using a three-section $\lambda/4$ transformer. Different impedances are realized by changing the inner conductor diameter. Abrupt changes in line dimensions cause not only reflections but also reactive fields and reactive energy storages. In an equivalent circuit these can be modeled using shunt susceptances. In an accurate analysis and design these reactive components must be taken into account.

Instead of using a multisection transformer, we can use a tapered section at least $\lambda_g/2$ long, as shown in Figure 4.21(b). The tapering may be linear or follow other mathematical functions leading to different frequency responses.

4.3.4 Resistive Matching

Matching of a load can be improved simply by introducing an attenuator in front of the load, as shown in Figure 4.22. This may be a useful solution, for example, in a measurement application when a wide measurement bandwidth is required but the power loss is not a problem.

Let us assume that the load reflection coefficient is ρ_L and the insertion loss of an attenuator matched to the line is L [see (5.32)]. If the incident power to the attenuator is P, power after the attenuator is P/L. From this power, a part $\left(1 - |\rho_L|^2\right) \times P/L$ is absorbed to the load and a part $|\rho_L|^2 \times P/L$ is reflected. The reflected power is further attenuated in the attenuator to a value of $|\rho_L|^2 \times P/L^2$. When compared to a situation without an attenuator, the power reflection coefficient decreases from a value of $|\rho_L|^2$ to a value of $|\rho_L|^2/L^2$. The drawback of this method is that the power absorbed to the load is at maximum P/L. The attenuator is realized in integrated circuits using resistors shown in Figure 4.23. Two applications of resistive matching are illustrated in Figure 4.24.

A better solution than the attenuator is an isolator (see Section 6.2.3) placed in front of the load. An ideal isolator is lossless in the forward direction but absorbs the backward reflected wave fully. The reflected power is also lost in this case but more power is available to the load, although in practice

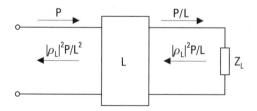

Figure 4.22 Resistive matching with an attenuator.

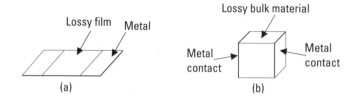

Figure 4.23 Resistive lumped elements for integrated circuits: (a) planar resistor; and (b) chip resistor.

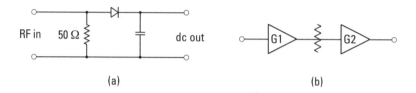

Figure 4.24 Applications of resistive matching: (a) a diode detector; and (b) an amplifier chain.

an isolator also has some attenuation in the forward direction. Furthermore, it does not fully block the backward reflected wave and its ports are not fully matched to the line.

References

[1] Bryant, G. H., *Principles of Microwave Measurements,* London, England: Peter Peregrinus, 1988.

[2] Smith, P. H., "Transmission Line Calculator," *Electronics,* Vol. 12, No. 1, 1939, pp. 29–31.

[3] Collin, R. E., *Foundations for Microwave Engineering,* 2nd ed., New York: IEEE Press, 2001.

[4] Matthaei, G. L., L. Young, and E. M. T. Jones, *Microwave Filters, Impedance-Matching Networks, and Coupling Structures,* Dedham, MA: Artech House, 1980.

5

Microwave Circuit Theory

Microwave circuits are composed of many parts and blocks, such as transmission lines, filters, and amplifiers. It was shown in Chapter 3 how the field distributions within the waveguides could be solved using Maxwell's equations and boundary conditions. In principle, whole circuits could be analyzed this way. However, this is very cumbersome, and often the knowledge of the field distributions is of no use.

Usually one wants to know how the wave is transmitted through the circuit or reflected from it. Therefore, the circuit can be considered to be a "black box" that has one or more ports. It is sufficient to know the transfer functions between the ports; it is not necessary to know what happens inside the circuit. Thus, the operation of the circuit can be described with only a few parameters. The transfer function of a system comprising of cascaded circuits can be obtained using these parameters. In the circuit theory, Z- and Y-parameters are commonly used. However, the scattering or S-parameters are best suited for describing the operation of a microwave circuit.

5.1 Impedance and Admittance Matrices

The voltages and currents of a low-frequency circuit can be defined uniquely. In case of a high-frequency circuit this is not necessarily true. Voltages and currents can be defined uniquely only for a transmission line that carries a pure TEM mode. For example, the voltage and current of a rectangular waveguide can be defined in several ways. In such a line, the electric and magnetic fields and the power propagating in the waveguide are more fundamental quantities than the voltage and current. However, it would be useful if the operation of a high-frequency circuit could be described in terms of voltages, currents, and impedances because then the methods of the circuit theory could be used.

Figure 5.1 shows a circuit having n ports. There is a short homogeneous transmission line at each port. The reference plane (within this line) of each port has to be defined clearly because the parameters of the circuit depend on the positions of the reference planes. Let us assume that only the fundamental TEM mode is propagating into and out of the ports. The discontinuities of the circuit generate higher-order TE and TM modes, which usually are not able to propagate. The reference planes have to be far enough from these discontinuities so that the fields of the nonpropagating modes are well attenuated. For each port i, an entering voltage wave V_i^+ and current wave I_i^+ as well as a leaving voltage wave V_i^- and current wave I_i^- can be defined.

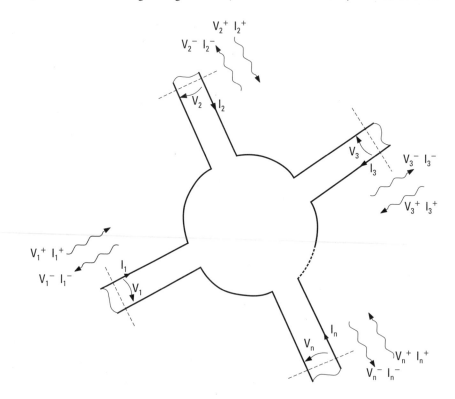

Figure 5.1 Circuit having n ports.

V_i^+, I_i^+, V_i^-, and I_i^- are the complex amplitudes of these sinusoidal waves. These equivalent voltage and current waves are defined so that (1) the voltage and current are proportional to the transverse electric and magnetic fields of the wave, respectively, (2) the product of the voltage and current gives the power of the entering or leaving wave, and (3) the ratio of the voltage and current is the characteristic impedance of the port.

The total voltage and the total current at port i are:

$$V_i = V_i^+ + V_i^- \tag{5.1}$$

$$I_i = I_i^+ - I_i^- \tag{5.2}$$

For a linear circuit, the voltage at port i is a linear function of the currents at all ports:

$$V_i = Z_{i1} I_1 + Z_{i2} I_2 + \ldots + Z_{in} I_n \tag{5.3}$$

The whole circuit can be described with the impedance matrix $[Z]$ as

$$\begin{bmatrix} V_1 \\ V_2 \\ \vdots \\ V_n \end{bmatrix} = \begin{bmatrix} Z_{11} & Z_{12} & \cdots & Z_{1n} \\ Z_{21} & Z_{22} & \cdots & Z_{2n} \\ \vdots & \vdots & \vdots & \vdots \\ Z_{n1} & Z_{n2} & \cdots & Z_{nn} \end{bmatrix} \begin{bmatrix} I_1 \\ I_2 \\ \vdots \\ I_n \end{bmatrix} \tag{5.4}$$

Correspondingly, currents are obtained from voltages using the admittance matrix $[Y]$:

$$\begin{bmatrix} I_1 \\ I_2 \\ \vdots \\ I_n \end{bmatrix} = \begin{bmatrix} Y_{11} & Y_{12} & \cdots & Y_{1n} \\ Y_{21} & Y_{22} & \cdots & Y_{2n} \\ \vdots & \vdots & \vdots & \vdots \\ Y_{n1} & Y_{n2} & \cdots & Y_{nn} \end{bmatrix} \begin{bmatrix} V_1 \\ V_2 \\ \vdots \\ V_n \end{bmatrix} \tag{5.5}$$

The impedance matrix [1] is an inverse matrix [2] of the admittance matrix, $[Z] = [Y]^{-1}$. The elements of the matrices, Z_{ij} and Y_{ij}, are called Z- and Y-parameters. For a reciprocal circuit, the matrices are symmetric: $Z_{ij} = Z_{ji}$ and $Y_{ij} = Y_{ji}$.

A two-port is the most common of the n-port circuits. Many different equivalent circuits can be used to realize the equations of a two-port [3, 4].

Figure 5.2 shows an equivalent circuit for a reciprocal two-port. The three Z-parameters for this T-circuit, Z_{11}, Z_{22}, and Z_{12}, are calculated or measured. If the load impedance $Z_L = -V_2/I_2$ is connected at port 2, the input impedance measured at port 1 is

$$Z_{1in} = Z_{11} - \frac{Z_{12}^2}{Z_{22} + Z_L} \tag{5.6}$$

By measuring the input impedances corresponding to three different load impedances, a set of three equations is obtained. The Z-parameters may then be solved from these equations.

The properties of a circuit composed of two-ports connected in series can be calculated from the transmission matrices $[T]$ of the two-ports. A transmission matrix is called also a chain or $ABCD$ matrix. A transmission matrix ties the input and output quantities as

$$\begin{bmatrix} V_1 \\ I_1 \end{bmatrix} = \begin{bmatrix} A & B \\ C & D \end{bmatrix} \begin{bmatrix} V_2 \\ I_2 \end{bmatrix} = [T] \begin{bmatrix} V_2 \\ I_2 \end{bmatrix} \tag{5.7}$$

The transmission matrix of a two-port can be calculated from its Z-parameters:

$$[T] = \begin{bmatrix} Z_{11}/Z_{21} & Z_{11}Z_{22}/Z_{21} - Z_{12} \\ 1/Z_{21} & Z_{22}/Z_{21} \end{bmatrix} \tag{5.8}$$

It should be noted that the positive output current I_2 is now defined to flow out of the two-port so that I_2 will be the input current to the following two-port. The transmission matrix of a circuit consisting of several two-ports in a series is obtained by multiplying the transmission matrices of the two-ports in the same order.

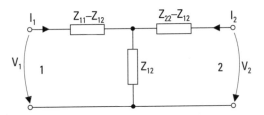

Figure 5.2 Equivalent T-circuit for a two-port.

Generally, the measurement of Z- and Y-parameters is difficult at microwave frequencies because the measurement of the total voltages and currents at the ports is difficult, and in the case of waveguides carrying TE or TM modes it is impossible. Furthermore, in the case of some active circuits, the load impedances needed in the measurement may cause instability in the circuit.

5.2 Scattering Matrices

The scattering or S-parameters [1, 5, 6] are defined using the voltage waves entering the ports, V_i^+, and leaving the ports, V_i^-. If the circuit in Figure 5.1 is linear and all its ports have the same characteristic impedance of Z_0, the voltage wave leaving port i may be written as

$$V_i^- = S_{i1} V_1^+ + S_{i2} V_2^+ + \ldots + S_{in} V_n^+ \qquad (5.9)$$

The whole circuit is described by the scattering matrix $[S]$ as

$$\begin{bmatrix} V_1^- \\ V_2^- \\ \vdots \\ V_n^- \end{bmatrix} = \begin{bmatrix} S_{11} & S_{12} & \cdots & S_{1n} \\ S_{21} & S_{22} & \cdots & S_{2n} \\ \vdots & \vdots & \vdots & \vdots \\ S_{n1} & S_{n2} & \cdots & S_{nn} \end{bmatrix} \begin{bmatrix} V_1^+ \\ V_2^+ \\ \vdots \\ V_n^+ \end{bmatrix} \qquad (5.10)$$

or $[V^-] = [S][V^+]$. The power flowing into port i is $|V_i^+|^2/(2Z_0)$, and the power flowing out of port i is $|V_i^-|^2/(2Z_0)$.

Usually, all the ports of a microwave circuit have similar connectors, such as 50-Ω coaxial connectors or waveguide flanges, and the characteristic impedances of the ports have the same value. However, in a general case, the characteristic impedances Z_{0i} may have different values. For example, the ports of a coaxial-to-waveguide adapter have different characteristic impedances. Then, the voltage waves should be normalized as

$$a_i = \frac{V_i^+}{\sqrt{Z_{0i}}} \qquad (5.11)$$

$$b_i = \frac{V_i^-}{\sqrt{Z_{0i}}} \qquad (5.12)$$

The total voltage and current are expressed using the normalized voltage waves as

$$V_i = V_i^+ + V_i^- = \sqrt{Z_{0i}}(a_i + b_i) \tag{5.13}$$

$$I_i = \frac{1}{Z_{0i}}(V_i^+ - V_i^-) = \frac{1}{\sqrt{Z_{0i}}}(a_i - b_i) \tag{5.14}$$

The power flowing into port i is $|a_i|^2/2$, and the power flowing out of port i is $|b_i|^2/2$. The scattering matrix presentation using normalized waves is now

$$\begin{bmatrix} b_1 \\ b_2 \\ \vdots \\ b_n \end{bmatrix} = \begin{bmatrix} S_{11} & S_{12} & \cdots & S_{1n} \\ S_{21} & S_{22} & \cdots & S_{2n} \\ \vdots & \vdots & \vdots & \vdots \\ S_{n1} & S_{n2} & \cdots & S_{nn} \end{bmatrix} \begin{bmatrix} a_1 \\ a_2 \\ \vdots \\ a_n \end{bmatrix} \tag{5.15}$$

or $[b] = [S][a]$.

If all the ports are terminated with matched loads, the reflection coefficient for port i is $\rho_i = S_{ii} = b_i/a_i$, and the transducer power gain from port j to port i is $G_{ij} = |S_{ij}|^2 = |b_i/a_j|^2$.

The scattering matrix of a reciprocal circuit is symmetrical: $S_{ij} = S_{ji}$. In other words, the transposed matrix is the same as the matrix itself: $[S]^T = [S]$. A reciprocal circuit operates the same way, regardless of the direction of the power flow. Most passive circuits are reciprocal; circuits that include ferrite components are the exceptions.

If the circuit has no loss, the sum of the powers flowing into the ports equals the sum of the powers flowing out of the ports:

$$\sum_{i=1}^{n} |a_i|^2 = \sum_{i=1}^{n} |b_i|^2 = \sum_{i=1}^{n} \left| \sum_{j=1}^{n} S_{ij} a_j \right|^2 \tag{5.16}$$

If all the voltage waves a_i are chosen to be zero, except a_k, then

$$\sum_{i=1}^{n} |S_{ik}|^2 = \sum_{i=1}^{n} S_{ik} S_{ik}^* = 1 \tag{5.17}$$

Thus, for any column of the scattering matrix of a lossless circuit, the sum of the squares of the scattering parameters is 1. The same applies for all rows. If the voltage waves a_k and a_l are chosen to be nonzero and other waves entering the circuit are zero, it can be proven that

$$\sum_{i=1}^{n} S_{ik} S_{il}^* = 0 \qquad (5.18)$$

For any two columns, the scattering parameters of a lossless circuit fulfill this equation. A similar equation applies for any two rows. The scattering matrix of a lossless circuit is unitary; that is, the transposed scattering matrix is equal to the inverse of the complex conjugate of the scattering matrix.

Scattering matrices of some simple circuits:

- *A lossless transmission line having a length of l and a characteristic impedance of Z_0, as shown in Figure 5.3.* Z_0 is also the characteristic impedance of both ports. When one of the ports is terminated with a matched load, the reflection coefficient of the other port is zero. Thus, $S_{11} = S_{22} = 0$. If the voltage wave entering port 1 is $a_1 = 1$, the voltage wave leaving port 2 is $b_2 = e^{-j\beta l}$, and $S_{21} = b_2/a_1 = e^{-j\beta l}$. Due to the symmetry, $S_{12} = S_{21}$.

- *A joint of two transmission lines, as shown in Figure 5.4.* The characteristic impedances of the transmission lines and ports are Z_{01} and Z_{02}. The reference planes of the ports are located at a distance of

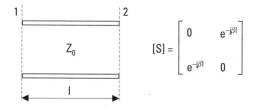

Figure 5.3 Section of a lossless transmission line and its scattering matrix.

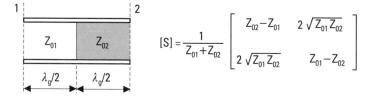

Figure 5.4 Joint of two transmission lines and its scattering matrix.

$n\lambda_g/2$ from the junction. If $a_1 = 1$ and $a_2 = 0$, then $b_1 = \rho = (Z_{02} - Z_{01})/(Z_{01} + Z_{02}) = S_{11}$. The voltage transmission coefficient is $\tau = 1 + \rho$. The normalized voltage wave b_2 is obtained from τ by using (5.11) and (5.12): $b_2 = (1 + \rho)\sqrt{Z_{01}/Z_{02}} = 2\sqrt{Z_{01}Z_{02}}/(Z_{01} + Z_{02}) = S_{21}$. Correspondingly, if $a_1 = 0$ and $a_2 = 1$, $S_{22} = \rho$ and $b_1 = (1 - \rho)\sqrt{Z_{02}/Z_{01}} = 2\sqrt{Z_{01}Z_{02}}/(Z_{01} + Z_{02}) = S_{12}$, which may also be recognized directly due to the reciprocity.

- *A load having an impedance of Z_L is a one-port circuit.* Its scattering matrix has only one scattering parameter: $S_{11} = \rho_L = (Z_L - Z_0)/(Z_L + Z_0)$, the voltage reflection coefficient of the load terminating a transmission line.

The measurement of scattering parameters is much easier than the measurement of the Z- or Y-parameters. For example, S_{11} is obtained by measuring the voltage reflection coefficient $\rho_1 = b_1/a_1$ at port 1, as all the other ports are terminated with their characteristic impedance Z_{0i} and therefore $a_2 \ldots a_n = 0$. It is also an advantage that changing the position of a reference plane only changes the phases of the scattering parameters. For example, if the reference plane of port 1 of a two-port is moved outward an electrical distance of $\beta l = \theta$, S_{11} changes to $e^{-2j\theta}S_{11}$, S_{12} to $e^{-j\theta}S_{12}$, and S_{21} to $e^{-j\theta}S_{21}$, while S_{22} remains unchanged.

The transmission matrix $[T]$ relates the input waves to output waves. Thus, in the case of a two-port we have

$$\begin{bmatrix} b_2 \\ a_2 \end{bmatrix} = \begin{bmatrix} T_{11} & T_{12} \\ T_{21} & T_{22} \end{bmatrix} \begin{bmatrix} a_1 \\ b_1 \end{bmatrix} \tag{5.19}$$

The transmission matrix is calculated from the scattering parameters as

$$[T] = \begin{bmatrix} S_{21} - S_{11}S_{22}/S_{12} & S_{22}/S_{12} \\ -S_{11}/S_{12} & 1/S_{12} \end{bmatrix} \tag{5.20}$$

The transmission matrix of a circuit consisting of blocks connected in series is obtained by multiplying the transmission matrices of the blocks.

5.3 Signal Flow Graph, Transfer Function, and Gain

A signal flow graph [7–9] is a graphical representation of the scattering matrix. It illustrates the equations governing the operation of a circuit. The equations for such transfer functions as gain and reflection coefficient can be derived with the aid of signal flow graphs. Even the analysis of a circuit, which has more than one internal reflection leading to an infinite number of reflected waves, may be kept clear using a signal flow graph.

In a flow graph, there are two nodal points for each port. The values of the voltage waves, a_i and b_i, are assigned to these nodes. The nodes are connected with branches whose gains correspond to the scattering parameters. Signal may flow between two nodes along a branch only to that direction given by the arrow, that is, from node a to node b. Figure 5.5 shows the signal flow graphs for a two-port and three-port.

A given transfer function can be solved from a signal flow graph by using the simplification rules explained here and shown in Figure 5.6 [7]:

- Two branches in a series, Figure 5.6(a), with no other branches connected to the common node, can be replaced with one branch whose gain is the product of the gains of the two branches:

$$V_3 = S_{32} V_2 = S_{32} S_{21} V_1 \qquad (5.21)$$

The normalized voltage waves a_i and b_i are denoted here with V_i.

- Two branches in parallel, Figure 5.6(b), can be replaced with a single branch whose gain is the sum of the gains of the two branches:

$$V_2 = S_a V_1 + S_b V_1 = (S_a + S_b) V_1 \qquad (5.22)$$

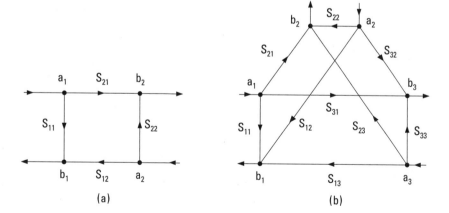

Figure 5.5 Signal flow graph for (a) a two-port and (b) a three-port.

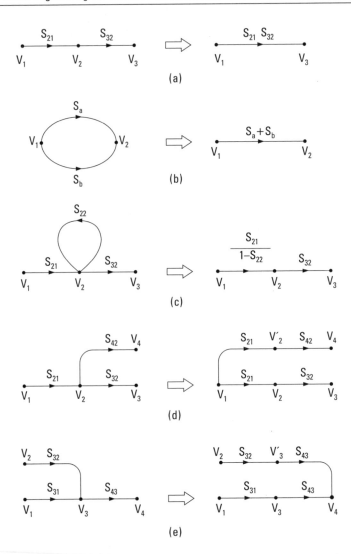

Figure 5.6 Simplification of flow graphs: (a) branches in series; (b) branches in parallel; (c) self-loop; (d) duplication of node with duplication of feeding branch; and (e) duplication of node with duplication of leaving branch.

- A self-loop connected to a node can be eliminated, if the gain of the branch(es) feeding the node is divided by 1 minus the gain of the loop, because from $V_2 = S_{21} V_1 + S_{22} V_2$ it follows

$$V_2 = \frac{S_{21}}{1 - S_{22}} V_1 \qquad (5.23)$$

- A node can be duplicated by duplicating the branch(es) feeding the node, Figure 5.6(d), or by duplicating the branch leaving the node, Figure 5.6(e).

The following examples illustrate how flow graphs can be simplified and transfer functions solved.

Example 5.1

Derive the input reflection coefficient ρ_{in} for a two-port when the output port (port 2) is terminated with a load impedance Z_L. The characteristic impedance of both ports is Z_0.

Solution

The voltage reflection coefficient for the load is $\rho_L = (Z_L - Z_0)/(Z_L + Z_0)$. This is also the gain of the branch connected to the output port in the flow graph of Figure 5.7(a). The node a_2 is then duplicated by duplicating the branch ρ_L [Figure 5.7(b)]. The gain of the self-loop is $S_{22}\rho_L$ according to the rule of branches in series. Then the self-loop is eliminated [Figure 5.7(c)].

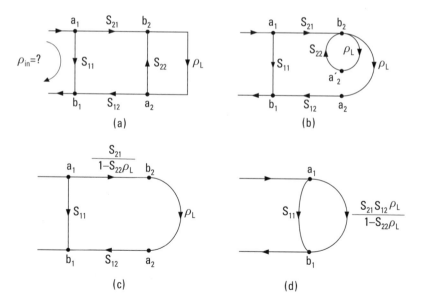

Figure 5.7 Solving the input reflection coefficient for a two-port using a flow graph and its simplification rules: (a) a flow-graph presentation of a terminated two-port; (b) duplication of a node; (c) elimination of a self-loop; and (d) combination of branches in a series.

The rule of branches in series is used again [Figure 5.7(d)]. The input reflection coefficient is obtained by applying the rule of branches in parallel:

$$\rho_{in} = S_{11} + \frac{S_{21} S_{12} \rho_L}{1 - S_{22} \rho_L} \qquad (5.24)$$

Example 5.2

A lossless transmission line is connected between a generator and load. The length of the line is $l = n\lambda_g$ (n is integer) and its characteristic impedance is Z_0, Figure 5.8(a). The load impedance is Z_L. The output impedance of the generator is Z_S. What is the load voltage V_L, if the generator voltage is V_S?

Solution

It is not necessary to normalize the voltages because both ports of the line (two-port) have the same characteristic impedance. The branches representing S_{11} and S_{22} are not drawn in Figure 5.8(b) because their gain is zero. Now $S_{21} = S_{12} = e^{-j\beta l} = 1$. The node having a voltage of $V_S/2$ represents the generator because this voltage corresponds to available power of $V_S^2/(8Z_S)$ of the generator. The voltage transmission coefficient from the generator to the line is $1 - \rho_S$. A branch having a gain of $1 + \rho_L$ is added for the calculation of the load voltage V_L. By duplicating the node V_2^-, using the rule of branches in series, and eliminating the self-loop, the flow graph of Figure 5.8(c) is obtained. From this we get

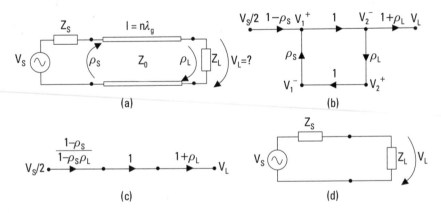

(a)   (b)   (c)   (d)

Figure 5.8 Solving the load voltage using flow graphs: (a) a terminated $n\lambda_g$ transmission line fed from a generator; (b) its flow-graph presentation; (c) elimination of a self-loop; and (d) an equivalent circuit of the flow graph presented in (c), equivalent to the circuit in (a).

$$V_L = \frac{(1 - \rho_S)(1 + \rho_L)}{1 - \rho_S \rho_L} \times \frac{V_S}{2}$$

Because the reflection coefficients are $\rho_S = (Z_S - Z_0)/(Z_S + Z_0)$ and $\rho_L = (Z_L - Z_0)/(Z_L + Z_0)$, the load voltage is $V_L = Z_L V_S/(Z_S + Z_L)$, which may be seen also from Figure 5.8(d) by using voltage division.

5.3.1 Mason's Rule

Instead of the flow graph simplification, transfer functions can also be found by using Mason's rule [10]. According to Mason's rule, the ratio of a dependent variable (voltage of a node) to an independent variable produced by a source (voltage of the feed node) is

$$T = \frac{P_1\left[1 - \sum L(1)^1 + \sum L(2)^1 - \ldots\right] + P_2\left[1 - \sum L(1)^2 + \sum L(2)^2 - \ldots\right] + P_3[1 - \ldots]}{1 - \sum L(1) + \sum L(2) - \sum L(3) + \ldots}$$

(5.25)

where

$P_1, P_2, \ldots$ are the gains of the forward paths between the input and output nodes;

$\sum L(1), \sum L(2), \ldots$ are the sums of the loop gains of the first order, second order, and so on;

$\sum L(1)^1, \sum L(2)^1, \ldots$ are the sums of the loop gains of the first order, second order, and so on, for such loops, which do not touch path 1;

$\sum L(1)^2, \sum L(2)^2, \ldots$ are the sums of the loop gains of the first order, second order, and so on, for such loops, which do not touch path 2.

A path is a continuous succession of branches having arrows pointing to the same direction. It is either a forward path connecting the input node to the output node, or a loop, which originates and terminates on the same node. A path passes each node in the loop only once. The path gain is the product of all the gains in the path. The loop gain is the product of the gains in the loop. The loop gain of the first order means the gain of an individual loop; the loop gain of the second order means the product of the gains of two nontouching loops, and so on. Nontouching loops are separate loops that do not touch each other at any node.

Example 5.3

A generator and a load are connected to a two-port, as in Figure 5.9. Find the transducer power gain, that is, the ratio of the power coupled to the load, P_L, to the available power of the generator, $P_{S,a}$. The characteristic impedance is Z_0.

Solution

In the flow graph, a_S and a_L are normalized voltages corresponding to the available power of the generator and the power coupled to the load, respectively. There is only one path from the input node a_S to the output node a_L. Its gain is

$$P_1 = (1 - \rho_S)\sqrt{Z_S/Z_0}\,S_{21}(1 + \rho_L)\sqrt{Z_0/Z_L}$$

There are three loops, and the sum of their gains is

$$\sum L(1) = S_{11}\rho_S + S_{22}\rho_L + S_{21}\rho_L S_{12}\rho_S$$

The loops $S_{11}\rho_S$ and $S_{22}\rho_L$ are nontouching; thus,

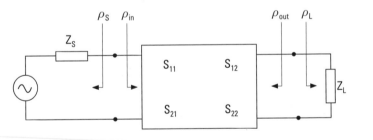

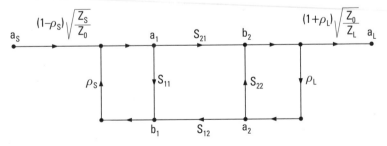

Figure 5.9 Two-port connected between a generator and a load.

$$\sum L(2) = S_{11}\rho_S S_{22}\rho_L$$

All loops touch path P_1 and therefore

$$\sum L(1)^1 = \sum L(2)^1 = \ldots = 0$$

Using (5.25), the voltage of the output node is

$$a_L = \frac{(1-\rho_S)S_{21}(1+\rho_L)\sqrt{Z_S/Z_L}}{1-S_{11}\rho_S - S_{22}\rho_L - S_{21}\rho_L S_{12}\rho_S + S_{11}\rho_S S_{22}\rho_L} \times a_S$$

5.3.2 Gain of a Two-Port

The final expression of the above solution gives us a good basis to present different definitions of the gain of a two-port. The *transducer power gain* (G_t) can be presented in several ways:

$$
\begin{aligned}
G_t &= \frac{P_L}{P_{S,a}} = \frac{|a_L|^2}{|a_S|^2} = \frac{|S_{21}|^2(1-|\rho_S|^2)(1-|\rho_L|^2)}{|(1-S_{11}\rho_S)(1-S_{22}\rho_L)-S_{12}S_{21}\rho_S\rho_L|^2} \\
&= \frac{|S_{21}|^2(1-|\rho_S|^2)(1-|\rho_L|^2)}{|1-\rho_S\rho_{in}|^2|1-S_{22}\rho_L|^2} \\
&= \frac{|S_{21}|^2(1-|\rho_S|^2)(1-|\rho_L|^2)}{|1-S_{11}\rho_S|^2|1-\rho_{out}\rho_L|^2}
\end{aligned}
\tag{5.26}
$$

where ρ_{out} is the reflection coefficient of the output port 2.

The *power gain* (G_p) of a two-port is defined as the ratio of the power coupled to the load, P_L, to the power coupled to the two-port, P_{in}. Using the flow graph we obtain

$$G_p = \frac{P_L}{P_{in}} = \frac{|a_L|^2}{|a_1|^2(1-|\rho_{in}|^2)} = \frac{|S_{21}|^2(1-|\rho_L|^2)}{|1-S_{22}\rho_L|^2(1-|\rho_{in}|^2)}$$

$$\tag{5.27}$$

The *available power gain* (G_a) is defined as the ratio of the available output power of the two-port, $P_{out,a}$, to the available power of the generator, $P_{S,a}$:

$$G_a = \frac{P_{out,a}}{P_{S,a}} = \frac{P_L(\rho_L = \rho_{out}^*)}{P_{S,a}} = \frac{|S_{21}|^2(1 - |\rho_S|^2)}{|1 - S_{11}\rho_S|^2(1 - |\rho_{out}|^2)}$$

(5.28)

The *maximum available power gain* $(G_{a,max})$ is the available power gain in that case when the input port is conjugate-matched to the generator:

$$G_{a,max} = \frac{P_L(\rho_L = \rho_{out}^*)}{P_{in}(\rho_S = \rho_{in}^*)}$$

(5.29)

How $G_{a,max}$ can be expressed using the scattering parameters of a two-port is presented in Chapter 8, (8.28). In a unilateral case $(S_{12} = 0)$, the maximum available power gain is

$$G_{a,max} = \frac{|S_{21}|^2}{(1 - |S_{11}|^2)(1 - |S_{22}|^2)}$$

(5.30)

The *insertion gain* (G_i) is the ratio of the power coupled to the load from the two-port, P_L, to the power coupled to the load directly from the generator, P_d (no two-port between):

$$G_i = \frac{P_L}{P_d} = \frac{|S_{21}|^2|1 - \rho_S\rho_L|^2}{|1 - \rho_S\rho_{in}|^2|1 - S_{22}\rho_L|^2}$$

(5.31)

If both the generator and load are matched to the characteristic impedance Z_0, $\rho_S = \rho_L = 0$ and $G_i = |S_{12}|^2$. The inverse of G_i is called the insertion loss:

$$L_i = \frac{1}{G_i} = \frac{P_d}{P_L}$$

(5.32)

The insertion gain and insertion loss are parameters, which can be measured directly. Other gains of a two-port may be calculated from measured scattering parameters and impedances Z_S and Z_L.

References

[1] Kuh, E. S., and R. A. Rohrer, *Theory of Linear Active Networks,* San Francisco, CA: Holden-Day, 1967.

[2] Lay, D. C., *Linear Algebra and Its Applications,* 3rd ed., Reading, MA: Addison Wesley, 2002.

[3] Collin, R. E., *Foundations for Microwave Engineering,* 2nd ed., New York: IEEE Press, 2001.

[4] Ramo, S., J. Whinnery, and T. van Duzer, *Fields and Waves in Communication Electronics,* New York: John Wiley & Sons, 1965.

[5] Belevitch, V., "Transmission Losses in 2n-Terminal Networks," *Journal of Applied Physics,* Vol. 19, No. 7, 1948, pp. 636–638.

[6] Montgomery, C. G., R. H. Dicke, and E. M. Purcell, *Principles of Microwave Circuits,* Radiation Laboratory Series, New York: McGraw-Hill, 1948.

[7] Kuhn, N., "Simplified Signal Flow Graph Analysis," *Microwave Journal,* November 1963, pp. 59–66.

[8] Bryant, G. H., *Principles of Microwave Measurements,* London, England: Peter Peregrinus, 1988.

[9] Nyfors, E., and P. Vainikainen, *Industrial Microwave Sensors,* Norwood, MA: Artech House, 1989.

[10] Mason, S. J., "Feedback Theory: Further Properties of Signal Flow Graphs," *IRE Proc.,* Vol. 44, July 1956, pp. 920–926.

6

Passive Transmission Line and Waveguide Devices

Transmitters and receivers are composed of many kinds of passive and active devices. Some important passive devices based on sections of transmission lines or waveguides are covered in this chapter. Frequency-selective passive devices, resonators and filters, are the topic of Chapter 7. Standardized symbols for various passive devices are shown in Figure 6.1. Most passive devices are reciprocal; only isolators and circulators, which are based on ferrites, are nonreciprocal.

Components or devices used in radio equipment at various frequency ranges can be divided into three groups, according to their size in wavelengths:

1. Lumped components, such as capacitors and coils, are usable up to UHF and even higher frequencies. Their size is small compared to a wavelength. As the frequency increases, lumped elements become lossy and their parasitic reactances and radiation loss increase. For example, a capacitor may become a resonant circuit as a result of the parasitic inductances of the connecting wires.

2. Distributed components are made of sections of transmission lines or waveguides. Their size is comparable to a wavelength, and the phase differences between the parts of a component are significant. Distributed components are used at microwave and millimeter-wave ranges. However, waveguide components eventually become lossy and difficult to fabricate as the frequency increases.

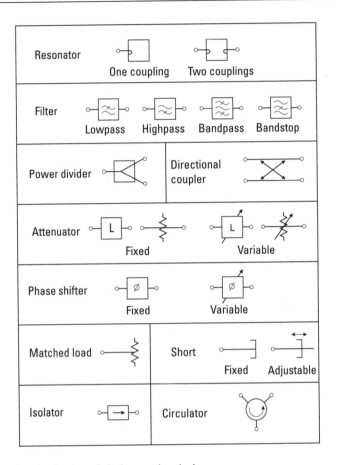

Figure 6.1 Standardized symbols for passive devices.

3. Quasioptical components handle waves propagating in a beam in free space. The dimensions of quasioptical components are larger than a wavelength. They are used in millimeter-wave and submillimeter-wave systems.

6.1 Power Dividers and Directional Couplers

Power dividers and directional couplers are components that split the input signal into two or more output ports. They may also be used as power combiners. Power dividers usually are three-port devices. Directional couplers have four ports and can separate waves propagating into opposite directions on the line. Directional couplers are used in impedance measurement and for taking a sample of a signal. Hybrids are 3-dB directional couplers with either a 90° or 180° phase difference between their output signals. Hybrids are needed in many mixers, modulators, and demodulators.

6.1.1 Power Dividers

The T-junctions shown in Figure 6.2 are simple power dividers. However, all the ports of a lossless three-port circuit cannot be matched. We can prove this by considering the properties of the scattering matrices. A passive, reciprocal, and matched three-port would have a scattering matrix, as

$$[S] = \begin{bmatrix} 0 & S_{12} & S_{13} \\ S_{12} & 0 & S_{23} \\ S_{13} & S_{23} & 0 \end{bmatrix} \tag{6.1}$$

As we stated in Chapter 5, the scattering matrix of a lossless circuit is unitary, from which it follows that

$$|S_{12}|^2 + |S_{13}|^2 = 1 \tag{6.2}$$

$$|S_{12}|^2 + |S_{23}|^2 = 1 \tag{6.3}$$

$$|S_{13}|^2 + |S_{23}|^2 = 1 \tag{6.4}$$

$$S_{13}^* S_{23} = 0 \tag{6.5}$$

$$S_{23}^* S_{12} = 0 \tag{6.6}$$

$$S_{12}^* S_{13} = 0 \tag{6.7}$$

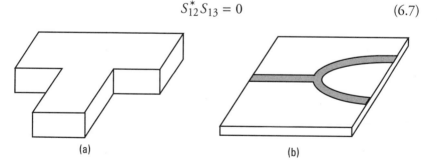

(a)   (b)

Figure 6.2 T-junctions: (a) a waveguide junction; (b) a microstrip line junction.

According to (6.5) through (6.7) at least two of the parameters S_{12}, S_{13}, and S_{23} are zero. However, this is in contradiction with at least one of (6.2) through (6.4). Thus, such a circuit cannot exist.

Let us consider the matching problem of a lossless T-junction with an equivalent circuit shown in Figure 6.3(a). The parallel susceptance B represents the reactive fields produced by the discontinuity of the junction. The characteristic impedances of the ports are Z_1, Z_2, and Z_3. Let us assume that $B = 0$. We then choose $Z_2 = Z_3 = 2Z_1$ and assume that the ports are terminated with load impedances equal to their characteristic impedances. Now port 1 is matched: The input impedance is Z_1 and the power fed to port 1 is split evenly to the loads of ports 2 and 3. However, ports 2 and 3 are not matched because their input impedance is $2Z_1/3$ (Z_1 and $2Z_1$ in parallel) instead of $2Z_1$.

All ports of a three-port divider can be matched by using resistive elements. Figure 6.3(b) shows a matched power divider containing lumped resistors. One half of the power coupled to the input port is absorbed in these resistors.

The isolation of the output ports of these power dividers is poor since a part of the power reflected from a mismatched output load is coupled to the other output port. The Wilkinson power divider shown in Figure 6.4 avoids this disadvantage. All the ports are matched to a characteristic impedance Z_0 if the quarter-wave-long sections have a characteristic impedance of $\sqrt{2}Z_0$, and the output ports 2 and 3 are connected with a lumped resistor having a resistance $2Z_0$. This circuit is also lossless if the ports are terminated with a matched load, that is, with an impedance of Z_0.

For all the power dividers discussed so far, the ratio of output powers equals 1. However, this ratio can be chosen freely by modifying the parameters of the circuits.

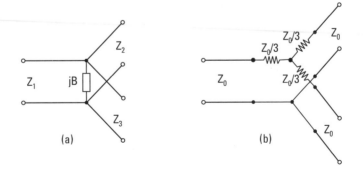

Figure 6.3 Equivalent circuits of power dividers: (a) lossless T-junction and (b) resistive power divider.

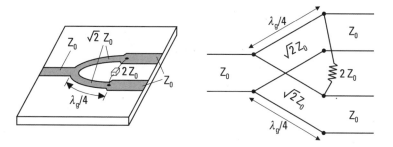

Figure 6.4 Wilkinson power divider.

6.1.2 Coupling and Directivity of a Directional Coupler

Let us consider the directional coupler shown in Figure 6.5 and assume that it is ideal. If a wave is fed from a signal source into port 1, it will couple to ports 2 and 4 but not at all to port 3. Similarly, if port 2 is the input port, ports 1 and 3 are output ports and port 4 is an isolated port. An ideal directional coupler is also lossless, and all of its ports can be matched. If all the ports are terminated with a matched load, the input reflection coefficients are zero. In practice, these properties can be achieved only approximately.

Let us assume that the power coupled into the input port 1 is P_1 and the powers coupled from ports 2, 3, and 4 to the matched terminations are P_2, P_3, and P_4, respectively. The coupling C and directivity D in decibels are defined as

$$C = 10 \, \log \frac{P_1}{P_4} \qquad (6.8)$$

$$D = 10 \, \log \frac{P_4}{P_3} \qquad (6.9)$$

Usually, most of the input power couples to the termination of the main line at port 2. The coupling describes the power coupled from the main line to the side line and is designed to a value that depends on the

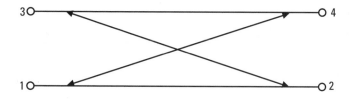

Figure 6.5 Directional coupler.

application, typically 3 dB to 30 dB. The directivity describes the leakage to the isolated port and should be as large as possible; a good directivity may be 30 dB to 40 dB. The isolation between the input port and the isolated port is $C + D$ in decibels.

A directional coupler with a good directivity can discriminate between the waves propagating in opposite directions on a line. However, mismatches of the output loads may worsen the effective directivity. Let us consider the situation illustrated in Figure 6.6. A signal source is connected at port 1, an unknown load with a reflection coefficient of ρ_L is connected at port 2, and matched power meters are connected to ports 3 and 4. In an ideal case the power meter readings are

$$P_3 = |\rho_L|^2 \left(1 - \frac{1}{10^{C/10}} \right) \frac{1}{10^{C/10}} P_1 \text{ and } P_4 = \frac{1}{10^{C/10}} P_1$$

from which the magnitude of the reflection coefficient can be solved. If the directional coupler has a finite directivity, and the signal source and power meters are mismatched, several waves will disturb the measurement and cause errors. An accurate analysis is complicated since there will be multiple reflections between the mismatches. The analysis may be carried out using a flow graph. Approximate error limits may be calculated by taking only the first reflections into account. When summing up the waves propagated to the power meters via different paths, both the amplitudes and phases of the waves must be taken into consideration. Summing up the powers of individual waves is not correct.

6.1.3 Scattering Matrix of a Directional Coupler

Let us next derive the scattering matrix of an ideal directional coupler. Because ports 1 and 3 as well ports 2 and 4 are isolated from each other,

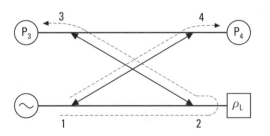

Figure 6.6 Measuring the magnitude of the reflection coefficient with a directional coupler.

$S_{13} = S_{24} = 0$. Let us assume that ports 1 and 2 are matched, or $S_{11} = S_{22} = 0$. Due to the reciprocity $S_{ij} = S_{ji}$. Thus, the scattering matrix is

$$[S] = \begin{bmatrix} 0 & S_{12} & 0 & S_{14} \\ S_{12} & 0 & S_{23} & 0 \\ 0 & S_{23} & S_{33} & S_{34} \\ S_{14} & 0 & S_{34} & S_{44} \end{bmatrix} \qquad (6.10)$$

The scattering matrix of a lossless circuit is unitary. From rows 1 and 4 we get $S_{14}S_{44}^* = 0$ and from rows 2 and 3 $S_{23}S_{33}^* = 0$. Because S_{14} and S_{23} are nonzero, parameters S_{33} and S_{44} must be zero, and ports 3 and 4 must be matched. From rows 1 and 3 and from rows 2 and 4 we get the following equations, respectively,

$$S_{12}S_{23}^* + S_{14}S_{34}^* = 0 \qquad (6.11)$$

$$S_{12}S_{14}^* + S_{23}S_{34}^* = 0 \qquad (6.12)$$

Because, for example $|S_{12}S_{23}^*| = |S_{12}||S_{23}|$, (6.11) and (6.12) can be written as

$$|S_{12}||S_{23}| = |S_{14}||S_{34}| \qquad (6.13)$$

$$|S_{12}||S_{14}| = |S_{23}||S_{34}| \qquad (6.14)$$

By dividing the left side and right side of (6.13) with the corresponding sides of (6.14), we get $|S_{23}|/|S_{14}| = |S_{14}|/|S_{23}|$, which means that $|S_{14}| = |S_{23}|$. Hence the coupling between ports 1 and 4 is equal to that between ports 2 and 3. Now, from (6.13) it follows that $|S_{12}| = |S_{34}|$.

The reference planes of ports 1 and 3 can be chosen so that S_{12} and S_{34} are real and positive numbers equal to α, and the reference plane of port 4 so that S_{14} is an imaginary number $j\beta$ (β is real and positive). From (6.11) it follows that also $S_{23} = j\beta$. Due to the conservation of energy $|S_{12}|^2 + |S_{14}|^2 = 1$ or $\alpha^2 + \beta^2 = 1$. Thus, the scattering matrix of an ideal directional coupler can be written as

$$[S] = \begin{bmatrix} 0 & \alpha & 0 & j\beta \\ \alpha & 0 & j\beta & 0 \\ 0 & j\beta & 0 & \alpha \\ j\beta & 0 & \alpha & 0 \end{bmatrix} \tag{6.15}$$

The coupling C (as a power ratio, not in decibels) is $1/|S_{14}|^2 = 1/\beta^2$, or $\beta = \sqrt{1/C}$, and from this it follows that $\alpha = \sqrt{1 - 1/C}$.

The special cases of a directional coupler having a 3-dB coupling are called hybrids. The hybrid couplers can be classified into two categories, depending on whether the phase difference of the output waves is 90° or 180°. The scattering matrix of a 90° hybrid is

$$[S] = \frac{1}{\sqrt{2}} \begin{bmatrix} 0 & 1 & 0 & j \\ 1 & 0 & j & 0 \\ 0 & j & 0 & 1 \\ j & 0 & 1 & 0 \end{bmatrix} \tag{6.16}$$

The scattering matrix of a 180° hybrid is

$$[S] = \frac{1}{\sqrt{2}} \begin{bmatrix} 0 & 1 & 0 & 1 \\ 1 & 0 & -1 & 0 \\ 0 & -1 & 0 & 1 \\ 1 & 0 & 1 & 0 \end{bmatrix} \tag{6.17}$$

Ports 1 and 4 of a 180° hybrid are called the Σ ports, whereas ports 2 and 3 are called the Δ ports. When a wave enters a Σ port, the output waves have equal powers and are in the same phase. If a Δ port is the input port, the output waves are in an opposite phase.

6.1.4 Waveguide Directional Couplers

We may make a directional coupler by placing side by side two rectangular metal waveguides having coupling holes in the common wall [1]. Figure 6.7 shows a simple directional coupler having two holes $d = \lambda_g/4$ apart in the broad wall of the waveguides. Let us assume that the coupling factor of a single hole is B_f in the forward direction and B_b in the backward direction.

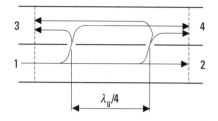

Figure 6.7 Two-hole waveguide directional coupler.

For example, if a wave is applied to port 1 and its field is equal to 1 in the lower waveguide at a hole, in the upper waveguide the fields of the waves propagating toward ports 3 and 4 are B_b and B_f, respectively. If the coupling factors are small, the fields in the lower waveguide at both holes have nearly equal amplitudes. The two paths from port 1 to port 4 have equal lengths, and the fields strengthen each other at port 4. If the coupling holes are identical, the coupling is in decibels

$$C = -20 \log\left(2|B_f|\right) \tag{6.18}$$

On the other hand, the paths from port 1 to port 3 have a difference of $\lambda_g/2$ in their lengths. The waves coupled through the holes to port 3 have opposite phases and cancel each other. Hence the directivity D is infinite.

The separation of the holes in the directional coupler of Figure 6.7 is $\lambda_g/4$ only at a single frequency. As the frequency deviates from this frequency, the directivity decreases. The frequency response of the directivity is

$$D = 20 \log \frac{2|B_f|}{|B_b||1 + e^{-j2\beta d}|} = 20 \log \frac{|B_f|}{|B_b|} + 20 \log \frac{1}{|\cos \beta d|} \tag{6.19}$$

The directivity can be interpreted as the sum of the directivity of a single hole and the directivity of the array of holes. A good directivity over a broad band can be achieved by using several coupling holes separated by $\lambda_g/4$ at the center frequency. As before, the coupling and directivity of a multihole coupler can be calculated by summing the fields at ports 3 and 4. By choosing the sizes of the holes properly, different frequency responses, such as the Butterworth or Chebyshev response, can be realized for the directivity [2].

The waveguide junction shown in Figure 6.8 is called the magic T-junction. It operates as a 180° hybrid. A wave applied to port 1 (Σ) is

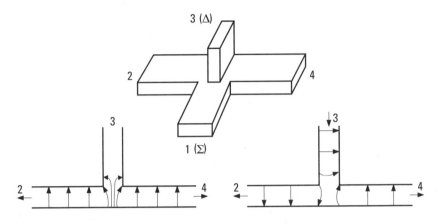

Figure 6.8 Magic T-junction and its field patterns.

divided into ports 2 and 4 equally and in the same phase, due to symmetry. The electric field distribution has an even symmetry with respect to the middle line of port 3, whereas the field of the TE_{10} mode has an odd symmetry. Therefore, a wave cannot couple from port 1 to port 3. Also, a wave applied to port 3 (Δ) is divided into ports 2 and 4 with equal amplitude, but now the output waves have an opposite phase.

6.1.5   Microstrip Directional Couplers

Let us consider two parallel microstrip lines that are placed so close to each other that the fields of the lines couple to each other. Then a wave propagating in one line can excite a wave in the other line. The fields of a coupled line can be presented as a superposition of an even mode and an odd mode, shown in Figure 6.9. In case of the even mode the currents of the lines are equal and in the same direction; in case of the odd mode they are equal but in the opposite directions. A coupled line may be represented with an even-mode characteristic impedance Z_{0e} and an odd-mode characteristic impedance Z_{0o}, which are characteristic impedances of one of the strip

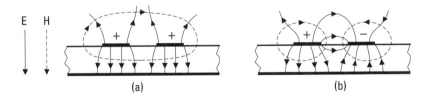

Figure 6.9 Fields of (a) the even mode and (b) the odd mode in a coupled microstrip line.

conductors relative to the ground when the coupled line is operated in the even mode or odd mode, respectively. The graph in Figure 6.10 gives these impedances when the relative permittivity of the substrate is 10.

The microstrip lines shown in Figure 6.11(a) are coupled to each other over a length of l. Let us assume that a signal source is at port 1 and other ports are terminated with loads having an impedance of Z_0. It can be proven that all the ports are matched if

$$Z_0 = \sqrt{Z_{0e} Z_{0o}} \tag{6.20}$$

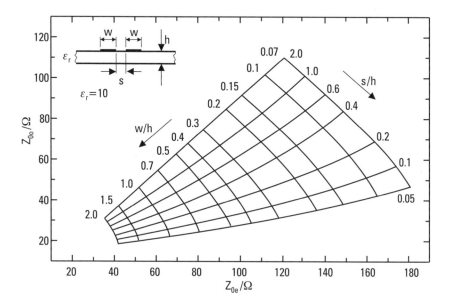

Figure 6.10 Even-mode and odd-mode characteristic impedances of coupled microstrip lines; $\epsilon_r = 10$.

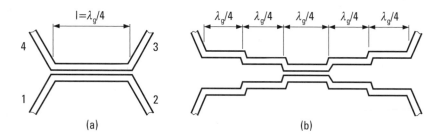

Figure 6.11 Directional couplers based on coupled microstrip lines: (a) single-element coupler; and (b) multielement coupler.

When $l = \lambda_g/4$ the coupling to port 4 reaches its maximum value and no signal is coupled to port 3. Thus, this device operates as a directional coupler. (Note that the coupled port is on the same end as the input port, unlike in Figures 6.6 and 6.7.) The characteristic impedances of the coupled line depend on Z_0 and on the voltage coupling coefficient $K = |V_4/V_1|$ as

$$Z_{0e} = Z_0 \sqrt{\frac{1 + K}{1 - K}} \qquad (6.21)$$

$$Z_{0o} = Z_0 \sqrt{\frac{1 - K}{1 + K}} \qquad (6.22)$$

Equations (6.20) through (6.22) are valid if the even-mode and odd-mode waves propagate at the same speed. In a coupled microstrip line, this is not exactly true, and the directivity is worse than in an ideal case. The structure of Figure 6.11(a) is best suited for realizing a weak coupling (large C). The lines would be impractically close to each other to achieve a strong coupling. The single-element coupler has a bandwidth that may be too narrow for some applications. A broadband directional coupler is obtained by connecting quarter-wave sections with appropriate couplings, as in Figure 6.11(b).

The directional coupler shown in Figure 6.12 is called the Lange coupler and is suitable for realizing strong couplings as 3 dB to 6 dB. It is made of several coupled lines bonded together with thin wires.

The ring coupler illustrated in Figure 6.13(a) is a 180° hybrid. Its scattering matrix is obtained by multiplying the matrix of (6.17) by $-j$, if

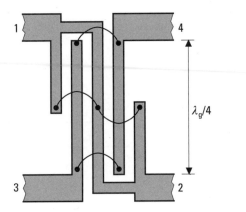

Figure 6.12 Lange coupler.

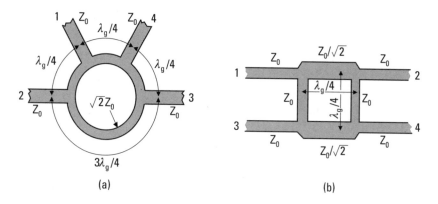

Figure 6.13 Hybrids: (a) ring hybrid; and (b) branch-line hybrid.

the reference planes are at the T-junctions. The characteristic impedances of the ports are Z_0 and that of the $3\lambda_g/2$-long ring is $\sqrt{2}Z_0$. A wave applied to port 1 (Σ) does not couple to port 3 because the two paths have a difference in length of $\lambda_g - \lambda_g/2 = \lambda_g/2$, but it couples to ports 2 and 4 in the same phase. A wave applied to port 2 (Δ) couples to ports 1 and 3 in an opposite phase.

The branch-line coupler shown in Figure 6.13(b) is a 90° hybrid. The $\lambda_g/4$-long branches have characteristic impedances of Z_0 and $Z_0/\sqrt{2}$. For example, a wave applied to port 1 couples to ports 2 and 4 with a phase difference of 90°, and port 3 is isolated from port 1. Both ring and branch-line couplers can be modified so that the ratio of output powers differs from 1.

Example 6.1

Design a 50-Ω microstrip directional coupler operating at 1 GHz with a coupling of $C = 15$ dB. The properties of the substrate are: $\epsilon_r = 10$, $h = 0.254$ mm, $t = 5\ \mu$m. Use the structure presented in Figure 6.11(a).

Solution

The voltage-coupling coefficient corresponding to a 15-dB coupling is $K = \sqrt{1/10^{1.5}} = 0.1778$. From (6.12) and (6.13) we get $Z_{0e} = 59.8\Omega$ and $Z_{0o} = 41.8\Omega$. We use the graph of Figure 6.10 for $\epsilon_r = 10$, and read $w/h = 0.9$ and $s/h = 0.9$. Thus, both the width of strips forming the coupled line and their separation is 0.23 mm. According to (3.85), the effective relative permittivity is $\epsilon_{reff} = 6.69$. The length of the coupled line section is $\lambda/4 = c/(4f\sqrt{\epsilon_{reff}}) = 29.0$ mm. The strip width of 50-Ω lines is 0.234 mm.

6.2 Ferrite Devices

Ferrites are ceramic materials that possess a high resistivity and that behave nonreciprocally when embedded in a magnetic field. Ferrite devices such as isolators, circulators, attenuators, phase shifters, modulators, and switches are based on these properties [3].

6.2.1 Properties of Ferrite Materials

Ferrites are oxides of ferromagnetic materials, such as iron, to which another oxide has been added as an impurity. According to their molecular structure, ferrites are divided into garnets ($3M_2O_3 \cdot 5Fe_2O_3$), spinels ($MO \cdot Fe_2O_3$), and hexaferrites. In garnets M is a lantanid like yttrium, gadolinium, or samarium. In spinels M is mangan, manganese, iron, zinc, nickel, or cadmium. The impurities increase the resistivity of the ferrite to as much as 10^{14} times higher than the resistivity of metals. Typically, the relative permittivity ϵ_r is 10 to 20, whereas the relative permeability μ_r may be up to VHF band 1,000 or even more.

In ferromagnetic materials, strong interactions between atomic magnetic moments force them to line up parallel to each other. Ferromagnetic materials are able to retain magnetization when the magnetizing field is removed.

Atoms behave as magnetic dipoles because of the spin of their electrons. The orbital movement of the electrons about the nucleus also causes a small magnetic moment, but its effect is less important for the magnetic properties of materials. We can imagine that an electron is rotating about its axis producing a magnetic dipole moment

$$|\mathbf{m}| = \frac{eh}{4\pi m_e} = 9.27 \times 10^{-24} \text{ Am}^2 \tag{6.23}$$

where e is the magnitude of the electron charge, h is Planck's constant, and m_e is the mass of an electron. The spin angular momentum of an electron is

$$|\mathbf{P}| = \frac{h}{4\pi} \tag{6.24}$$

The vectors $\mathbf{m}$ and $\mathbf{P}$ point to opposite directions. The ratio of their magnitudes, the gyromagnetic ratio, is

$$\gamma = \left|\frac{m}{P}\right| = \frac{e}{m_e} = 17.6 \text{ MHz/gauss} \qquad (6.25)$$

A static magnetic field having a flux density $\mathbf{B_0} = B_0\,\mathbf{u_z}$ exerts on an electron a torque of ($\mathbf{m} = -\gamma\mathbf{P}$):

$$\mathbf{T} = \mathbf{m} \times \mathbf{B_0} = -\gamma\mathbf{P} \times \mathbf{B_0} \qquad (6.26)$$

Because of this torque, the electrons and their magnetic dipoles precess as gyroscopes. The angle of precession, ϕ, is shown in Figure 6.14. The rate of change of the angular momentum equals the torque, or $d\mathbf{P}/dt = \mathbf{T}$. Thus the equation of motion for a magnetic dipole is

$$\frac{d\mathbf{m}}{dt} = -\gamma\mathbf{m} \times \mathbf{B_0} \qquad (6.27)$$

From this we can solve the angular frequency of precession (called the Larmor frequency):

$$\omega_0 = \gamma B_0 \qquad (6.28)$$

Let us assume that both a static magnetic field with a flux density of B_0 and a field of a high-frequency wave propagating into the z direction interact with an electron. The wave is circularly polarized in the xy-plane

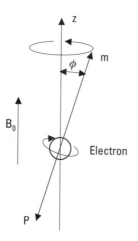

Figure 6.14 An electron precessing in magnetic field.

and has a flux density of B_1 ($<< B_0$). For a left-handed wave, $\mathbf{B}_1 = \mathbf{B}_1^- = B_1(\mathbf{u_x} + j\mathbf{u_y})$. Now the total magnetic field is tilted by an angle of $\theta = \arctan(B_1/B_0)$ with respect to the z-axis and precesses with the angular frequency of the wave, ω. The torque due to the field produces precession of electrons in the counterclockwise direction in synchronism with the propagating wave, and therefore $\phi < \theta$. From the equation of motion we solve the component of the magnetic dipole moment m^- that rotates in synchronism with the left-handed circularly polarized wave

$$m^- = \frac{\gamma m_0 B_1}{\omega_0 + \omega} \tag{6.29}$$

where $m_0 = m \cos \phi$. Correspondingly, for a right-handed wave $\mathbf{B}_1 = \mathbf{B}_1^+ = B_1(\mathbf{u_x} - j\mathbf{u_y})$, both fields produce precession in the clockwise direction, and therefore $\phi > \theta$, and

$$m^+ = \frac{\gamma m_0 B_1}{\omega_0 - \omega} \tag{6.30}$$

In ferromagnetic materials, the magnetic dipole moments are aligned parallel in regions called magnetic domains, even when no external field is present. When an external field is applied, the domains tend to orient parallel to the field. The magnetization of the material, or the magnetic dipole moment per unit volume, is $\mathbf{M} = N\mathbf{m}$, where N is the effective number of electrons per unit volume. When the external field increases, nearly all magnetic moments are aligned parallel to the field and a saturation magnetization $\mathbf{M_S}$ is finally reached. Then the whole ferrite body behaves like a large magnetic dipole. The magnetic flux density in a saturated ferrite is

$$\mathbf{B} = \mu_0(\mathbf{H}_0 + \mathbf{M_S}) \tag{6.31}$$

As for a single electron, an equation of motion can be derived for magnetization. Equations analogous to (6.29) and (6.30) are obtained for circularly polarized waves by replacing m_0 with Nm_0. From these it follows that the effective permeabilities for right-handed and left-handed circularly polarized waves are

$$\mu^+ = \mu_0 \mu_r^+ = \mu_0 \left(1 + \frac{\gamma \mu_0 M_S}{\omega_0 - \omega} \right) \tag{6.32}$$

$$\mu^- = \mu_0\mu_r^- = \mu_0\left(1 + \frac{\gamma\mu_0 M_S}{\omega_0 + \omega}\right) \qquad (6.33)$$

when $B_1 \ll B_0$ (small-signal conditions) and $M = M_S$. The matrix presentation is

$$\begin{bmatrix} B^+ \\ B^- \\ B_z \end{bmatrix} = \mu_0 \begin{bmatrix} \mu_r^+ & 0 & 0 \\ 0 & \mu_r^- & 0 \\ 0 & 0 & 1 \end{bmatrix} \begin{bmatrix} H^+ \\ H^- \\ H_z \end{bmatrix} \qquad (6.34)$$

Thus the phase constant of a right-handed wave, $\beta^+ = \omega\sqrt{\epsilon\mu^+}$, and that of a left-handed wave, $\beta^- = \omega\sqrt{\epsilon\mu^-}$, are different.

6.2.2 Faraday Rotation

Let us consider a situation in which a plane wave propagates in ferrite in the z direction. A uniform, static magnetic field pointing to the z direction is applied over the ferrite. The wave is linearly polarized and the electric field is directed along the x-axis at $z = 0$. A linearly polarized wave can be divided into two orthogonal circularly polarized waves, as

$$\mathbf{E} = \mathbf{u_x}E_0 = (\mathbf{u_x} + j\mathbf{u_y})\frac{E_0}{2} + (\mathbf{u_x} - j\mathbf{u_y})\frac{E_0}{2} \qquad (6.35)$$

The phase constants of these two components are β^- and β^+. At $z = l$ the electric field is

$$\mathbf{E} = (\mathbf{u_x} + j\mathbf{u_y})\frac{E_0}{2}e^{-j\beta^- l} + (\mathbf{u_x} - j\mathbf{u_y})\frac{E_0}{2}e^{-j\beta^+ l} \qquad (6.36)$$

This can be written as

$$\mathbf{E} = E_0 e^{-j(\beta^- + \beta^+)l/2}\{\mathbf{u_x}\cos[(\beta^+ - \beta^-)l/2] - \mathbf{u_y}\sin[(\beta^+ - \beta^-)l/2]\} \qquad (6.37)$$

The phase shift of the resultant wave is $(\beta^- + \beta^+)l/2$ and the tilt angle with respect to the x-axis is

$$\theta = \arctan (E_y / E_x) = -(\beta^+ - \beta^-) \frac{l}{2} \qquad (6.38)$$

Hence the tilt angle of the polarization vector changes as the wave propagates in a ferrite. This phenomenon is called the Faraday rotation. A typical change is 100° per centimeter at 10 GHz.

If the direction of propagation is reversed, the tilt angle rotates in the same direction with respect to the coordinate system. Therefore, as the wave propagates back from $z = l$ to $z = 0$, the tilt angle does not return back from θ to 0° but its value becomes 2θ. Consequently, the Faraday rotation is a nonreciprocal phenomenon.

Figure 6.15 shows how the phase and attenuation constants typically behave in a ferrite. When $\omega_0 > \omega$, $\beta^+ > \beta^-$, and when $\omega_0 < \omega$, $\beta^+ < \beta^-$. Thus, the direction of the Faraday rotation depends on whether the signal frequency is smaller or larger than the resonance frequency. Close to the resonance, the attenuation constant α^+ is large. Well below the resonance frequency, the attenuation constant is small, but then the difference between β^+ and β^- is small and the tilt angle rotates slowly.

Example 6.2

A linearly polarized wave at a frequency of $f = 3$ GHz propagates in a ferrite into the direction of a static magnetic field with a flux density $B_0 = 0.14$ Wb/m². The ferrite has a saturation magnetization of $\mu_0 M_S = 0.2$ Wb/m² and a relative permittivity of $\epsilon_r = 10$. Find the length of such a ferrite body that rotates the tilt angle by 90° as a wave passes through it.

Solution

Using (6.25) and (6.28) we find the resonance frequency $\omega_0 = \gamma B_0 = 24.64 \times 10^9$ 1/s. Note that 1 Wb/m² = 1 T = 10^4 gauss. The angular frequency

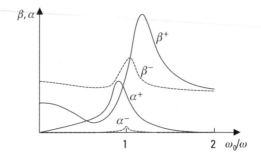

Figure 6.15 Phase and attenuation constants for propagation in ferrite.

of the wave is $\omega = 2\pi f = 18.85 \times 10^9$ 1/s. From (6.32) and (6.33) we get the effective permeabilities for right-handed and left-handed circularly polarized waves as $\mu^+ = 7.08\mu_0$ and $\mu^- = 1.81\mu_0$, respectively. Correspondingly, the phase constants are $\beta^+ = \sqrt{\epsilon_r\mu_r^+}\,\omega/c = 8.41\,\omega/c$ and $\beta^- = \sqrt{\epsilon_r\mu_r^-}\,\omega/c = 4.25\,\omega/c$. Because $\beta^+ > \beta^-$, the angle θ is negative and the tilt angle rotates counterclockwise as the wave propagates. By setting $\theta = -\pi/2$ in (6.38) we solve $l = \pi/(\beta^+ - \beta^-) = 12$ mm. Also, lengths producing a rotation of $\theta = -\pi/2 - n\pi$ (n is a positive integer) give a tilt angle of $-90°$ for the output wave. If the wave would propagate to the direction opposite to the field, the tilt angle would rotate clockwise, as seen to the direction of propagation, but in the same direction with respect to the coordinate system as before.

6.2.3 Isolators

An ideal isolator passes signals in the forward direction without loss but totally absorbs signals propagating in the reverse direction. In practice, the insertion loss may be below 0.5 dB in the forward direction and more than 20 dB in the reverse direction for a good isolator. Isolators are used for matching and for stabilizing oscillators against frequency changes due to varying load impedance.

The operation of an isolator may be based on a ferromagnetic resonance, on shifting of field pattern, or on the Faraday rotation. Figure 6.16 shows a waveguide isolator. There is a ferrite rod in a circular waveguide in a static magnetic field. Because of the Faraday rotation, the polarization of a wave propagating in the forward direction turns 45° clockwise in the ferrite. This wave does not attenuate significantly in the resistive cards at the input and output, because the electric field is now perpendicular to both cards. The polarization of a reverse wave turns 45° counterclockwise, as seen, to the

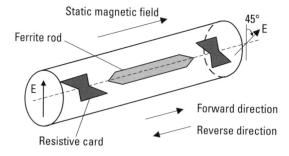

Figure 6.16 Waveguide isolator based on the Faraday rotation.

direction of propagation. The electric field is now parallel to the resistive card at the output (output for reverse direction) and the wave is absorbed.

6.2.4 Circulators

An ideal circulator is an n-port device, which passes a signal applied in port 1 to port 2, a signal applied in port 2 to port 3, and finally a signal applied in port n to port 1. Usually, a circulator has three ports.

A three-port circulator can be used as an isolator by terminating one of the ports with a matched load. Circulators are used to separate the input and output ports of such devices that are based on reflection (e.g., reflection amplifier). Circulators are also used in radars to couple the transmitted power to the antenna and the echo signals from the antenna to the receiver.

A circulator may be based on the Faraday rotation or on a direction-dependent phase shift. The Y-junction circulator is the most common type. A cylindrical ferrite is placed in the middle of a symmetric junction, as shown in Figure 6.17. A static magnetic field is along the axis of the cylinder. The operation of this circulator may be explained by two degenerate resonance modes whose resonance frequencies differ due to the magnetic field [4, 5]. The operation range is between these two resonance frequencies.

6.3 Other Passive Components and Devices

In addition to the reciprocal power dividers and directional couplers and nonreciprocal ferrite devices, many other passive devices and components

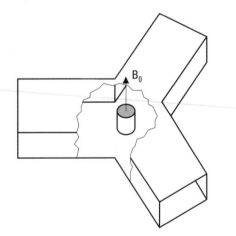

Figure 6.17 Y-junction circulator.

are needed in radio engineering. Terminations, attenuators, phase shifters, connectors, and adapters are briefly discussed here.

6.3.1 Terminations

Terminations are single-port components that are used for terminating transmission lines, waveguides, and ports of different devices. Matched loads (in an ideal case $\rho = 0$), shorts or short circuits ($\rho = -1$), and open ends or open circuits ($\rho = +1$) are terminations that are commonly used in measurements and in the calibration of measurement equipment.

A matched load absorbs all the power that is incident on it. Therefore, the impedance of a matched load equals the characteristic impedance of the line it terminates. A matched load can be realized by inserting a wedge, card, or pyramid made of lossy material in the waveguide, as shown in Figure 6.18(a). The length of the load should be at least one wavelength. A matched load is often adjustable; that is, the position of the absorber can be adjusted. Then, in measurements requiring a good accuracy, we may eliminate the effect of reflection from a nonideal matched load by performing the measurements with several positions of the load. A good matched load may have a *VSWR* less than 1.01. In a microstrip line, a matched load can be realized by terminating the line with a thin-film resistor followed by a shorting pin, as illustrated in Figure 6.18(b).

An ideal short circuit reflects the incident power totally. As a matched load, a short also may be fixed or adjustable. With an adjustable short we can realize a desired reactance: The impedance in a lossless line at a distance of l from the short is

$$Z = jZ_0 \tan \beta l \tag{6.39}$$

A metal block tightly fit in a coaxial line or waveguide serves as a simple short. However, in such a short the contact between the line and metal block is erratic if the short is moved. Figure 6.19 shows a structure

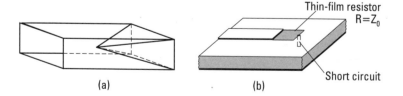

Thin-film resistor
$R=Z_0$

Short circuit

(a)   (b)

Figure 6.18 Matched loads: (a) in waveguide; and (b) in microstrip line.

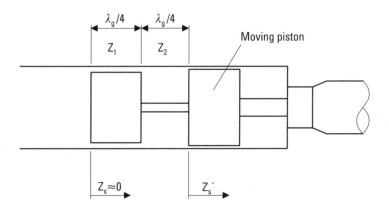

Figure 6.19 Adjustable short.

that is better suited for an adjustable short. It is made of high- and low-impedance quarter-wave sections that operate as impedance inverters. If the characteristic impedances of the low-impedance and high-impedance sections are Z_1 and Z_2, respectively, the input impedance is

$$Z_s = \left(\frac{Z_1}{Z_2}\right)^2 Z_s' \qquad (6.40)$$

where Z_s' is the impedance indicated in Figure 6.19. Thus Z_s is much lower than Z_s', which already has a low value. The disadvantage of this short is its narrow bandwidth, about 10%; the length of the sections is a quarter wavelength only at a single frequency.

Often an open-ended line does not correspond well to an ideal open circuit. The fringing fields of an open end of a coaxial line may be modeled as a small capacitor or as an extension of the line. An open-ended waveguide radiates effectively and operates as an antenna; thus, it does not resemble an open circuit at all. An open-ended microstrip line is quite a good open circuit; it only needs to be slightly shortened to compensate for the length extension due to a fringing field.

6.3.2 Attenuators

An ideal attenuator passes a given part of the incident power, absorbs the rest, and has matched ports. Lowering a power level, improving impedance matching, and measuring power ratios are applications of attenuators. The value of attenuation may be fixed or adjustable.

Figure 6.20(a) shows two fixed coaxial attenuators made of series-connected and parallel-connected resistors in a T and π configuration. In a microstrip circuit, T and π attenuators can be realized with the same principle using thin-film resistors. Figure 6.20(b) shows a simple microstrip line attenuator. The waveguide attenuator shown in Figure 6.20(c) has a resistive card in the middle of the broad wall along the direction of the E field. The card is tapered to ensure good matching.

Figure 6.21 shows a continuously adjustable waveguide attenuator. It has a rotating, circular waveguide section between a rectangular input and output waveguide. All three sections contain thin resistive cards. The input signal passes the first card with a negligible attenuation because the electric field of the TE_{10} wave mode is perpendicular to the card. Then the wave enters through a transition to the circular waveguide. The attenuation is adjusted by rotating the circular waveguide section and the resistive card within it. The field of the TE_{11} wave mode can be divided into two compo-

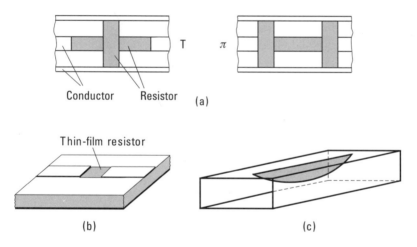

Figure 6.20 Fixed attenuators: (a) coaxial attenuators, T- and π-type; (b) microstrip attenuator; and (c) waveguide attenuator.

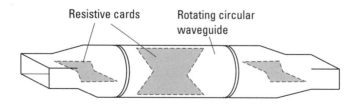

Figure 6.21 Adjustable waveguide attenuator.

nents, one perpendicular to the card and the other parallel to it. The latter component is absorbed by the card; the former component enters the output waveguide in which again its component parallel to the resistive card is absorbed. We can show that the attenuation in decibels is [1]

$$L = -40 \log (\sin \theta) \text{ dB} \qquad (6.41)$$

where θ is the angle between the electric field at the input and the plane of the resistive card in the circular section.

6.3.3 Phase Shifters

An ideal phase shifter is lossless and matched; it only shifts the phase of the output wave, or in other words, changes the phase difference between the output and input waves. Phase shifters are needed, for example, in phased antenna arrays.

An adjustable waveguide phase shifter can be realized by replacing the resistive card of the attenuator in Figure 6.20(c) with a dielectric card whose depth in the waveguide is adjustable. A structure resembling the attenuator in Figure 6.21 also operates as a phase shifter when the resistive cards are replaced with dielectric cards having proper lengths [1]. Electrically controlled phase shifters are much faster than mechanical phase shifters. They are often based on semiconductor devices such as *p-i-n* diodes or *field effect transistors* (FETs).

6.3.4 Connectors and Adapters

Connectors are needed to join different lines, devices, and circuit blocks together. An ideal connector is matched and lossless. Practical connectors cause small discontinuities. Therefore, unnecessary use of connectors should be avoided. The quality of connectors gets more and more important as the frequency gets higher.

Figure 6.22 shows some common coaxial connectors used at RF and microwave frequencies. An APC-7 connector is a precision connector that is used in measurements requiring good accuracy and repeatability. It is a sexless connector whose inner diameter of its outer conductor is 7 mm. SMA and N connectors are good enough for most cases. These connectors can be either male or female type. BNC connectors work best at frequencies below 1 GHz; at higher frequencies they may radiate. Waveguide components have flanges at their ports. Alignment pins on the flanges ensure accurate connection.

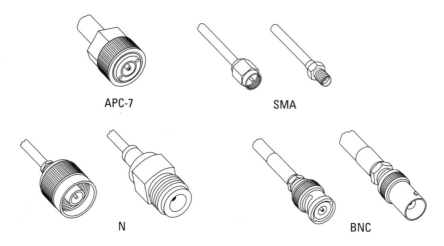

Figure 6.22 Some common coaxial connectors.

Adapters are needed to connect components having connectors of different types or of the same sex. Figure 6.23(a) shows a transition from a coaxial line to a microstrip line. Coaxial and waveguide components can be connected using the adapter illustrated in Figure 6.23(b).

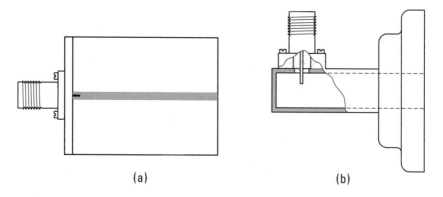

Figure 6.23 (a) Coaxial-to-microstrip transition; and (b) waveguide-to-coaxial adapter.

References

[1]   Collin, R. E., *Foundations for Microwave Engineering*, 2nd ed., New York: IEEE Press, 2001.

[2]   Pozar, D. M., *Microwave Engineering*, 2nd ed., New York: John Wiley & Sons, 1998.

[3]   Rodrigue, G. P., "A Generation of Microwave Ferrite Devices," *Proc. IEEE,* Vol. 76, No. 2, 1988, pp. 121–137.

[4]   Fay, C. E., and R. L. Comstock, "Operation of the Ferrite Junction Circulator," *IEEE Trans. on Microwave Theory and Techniques,* Vol. 13, No. 1, 1965, pp. 15–27.

[5]   Lahey, J., "Junction Circulator Design," *Microwave Journal,* Vol. 32, No. 11, 1989, pp. 26–45.

7

Resonators and Filters

Transmission line and waveguide devices, discussed in Chapter 6, would ideally operate over a broad bandwidth. However, the useful bandwidth may be limited, for example, by the frequency dependence of the line sections that have proper electrical lengths only at the design frequency. Resonators and filters are intentionally frequency-selective devices.

7.1 Resonators

Resonators are used for stabilizing the frequency of oscillators, as building blocks of filters, as sensors in material measurements, and so on.

There are a large number of different resonator structures. Lumped components, coils and capacitors, are usable in realizing resonators at radio frequencies. Resonators based on the piezoelectric effect in a quartz crystal operate up to the VHF range. In micromechanical resonators made using *microelectromechanical systems* (MEMS) technology, electrical signals are coupled with the mechanical vibrations of a resonating beam [1]. Micromachined beam resonators may soon become usable at the UHF range. An open-circuited or short-circuited line, a closed metal cavity, a cylindrical pill made of a ceramic material, and a sphere made of ferrite (yttrium iron garnet, YIG) are examples of resonators operating at microwave frequencies. Open quasioptical resonators become usable in the millimeter-wave range and at higher frequencies.

7.1.1 Resonance Phenomenon

A resonator is a structure having a natural frequency of oscillation. A circuit consisting of a coil and a capacitor, shown in Figure 7.1, forms a simple electromagnetic resonator. At first the switch is open and the capacitor is charged to a voltage V. The electric field of the capacitor contains an energy of $W_e = CV^2/2$, where C is the capacitance of the capacitor. After the switch is closed, a current starts to flow through the coil. When the capacitor has completely discharged, the current I is at maximum and the whole energy of the circuit is in the magnetic field of the coil. This energy is $W_m = LI^2/2$, where L is the inductance of the coil. Then the current will again charge the capacitor, but now the polarity of the voltage is reversed. At resonance, the average energy in the electric field $CV^2/4$ is equal to the average energy in the magnetic field $LI^2/4$. The resonance frequency of the circuit is

$$f_r = \frac{1}{2\pi\sqrt{LC}} \tag{7.1}$$

If energy is applied to the circuit from an external source at the resonance frequency and in the correct phase, the energy contained in the circuit will increase. However, due to losses in the circuit, the energy does not increase indefinitely. The losses are modeled with a conductance G in a parallel resonant circuit and with a resistance R in a series resonant circuit, as shown in Figure 7.2. Also, resonators made of transmission lines and waveguides can be modeled with equivalent circuits containing lumped elements.

7.1.2 Quality Factor

The quality factor of a resonator is defined as

$$Q = \frac{\omega_r W}{P_l} \tag{7.2}$$

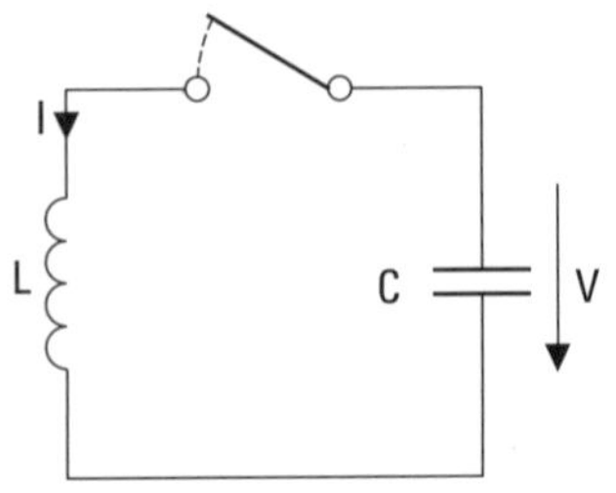

Figure 7.1 Resonator composed of a coil and a capacitor.

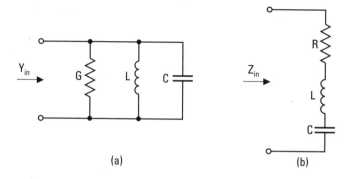

Figure 7.2 (a) Parallel resonant circuit; and (b) series resonant circuit.

where $\omega_r = 2\pi f_r$ is the angular resonance frequency, W is the energy stored in the resonator, and P_l is the power loss in the resonator.

When the energy source of the resonator is closed off, the stored energy decreases from its original value W_0 exponentially as $W(t) = W_0 e^{-j\delta t}$. The damping factor $\delta = \omega_r/(2Q)$ describes how fast the energy in the resonator decreases. Conversely, when the energy source is switched on, the energy increases from zero to its final value W_0 as $W(t) = W_0(1 - e^{-j\delta t})$. The larger the quality factor, the longer the time required to charge or discharge the resonator.

Let us consider the parallel resonant circuit in Figure 7.2(a). The analysis of a series resonant circuit is a dual case: We replace G with R, interchange C and L, replace admittance quantities with impedance quantities, and replace current sources with voltage sources. Because the power loss of the parallel resonant circuit is $P_l = GV^2/2$, the quality factor is

$$Q = \frac{\omega_r W}{P_l} = \frac{\omega_r CV^2/2}{GV^2/2} = \frac{\omega_r C}{G} = \frac{1}{G\omega_r L} \qquad (7.3)$$

The input admittance of the resonator is

$$Y_{in} = G + j\omega C + \frac{1}{j\omega L} \qquad (7.4)$$

At the resonance frequency, the input admittance is real: $Y_{in} = G$. At frequencies close to the resonance, the input impedance is approximately

$$Y_{in} \approx G + j\Delta\omega 2C = G\left(1 + j2Q\frac{\Delta\omega}{\omega_r}\right) = G + jB \qquad (7.5)$$

where $\Delta\omega = \omega - \omega_r \left(|\Delta\omega| \ll \omega_r \right)$, Hence on the Smith chart the input impedance moves on a constant-conductance circle as the frequency changes. Close to the resonance frequency, the susceptance B is directly proportional to the frequency deviation $\Delta f = \Delta\omega/(2\pi)$ from the resonance frequency f_r.

Let us assume that an ac current source is connected to the parallel resonant circuit above. At resonance $B = 0$, and current flows through the conductance G. The power loss in the resonator is now at its maximum. The more the frequency deviates from f_r, the larger the magnitude of the susceptance and the smaller the current through the conductance. As $\Delta\omega = \pm\Delta\omega_{3dB} = \pm\omega_r/(2Q)$, the real and imaginary parts of the input impedance are equal, the magnitude of the admittance is $\sqrt{2}G$, and the phase of the admittance is $\pm\pi/4$. Then the power loss in the resonator is half of that at the resonance frequency. Thus the quality factor may also be defined with the half-power frequencies illustrated in Figure 7.3 as

$$Q = \frac{\omega_r}{2\Delta\omega_{3dB}} = \frac{f_r}{2\Delta f_{3dB}} \tag{7.6}$$

In other words, the quality factor of a resonator is a measure of its selectivity. The higher the quality factor, the narrower the frequency response of a resonator.

7.1.3 Coupled Resonator

A resonator may have one, two, or more couplings to the external circuit. Figure 7.4 shows the normalized equivalent circuits of resonators having one

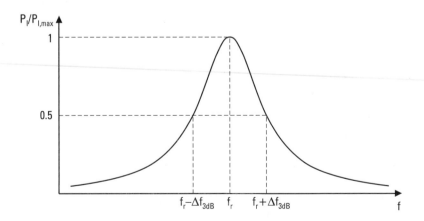

Figure 7.3 Power absorbed in a resonator.

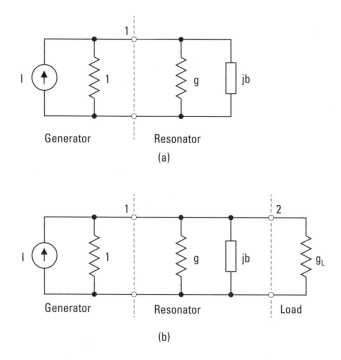

Figure 7.4 Equivalent circuits of resonators: (a) one coupling; and (b) two couplings.

and two couplings. A generator (current source) having a normalized output admittance of 1 is connected to port 1. The load admittance at port 2 of the resonator having two couplings is g_L.

Let us consider at first the resonator with one coupling. The normalized input impedance is

$$y_{in} = g + jb \qquad (7.7)$$

The total conductance of the circuit is $1 + g$, whereas that of the resonator alone is g. Therefore, the resonance curve such as that in Figure 7.3 has a peak that is broader by a factor of $(1 + g)/g$ when the external coupling is taken into account.

The power loss in the circuit is divided into two parts, for each of which we can define a quality factor. The unloaded quality factor Q_0 is related to the loss in the resonator. Absorption in the metal walls and in the dielectric medium and radiation into free space are the sources of this loss. Q_0 can be obtained from those frequencies $f_r \pm \Delta f_0$ at which $g = b$:

$$Q_0 = \frac{f_r}{2\Delta f_0} \qquad (7.8)$$

The external quality factor Q_e is a measure of losses in the external circuit. From those frequencies $f_r \pm \Delta f_e$ at which $1 = b$, we get

$$Q_e = \frac{f_r}{2\Delta f_e} \qquad (7.9)$$

The loaded quality factor Q_L describes the losses of the whole circuit. From frequencies $f_r \pm \Delta f_L$ at which $1 + g = b$, we get

$$Q_L = \frac{f_r}{2\Delta f_L} \qquad (7.10)$$

Because the power loss is inversely proportional to the corresponding quality factor, we can combine different loss components as

$$\frac{1}{Q_L} = \frac{1}{Q_0} + \frac{1}{Q_e} \qquad (7.11)$$

or in other words, the total loss equals the sum of the loss in the resonator and the loss in the external circuit.

Figure 7.5 illustrates how the quality factors can be obtained from the input admittance $y_{in}(f)$ presented on the Smith chart. From the intersection points of $y_{in}(f)$ with the lines $b = g$, $b = 1$, and $b = 1 + g$, we get the frequency deviations Δf_0, Δf_e, and Δf_L, from which we calculate Q_0, Q_e, and Q_L using (7.8) through (7.10).

If $Q_e > Q_0$ ($1 < g$), the resonator loss at the resonance is larger than the loss in the external circuit; the resonator is undercoupled. For an overcoupled resonator, $Q_e < Q_0$ ($1 > g$), and the resonator loss at the resonance is smaller than the external loss. The coupling is called critical when $Q_e = Q_0$; then the resonator is matched to the generator at resonance.

For a resonator having two couplings we can define two external quality factors: Q_{e1} for port 1 and Q_{e2} for port 2. The elements of the equivalent circuits can also be represented using the quality factors as $g = Q_{e1}/Q_0$, $g_L = Q_{e1}/Q_{e2}$, and $b = gQ_0 2\Delta f/f_r = Q_{e1} 2\Delta f/f_r$. The transducer power loss of the resonator is

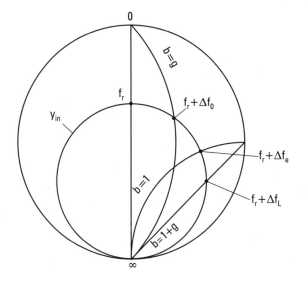

Figure 7.5 Solving the quality factors of a resonator from the input admittance versus frequency on the Smith chart. Input admittance y_{in} of an overcoupled resonator is presented.

$$L = \frac{P_a}{P_L} = \frac{(1 + g + g_L)^2 + b^2}{4g_L} = \frac{Q_{e1} Q_{e2}}{4Q_L^2} \left[1 + Q_L^2 \left(\frac{2\Delta f}{f_r} \right)^2 \right]$$

(7.12)

where $P_a = I^2/4$ is the available power from the current source and P_L is the power coupled to the load.

7.1.4 Transmission Line Section as a Resonator

Let us consider a section of a short-circuited transmission line with a length l, shown in Figure 7.6. Its series resistance, series inductance, and parallel capacitance per unit length are R', L', and C', respectively. For an air-filled line the parallel conductance may be neglected. The input impedance of the line is

$$Z_{in} = Z_0 \tanh (j\beta l + \alpha l) = Z_0 \frac{\tanh \alpha l + j \tan \beta l}{1 + j \tan \beta l \tanh \alpha l}$$

(7.13)

We assume that the total loss is small so that $\tanh \alpha l \approx \alpha l$. Close to the frequency f_r, at which $l = \lambda_g/2$, $\tan \beta l = \tan (\pi + \pi \Delta f/f_r) = \tan (\pi \Delta f/f_r) \approx \pi \Delta f/f_r$. Now (7.13) simplifies to

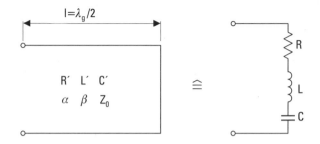

Figure 7.6 Short-circuited $\lambda_g/2$-long transmission line and its equivalent circuit.

$$Z_{in} \approx Z_0(\alpha l + j\pi \Delta f / f_r) \qquad (7.14)$$

The resistance is constant and the reactance is directly proportional to the frequency deviation; thus a short-circuited $\lambda_g/2$-long transmission line resembles a series resonant circuit. Because $Z_0 = \sqrt{L'/C'}$, $\alpha = (R'/2)\sqrt{C'/L'}$, and $\beta l = \omega_r l \sqrt{L'C'} = \pi$, then

$$Z_{in} \approx R'l/2 + jL'l\Delta f \qquad (7.15)$$

On the other hand, close to the resonance frequency, the input impedance of a series resonant circuit made of lumped elements is

$$Z_{in} \approx R + j2L\Delta f \qquad (7.16)$$

By comparing (7.15) and (7.16), we see the relationship between the distributed quantities and the lumped elements of the equivalent circuit: $R = R'l/2$, $L = L'l/2$, and $C = 1/(\omega_r^2 L) = 1/(\omega_r^2 Z_0^2 C'l/2)$.

The reactance of a short-circuited 50-Ω line and that of a corresponding LC series resonant circuit are compared in Figure 7.7. We see that close to the resonance frequency these two circuits have nearly similar properties. The quality factor of the transmission-line resonator is

$$Q = \frac{\omega_r L}{R} = \frac{\omega_r L'}{R'} = \frac{\beta}{2\alpha} \qquad (7.17)$$

As before, we can show that an open-circuited $\lambda_g/4$-long line corresponds to a series resonant circuit, whereas a short-circuited $\lambda_g/4$-long line and an open-circuited $\lambda_g/2$-long line correspond to a parallel resonant circuit.

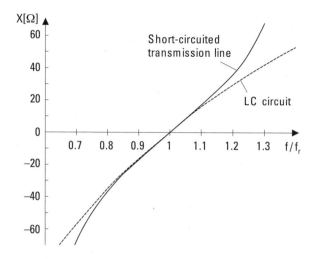

Figure 7.7 The reactance *X* versus frequency for a short-circuited transmission line and an LC series resonant circuit. The length of the line is $\lambda_g/2$ at f_r.

7.1.5 Cavity Resonators

Metal cavities can be used as resonators at microwave frequencies. A cavity resonator has a closed structure, except for the couplings to the external circuit, and thus has no radiative loss. The quality factor of a cavity resonator may by high—several thousands or even more.

Often a cavity resonator is made of a section of a waveguide or a coaxial line short-circuited at both ends. At resonance a standing wave is formed in the cavity as the wave bounces back and forth between the ends. Thus the length of the cavity is half of a wavelength or a multiple of that at the resonance frequency. A given cavity has an infinite number of resonance frequencies, unlike a resonator made of lumped elements.

Figure 7.8 shows three ways to couple a field into a cavity or from it: a loop, a probe, and a hole. A prerequisite for an efficient coupling is that

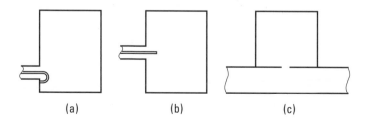
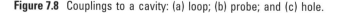

Figure 7.8 Couplings to a cavity: (a) loop; (b) probe; and (c) hole.

the fields of the resonance mode have some common components with the fields of the coupling element. Therefore, a loop at the maximum of the magnetic field perpendicular to the field or a probe at the maximum of the electric field along the field works as a good coupling element. In order for the hole coupling to be successful, the fields of the waveguide and cavity should have some common components at the coupling hole. Different resonance modes that may be excited at a given frequency can often be discriminated by choosing the proper position for the coupling element. The coupling coefficient $\beta_{ci} = Q_0/Q_{ei}$ at port i is used to describe the strength of the coupling.

Close to the resonance, a cavity resonator may be modeled with a parallel resonant or series resonant RLC circuit. A parallel resonant circuit may be transformed into a series resonant circuit and vice versa by changing the position of the reference plane at which the resonator input is assumed to be. Often it is more practical to treat a cavity resonator with its quality factors.

Let us consider the air-filled rectangular cavity shown in Figure 7.9 [2]. We can regard it as a section of a rectangular waveguide having short circuits at planes $z = 0$ and $z = d$. The phase constant of the TE_{nm} and TM_{nm} wave modes is

$$\beta_{nm} = \sqrt{k_0^2 - \left(\frac{n\pi}{a}\right)^2 - \left(\frac{m\pi}{b}\right)^2} \qquad (7.18)$$

where $k_0 = \omega\sqrt{\mu_0 \epsilon_0} = 2\pi/\lambda_0$. Since at resonance the length of the cavity is $l\lambda_g/2$ (l is integer),

$$\beta_{nm} = \frac{l\pi}{d} \qquad (7.19)$$

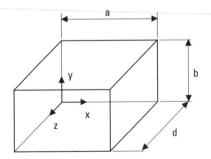

Figure 7.9 Rectangular cavity resonator.

From (7.18) and (7.19) we solve

$$k_0 = k_{nml} = \sqrt{\left(\frac{n\pi}{a}\right)^2 + \left(\frac{m\pi}{b}\right)^2 + \left(\frac{l\pi}{d}\right)^2} \qquad (7.20)$$

Resonance frequencies corresponding to these discrete values of k_{nml} are

$$f_{nml} = \frac{c k_{nml}}{2\pi} = \frac{c}{2}\sqrt{\left(\frac{n}{a}\right)^2 + \left(\frac{m}{b}\right)^2 + \left(\frac{l}{d}\right)^2} \qquad (7.21)$$

This equation is valid for both the TE_{nm} and TM_{nm} wave modes. Resonance modes having the same resonance frequency but a different field distribution are called degenerate modes.

Let us study in more detail the resonance mode TE_{101}, that is, a resonance that is excited in a cavity that is half-wave long at the fundamental wave mode TE_{10}. This is the mode having the lowest resonance frequency if $b < a < d$. We find the field distribution by summing up waves propagating into the $+z$ and $-z$ directions:

$$E_y = (E^+ e^{-j\beta z} + E^- e^{j\beta z}) \sin\frac{\pi x}{a} \qquad (7.22)$$

$$H_x = -\frac{1}{Z_{TE}}(E^+ e^{-j\beta z} - E^- e^{j\beta z}) \sin\frac{\pi x}{a} \qquad (7.23)$$

$$H_z = \frac{j\lambda}{\eta 2a}(E^+ e^{-j\beta z} + E^- e^{j\beta z}) \cos\frac{\pi x}{a} \qquad (7.24)$$

Because $E_y = 0$ at $z = 0$, $E^- = -E^+$. E_y must also be zero at $z = d$, which leads to $\beta = \pi/d$. By denoting $E_0 = -2jE^+$, we get

$$E_y = E_0 \sin\frac{\pi x}{a} \sin\frac{\pi z}{d} \qquad (7.25)$$

$$H_x = -j\frac{E_0}{\eta}\frac{\lambda}{2d}\sin\frac{\pi x}{a}\cos\frac{\pi z}{d} \qquad (7.26)$$

$$H_z = j\frac{E_0}{\eta}\frac{\lambda}{2a}\cos\frac{\pi x}{a}\sin\frac{\pi z}{d} \qquad (7.27)$$

The energy stored is the maximum energy of the electric field because then the energy of the magnetic field is zero. This energy is

$$W = \frac{\epsilon_0}{2} \int_0^d \int_0^b \int_0^a |E_y|^2 \, dx \, dy \, dz = \frac{\epsilon_0 abd}{8} E_0^2 \qquad (7.28)$$

The loss can be calculated if the surface current J_s and the surface resistance R_s are known on all walls of the cavity. The surface current, or current per unit width, is

$$\mathbf{J_s} = \mathbf{n} \times \mathbf{H} \qquad (7.29)$$

where $\mathbf{n}$ is a unit vector perpendicular to the surface. Equations (7.25) through (7.27) are valid in case of ideal, lossless conductors but they can be applied with good accuracy in case of low-loss conductors. The power loss is obtained by integrating over all the surfaces of the cavity:

$$P_l = \frac{R_s}{2} \int_S |J_s|^2 \, dS = \frac{R_s \lambda^2}{8\eta^2} E_0^2 \left[\frac{ab}{d^2} + \frac{bd}{a^2} + \frac{1}{2} \left(\frac{a}{d} + \frac{d}{a} \right) \right] \qquad (7.30)$$

By combining (7.28) and (7.30) we get the quality factor of TE_{101} mode as

$$Q = \frac{\omega_r W}{P_l} = \frac{\pi \eta}{4 R_s} \left[\frac{2b(a^2 + d^2)^{3/2}}{ad(a^2 + d^2) + 2b(a^3 + d^3)} \right] \qquad (7.31)$$

The quality factor of a cubical ($a = b = d$) cavity is

$$Q = \frac{\sqrt{2}\pi}{6} \frac{\eta}{R_s} = 0.742 \frac{\eta}{R_s} \qquad (7.32)$$

If the cavity is filled with a lossy dielectric having a permittivity of $\epsilon = \epsilon' - j\epsilon''$, the quality factor describing the dielectric loss is [3]

$$Q_d = \frac{\epsilon'}{\epsilon''} \qquad (7.33)$$

This equation is valid for all resonance modes.

Example 7.1

A cubical cavity resonator made of copper has a side length of 20 mm. Find the resonance frequency of the fundamental mode and the quality factor.

Solution

The fundamental mode is TE_{101}. When $a = b = d = 20$ mm, $n = l = 1$, and $m = 0$, we get, from (7.21), the resonance frequency as $f_{101} = 10.6$ GHz. The conductivity of copper is $\sigma = 5.8 \times 10^7$ S/m. At the resonance frequency the surface resistance is $R_s = \sqrt{\omega\mu_0/(2\sigma)} = 0.027\Omega$. From (7.31) or (7.32) we solve $Q = 10,400$. In practice Q is lower because R_s is higher due to surface roughness and because couplings have some loss.

In principle, the quality factor of other resonance modes may be calculated the same way as the quality factor of the TE_{101} mode. Note that the name of a resonance mode also depends on the choice of the coordinate system. For example, the TE_{101} mode is called the TM_{110} mode if the y-axis is chosen to be "the direction of propagation." At a given frequency, the higher the order of the resonance mode, the larger the cavity needed. As the size of the cavity increases, the ratio of the volume to the surface area increases, leading to a higher quality factor. In the case of a large cavity, however, the resonance frequencies of different modes are close to each other, and it is difficult to excite only a particular mode.

A cylindrical cavity is a section of a circular waveguide. The lowest order resonance mode is TE_{111}. At this mode the height of the cylinder is $\lambda_g/2$ at the fundamental mode TE_{11}. The resonance mode TE_{011} of a cylindrical cavity is exceptionally important. This mode has a high quality factor and no axial surface currents, which facilitates the realization of an adjustable cavity because the moving short does not need to make a good contact with the cylinder walls.

7.1.6 Dielectric Resonators

It is not possible to make high-quality resonators with microstrip techniques because microstrip lines are rather lossy and radiate easily. However, dielectric resonators [4] can easily be used in connection with microstrip circuits.

Dielectric resonators are usually small, cylindrical pills made of ceramic materials such as $Ba_2Ti_9O_{20}$, $BaTi_4O_9$, or $(Zr\text{-}Sn)TiO_4$. Such materials have a good temperature stability, low loss, and high dielectric constant, typically $\epsilon_r = 10$ to 100. Because of the large dielectric constant, the size of a dielectric resonator is much smaller than the size of a cavity resonator operating at the same frequency. Electric and magnetic fields concentrate within the resonator, but part of the field is outside the cylinder and this part may be employed in coupling. The radiation loss is low and the quality factor is mainly determined by the loss in the dielectric material. The unloaded quality factor Q_0 is typically 4,000 to 10,000 at 10 GHz. A given resonator can operate at several resonance modes, of which the $TE_{01\delta}$ mode is the most used.

Dielectric resonators are used in filters and transistor oscillators at frequencies from 1 to 50 GHz. If the frequency of an oscillator is stabilized with a dielectric resonator, it is called a *dielectric resonator oscillator* (DRO). Figure 7.10 shows how a DRO is coupled to a microstrip line. The magnetic fields of the line and the resonator have common components. The resonator is simply placed on the substrate, and the strength of the coupling can be adjusted by changing the distance of the resonator from the strip. To reduce radiation loss, the structure is enclosed within a metal case.

7.2 Filters

A resonator with two couplings passes through signals having frequencies near the resonance frequency; in other words, it acts as a bandpass filter. A hollow metal waveguide acts as a highpass filter, because it has a cutoff frequency that depends on the dimensions.

In general a filter is a two-port, which prevents propagation of undesired signals while desired signals pass it. In an ideal case, there is no insertion loss in the passband, but the attenuation in the stopband is infinite. Depending on the appearance of these bands, the filter is said to be a bandpass, bandstop, lowpass, or highpass filter. An ideal filter has a linear phase response, which allows a signal containing several frequency components to pass through

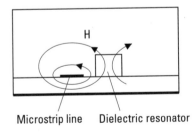

Microstrip line   Dielectric resonator

Figure 7.10 Dielectric resonator coupled to a microstrip line.

without distortion. Filters are used also for multiplexing (combining signals at different frequencies) and demultiplexing (separating signals at different frequencies). Also, reactive impedance matching circuits, tuning circuits in oscillators and amplifiers, delay lines, and slow-wave structures act as filters.

In the design of filters, two basic methods are used: the image parameter method and insertion loss method [3, 5, 6]. In the image parameter method, simple filter sections are cascaded to provide the desired passband-stopband characteristics. However, the required frequency response for the whole frequency range cannot be exactly synthesized. An iterative design process is used to improve the frequency response. On the contrary, the insertion loss method allows the synthesis of an exact response. We study the insertion loss method in more detail in the following section.

A filter design using the insertion loss method gives as a result a circuit consisting of lumped elements. At microwave frequencies, distributed elements are used instead of lumped ones as already discussed in Chapter 4. To realize distributed elements corresponding to the desired lumped elements, we use transmission line sections and aid the design with Richards' transformation, the Kuroda identities, as well as the impedance and admittance inverters.

7.2.1 Insertion Loss Method

In the insertion loss method, the filter design and synthesis is started by choosing the desired frequency response. This is followed by calculation of the normalized (in terms of frequency and impedance) component values for a lowpass filter prototype. These normalized component values can also be obtained from tables presented in the literature [6]. Then the normalized filter is converted to the desired frequency band and impedance level.

The insertion loss of a filter containing only reactive elements is obtained from its reflection coefficient as

$$L = \frac{1}{1 - |\rho(\omega)|^2} \tag{7.34}$$

The power reflection coefficient $|\rho(\omega)|^2$ of all realizable linear, passive circuits can be expressed as a polynomial of ω^2, that is, it is an even function of ω. It follows from this fact that the insertion loss of (7.34) can always be written as [3, 7]

$$L = 1 + \frac{P(\omega^2)}{Q^2(\omega)} \tag{7.35}$$

where P is a polynomial of ω^2 and Q is a polynomial of ω.

The most frequently used filter responses are the maximally flat and Chebyshev responses. In the following we study these filter responses in more detail.

Maximally Flat Response   The maximally flat response is also called the *binomial* or *Butterworth response*. It provides the flattest possible passband for a given order of the filter, that is, in practice for a given number of reactive elements. The insertion loss for the lowpass filter prototype is

$$L = 1 + k^2 \left(\frac{\omega}{\omega_c} \right)^{2N} \tag{7.36}$$

where N is the order of the filter and ω_c is its cutoff (angular) frequency. Note that here $Q^2(\omega) = 1$. The passband is from 0 to ω_c, and at ω_c the insertion loss is $L = 1 + k^2$. Most often the band edge is chosen to be the 3-dB point, and then $k = 1$. At frequencies well above the cutoff frequency ($\omega \gg \omega_c$) the insertion loss is $L \approx k^2(\omega/\omega_c)^{2N}$ and, thus, it increases $20N$ dB per decade.

Chebyshev Response   The Chebyshev response is often also called the *equal-ripple response*. The insertion loss is

$$L = 1 + k^2 T_N^2 \left(\frac{\omega}{\omega_c} \right) \tag{7.37}$$

where T_N is the Nth order Chebyshev polynomial, which can also be written as

$$T_N \left(\frac{\omega}{\omega_c} \right) = \cos \left[N \arccos \left(\frac{\omega}{\omega_c} \right) \right] \tag{7.38}$$

when $0 \le \omega/\omega_c \le 1$, and

$$T_N \left(\frac{\omega}{\omega_c} \right) = \cosh \left[N \, \mathrm{arcosh} \left(\frac{\omega}{\omega_c} \right) \right] \tag{7.39}$$

when $\omega/\omega_c \geq 1$. In the passband, L varies between values 1 and $1 + k^2$. At $\omega = 0$ the insertion loss is $L = 1$ if N is odd, and $L = 1 + k^2$, if N is even. When $\omega \gg \omega_c$, $L \approx k^2 (2\omega/\omega_c)^{2N}/4$, which is to say, the insertion loss increases $20N$ dB per decade, as is also the case with a maximally flat response. The insertion loss is, however, $2^{2N}/4$ times larger than that of a maximally flat response of the same order. In Figure 7.11 these responses are compared to each other.

Other important filter responses are the elliptic amplitude response and the linear phase response. The insertion loss of the maximally flat and Chebyshev responses increases monotonically in the stopband. In some applications a given minimum stopband insertion loss is adequate but a sharper cutoff response is desired. In such a case an elliptic filter is a good choice [8]. In some other applications (e.g., in multiplexers) a phase response as linear as possible is desired. Then a linear phase filter is the correct choice. However, a good phase response and a sharp cutoff response are incompatible requirements, so in designing a filter for a good phase response one must compromise with the amplitude response.

A normalized lowpass filter consists of shunt (parallel) capacitors and series inductors g_k. The generator source impedance is $g_0 = 1\Omega$ or the source admittance is $g_0 = 1S$, depending on whether the filter prototype starts with a shunt capacitor or with a series inductor, respectively, and the cutoff

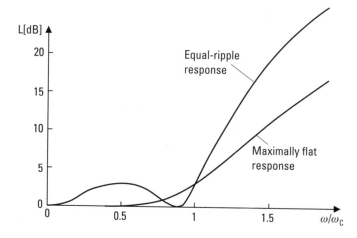

Figure 7.11 Maximally flat and Chebyshev (equal-ripple) responses of a lowpass filter ($N = 3$, $k = 1$).

frequency is $\omega_c = 1$. The order N of the filter is the number of reactive elements in the filter. As already discussed, the first element may be a shunt element, as in Figure 7.12(a), or a series element, as in Figure 7.12(b). The response in both cases is the same. The element g_{N+1} is the load resistance if g_N is a shunt capacitor, and the load conductance if g_N is a series inductor.

With the equivalent circuits presented in Figure 7.12, it is possible to calculate the component values that provide a given response. For the maximally flat response the prototype component values are $g_0 = 1$, $g_{N+1} = 1$, and

$$g_k = 2 \sin \left[\frac{(2k - 1)\pi}{2N} \right] \tag{7.40}$$

where $k = 1 \ldots N$. For the Chebyshev response, calculation of the component values is more difficult, so we omit it here. Tables 7.1 through 7.3 represent element values for maximally flat and Chebyshev (equal ripple) lowpass filter prototypes.

After the lowpass filter prototype design is completed, the circuit designed is converted to the correct frequency and correct impedance level.

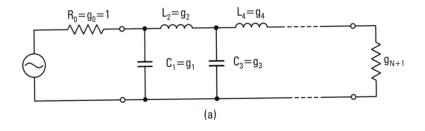

(a)

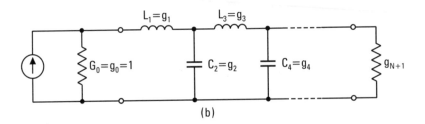

(b)

Figure 7.12 Lowpass filter prototypes: beginning with (a) a parallel element, and (b) a series element.

Table 7.1

Element Values for the Maximally Flat Lowpass Filter Prototype

$(g_0 = 1, \; \omega_c = 1)$

N	g_1	g_2	g_3	g_4	g_5	g_6	g_7
1	2.0000	1.0000					
2	1.4142	1.4142	1.0000				
3	1.0000	2.0000	1.0000	1.0000			
4	0.7654	1.8478	1.8478	0.7654	1.0000		
5	0.6180	1.6180	2.0000	1.6180	0.6168	1.0000	
6	0.5176	1.4142	1.9318	1.9318	1.4142	0.5176	1.0000

Source: [6].

Table 7.2

Element Values for a Chebyshev Lowpass Filter Prototype

$(g_0 = 1, \; \omega_c = 1, \text{ ripple } 0.5 \text{ dB})$

N	g_1	g_2	g_3	g_4	g_5	g_6	g_7
1	0.6986	1.0000					
2	1.4029	0.7071	1.9841				
3	1.5963	1.0967	1.5963	1.0000			
4	1.6703	1.1926	2.3661	0.8419	1.9841		
5	1.7058	1.2296	2.5408	1.2296	1.7058	1.0000	
6	1.7254	1.2479	2.6064	1.3137	2.4758	0.8696	1.9841

Source: [6].

Table 7.3

Element Values for a Chebyshev Lowpass Filter Prototype

$(g_0 = 1, \; \omega_c = 1, \text{ ripple } 3.0 \text{ dB})$

N	g_1	g_2	g_3	g_4	g_5	g_6	g_7
1	1.9953	1.0000					
2	3.1013	0.5339	5.8095				
3	3.3487	0.7117	3.3487	1.0000			
4	3.4389	0.7483	4.3471	0.5920	5.8095		
5	3.4817	0.7618	4.5381	0.7618	3.4817	1.0000	
6	3.5045	0.7685	4.6061	0.7929	4.4641	0.6033	5.8095

Source: [6].

If the generator resistance is R_0, the scaled element values (symbols with prime) are

$$L'_k = R_0 L_k \tag{7.41}$$

$$C'_k = C_k/R_0 \tag{7.42}$$

$$R'_L = R_0 R_L \tag{7.43}$$

where L_k, C_k, and R_L are the prototype values g_k and g_{N+1}. Figure 7.13 shows the scaling of the cutoff frequency from 1 to ω_c, and the transformations to a highpass, bandpass, and bandstop filter. In a bandpass filter, an LC series circuit corresponds to a series inductor of the lowpass prototype, and an LC parallel circuit corresponds to a shunt capacitor of the lowpass prototype. On the other hand, in a bandstop filter, an LC parallel circuit corresponds to a series inductor, and an LC series circuit corresponds to a shunt capacitor of the lowpass prototype. In the equations for Figure 7.13, $\omega_0 = \sqrt{\omega_1 \omega_2}$, $\Delta = (\omega_2 - \omega_1)/\omega_0$, and ω_1 and ω_2 are the limits of the filter frequency band.

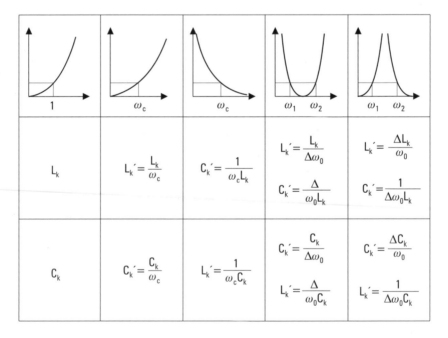

Figure 7.13 Frequency scaling and transformations of a lowpass filter prototype, $\omega_0 = \sqrt{\omega_1 \omega_2}$, $\Delta = (\omega_2 - \omega_1)/\omega_0$.

The insertion-loss frequency response of a lowpass filter provides a frequency response of a highpass filter, when in (7.36) and (7.37) ω/ω_c is replaced with ω_c/ω. The frequency response of a bandpass filter is obtained by replacing ω/ω_c with the term $(\omega/\omega_0 - \omega_0/\omega)/\Delta$, and that of a bandstop filter by replacing ω/ω_c with the term $\Delta/(\omega/\omega_0 - \omega_0/\omega)$.

7.2.2 Design of Microwave Filters

At microwave frequencies we have two major problems in realizing the synthesized filters. First, good lumped elements do not exist; instead we must use distributed elements. The frequency behavior of the distributed elements is more complicated than that of the lumped ideal ones, which makes the filter synthesis difficult. However, design of a narrow-band filter is easy, because over a narrow bandwidth many distributed elements may be modeled by ideal inductors and capacitors. Second, the filter elements should be physically close to each other (in wavelength scale), which is often impossible in practice. Therefore, transmission line sections must be used to separate the filter elements.

Richards' transformation is used to transform the lumped elements into sections of transmission lines. Richards' transformation [9]

$$\Omega = \tan \beta l = \tan (\omega l/v_p) \tag{7.44}$$

maps the ω plane to the Ω plane. By replacing ω with Ω, we can write the reactance of an inductor and the susceptance of a capacitor, respectively, as

$$jX_L = j\Omega L = jL \tan \beta l \tag{7.45}$$

$$jB_C = j\Omega C = jC \tan \beta l \tag{7.46}$$

This means that an inductor can be replaced with a short-circuited stub having an electrical length of βl and a characteristic impedance of L. Accordingly, a capacitor can be replaced with an open-circuited stub having an electrical length of βl and a characteristic impedance of $1/C$. The cutoff frequency of the transformed filter is the same as that of the prototype ($\omega_c = 1$), if $\Omega = 1 = \tan \beta l$, or $l = \lambda_g/8$. At frequencies where ω differs a lot from ω_c, the response of the transformed filter differs considerably from the response of the prototype. The response is periodic, repeating every $4\omega_c$.

With the aid of the Kuroda identities [5, 10, 11] we can separate the transmission line stubs physically from each other, transform the series stubs into parallel stubs (or vice versa), and also transform characteristic impedances to a more easily realizable level. Figure 7.14 shows the four Kuroda identities, where an inductance represents a short-circuited stub, a capacitance represents an open-circuited stub, and a box represents a transmission line with a characteristic impedance marked in the box. All stubs are of the same length—for example, $\lambda_g/8$ at the angular frequency of ω_c—and $n^2 = 1 + Z_2/Z_1$.

Example 7.2

Design a lowpass microstrip filter with the following characteristics: cutoff frequency of 3 GHz, Chebyshev response with $N = 3$, ripple of 0.5 dB, and filter impedance of 50Ω.

Solution

The element values for the prototype filter are $g_0 = G_0 = 1$, $g_1 = L_1 = 1.5963$, $g_2 = C_2 = 1.0967$, $g_3 = L_3 = 1.5963$, and $g_4 = G_L = 1$; see Table 7.2 and Figure 7.15(a). Using Richards' transformation, we can transform the inductances into series stubs and the capacitance into a parallel stub, as shown in Figure 7.15(b). The length of all stubs is $\lambda_g/8$ at 3 GHz. Because

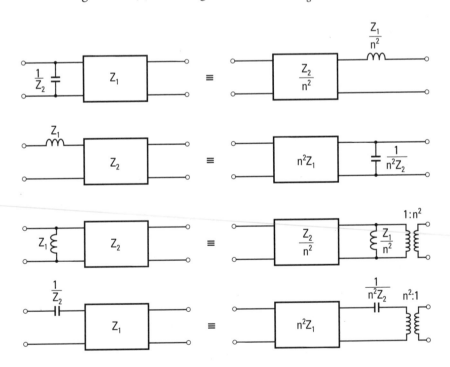

Figure 7.14 The four Kuroda identities.

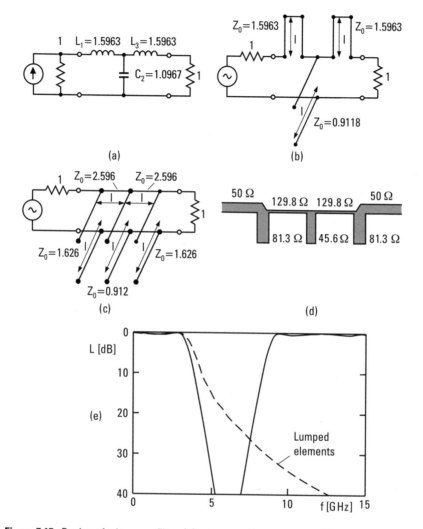

Figure 7.15 Design of a lowpass filter: (a) a lowpass filter prototype; (b) lumped inductors and capacitors converted to transmission line stubs ($l = \lambda_g/8$ at 3 GHz) using Richards' transformation; (c) series stubs transformed to parallel stubs using a Kuroda identity; (d) microstrip layout of the filter; and (e) calculated frequency response.

the series stubs cannot be realized with microstrip lines, we transform them into parallel stubs using a Kuroda identity. In order to be able to do that, we first add a transmission line section with a length of $\lambda_g/8$ and a characteristic impedance of $Z_0 = 1$ into both ends of the filter. These sections do not affect the filter response because the generator and load are matched to these lines. The second Kuroda identity of Figure 7.14, with $Z_1 = 1.5963$, $Z_2 = 1$, $n^2 = 1 + Z_2/Z_1 = 1.6264$, $n^2Z_1 = 2.596$, and $1/(n^2Z_2) = 0.615$, is then used for both ends of the filter. The result is shown in Figure 7.15(c). Finally, the impedances are scaled by multiplying by 50Ω, and the line lengths are calculated to be $\lambda_g/8$ at 3 GHz. The stub characteristic impedances are $50n^2Z_2 = 81.3\Omega$, $50/\tilde{C}_2 = 45.6\Omega$, and 81.3Ω, and the transmission line sections between the stubs have a characteristic impedance of $50n^2Z_1 = 129.8\Omega$. In order to find the exact line lengths and widths we should know the characteristics of the substrate and use (3.85) through (3.93). However, a schematic layout is presented in Figure 7.15(d), and its calculated frequency response is presented in Figure 7.15(e). When this response is compared with that of a filter made of lumped elements, we observe that in the passband the responses are nearly equal, but above the cutoff frequency the insertion loss of the microstrip filter increases more quickly and the response has another passband at 12 GHz.

As in the preceding example, in most filters we want to use only parallel (or series) elements. In the microwave region we often prefer parallel stubs. In addition to the Kuroda identities, this transformation can also be done using impedance or admittance inverters. The impedance inverters are also called the K-inverters and the admittance inverters the J-inverters. For example, an ideal quarter-wave transformer is both a K- and a J-inverter. It transforms a load impedance Z_L into an impedance $Z_{in} = K^2/Z_L$ or a load admittance Y_L into an admittance $Y_{in} = J^2/Y_L$. Here K is the characteristic impedance and J the characteristic admittance of the transformer. A quarter-wave transformer, however, behaves approximately as an ideal inverter only over a narrow bandwidth, and therefore this method is suitable only for narrow-band filters. Figure 7.16 shows how a bandpass filter is transformed into a filter circuit consisting only of either series or parallel resonators. The characteristic impedance values of the impedance and admittance inverters are presented in Table 7.4.

R_{aG}, R_{aL}, L_{ak}, and C_{ak} can be chosen freely, as long as the resonance frequency of the resonant circuits is the same as the filter center frequency or $\omega_0 = 1/\sqrt{L_{ak}C_{ak}}$ and the impedance values of the inverters are calculated according to Table 7.4. We may also choose a value 1 for R_{aG} and R_{aL}, as well as for the inverters, and then calculate values for L_{ak} and C_{ak} starting from one end of the filter. The LC parallel or series resonant circuits can be realized, for example, with open- and short-circuited transmission line stubs with a length of $\lambda_g/4$ or its multiple (see also Section 7.1.4). The characteristic impedance of a short-circuited stub with a length of $\lambda_g/4$ must

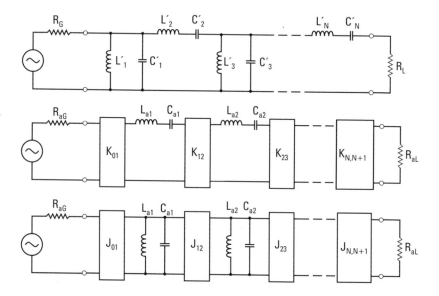

Figure 7.16 A bandpass filter, and the same filter transformed using impedance and admittance inverters.

Table 7.4
Characteristics of the Impedance and Admittance Inverters ($k = 1 \ldots N - 1$)

	k/N odd	k/N even
K_{01}	$(L'_1 R_{aG}/C_{a1} R_G)^{1/2}$	$(L' R_{aG}/C_{a1} R_G)^{1/2}$
$K_{k,k+1}$	$(L_{ak} L_{ak+1}/C'_k L'_{k+1})^{1/2}$	$(L_{ak} L_{ak+1}/L'_k C'_{k+1})^{1/2}$
$K_{N,N+1}$	$(L_{aN} R_{aL}/C'_N R_L)^{1/2}$	$(L_{aN} R_{aL} R_L/L'_N)^{1/2}$
J_{01}	$(C_{a1}/C'_1 R_{aG} R_G)^{1/2}$	$(C_{a1}/C'_1 R_{aG} R_G)^{1/2}$
$J_{k,k+1}$	$(C_{ak} C_{ak+1}/C'_k L'_{k+1})^{1/2}$	$(C_{ak} C_{ak+1}/L'_k C'_{k+1})^{1/2}$
$J_{N,N+1}$	$(C_{aN}/C'_N R_{aL} R_L)^{1/2}$	$(C_{aN} R_L/L'_N R_{aL})^{1/2}$

be $Z_0 = (\pi/4)\sqrt{L_{ak}/C_{ak}}$, which may be difficult to realize because of its low value.

Example 7.3

Design a bandpass filter with the following specifications: maximally flat response with $N = 3$, frequency range from 950 to 1,050 MHz, filter impedance of 50Ω.

Solution

Now f_1 = 950 MHz, f_2 = 1,050 MHz, and f_0 = 998.7 MHz. From Table 7.1 we can read the element values for the lowpass filter prototype: g_0 = R_G = 1, $g_1 = C_1 = 1$, $g_2 = L_2 = 2$, $g_3 = C_3 = 1$, $g_4 = R_L = 1$. Let us transform the lowpass prototype into a bandpass filter using the equations presented in Figure 7.13: $C_1' = C_1/\Delta\omega_0 = C_1/(\omega_2 - \omega_1) = 1.592 \times 10^{-9}$ $= C_3'$, $L_2' = L_2/(\omega_2 - \omega_1) = 3.183 \times 10^{-9}$. L_1', C_2', and L_3' are obtained from condition $L_k'C_k' = 1/\omega_0^2$. L_2' and C_2' form a series resonant circuit in series. Let us transform this into a shunt element using a J-inverter. We can choose $R_{aG} = 1$ and $J = 1$. From Table 7.4 we obtain $C_{a1} = C_1'$, $C_{a2} = L_2'$, $C_{a3} = C_3'$, and $R_{aL} = 1$. The parallel resonant circuits can be realized with short-circuited stubs with a length of $\lambda_g/4$. From equation $z_k = (\pi/4)\sqrt{L_{ak}/C_{ak}} = \pi/(4\omega_0 C_{ak})$ we obtain the normalized characteristic impedances of the lines: $z_1 = z_3 = 0.079$ and $z_2 = 0.039$. The characteristic impedances of the short-circuited parallel stubs are $Z_1 = Z_3 = 4.0\Omega$ and $Z_2 = 2.0\Omega$. Between these stubs there are inverters with a 50-Ω characteristic impedance and a $\lambda_g/4$ length. The short-circuited stubs may also be $3\lambda_g/4$ long and then the characteristic impedances are three times these values. However, they are still extremely hard to realize and the response differs even more from the response obtained with a filter formed with lumped elements.

7.2.3 Practical Microwave Filters

A large number of different possible structures can be used to realize a synthesized filter. In the following we briefly describe some commonly used filter structures. Other filters and their design rules are presented in the literature [6].

A simple lowpass filter can be realized by coupling short transmission line sections in series, with alternating low and high characteristic impedances. A short (electrical length $\beta l < \pi/4$) line with a high characteristic impedance Z_0 corresponds approximately to a series reactance of

$$X \approx Z_0 \beta l \qquad (7.47)$$

Accordingly, a short line with a low characteristic impedance corresponds to a parallel susceptance of

$$B \approx \beta l/Z_0 \qquad (7.48)$$

From the element values of the prototype filter we can calculate the required electrical lengths of the lines. The ratio of the high and low impedance should be as high as possible. The longer the line sections, the further from the ideal the response will be. Usually there are also passbands at higher frequencies. Figure 7.17 shows a microstrip layout of such a stepped-impedance filter with six line sections. One must also remember that an abrupt change in the microstrip line width causes a fringing capacitance, which must be taken into account in determining the lengths of the sections.

The bandpass and bandstop filters consist of series and parallel resonant circuits. In the microwave region the resonators can be realized in various ways, and then filters can be constructed from them in a number of ways. Figure 7.18(a) shows a bandpass filter consisting of open-circuited $\lambda_g/2$ long microstrip lines that are side-coupled over a length of $\lambda_g/4$ to each other [12]. This structure is suitable for filters with a passband width less than 20%. Figure 7.18(b) shows a microstrip bandpass filter consisting of end-coupled $\lambda_g/2$ resonators. The small gap between the line ends corresponds to a series capacitance. This capacitance is necessarily rather small due to

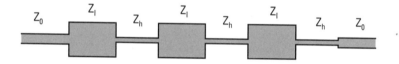

Figure 7.17 Microstrip layout of a stepped-impedance lowpass filter.

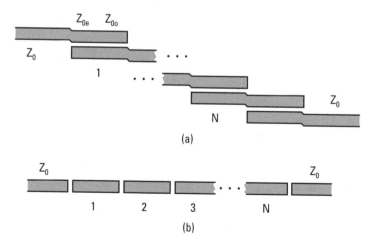

Figure 7.18 Microstrip layouts of bandpass filters: (a) side-coupled line resonators; and (b) capacitive-gap coupled (end-coupled) line resonators.

limitations in fabricating small gaps using microstrip techniques, and therefore the resulting bandwidth is rather small.

A comb-line filter consists of resonators with a length less than $\lambda_g/4$, which are grounded in one end and capacitively loaded in the other end. Figure 7.19(a) shows a comb-line filter consisting of rectangular or circular metal posts in a rectangular metal box. By adding a metal plate to the end of each capacitively loaded resonator, the end capacitance can be increased. A fine-tuning of the resonance frequency may be done with tuning screws.

An interdigital filter also consists of $\lambda_g/4$-long resonators, which are grounded in one end and open in the other end, as shown in Figure 7.19(b). This structure is suitable for a broad bandpass filter. The comb-line and interdigital filters can also be manufactured using microstrip medium.

Figure 7.20 shows a bandpass filter made in a metal waveguide from iris-coupled resonators. The resonator cavities are $\lambda_g/2$ long and separated by thin metal walls, each containing a rectangular or circular inductive iris. The resonance frequency of each individual resonator can be tuned with a tuning screw through the broad waveguide wall in the middle of the resonator.

A waveguide-cavity filter, a comb-line filter, or an interdigital filter can be made much smaller if the metal housing is filled with a ceramic of

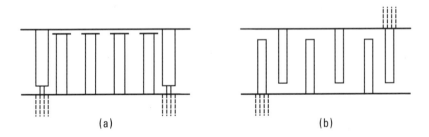

Figure 7.19 (a) Comb-line filter; and (b) interdigital filter.

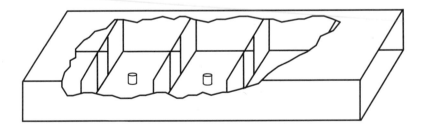

Figure 7.20 Bandpass filter made from waveguide cavities coupled through inductive irises.

high permittivity ($\epsilon_r = 10$ to 100). Such a ceramic interdigital filter at 5 GHz with a 100 MHz passband may have dimensions of $10 \times 4 \times 3$ mm^3, and its insertion loss is typically 1 dB. Ceramic filters are used also in mobile phones as duplex filters, with dimensions like $10 \times 5 \times 2$ mm^3, but in this application such dimensions are considered large, and the tendency is to move to using *surface acoustic wave* (SAW) or *bulk acoustic wave* (BAW) filters [13, 14].

A SAW filter is based on an acoustic wave propagating on the surface of a piezoelectric medium. The SAW filters are bandpass filters of a small size. The electric signal is transformed into an acoustic wave with an interdigital transducer and vice versa, as shown in Figure 7.21. The SAW filters are usable to frequencies over 2 GHz. A 2-GHz SAW filter chip has an area of 1×1 mm^2, but with the package it requires a somewhat larger area. Insertion loss is typically 2 dB to 3 dB. A BAW filter is even smaller and provides somewhat higher frequency selectivity because of higher Q compared to SAW.

Although the basic filter theory has been around for a long time, there are continuing advances in the synthesis methods. In particular, there are continuous technological advances in SAW and BAW filters, in MEMS tuning of micromechanical microwave filters, and in the more conventional filter structures where high-temperature superconductors are now successfully utilized.

Interdigital transducer

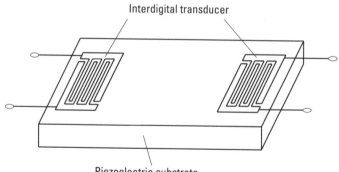

Piezoelectric substrate

Figure 7.21 SAW filter.

References

[1] Nguyen, C. T.-C., "Frequency-Selective MEMS for Miniaturized Low-Power Communication Devices," *IEEE Trans. Microwave Theory and Techniques,* Vol. 47, No. 8, 1999, pp. 1486–1503.

[2]   Ramo, S., J. Whinnery, and T. van Duzer, *Fields and Waves in Communication Electronics*, New York: John Wiley & Sons, 1965.

[3]   Collin, R. E., *Foundations for Microwave Engineering*, 2nd ed., New York: IEEE Press, 2001.

[4]   Kajfez, D., and P. Guillon, (eds.), *Dielectric Resonators*, Oxford, MS: Vector Fields, 1990.

[5]   Pozar, D. M., *Microwave Engineering*, 2nd ed., New York: John Wiley & Sons, 1998.

[6]   Matthaei, G. L., L. Young, and E. M. T. Jones, *Microwave Filters, Impedance-Matching Networks, and Coupling Structures*, Dedham, MA: Artech House, 1980.

[7]   Fano, R. M., and A. W. Lawson, "The Theory of Microwave Filters," G. L. Ragan, (ed.), *Microwave Transmission Circuits*, Radiation Laboratory Series, New York: McGraw-Hill, 1948.

[8]   Zverev, A. I., *Handbook of Filter Synthesis*, New York: John Wiley & Sons, 1967.

[9]   Richards, P. I., "Resistor-Transmission-Line Networks," *Proc. IRE*, Vol. 36, February 1948, pp. 217–220.

[10]   Ozaki, H., and J. Ishii, "Synthesis of a Class of Stripline Filters," *IRE Trans. on Circuit Theory*, Vol. CT-5, June 1958, pp. 104–109.

[11]   Matsumoto, A., *Microwave Filters and Circuits*, New York: Academic Press, 1970.

[12]   Cohn, S. B., "Parallel-Coupled Transmission-Line-Resonator Filter," *IRE Trans. on Microwave Theory and Techniques*, Vol. 6, April 1958, pp. 223–231.

[13]   Campbell, C. K., "Application of Surface Acoustic and Shallow Bulk Acoustic Wave Devices," *Proc. IEEE*, Vol. 77, No. 10, 1989, pp. 1453–1484.

[14]   Special Issue on Modeling, Optimization, and Design of Surface and Bulk Acoustic Wave Devices, *IEEE Trans. on Ultrasonics, Ferroelectrics, and Frequency Control*, Vol. 48, No. 5, 2001, pp. 1161–1479.

8

Circuits Based on Semiconductor Devices

In Section 1.4 we discussed early development of the radio. At first both the transmitter and receiver were based on a spark gap. Then came a coherer as a detector, and an electron tube was invented in 1904. Nowadays semiconductor devices have replaced electron tubes in most applications.

8.1 From Electron Tubes to Semiconductor Devices

Electron tubes came into wide use in radio engineering in the 1910s. They were used as oscillators, modulators, amplifiers, mixers, and detectors. A suitable electron tube was developed for different applications: diode, triode, tetrode, pentode, hexode, heptode, and octode. The names of the different electron tubes are based on the number of electrodes: a diode has only a cathode and an anode; a triode has in addition one grid, which can be used to control the current from the anode to the cathode by a small applied voltage the same way as is done today in the field-effect transistor (see Section 8.2.2); a tetrode has two grids; and so on. Although the transistor was invented in 1948 and a semiconductor diode earlier, electron tubes are still in use. They are used as transmitter tubes in LF, MF, HF, and VHF radio broadcasting stations, and in some military electronics because of their high tolerance for strong electromagnetic pulses.

Currently, in most radio applications we use semiconductor devices for signal generation, amplification, detection, and so on. The advantages of the semiconductor devices over the electron tubes are their small size, low weight, low supply voltage, and long lifetime.

Circuits based on semiconductor devices may be either active or passive. A circuit is said to be active if it generates RF power from dc power (oscillator) or it amplifies an RF signal (amplifier). In a broader sense, we can consider some other circuits as active: A mixer, frequency multiplier, detector, modulator, and demodulator are all active because they convert power from one frequency to another. However, not all circuits containing semiconductor devices, that is, diodes and transistors, are active. They are also used to realize switches, attenuators, phase shifters, and loads needed in impedance matching (e.g., active matching in MMICs). Figure 8.1 presents standardized drawing symbols of some circuits based on semiconductor components.

8.2 Important Semiconductor Devices

Semiconductor technology has advanced rapidly during the last decades. Several types of diodes and transistors are available for RF and microwave applications. The fastest transistors are usable at frequencies over 200 GHz and the fastest diodes at frequencies over 3 THz. The structures and operation principles of the most important diodes and transistors are treated in this section. A more detailed analysis of their physics can be found in the literature [1–3].

8.2.1 Diodes

The simplest semiconductor diode is the *p-n* diode shown in Figure 8.2(a). It is based on the interface of *p*- and *n*-type semiconductors. The semiconductor is most often silicon (Si), germanium (Ge), or gallium arsenide (GaAs).

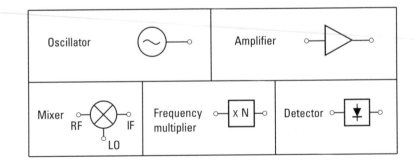

Figure 8.1 Drawing symbols for circuits based on semiconductor devices.

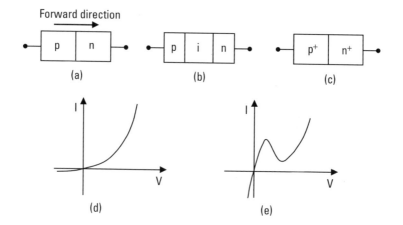

Figure 8.2 (a) *p-n* diode; (b) *p-i-n* diode; (c) tunnel diode; (d) *I–V* characteristic of a *p-n* diode; and (e) *I–V* characteristic of a tunnel diode.

In a *p-n* junction, current is carried by minority carriers, that is, by holes injected into the *n*-side and by electrons injected into the *p*-side. In the forward direction the current increases exponentially as the applied voltage increases as shown in Figure 8.2(d). In the reverse direction only a small saturation current flows. Because of the large diffusion capacitance due to the minority carriers, the use of the *p-n* diode is limited to low frequencies, a few hundred MHz at maximum. The *p-n* diode is used in rectifiers and detectors.

A reverse-biased *p-n* diode is used as a varactor, that is, as a voltage-dependent capacitor. It is used as an electrically controlled tuning element, but also in modulators, switches, frequency multipliers, and parametric amplifiers.

When an intrinsic (undoped) semiconductor layer is added in between the *p*- and *n*-regions, a *p-i-n* diode, shown in Figure 8.2(b), is formed. The intrinsic semiconductor layer decreases considerably the junction capacitance, and therefore the *p-i-n* diode is well suited to many microwave circuits. It is used in rectifiers, modulators, attenuators, switches, phase shifters, and limiters.

A tunnel diode is a *p-n* junction with both sides very heavily doped, as shown in Figure 8.2(c). The depletion region becomes very narrow and therefore allows a remarkable tunneling current at a low forward bias. Its *I–V* curve has a negative differential resistance region, as shown in Figure 8.2(e). The tunnel diode is well suited to oscillators and detectors.

In a forward-biased *p-i-n* diode, carriers are accumulated in the *i*-region and therefore the diffusion capacitance is high. However, this accumulated charge is suddenly released when the bias is reversed: A short reverse current pulse is generated. This extremely nonlinear behavior is utilized in the step-recovery diode, which is used in frequency multipliers and comb generators for producing frequencies of high harmonic number [4].

The most important diode suitable for microwave detectors, mixers, and frequency multipliers is the Schottky diode. It is an interface between an n-type semiconductor (Si or GaAs) and a metal (Au, Pt, or Ti). Minority carriers (holes) play a negligible role, and therefore a Schottky diode is very fast, that is, it can switch from a conducting state to a nonconducting state very quickly. GaAs-Schottky diodes are used up to 3 THz.

A Schottky diode can be contacted and packaged in many ways. In Figure 8.3(a) an unpackaged, whisker-contacted Schottky diode is shown. There are many small anodes on the surface of the GaAs chip; one of them is contacted to the embedding circuit with a sharp wire, a whisker. The planar Schottky diode shown in Figure 8.3(d) can be used as a flip-chip component on a microstrip circuit, it can be encapsulated as a beam-lead diode, or it can be integrated monolithically.

Figure 8.3(b) shows an equivalent circuit of a Schottky diode. It consists of a voltage-dependent junction resistance R_j, a voltage-dependent junction

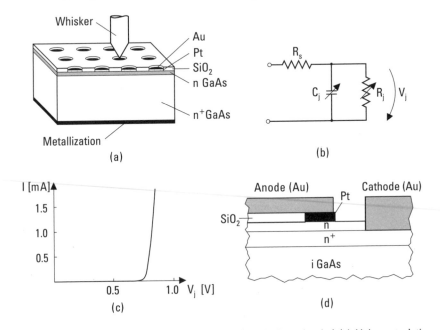

Figure 8.3 Schottky diode: (a) GaAs diode chip; (b) equivalent circuit; (c) I–V characteristic; and (d) planar diode.

capacitance C_j, and a series resistance R_s. When the Schottky diode is connected to a circuit, it always has a series inductance as well and may have an extra fringing capacitance which both decrease its performance.

The I–V characteristic shown in Figure 8.3(c) is exponential as

$$I(V_j) = I_s(e^{\alpha V_j} - 1) \tag{8.1}$$

$$\alpha = \frac{q}{\eta kT} = \frac{1}{V_0} \tag{8.2}$$

where I_s is the saturation current, q is the magnitude of the electron charge, η is the ideality factor, k is Boltzmann's constant, and T is the absolute temperature. The ideality factor of a good diode at room temperature is slightly above unity. The junction differential resistance is obtained from the I–V characteristic as

$$R_j = \left(\frac{dI}{dV_j}\right)^{-1} = \frac{1}{\alpha(I + I_s)} \approx \frac{V_0}{I} \tag{8.3}$$

The junction capacitance is also voltage dependent and behaves as

$$C_j(V_j) = \frac{C_{j0}}{(1 - V_j/\phi_i)^{\gamma}} \tag{8.4}$$

where C_{j0} is the junction capacitance at zero voltage, ϕ_i is the contact potential, and γ is a constant depending on the doping profile of the epitaxial layer. For a GaAs–Pt junction ϕ_i is about 1 V. If the doping profile is abrupt, we have $\gamma = 0.5$.

When a Schottky diode is used as a detector or mixer, its figure of merit is the cutoff frequency:

$$f_c = \frac{1}{2\pi R_s C_j} \tag{8.5}$$

The series resistance R_s is mainly due to the low mobility of electrons in the undepleted epitaxial layer; it is also called the spreading resistance. At the cutoff frequency, one half of the voltage applied over the diode is over the series resistance. The cutoff frequency should be much higher than the operating frequency ($f_c \geq 10f$). A Schottky varactor has basically the same structure and equivalent circuit as the mixer diode; its behavior is based on the voltage-dependent capacitance, and it is used in frequency multipliers.

In oscillators a device with negative resistance is needed. Besides the tunnel diode, a Gunn diode and an *impact ionization avalanche transit time* (IMPATT) diode have a negative resistance region in their *I–V* characteristics.

The Gunn diode, named for its inventor but also called a *transferred electron device* (TED), is not a rectifying diode but rather a piece of *n*-type bulk semiconductor. Its negative resistance is based on the properties of the energy band structure of the III–V semiconductors, such as GaAs or *indium phosphide* (InP). In these semiconductors, electrons with sufficiently high energy transfer from the main valley of the conduction band to a satellite valley, where their effective mass is higher and their mobility lower than in the main valley. Therefore, above a given electric field $E = E_T$ the average drift velocity of electrons decreases while E increases; in other words, the differential resistance of the semiconductor is negative. Figure 8.4 illustrates the energy band structure and current density versus electric field in *n*-type GaAs.

Figure 8.5(a) presents different structures of the IMPATT diode. When a sufficiently high reverse voltage is applied over the diode, an avalanche breakdown (electron-hole pairs are rapidly and increasingly created) occurs in the *p-n* interface, where the electric field is highest. For example, in a p^+-n-n^+ structure the holes go directly to the p^+-region but the electrons drift through the *n*-region (so-called drift region) to the n^+-contact. When an alternating voltage is applied over the diode in addition to the dc bias, the phase of the generated electron pulse is 90° behind the voltage phase. With a proper thickness of the *n*-layer, an additional phase shift of 90° occurs, due to the drift time. Then the current and voltage of the diode are

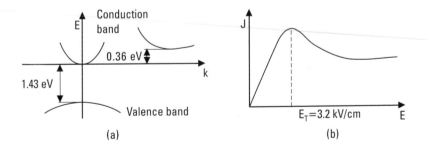

Figure 8.4 (a) Energy band structure and (b) current density versus electric field in *n*-type GaAs.

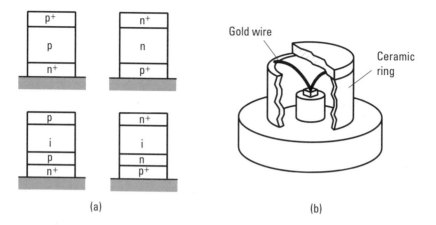

Figure 8.5 IMPATT diode: (a) different structures; and (b) encapsulated diode.

in opposite phase, that is, its resistance is negative. An IMPATT diode must be encapsulated so that the heat generated in the diode is effectively transferred away.

8.2.2 Transistors

The most common transistor in RF applications up to a few gigahertz is the bipolar transistor. In a bipolar transistor both electrons and holes act as current carriers. A bipolar transistor is usually made of silicon. Figure 8.6 shows an *n-p-n* type bipolar transistor. Between the emitter (E) and collector (C) there is a thin base (B) layer. In RF applications the transistor is usually in common-emitter connection, that is, the emitter is grounded. Proper bias voltages are applied to the base-emitter and collector-base junctions; then a small change in the base current, ΔI_B, causes a large change in the collector current, ΔI_C. The small-signal gain is

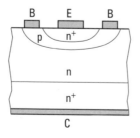

Figure 8.6 Bipolar transistor.

$$\beta = \frac{\Delta I_C}{\Delta I_B} \qquad (8.6)$$

Parasitic capacitances and resistances and the drift times of carriers limit the highest usable frequency of the bipolar transistor.

A *heterojunction bipolar transistor* (HBT) is a faster version of the bipolar transistor. Here *heterojunction* means an interface of two different semiconductors; for example, the emitter is of Si and the base of SiGe, or the emitter is of AlGaAs and the base of GaAs. Because of the heterojunction, the base can be doped very heavily, and therefore the base resistance is small and the transistor is operational at high frequencies.

Metal-oxide-semiconductor field-effect transistors (MOSFETs) and *metal-semiconductor field-effect transistors* (MESFETs) are field-effect transistors for RF and microwave applications. MOSFETs fabricated using *complementary metal-oxide-semiconductor* (CMOS) technology, commonly used for digital microcircuits, are applicable for analog RF circuits up to several gigahertz.

GaAs MESFETs are useful up to millimeter wavelengths. Figure 8.7 shows a cross section of a MESFET and its small-signal equivalent circuit. There is a thin n-type layer on an undoped substrate. This layer forms the transistor channel, where electrons act as carriers. On the surface of the channel layer there are two ohmic contacts, the source (S) and the drain (D), and between them a short gate (G) contact, which forms with the semiconductor a reverse-biased Schottky junction. As in the Schottky diode, there is a depletion layer in the channel under the gate; the width of the depletion layer depends on the gate voltage. Therefore, the gate voltage V_{GS} can be used to control the current between the source and drain, I_{DS}. The ratio of the changes in I_{DS} and V_{GS} with a constant V_{DS} is called the transconductance

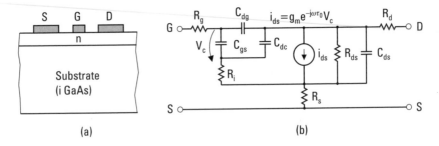

Figure 8.7 Metal-semiconductor field-effect transistor (MESFET): (a) structure; (b) equivalent circuit.

$$g_m = \frac{\partial I_{DS}}{\partial V_{GS}} \tag{8.7}$$

The frequency at which the short-circuit current gain is 1, is approximately

$$f_T \approx \frac{g_m}{2\pi C_{gs}} \approx \frac{v_s}{2\pi L} \tag{8.8}$$

where C_{gs} is the capacitance between the gate and source, v_s is the saturation velocity of carriers, and L is the gate length. The maximum oscillation frequency, or frequency at which the power gain is unity, is

$$f_{max} \approx \frac{f_T}{2} \sqrt{\frac{R_{ds}}{R_g + R_i + R_s}} \tag{8.9}$$

The cutoff frequency can be made high if the gate is made short. Typically L is below 1 μm.

A *high electron mobility transistor* (HEMT) or *heterojunction field-effect transistor* (HFET) is a MESFET based on a heterojunction. In the HEMT shown in Figure 8.8 an interface between n-type AlGaAs and undoped GaAs forms the heterojunction. At the interface, on the side of GaAs, a very thin potential well is formed, due to the mismatch of energy bands. The potential well is so thin that the electrons attracted by the lower potential form a two-dimensional electron gas in the well. Because the electrons drift in the undoped semiconductor, they are not experiencing collisions with impurity ions and therefore their mobility is higher than in a doped semiconductor. Thus, a HEMT is faster than a conventional MESFET. HEMTs made using InP technology are operational up to 200 GHz.

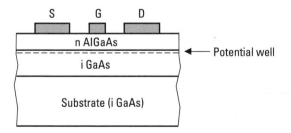

Figure 8.8 Structure of the HEMT.

8.3 Oscillators

An oscillator is a circuit that transfers dc power to RF power [5–8]. The generated RF signal may be sinusoidal or distorted because of containing harmonic components. Important characteristics of an oscillator are its frequency and tuning range, output power, frequency stability, and spectral purity.

An oscillator may be modeled either as a feedback circuit providing a nonzero output voltage for zero-input voltage or as a one-port circuit having negative resistance. In this text we use the latter concept. An active element having a negative resistance may be a diode or a potentially unstable transistor (more about the stability of a transistor in Section 8.4). Figure 8.9 shows a simplified equivalent circuit of an oscillator: A passive load impedance Z_L is connected to the input impedance Z_{in} of an active component. The impedance of the active element depends on both current and frequency, that is,

$$Z_{in}(I, f) = R_{in}(I, f) + jX_{in}(I, f) \qquad (8.10)$$

The load impedance depends on frequency:

$$Z_L(f) = R_L(f) + jX_L(f) \qquad (8.11)$$

Before an oscillation starts, the circuit must be in an unstable state, that is, $R_{in} + R_L < 0$. Because R_L is always positive, R_{in} must be negative. Then any disturbance or noise may cause oscillation at some frequency f. When the current increases due to oscillation, R_{in} must change to less

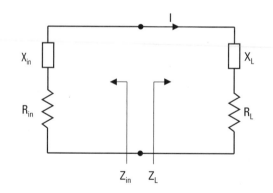

Figure 8.9 A simplified equivalent circuit of an oscillator.

negative. A properly designed oscillator settles down in a stable operation. Then, according to Kirchoff's law $(Z_{in} + Z_L)I = 0$, or

$$R_{in}(I_0, f_0) + R_L(f_0) = 0 \qquad (8.12)$$

$$X_{in}(I_0, f_0) + X_L(f_0) = 0 \qquad (8.13)$$

The final, stable oscillation frequency f_0 is usually different from the original frequency. In a stable condition, any disturbances of current or voltage are damped, and after a disturbance the oscillator rapidly returns into its stable state.

The load is a circuit with a high quality factor Q; it is for example an *LC* circuit, quartz crystal, cavity, YIG, or dielectric resonator. Then X_L changes fast as a function of frequency, and the reactance equation, (8.13), determines the oscillation frequency. In practice, R_L is nearly independent of frequency. The higher the Q, the more stable the oscillation state. The oscillation may also be stabilized by using injection locking or phase locking. In the injection locking, a weak signal from an accurate frequency standard is fed into the oscillator. In the phase locking, the output frequency is compared to an accurate signal derived from a frequency standard (see Section 11.1). The frequency standard is usually a crystal-controlled oscillator, the frequency of which may be further stabilized by controlling the temperature of the quartz crystal.

Suitable diodes having a potential negative resistance for an oscillator are Gunn, IMPATT, and tunnel diodes. Only a proper bias voltage is needed to produce a negative resistance. A transistor oscillator may be based on a bipolar transistor in the common-emitter connection, or on an FET in the common-gate connection. Other configurations are also possible. A negative resistance is realized by connecting to the input port of the transistor a load, which makes the transistor unstable. Then the reflection coefficient seen toward the transistor in the output port is greater than unity; that is, the real part of the impedance is negative. The instability may be increased with feedback.

Bipolar transistors are used in oscillators up to about 20 GHz. HBT operates at higher frequencies, up to 50 GHz. These both have 10 dB to 15 dB lower phase noise, that is, a cleaner spectrum near the oscillation frequency, than an FET oscillator has. MESFET is suitable for oscillators up to 100 GHz and HEMT to 200 GHz. The Gunn oscillator operates in the fundamental mode to about 100 GHz, and in harmonic mode up to 200 GHz. IMPATT oscillators are used even at 300 GHz. The spectrum of an IMPATT oscillator is rather noisy. The amplitude noise is especially strong; that is, the spectrum is noisy even far away from the oscillation frequency. Output powers available from semiconductor oscillators are presented in Figure 8.10. Tube oscillators provide much higher powers; for example, a klystron at 1 GHz or a gyrotron at 100 GHz may produce over 1 MW.

There are several alternative ways to tune the oscillation frequency. According to (8.13), the frequency f_0 depends on the reactance of both the active element and the load. Therefore the frequency can be tuned either mechanically or electrically. The resonance frequency of a cavity is tuned by changing its length, for example, by moving a short circuit in the end of the cavity. A Gunn oscillator may be tuned mechanically over an octave, and an IMPATT oscillator over ±10%. The resonance frequency of a dielectric resonator is tunable mechanically about ±2% by changing the distance of a metal plate or a screw above the resonator pill. With bias tuning the Gunn oscillator frequency changes about ±1%, and that of an IMPATT oscillator over ±5%. As mentioned before, a varactor is a voltage-dependent capacitor. With a varactor in the embedding circuit, a transistor oscillator may be tuned electrically about an octave. The varactor tuning is also often

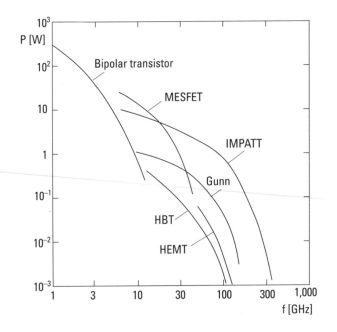

Figure 8.10 Output powers available from semiconductor oscillators.

used in oscillators stabilized with a DRO, but then the tuning range is small. A varactor tuning (Schottky varactor) is used up to 50 GHz. Such a voltage-tuned oscillator is often called a *voltage-controlled oscillator* (VCO).

Figure 8.11 shows a 5.43-GHz transistor oscillator on a microstrip. A bipolar transistor is in the common-collector connection. The base impedance is made to be in an unstable region. The frequency is determined by a DRO and may be tuned electrically about ±1 MHz by changing the dc bias of a varactor.

Signal generators, especially sweepers, often utilize transistor oscillators, the frequency of which is tuned using a *yttrium iron garnet* (YIG) resonator. The YIG material is ferrite. In a static magnetic field the YIG resonator has a resonance at microwave frequencies. The YIG resonators are spherical, having a diameter of 0.2 mm to 2 mm. The resonator is coupled to the embedding network with a current loop around the sphere, as shown in Figure 8.12. The unloaded Q is about 10,000. The resonance frequency depends linearly on the magnetic field strength, which in turn depends linearly on the dc current of the magnet coil. The frequency tuning range can be 2–3 octaves, making it very useful for sweep generators. The YIG resonators are used up to 50 GHz.

The electric frequency tuning of an oscillator is also utilized in phase locking, frequency modulation, and demodulation. *Frequency modulation* (FM) (see Section 11.3) may be realized by modulating the control voltage of a VCO. Demodulation of an FM signal can be made by phase locking the frequency of a VCO to the received signal. The VCO control voltage is then the demodulated FM signal.

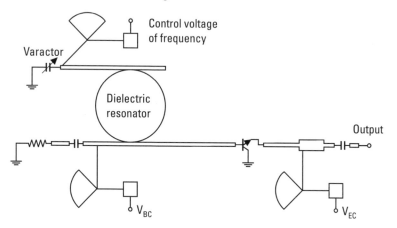

Figure 8.11 Microstrip layout of a transistor oscillator stabilized with a dielectric resonator and voltage tuned with a varactor.

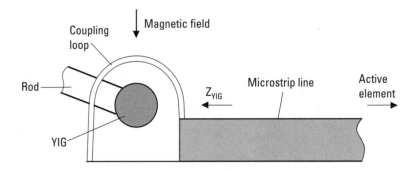

Figure 8.12 YIG resonator coupled to an oscillator circuit.

8.4 Amplifiers

Amplifiers based on semiconductor devices are of either transmission (trans-conductance) or reflection type. In transconductance type amplifiers, bipolar and field-effect transistors are used as active elements. Silicon bipolar transistors are applicable up to 10 GHz, HBTs to 50 GHz, GaAs-MESFETs to 100 GHz, and HEMTs to 200 GHz. Transistor amplifiers are used as *low-noise preamplifiers* (LNAs) in receivers, as *power amplifiers* (PAs) in transmitters, and as *intermediate frequency* (IF) amplifiers in both receivers and transmitters.

8.4.1 Design of Small-Signal and Low-Noise Amplifiers

In the following we study the design of a narrowband, small-signal amplifier (for more details, see [7–10]). The design of matching circuits may be based on the equivalent circuit of the transistor or its scattering parameters. We use the S-parameters as the starting point. Figure 8.13 presents a two-port

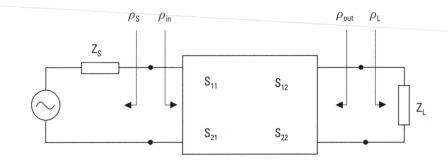

Figure 8.13 A two-port as an amplifier.

(a transistor), the S-parameters of which are determined in reference to the reference impedance Z_0 (characteristic impedance of the transmission line). The small-signal S-parameters of a transistor depend on frequency and operating point, that is, on bias voltages and currents. The manufacturer usually reports typical values of the S-parameters (in reference to 50Ω) versus frequency in a few operating points. The load impedance of the two-port is Z_L, and the impedance of the feeding generator is Z_S. The reflection coefficients of the terminations in the input and output are

$$\rho_S = \frac{Z_S - Z_0}{Z_S + Z_0} \tag{8.14}$$

$$\rho_L = \frac{Z_L - Z_0}{Z_L + Z_0} \tag{8.15}$$

The input reflection coefficient seen toward the two-port can be presented using the normalized voltage waves as

$$\rho_{in} = \frac{b_1}{a_1} \tag{8.16}$$

Accordingly, in the output we have

$$\rho_L = \frac{a_2}{b_2} \tag{8.17}$$

We can solve ρ_{in} using a signal flow graph, as we did in Section 5.3; see (5.24):

$$\rho_{in} = S_{11} + \frac{S_{21}S_{12}\rho_L}{1 - \rho_L S_{22}} = \frac{S_{11} - \rho_L \Delta}{1 - \rho_L S_{22}} \tag{8.18}$$

where

$$\Delta = S_{11}S_{22} - S_{12}S_{21} \tag{8.19}$$

The output reflection coefficient seen toward the two-port is

$$\rho_{out} = \frac{S_{22} - \rho_S \Delta}{1 - \rho_S S_{11}} \tag{8.20}$$

A transistor amplifier provides the maximum available power gain $G_{a,max}$ when both ports are conjugately matched. This condition can be written as

$$\rho_{in} = \rho_S^* \text{ and } \rho_{out} = \rho_L^* \tag{8.21}$$

By substituting these into (8.18) and (8.20) we obtain generator and load reflection coefficients (in reference to $50\,\Omega$) ρ_{SM} and ρ_{LM}, respectively, that both the input and output are simultaneously matched:

$$\rho_{SM} = \frac{B_1 \mp \sqrt{B_1^2 - 4|C_1|^2}}{2C_1} \tag{8.22}$$

$$\rho_{LM} = \frac{B_2 \mp \sqrt{B_2^2 - 4|C_2|^2}}{2C_2} \tag{8.23}$$

where

$$B_1 = 1 + |S_{11}|^2 - |S_{22}|^2 - |\Delta|^2 \tag{8.24}$$

$$B_2 = 1 - |S_{11}|^2 + |S_{22}|^2 - |\Delta|^2 \tag{8.25}$$

$$C_1 = S_{11} - \Delta S_{22}^* \tag{8.26}$$

$$C_2 = S_{22} - \Delta S_{11}^* \tag{8.27}$$

If $B_1 > 0$ and $|B_1/2C_1| > 1$, one must select the negative sign in front of the square root in (8.22) in order to have $|\rho_{SM}| < 1$, that is, to be able to realize the input matching circuit using passive elements. Accordingly, for the output, if $B_2 > 0$ and $|B_2/2C_2| > 1$, one must select the negative sign in (8.23). For a unilateral transistor ($S_{12} = 0$), $\rho_{SM} = S_{11}^*$ and $\rho_{LM} = S_{22}^*$.

The maximum available power gain can be presented in the following form:

$$G_{a,max} = \frac{|S_{21}|}{|S_{12}|}\left(K - \sqrt{K^2 - 1}\right) \tag{8.28}$$

where

$$K = \frac{1 - |S_{11}|^2 - |S_{22}|^2 + |\Delta|^2}{2|S_{12}S_{21}|} \qquad (8.29)$$

The use of (8.28) requires that $K \geq 1$; otherwise $G_{a,max}$ becomes complex.

Generally, the matching circuit provides the maximum available power gain only at the design frequency. When the frequency moves away from the design frequency, gain decreases rapidly. The bandwidth can be made wider if we are satisfied with a gain lower than $G_{a,max}$. In that case a small mismatch is purposely designed in both the input and output. Design is aided by using constant gain circles drawn on the Smith chart.

A transistor amplifier is not necessarily stable. Oscillation is possible if the real part of the input or output impedance is negative. This means that $|\rho_{in}| > 1$ or $|\rho_{out}| > 1$. If $|\rho_{in}| < 1$ and $|\rho_{out}| < 1$ with all generator and load impedance values, the amplifier is unconditionally stable. In other cases the amplifier is potentially unstable. From conditions $|\rho_{in}| = 1$ or $|\rho_{out}| = 1$ we can calculate boundaries for the stable regions of input and output impedances. On the Smith chart these boundaries are circles, as shown in Figure 8.14. The output impedance stability circle is defined by the center point c_L and radius r_L as

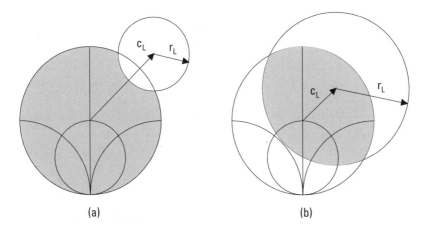

(a)   (b)

Figure 8.14 Output stability circles on the Smith chart. Shaded areas are stable when $|S_{11}| < 1$. The center point of the Smith chart is (a) outside the stability circle, and (b) inside the circle.

$$c_L = \frac{(S_{22} - \Delta S_{11}^*)^*}{|S_{22}|^2 - |\Delta|^2} \tag{8.30}$$

$$r_L = \left| \frac{S_{12} S_{21}}{|S_{22}|^2 - |\Delta|^2} \right| \tag{8.31}$$

Either the inside or outside of the stability circle presents the stable region. If $|S_{11}| < 1$, the center point of the Smith chart is in the stable region. If, however, $|S_{11}| > 1$, the Smith chart center point is in the unstable region. The center point c_S and radius r_S of the input stability circle are obtained by replacing S_{22} with S_{11} and vice versa in (8.30) and (8.31). It can be proven that the necessary and sufficient conditions for the unconditional stability are $K > 1$ and $|\Delta| < 1$. It may be worth checking that ρ_S and ρ_L are in the stable region not only at the operating frequency but also at other frequencies.

In addition to gain and stability, a third important characteristic of an LNA is its noise factor F (for more detail see Section 11.2). A transistor has four noise parameters: minimum noise factor F_{min}, magnitude and phase of optimum input reflection coefficient ρ_{opt} ($F = F_{min}$, when $\rho_S = \rho_{opt}$), and equivalent noise resistance R_n [11]. The noise factor can be presented as a function of the generator admittance $Y_S = 1/Z_S$ as

$$F = F_{min} + \frac{R_n}{G_S} |Y_S - Y_{opt}|^2 \tag{8.32}$$

where G_S is the real part of Y_S and Y_{opt} is the admittance corresponding to ρ_{opt}. The load impedance Z_L affects the gain but not the noise factor. In general, it is not possible to obtain the minimum noise factor and maximum gain simultaneously, but one must make a compromise. This can be helped by using constant noise circles calculated from (8.32) on the Smith chart, together with constant gain circles as shown Figure 8.15.

In addition to the design of matching circuits according to proper ρ_S and ρ_L, the completion of the design work requires also design of circuits for bias voltages. Figure 8.16 shows an example of a practical realization: a 22-GHz HEMT amplifier. The low-impedance microstrip line sections in the input and output provide ρ_S for the minimum noise factor and ρ_L for the conjugate match of output (in order to optimize gain). Bias voltages to the gate and drain are supplied through high-impedance lines. At a distance of $\lambda/4$ from the feed point there is a radial stub short circuit in each of

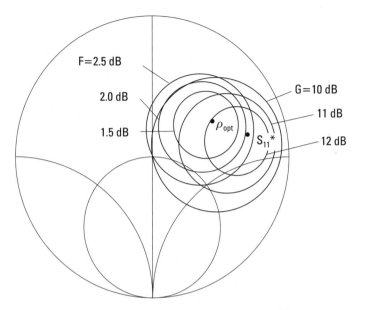

Figure 8.15 Constant gain and noise circles of an amplifier on the Smith chart. *F* and *G* versus Z_S when the output is matched.

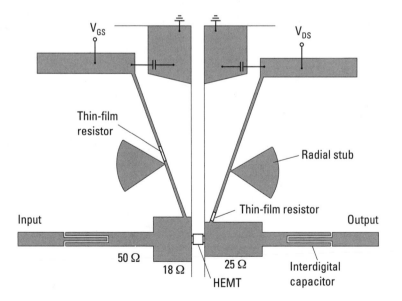

Figure 8.16 A 22-GHz HEMT amplifier (a microstrip circuit).

these lines. These are needed in order to have the bias circuits seen as open circuits from the transistor. The function of the thin-film resistors is to prevent low-frequency oscillations. The interdigital capacitors in input and output prevent dc from flowing out, but are only negligible series reactances at RF.

Example 8.1

Design a transistor amplifier at 4 GHz for maximum available gain. The scattering parameters in the desired operation point $V_{DS} = 3$ V and $I_{DS} = 10$ mA are $S_{11} = 0.70\angle{-115°}$, $S_{21} = 2.50\angle{70°}$, $S_{12} = 0.04\angle{55°}$, and $S_{22} = 0.65\angle{-40°}$.

Solution

First we must check the stability of the transistor. From (8.19) we obtain $\Delta = 0.544\angle{-150°}$, and from (8.29) $K = 1.917$. Therefore, the transistor is unconditionally stable at 4 GHz. We do not need to calculate the stability circles; they are totally outside the Smith chart. Next we calculate the reflection coefficients, providing a conjugate match in the input and output. From (8.24) through (8.27) we calculate $B_1 = 0.772$, $B_2 = 0.637$, $C_1 = 0.349\angle{-120°}$, and $C_2 = 0.273\angle{-47°}$. From (8.22) and (8.23) we obtain reflection coefficients $\rho_{SM} = 0.636\angle{120°}$ and $\rho_{LM} = 0.566\angle{47°}$. Equation (8.28) gives $G_{a,max} = 17.6 = 12.5$ dB. Because both ports are conjugate matched, it holds that $G_{a,max} = G_t = G_p = G_a$, which may be verified using (5.26) through (5.28). The matching circuits can be realized, for example, according to Figure 8.17 using open-circuited parallel stubs. All transmission

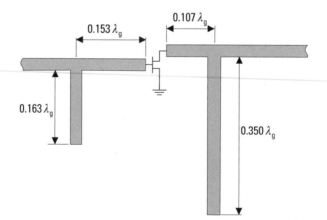

Figure 8.17 Microstrip matching circuits for an FET amplifier.

lines are 50-Ω microstrip lines. In this realization we have not taken into account the fringing components of the microstrip T-junctions and open ends [12]. Another often used matching method in transistor amplifiers is an alternating high-low-impedance line. A manual design of amplifiers and other circuits becomes excessively laborious if all parasitic effects are taken into account and the circuit has to operate over a broad band. Then use of a *computer-aided design* (CAD) package significantly facilitates the design.

8.4.2 Effect of Nonlinearities and Design of Power Amplifiers

In the previous study we assumed that the transistor characteristics did not depend on the signal level, that is, the transistor operates in linear, small-signal conditions. However, as the input power level increases, the nonlinearities of the transistor cause gain compression and generation of spurious frequency components.

As the input power level increases, the gain of an amplifier is constant at small signal levels but finally starts to decrease. Often the bias voltages limit the maximum output voltage. This saturation or gain compression is characterized by the 1-dB compression point, which is the output power at which the gain has decreased by 1 dB from its small-signal value.

Because of the compression, the output waveform is distorted. This distortion produces harmonics nf of a single input signal at frequency f and intermodulation products $mf_1 + nf_2$ (m, $n = \pm1, \pm2, \ldots$) of a two-tone input signal. The order of intermodulation products is defined to be $|m| + |n|$. Especially important are the third-order intermodulation products at frequencies $2f_1 - f_2$ and $2f_2 - f_1$ because they are close to frequencies f_1 and f_2, if $f_1 \approx f_2$. At low input signal levels, the power of third-order intermodulation products increases by 3 dB as the power of input signals having equal magnitudes increases by 1 dB. If there were no compression, the output powers of the desired signals at f_1 and f_2 and the third-order products would be equal at an output power level called the third-order intercept point, IP_3.

The dynamic range of an amplifier is that operating power range over which the amplifier has desirable characteristics. Noise usually sets the lower limit of dynamic range. The upper limit of the linear dynamic range may be defined as the 1-dB compression point. The spurious-free dynamic range is limited by the power level, which produces unacceptable intermodulation products.

In the design of a power amplifier, the theory presented here for getting proper ρ_S and ρ_L is valid only if the scattering parameters are measured in large-signal conditions, that is, at a power level corresponding to the real operation. A power amplifier is designed so that both input and output is conjugate matched, because this provides the maximum gain. Power amplifiers are divided into different classes. A class-A amplifier operates linearly. The bias voltages and signal amplitude are chosen so that output current flows during the full signal period, as shown in Figure 8.18. In a class-B amplifier the output current flows only during one-half of the period, and in a class-C amplifier less than one-half of the period. These amplifiers operate very nonlinearly but they transform dc power more effectively into RF power than a class-A amplifier. A good efficiency is obtained also with class-D, class-E, and class-F amplifiers in which the transistors operate as switches.

In comparing different power amplifiers, an often used figure-of-merit is the power-added efficiency

$$PAE = \frac{P_L - P_{in}}{P_{dc}} \tag{8.33}$$

where P_L is the RF power coupled to the load, P_{in} is the RF power coupled to the amplifier, and P_{dc} is the dc power absorbed by the amplifier. When a very high power level is needed, several amplifiers may be combined parallel using a power combiner (see Section 6.1).

8.4.3   Reflection Amplifiers

The reflection-type amplifier is based on the negative resistance of, for example, a Gunn or IMPATT diode. The power gain of a reflection-type amplifier is

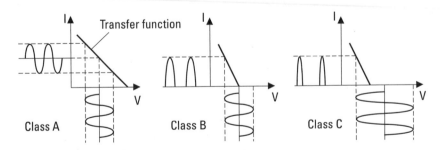

Figure 8.18 Current waveforms in class-A, class-B, and class-C amplifiers.

$$G = |\rho|^2 = \left|\frac{Z_d - Z_0}{Z_d + Z_0}\right|^2 \tag{8.34}$$

where Z_0 is the characteristic impedance of the transmission line and Z_d is the diode impedance. If for example $Z_0 = 50\Omega$ and $Z_d = -25\Omega$, gain is $G = (75/25)^2 = 9 = 9.5$ dB. The input and output signals can be separated by using a circulator according to Figure 8.19.

8.5 Frequency Converters (Mixers) and Frequency Multipliers

The output signal from a linear circuit has shape similar to that of the input signal; however, its amplitude may be higher (amplifier) or lower (attenuator). In a nonlinear circuit the signal is distorted, and the output signal (voltage V_o) is a nonlinear function of the input signal (voltage V_i) and can be presented as a power series

$$V_o = f(V_i) = AV_i + BV_i^2 + CV_i^3 + \ldots \tag{8.35}$$

Figure 8.20 illustrates the difference between a linear and nonlinear transfer function. If, in the case of a nonlinear transfer function, the input signal is weak and causes only a small perturbation in the vicinity of the operating point, the circuit can be considered linear for the signal; that is, $\delta V_o = A'\delta V_i$, where A' is the slope of the curve $f(V_i)$ in the operating

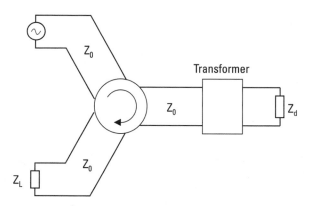

Figure 8.19 A reflection-type amplifier.

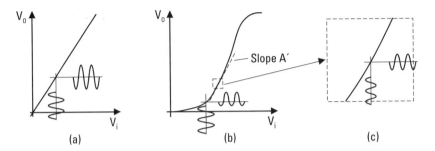

Figure 8.20 Transfer function of (a) a linear and (b) a nonlinear circuit, and (c) a linear small-signal condition.

point. We call this situation the small-signal condition. In a large-signal condition, several terms of (8.35) must be taken into account.

Let us assume that $V_i = V_1 \cos \omega_1 t + V_2 \cos \omega_2 t$. Then the term AV_i contains signal components at frequencies f_1 and f_2, term BV_i^2 contains components at frequencies 0 (dc), $2f_1$, $2f_2$, and $f_1 \pm f_2$, and term CV_i^3 contains components at frequencies f_1, f_2, $3f_1$, $3f_2$, $2f_1 \pm f_2$, and $2f_2 \pm f_1$ (a frequency may be also negative). We note that when a sinusoidal signal at frequency f_1 is fed to a nonlinear circuit, the output contains harmonics at frequencies mf_1, and when two sinusoidal signals at frequencies f_1 and f_2 are fed to a nonlinear circuit, the output contains components at frequencies $mf_1 + nf_2$ (m and n are integers). These nonlinear characteristics make possible the operation of a frequency converter, or a mixer and a frequency multiplier. Note that a mixer may also be based on a time-dependent linear circuit. In a circuit meant to be linear, such as a low-noise amplifier, the distortion due to nonlinearity produces unwanted frequency components.

8.5.1 Mixers

A mixer is a circuit that converts the frequency of a signal up or down so that the information contained in the signal is preserved. Upconverters are used in modulators and transmitters, downconverters in heterodyne receivers and demodulators. In Figure 8.21, a signal at frequency f_s and a local oscillator signal at f_{LO} are fed to a downconverter; then at the output we have a signal at a low intermediate frequency $f_{IF} = |f_s - f_{LO}|$. Processing of the signal at f_{IF} is much easier than that of the original signal at f_s. The conversion loss L_c is defined as

$$L_c = \frac{P_{s,av}}{P_{IF}} = \frac{\text{Available power at } f_s}{\text{Power coupled to load at } f_{IF}} \qquad (8.36)$$

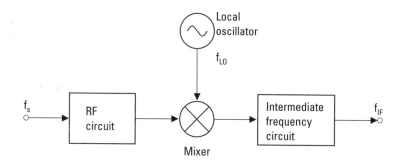

Figure 8.21 Mixer as a downconverter.

As in case of an amplifier, a mixer is linear for a low-power signal (P_s < $P_{LO}/100$) but at higher powers the output signal will be distorted. Thus we can define a 1-dB compression point and a third-order intercept point for a mixer, too.

The nonlinear element may be a diode or a transistor, most often a Schottky diode, bipolar transistor, or FET. Diode mixers are passive; transistor mixers may operate in an active mode and have some conversion gain. Transistor mixers suit well in integrated circuits. Operation of a diode mixer is based on the exponential *I–V* characteristic, but frequency conversion takes place also in the nonlinear capacitance. In a bipolar transistor the emitter-base junction forms a diode. Therefore, in a common-emitter connection the collector current depends exponentially on the base voltage. In an FET the drain current I_{DS} is a nonlinear function of the gate voltage V_{GS}. Especially a *dual-gate FET* (DGFET) is well suited as a mixer, because the RF signal can be fed to one gate and the local oscillator signal to another gate.

In case of a diode mixer, frequency conversion can be analyzed as follows; for equations see [13, 14]. Using the embedding impedances loading the diode at frequencies mf_{LO} we calculate the waveforms of the conductance $G_j(t) = 1/R_j(t)$ and capacitance $C_j(t)$ caused by the local oscillator signal and a possible dc bias. The better the diode corresponds to an ideal switch operating at f_{LO}, the more effective frequency conversion is. The signal (f_s) power is usually very small compared to the LO signal (f_{LO}) power; then from the signal's point of view the mixer is a linear, time-dependent circuit.

The operation of a mixer depends on conditions not only at the signal and IF frequency, but also at the sidebands $mf_{LO} \pm f_{IF}$ because power may convert from any sideband to another. Especially important is the image sideband $f_i = 2f_{LO} - f_s$. Frequencies $mf_{LO} \pm nf_{IF}$ ($n \geq 2$) are important only if the signal power level is of the same order as that of the LO. Using the Fourier series of $G_j(t)$ and $C_j(t)$ we can then calculate a frequency conversion matrix. With this and the load impedances we obtain conversion efficiencies between any two sidebands. Figure 8.22 illustrates the conversion from a frequency f_s to different sidebands.

In designing a mixer, it is important to find the correct load impedances at different sidebands. The conversion loss is at minimum when there is a conjugate match between the nonlinear element and the embedding network at signal and intermediate frequencies, and the other sidebands are terminated with proper, purely reactive loads. The noise optimum requires slightly different conditions the same way as in case of an amplifier. In practice, mixer design today is carried out with a CAD package employing a harmonic balance [13, 14] simulator.

Depending on which sidebands are selected as the signal bands, we have different mixers. A *single-sideband* (SSB) mixer converts the signal only from one sideband, either from the upper sideband $f_{LO} + f_{IF}$ or from the lower sideband $f_{LO} - f_{IF}$, to the intermediate frequency band. A *double-sideband* (DSB) mixer converts both sidebands to the IF band. Two DSB mixers can be combined to form an SSB mixer, which is then called an image-rejection mixer: The outputs of the individual mixers are combined in phase in case of the desired sideband while the outputs cancel each other in case of the image sideband. A harmonic mixer converts the sidebands of an LO harmonic $mf_{LO} \pm f_{IF}$ ($m \geq 2$) to the IF band.

There are a number of different mixer structures or architectures [14]. Figure 8.23 presents the principle of a single-ended, a balanced, and a double-balanced diode mixer, as well as of a double-balanced transistor mixer. For simplicity, the matching and bias circuits are omitted in Figure 8.23. At millimeter wavelengths the mixers are often single-ended waveguide mixers, where the signal and LO are fed to the diode along the same waveguide after combining them in a directional coupler. At RF and microwave frequencies most often balanced and double-balanced mixers are used, and signal and LO power are fed to the nonlinear elements using 3-dB hybrids (described

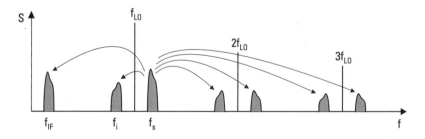

Figure 8.22 Conversion of signal power to different sidebands in a mixer.

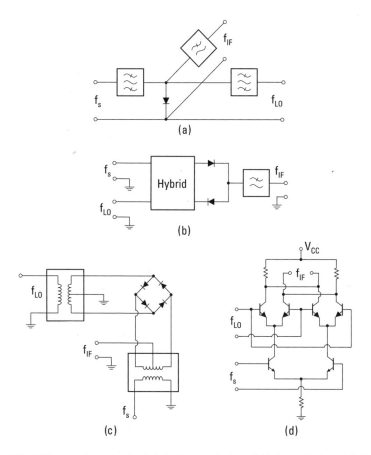

Figure 8.23 Different mixer circuits: (a) single-ended mixer; (b) balanced mixer; (c) double-balanced mixer; and (d) Gilbert cell mixer.

in Section 6.1). At low radio frequencies tapped transformers are used. The balanced and double-balanced mixers have many advantages over the single-ended mixer: There is a good isolation between the signal and LO ports, the AM noise of the LO is rejected, certain spurious signals are rejected, and the compression and intercept points are higher. In a double-balanced mixer there is a good isolation also between the IF and other ports. A disadvantage of balanced and double-balanced mixers is their higher LO power requirement. The Gilbert cell mixer shown in Figure 8.23(d) is a double-balanced transistor mixer, which is widely used in integrated circuits.

8.5.2 Frequency Multipliers

In a frequency multiplier, harmonic signals at frequencies nf are generated, and using a filter one of them is selected as the output signal. This way we can realize frequency doublers (x2), triplers (x3), quadruplers (x4), quintuplers (x5), and so on [15, 16]. A frequency multiplier helps in generating signals at high frequencies where it is otherwise difficult or impossible. Also a signal generated by a multiplier may have a more accurate frequency than a signal produced directly with an oscillator.

The nonlinear element may be either a diode (either resistive or capacitive diode, i.e., a varistor or a varactor, respectively) or a transistor. The multiplication efficiency η is defined as

$$\eta = \frac{\text{Power coupled to load at } nf}{\text{Available power from source at } f} \qquad (8.37)$$

In order to optimize the frequency multiplication efficiency, the nonlinear element must be conjugate matched to the embedding network at the input and output frequencies and terminated with proper, pure reactive loads at other harmonic frequencies. Especially important are the proper reactive terminations at the idler frequencies (intermediate harmonics between the fundamental and output frequency) in higher-order multipliers. The efficiency η of a multiplier based on a nonlinear reactive element is at maximum unity at any multiplication factor n, if both the nonlinear element and the embedding network are lossless (Manley–Rowe equations; see [17]). In practice the efficiency decreases rapidly versus an increasing multiplication factor. A positive, monotonically voltage-dependent nonlinear resistance can produce a multiplication efficiency of $1/n^2$ at maximum. The efficiency of a transistor multiplier may be greater than unity.

8.6 Detectors

Detecting a signal requires transforming it into a useful or observable form. In a diode detector an RF signal is transformed into a voltage proportional to the signal power. Operation of a detector is based on the nonlinearity of a diode, such as a Schottky or p-n diode. When a sinusoidal voltage is applied over the diode, the current contains, besides a component at the signal frequency, harmonic components and a dc component that is proportional to the signal power. Diode detectors are used for power measurement, automatic level control, AM demodulation, and so on.

Let us consider a Schottky diode, where the series resistance R_s and the junction capacitance C_j are assumed negligible. When a bias voltage V_B

and a small sinusoidal signal $V_s \cos \omega t$ are applied over the junction resistance (see Figure 8.24), the diode current can be presented as a series:

$$I(V_B + V_s \cos \omega t) = I_B + \alpha^2(I_s + I_B)\frac{V_s^2}{4} + \alpha(I_s + I_B)V_s \cos \omega t \quad (8.38)$$

$$+ \alpha^2(I_s + I_B)\frac{V_s^2}{4}\cos 2\omega t + \dots$$

Further terms are negligible if $\alpha V_s \ll 1$ [see α in (8.2)] or at room temperature $V_s \ll 25$ mV. I_B is the direct current caused by the bias voltage, $I(V_B)$. The second term is the dc component proportional to the signal power; that is, it is the useful component. According to (8.38), the junction can be considered as a voltage source with a voltage

$$V_o = \frac{\alpha V_s^2}{4} \quad (8.39)$$

and with an internal resistance R_j. The diode is said to follow the square law, because the useful signal is directly proportional to the RF power, that is, to the square of the signal voltage ($V_o \propto V_s^2$). The voltage sensitivity is the ratio of the detector output voltage V_o and the applied signal power P_s in an impedance-matched case, as in

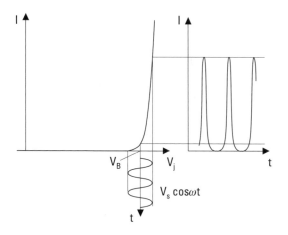

Figure 8.24 Current in a diode with an exponential *I–V* characteristic, when a dc bias and a sinusoidal signal are applied to the diode.

$$\beta_v = \frac{V_o}{P_s} = \frac{\alpha R_j}{2} \qquad (8.40)$$

If the parasitic elements R_s and C_j of the diode as well as the load resistance R_L are taken into account, we get the following expression [18] for the voltage sensitivity

$$\beta_v = \frac{V_L}{P_s} = \frac{\alpha R_j}{2} \times \frac{R_L}{(1 + R_s/R_j)(1 + R_s/R_j + \omega^2 C_j^2 R_s R_j)(R_j + R_s + R_L)} \qquad (8.41)$$

where V_L is the voltage over the load. R_s and C_j reduce the voltage sensitivity, which also decreases as the frequency or temperature are increased (α is proportional to temperature).

Figure 8.25 shows how a diode detector is connected into a circuit. In order to get all signal power absorbed into the diode, it must be matched to the transmission line, usually to 50Ω. Without a bias voltage, the junction resistance R_j may be very high and difficult to match. Furthermore, (8.41) shows that in order to maximize the voltage sensitivity, it should be $R_L \gg R_j$. Therefore, such a diode needs a small bias current in order to provide a proper R_j. Matching the diode over a wide frequency band is difficult. However, in practice we want a flat frequency response and, therefore, we must satisfy on lower voltage sensitivity than that given by (8.41). A lowpass filter is used in the output to prevent the RF and harmonic components from coupling to the load. A coil and a capacitor are needed to guarantee that both dc and RF currents can flow through the diode.

Figure 8.26 shows a typical power response of a diode detector. When the power level increases to a level over −20 dBm (dBm = decibels over

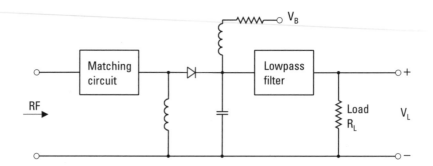

Figure 8.25 Equivalent circuit of a diode detector.

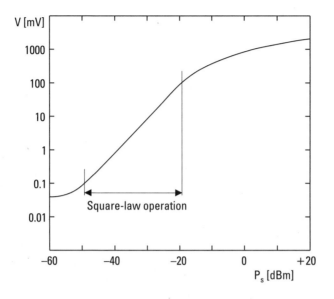

Figure 8.26 Response of a diode detector.

1 mW), the response no longer follows the square law. Finally, the output voltage will saturate. On the other hand, at very low power levels noise is the limiting factor.

8.7 Monolithic Microwave Circuits

Circuits consisting of microstrip lines, lumped passive elements (resistors, inductors, and capacitors), and semiconductor diodes and transistors may be integrated (connected without connectors) and be made very small. If components are soldered or bonded on a microstrip circuit, we call it a hybrid circuit. If a circuit is integrated directly on the surface of a semiconductor substrate, it is called a monolithic integrated circuit.

Up to about 2 GHz the monolithic circuits are made on Si; at higher frequencies the substrate is usually GaAs and these circuits are called *monolithic microwave integrated circuits* (MMICs). The advantages of the MMICs are their extremely small size, suitability to mass production, good repeatability, and high reliability. For example, a whole microwave amplifier can easily be fabricated on a GaAs chip with an area of 1 mm^2 and a thickness of 100 μm. Design and fabrication of a single MMIC becomes very expensive, but in mass production its price becomes reasonable. Microwave applications gaining from mass production of integrated circuits include mobile phones, satellite TV receivers, GPS receivers, and WLAN terminals.

From diodes the Schottky diode and from transistors both MESFET and HEMT are easily suited to GaAs-MMICs. The transmission lines are either microstrip lines or coplanar waveguides. Resistors are either ion-planted directly in GaAs or are thin metal films in the transmission lines. Inductors (coils) may be narrow microstrip lines in the form of a loop or a spiral; capacitors have either an interdigital or *metal-insulator-metal* (MIM) structure (see Figure 4.7). Grounding is realized by a metallized via in the substrate. Figure 8.27 presents a GaAs-MMIC with typical elements. Digital microwave circuits have been made using MMIC technology up to tens of gigahertz, analog circuits up to 200 GHz. Integrated optoelectronic circuits are made using similar technology. In designing MMICs, commercially available software packages are used for both electrical and layout design.

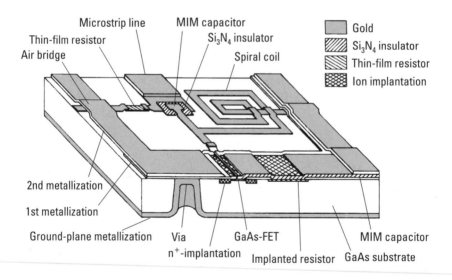

Figure 8.27 Monolithic microwave integrated circuit on gallium arsenide (GaAs-MMIC).

References

[1] Sze, S. M., *Semiconductor Devices, Physics, and Technology,* New York: John Wiley & Sons, 1985.

[2] Howes, M. J., and D. V. Morgan, *Gallium Arsenide Materials, Devices, and Circuits,* Chichester, England: John Wiley & Sons, 1986.

[3] Yngvesson, S., *Microwave Semiconductor Devices,* Boston, MA: Kluwer Academic Publishers, 1991.

[4] Zhang, J., and A. V. Räisänen, "Computer-Aided Design of Step Recovery Diode Frequency Multipliers," *IEEE Trans. on Microwave Theory and Techniques,* Vol. 44, No. 12, 1996, pp. 2612–2616.

[5] Gentili, C., *Microwave Amplifiers and Oscillators,* New York: McGraw-Hill, 1987.

[6] Rogers, R. G., *Low Phase Noise Microwave Oscillator Design,* Norwood, MA: Artech House, 1991.

[7] Liao, S. Y., *Microwave Circuit Analysis and Amplifier Design,* Englewood Cliffs, NJ: Prentice Hall, 1987.

[8] Abrie, P. L. D., *Design of RF and Microwave Amplifiers and Oscillators,* Norwood, MA: Artech House, 1999.

[9] Ha, T., *Solid-State Microwave Amplifier Design,* New York: John Wiley & Sons, 1981.

[10] Pozar, D. M., *Microwave Engineering,* 2nd ed., New York: John Wiley & Sons, 1998.

[11] Lange, J., "Noise Characterization of Linear Two-Ports in Terms of Invariant Parameters," *IEEE J. of Solid-State Circuits,* Vol. 2, No. 2, 1967, pp. 37–40.

[12] Hoffmann, R. K., *Handbook of Microwave Integrated Circuits,* Norwood, MA: Artech House, 1987.

[13] Held, D. N., and A. R. Kerr, "Conversion Loss and Noise of Microwave and Millimeter-Wave Mixers: Part I—Theory," *IEEE Trans. on Microwave Theory and Techniques,* Vol. 26, No. 2, 1978, pp. 49–55.

[14] Maas, S. A., *Microwave Mixers,* 2nd ed., Norwood, MA: Artech House, 1993.

[15] Räisänen, A. V., "Frequency Multipliers for Millimeter and Submillimeter Wavelengths," *Proc. IEEE,* Vol. 80, No. 11, 1992, pp. 1842–1852.

[16] Faber, M. T., J. Chramiec, and M. E. Adamski, *Microwave and Millimeter-Wave Diode Frequency Multipliers,* Norwood, MA: Artech House, 1995.

[17] Collin, R. E., *Foundations for Microwave Engineering,* 2nd ed., New York: IEEE Press, 2001.

[18] Bahl, I., and P. Bhartia, *Microwave Solid State Circuit Design,* New York: John Wiley & Sons, 1988.

9

Antennas

Antennas transmit and receive radio waves. They operate as matching devices from a transmission line to the free space and vice versa. An ideal antenna radiates all the power incident from the transmission line feeding the antenna. It radiates to (or receives from) desired directions; in other words, an antenna has a certain radiation pattern.

Antennas are needed in nearly all applications of radio engineering. The congestion of the radio spectrum due to the increasing number of users and applications sets increasingly strict requirements for antennas. A large number of antenna structures have been developed for different frequencies and applications. Antennas can be categorized, for example, into current element antennas, traveling-wave antennas, aperture antennas, and antenna arrays.

In this chapter, the fundamental concepts of antennas, the calculation of radiation pattern and other antenna quantities, different types of antennas, and the link between two antennas are treated. Antennas are the subject of many books [1–8].

9.1 Fundamental Concepts of Antennas

Antennas are *reciprocal* devices. That means that the properties of an antenna are similar both in the transmitting mode and in the receiving mode. For example, if a transmitting antenna radiates to certain directions, it can also receive from those directions—the same radiation pattern applies for both cases. The reciprocity does not apply if nonreciprocal components such as ferrite devices or amplifiers are integrated into the antenna. Also, a link between two antennas is reciprocal: The total loss is the same in both directions. However, magnetized plasma, such as in the ionosphere, between the antennas may cause Faraday rotation, making the link nonreciprocal.

The space surrounding an antenna can be divided into three regions according to the properties of the radiated field. Because the field changes smoothly, the boundaries between the regions are more or less arbitrary. The *reactive near-field region* is closest to the antenna. In this region, the reactive field component is larger than the radiating one. For a short current element, the reactive and radiating components are equal at a distance of $\lambda/(2\pi)$ from the element. For other current distributions this distance is shorter. As the distance increases, the reactive field decreases as $1/r^2$ or $1/r^3$ and becomes negligible compared to the radiating field. In the *radiating near-field region* or *Fresnel region*, the shape of the normalized radiation pattern depends on the distance. As the distance of the observation point changes, the difference in distances to different parts of the antenna changes essentially compared to the wavelength. In the *far-field region* or *Fraunhofer region*, the normalized radiation pattern is practically independent of the distance and the field decreases as $1/r$. The boundary between the near-field and far-field regions is usually chosen to be at the distance of

$$r = \frac{2D^2}{\lambda} \tag{9.1}$$

where D is the largest dimension of the antenna perpendicular to the direction of observation. At the boundary, the edges of a planar antenna are $\lambda/16$ farther away from the observation point P than the center of the antenna, as illustrated in Figure 9.1. This difference in distance corresponds to a phase

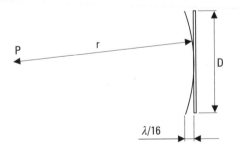

Figure 9.1 At the boundary of near-field and far-field regions.

difference of 22.5°. Because antennas are usually operated at large distances, the far-field pattern is of interest. It should be noted that at lower frequencies in case of small antennas, the outer limit of the reactive near-field region, $\lambda/(2\pi)$, is larger than the distance obtained from (9.1).

The coordinate system used for antenna analysis or measurements should be defined clearly. In analysis, the complexity of equations depends on the system. Figure 9.2 shows the spherical coordinate system that is often used. The elevation angle θ increases along a great circle from 0° to 180°. The azimuth angle ϕ is obtained from the projection of the directional vector in the xy-plane, and it is between 0° and 360°.

An antenna can be described by several properties, which are related to the field radiated by the antenna, for example, directional pattern, gain, and polarization. Due to the reciprocity, these properties also describe the ability of the antenna to receive waves coming from different directions and having different polarizations. The importance of different radiation properties depends on the application. As a circuit element an antenna also has an impedance, efficiency, and bandwidth. Often mechanical properties such as the size, weight, and wind load are also very important.

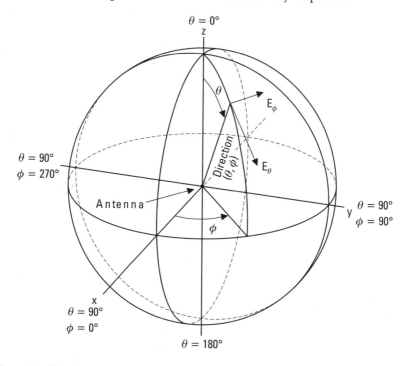

Figure 9.2 Spherical coordinate system used for antenna analysis and measurements.

An isotropic antenna that radiates at an equal strength to all directions is a good reference antenna but is not realizable in practice. A real antenna has a certain *radiation pattern,* which describes the field distribution as the antenna radiates. Often the radiation pattern means the same as the *directional pattern.* The directional pattern describes the power density $P(\theta, \phi)$ in watts per square meter or the electric field intensity $E(\theta, \phi)$ in volts per meter as a function of direction. Usually, the directional pattern is normalized so that the maximum value of the power density or electric field is 1 (or 0 dB). The normalized field $E_n(\theta, \phi)$ is equal to the square root of the normalized power density $P_n(\theta, \phi)$.

Often the antenna radiates mainly to one direction only. Then one main beam or the main lobe and possibly a number of lower maxima, sidelobes, can be distinguished, as in Figure 9.3(a). The directions of the lobes and nulls, the width of the main lobe, the levels of the sidelobes, and

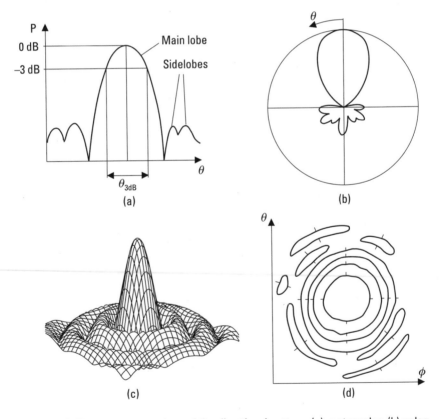

Figure 9.3 Different representations of the directional pattern: (a) rectangular; (b) polar; (c) three-dimensional; and (d) constant-value contours.

the depths of nulls can be obtained from the directional pattern. The half-power beamwidth, θ_{3dB} or ϕ_{3dB}, is often used as the measure of the main lobe width.

Figure 9.3 shows different representations of directional patterns. The rectangular representation is suitable for directive antennas having a narrow main beam. The polar representation is natural for an antenna radiating over a wide range of angles. Both rectangular and polar plots are two-dimensional cuts of the three-dimensional pattern. The directional patterns are often θ-cuts or ϕ-cuts. For a θ-cut, for example, the angle θ is constant and the angle ϕ is variable. The most important cuts are the cuts in the principal planes. The principal planes are orthogonal planes that intersect at the maximum of the main lobe, that is, at the boresight. For example, for a linearly polarized antenna, the principal planes are the E-plane and H-plane, which are the planes parallel to the electric field vector and magnetic field vector, respectively. The whole pattern can be represented as a three-dimensional or contour plot. The scale of different plots may be a linear power, a linear field, or a logarithmic (decibel) scale.

The number of different shapes of directional patterns is countless. A pencil beam antenna has a narrow and symmetrical main lobe. Such highly directional antennas are used, for example, in point-to-point radio links, satellite communication, and radio astronomy. The directional pattern of a terrestrial broadcasting antenna should be constant in the azimuth plane and shaped in the vertical plane to give a field strength that is constant over the service area. The directional pattern of an antenna in a satellite should follow the shape of the geographic service area.

The *directivity D* of an antenna is obtained by integrating the normalized power pattern $P_n(\theta, \phi)$ over the whole solid angle 4π:

$$D = \frac{4\pi}{\displaystyle\iint_{4\pi} P_n(\theta, \phi)\, d\Omega} \qquad (9.2)$$

where $d\Omega$ is an element of the solid angle. Because $P_n(\theta, \phi) = P(\theta, \phi)/P_{max}$, the directivity is the maximum power density divided by the average power density.

Example 9.1

The beam of an antenna is rotationally symmetric. Within the $1°$-wide beam, the pattern level is $P_n = 1$, and outside the beam the pattern level is

$P_n = 0$. (In practice, this kind of a beam is not realizable.) What is the directivity of this antenna?

Solution

Because the beamwidth is small, the section of the sphere corresponding to the beam can be approximated with a circular, planar surface. The beamwidth is $1° = \pi/180 = 0.01745$ radians. The solid angle of the beam is $\Omega_A = \iint_{4\pi} P_n(\theta, \phi)\, d\Omega = \pi \times 0.01745^2/4 = 2.392 \times 10^{-4}$ steradians (square radians). The directivity is $D = 4\pi/\Omega_A = 52,500$, which in decibels is $10 \log(52,500) = 47.2$ dB.

The *gain G* of an antenna is the ratio of the maximum radiation intensity produced by the antenna to the radiation intensity that would be obtained if the power accepted by the antenna were radiated equally in all directions. For an antenna having no loss, the gain is equal to the directivity. In practical antennas there are some conductor and dielectric losses. All the power coupled to the antenna is not radiated and the gain is smaller than the directivity:

$$G = \eta_r D \qquad (9.3)$$

where η_r is the *radiation efficiency*. If the power coupled to the antenna is P, the power radiated is $\eta_r P$, and the power lost in the antenna is $(1 - \eta_r)P$. Losses due to impedance and polarization mismatches are not taken into account in the definition of gain. The directivity and gain can also be given as functions of direction: $D(\theta, \phi) = P_n(\theta, \phi) \cdot D$, $G(\theta, \phi) = P_n(\theta, \phi) \cdot G$.

The *effective area A_{ef}* is a useful quantity for a receiving antenna. An ideal antenna with an area of A_{ef} receives from a plane wave, having a power density of S, the same power, $A_{ef}S$, as the real antenna. As shown in Section 9.6, the effective area is directly related to the gain as

$$A_{ef}(\theta, \phi) = \frac{\lambda^2}{4\pi} G(\theta, \phi) \qquad (9.4)$$

Thus, the effective area of an isotropic antenna is $\lambda^2/(4\pi)$. For an antenna having a radiating aperture, the aperture efficiency is defined as

$$\eta_{ap} = \frac{A_{ef}}{A_{phys}} \tag{9.5}$$

where A_{phys} is the physical area of the aperture.

The *phase pattern* $\psi(\theta, \phi)$ is the phase difference of the constant phase front radiated by the antenna and the spherical phase front of an ideal antenna. The position of the reference point where the spherical wave is assumed to emanate must be given. The *phase center* of an antenna is the reference point that minimizes the phase difference over the main beam. For example, the phase center of the feed antenna and the focal point of the reflector that is illuminated by the feed should coincide.

The *polarization* of an antenna describes how the orientation of the electric field radiated by the antenna behaves as a function of time. We can imagine that the tip of the electric field vector makes an ellipse during one cycle on a plane that is perpendicular to the direction of propagation (Figure 9.4). The polarization ellipse is defined by its axial ratio E_{max}/E_{min}, its tilt angle τ, and its sense of rotation. The special cases of the elliptical polarization are the linear polarization and the circular polarization. The polarization of an antenna is also a function of angle (θ, ϕ).

The field radiated by the antenna can be divided into two orthogonal components: the copolar and cross-polar field. Often the copolar component is used for the intended operation and the cross-polar component represents an unwanted radiation or an interference. Linear polarizations that are perpendicular to each other, as for example the vertical and horizontal polarizations, are orthogonal. The right-handed and left-handed circular polarization are orthogonal to each other as well.

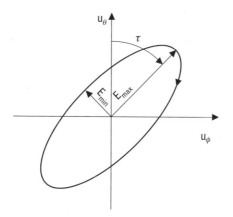

Figure 9.4 Polarization ellipse.

Generally, the polarization of an incoming wave and the polarization of an antenna are different, which causes a polarization mismatch. If the polarizations are the same, there will be no mismatch and the polarization efficiency is $\eta_p = 1$. In the case of orthogonal polarizations, no energy couples to the antenna and $\eta_p = 0$. If the wave is circularly polarized and the antenna is linearly polarized, one-half of the power incident on the effective area couples to the antenna, that is, $\eta_p = \frac{1}{2}$.

The quantities $P_n(\theta, \phi)$, $E_n(\theta, \phi)$, $D(\theta, \phi)$, $G(\theta, \phi)$, $A_{ef}(\theta, \phi)$, and $\psi(\theta, \phi)$ can be given for both copolar and cross-polar fields. An ideal antenna has no cross polarization. The cross-polar field of a practical antenna depends on the angle (θ, ϕ) and is often at minimum in the direction of the main beam. An antenna should have a low level of cross-polarization, for example in such applications where two channels are transmitted at the same frequency using two orthogonal polarizations.

All the power couples from the transmission line to the antenna and vice versa, if the *impedance Z* of the antenna is equal to the characteristic impedance of the transmission line (note that the characteristic impedance of a transmission line is real). A part of the power reflects back from an impedance mismatch. The impedance $Z = R + jX$ has a resistive part and a reactive part. The resistive part, $R = R_r + R_l$, is divided into the *radiation resistance R_r* and the loss resistance R_l. The power "absorbed" in the radiation resistance is radiated and the power absorbed in the loss resistance is transformed into heat in the antenna. The impedance of an antenna depends on its surroundings. The reflections coming from nearby objects, such as the head of a mobile phone user, alter the impedance. Due to the mutual couplings of elements in an antenna array, the impedance of an element embedded in the array differs from that of the element alone in free space.

The *bandwidth* of an antenna can be defined to be the frequency band in which the impedance match, gain, beamwidth, sidelobe level, cross-polarization level, or some other quantity is within the accepted limits.

The parameters of an antenna may also be adjustable. In case of an adaptive antenna, its impedance, radiation pattern, or some other characteristic can adapt according to the electromagnetic environment.

9.2 Calculation of Radiation from Antennas

The fields radiated by an antenna can be calculated using auxiliary quantities called the magnetic vector potential **A** and the electric vector potential **F**.

An antenna can be considered to be a sinusoidal current density distribution **J** in a volume V. At a point of space, the magnetic vector potential is

$$\mathbf{A} = \frac{\mu}{4\pi} \int\limits_{V} \frac{\mathbf{J} e^{-jkR}}{R} \, dV \qquad (9.6)$$

where R is the distance from a volume element dV to the point of observation and $k = 2\pi/\lambda$. If the currents flow on a surface S and the surface current density is $\mathbf{J_s}$, (9.6) can be written as

$$\mathbf{A} = \frac{\mu}{4\pi} \int\limits_{S} \frac{\mathbf{J_s} e^{-jkR}}{R} \, dS \qquad (9.7)$$

The electric field **E** and magnetic field **H** are calculated as

$$\mathbf{E} = -\frac{j\omega}{k^2} \nabla \times \nabla \times \mathbf{A} = -\frac{j\omega}{k^2} \nabla(\nabla \cdot \mathbf{A}) - j\omega\mathbf{A} \qquad (9.8)$$

$$\mathbf{H} = \frac{1}{\mu} \nabla \times \mathbf{A} \qquad (9.9)$$

In principle, the radiated fields can be calculated for all antennas using these equations. They are well suited for wire antennas that have a known current distribution.

An aperture antenna, such as a horn antenna, has an aperture or a surface from which the radiation seems to emanate. It may be difficult to find out the current distribution. Then it may be easier to calculate the radiated fields from the aperture fields $\mathbf{E_a}$ and $\mathbf{H_a}$. The aperture fields are replaced with surface currents that would produce the aperture fields. The magnetic field is replaced with a surface current having a density of

$$\mathbf{J_s} = \mathbf{n} \times \mathbf{H_a} \qquad (9.10)$$

where **n** is a unit vector normal to the surface of the aperture. The vector potential **A** corresponding to $\mathbf{J_s}$ is then calculated. The radiated field components are obtained from (9.8) and (9.9). The electric field of the aperture is replaced with a magnetic surface current having a density of

$$\mathbf{M_s} = -\mathbf{n} \times \mathbf{E_a} \qquad (9.11)$$

The electric vector potential is defined as

$$\mathbf{F} = \frac{\epsilon}{4\pi} \int_S \frac{\mathbf{M_s} e^{-jkR}}{R} \, dS \qquad (9.12)$$

The radiated field components corresponding to $\mathbf{M_s}$ are

$$\mathbf{E} = -\frac{1}{\epsilon} \nabla \times \mathbf{F} \qquad (9.13)$$

$$\mathbf{H} = -\frac{j\omega}{k^2} \nabla \times \nabla \times \mathbf{F} = -\frac{j\omega}{k^2} \nabla(\nabla \cdot \mathbf{F}) - j\omega \mathbf{F} \qquad (9.14)$$

The total radiated field is obtained by summing up the field components due to $\mathbf{J_s}$ and $\mathbf{M_s}$.

9.3 Radiating Current Element

Figure 9.5 shows a short current element at the origin. The element of a length dz along the z-axis carries an alternating sinusoidal current I_0, which is constant along the element. This kind of current element is also called

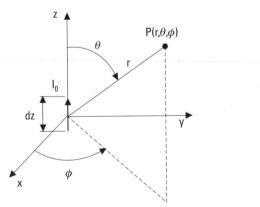

Figure 9.5 Radiating current element.

the Hertz dipole. In his experiments, Heinrich Hertz used end-loaded dipoles. Because of the capacitive loadings, currents could flow even at the ends of the dipole making a nearly constant current distribution possible. As explained in Chapter 2, a fluctuating current produces electromagnetic waves: The current produces a changing magnetic field, the changing magnetic field produces a changing electric field, the changing electric field produces a changing magnetic field, and so on.

The volume integral of the current density is $\int_V \mathbf{J}\, dV = I_0\, dz\mathbf{u_z}$ in the case of a current element. Therefore, the vector potential at a point $P(r,\ \theta,\ \phi)$ is

$$\mathbf{A} = \frac{\mu}{4\pi} \cdot \frac{I_0\, dz e^{-jkr}}{r} \mathbf{u_z} = A_z \mathbf{u_z} \tag{9.15}$$

The components of the vector potential in the spherical coordinate system are $A_r = A_z \cos\ \theta$, $A_\theta = -A_z \sin\ \theta$, and $A_\phi = 0$. Equations (9.8) and (9.9) give the components of the fields:

$$E_r = \frac{I_0\, dz}{4\pi} e^{-jkr} \left(\frac{2\eta}{r^2} + \frac{2}{j\omega\epsilon r^3} \right) \cos\ \theta \tag{9.16}$$

$$E_\theta = \frac{I_0\, dz}{4\pi} e^{-jkr} \left(\frac{j\omega\mu}{r} + \frac{\eta}{r^2} + \frac{1}{j\omega\epsilon r^3} \right) \sin\ \theta \tag{9.17}$$

$$H_\phi = \frac{I_0\, dz}{4\pi} e^{-jkr} \left(\frac{jk}{r} + \frac{1}{r^2} \right) \sin\ \theta \tag{9.18}$$

$$E_\phi = H_r = H_\theta = 0 \tag{9.19}$$

where η is the wave impedance in free space.

Those components of the field having a $1/r^2$ or $1/r^3$ dependence dominate at small distances but become negligible at larger distances. Far away from the element, the fields are

$$E_\theta = \frac{j\omega\mu I_0\, dz}{4\pi r} e^{-jkr} \sin\ \theta \tag{9.20}$$

$$H_\phi = \frac{E_\theta}{\eta} \tag{9.21}$$

Other components are negligible. The electric and magnetic fields are in phase and perpendicular to each other, just like in the case of a plane wave.

The power radiated by the current element is calculated by integrating the Poynting vector $\mathbf{S} = (1/2) \, \mathrm{Re} \, (\mathbf{E} \times \mathbf{H}^*)$ over a sphere surrounding the element. If the radius of the sphere, r, is much larger than dz, $\mathbf{S}$ is perpendicular to the surface of the sphere and the outflowing power per unit area is $S = |\mathbf{S}| = (1/2)|E_\theta H_\phi|$. The surface element for integration is selected as shown in Figure 9.6. The power radiated is

$$P = \int_0^\pi S 2\pi r^2 \sin\theta \, d\theta = 40\pi^2 I_0^2 \left(\frac{dz}{\lambda}\right)^2 \tag{9.22}$$

The radiation resistance of the current element is obtained by equating the radiated power with $P = (1/2) R_r I_0^2$:

$$R_r = 80\pi^2 \left(\frac{dz}{\lambda}\right)^2 \, \Omega \tag{9.23}$$

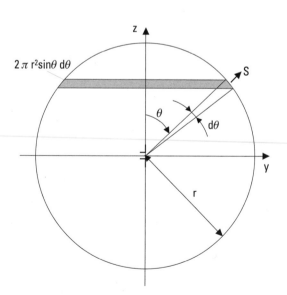

Figure 9.6 Integration of power density over a sphere.

9.4 Dipole and Monopole Antennas

Wire antennas are popular at frequencies below 1 GHz. The dipole antenna is the most often used wire antenna. It is a straight wire, which is usually split in the middle so that it can be fed by a transmission line.

It can be thought that a dipole shown in Figure 9.7 consists of current elements in a line. The far field is calculated by summing the fields produced by the current elements, that is, by integrating (9.20):

$$E_\theta = \frac{j\omega\mu}{4\pi} \int\limits_{-l/2}^{l/2} \frac{I(z)\,e^{-jkR(z)}}{R(z)} \sin\,\theta(z)\,dz \qquad (9.24)$$

where l is the length of the dipole. It can be assumed that the current distribution $I(z)$ is sinusoidal and at the ends of the wire the current is zero. This assumption applies well for a thin wire. The current distribution can be considered to be a standing wave pattern, which is produced as the current wave reflects from the end of the wire. The current distribution is

$$I(z) = \begin{cases} I_0 \sin\,[k(l/2 - z)], & \text{for } z > 0 \\ I_0 \sin\,[k(l/2 + z)], & \text{for } z < 0 \end{cases} \qquad (9.25)$$

where I_0 is the maximum current. Far away from the antenna at a point $P(r,\,\theta,\,\phi)$ it applies $\theta(z) \approx \theta$ and $1/R(z) \approx 1/r$, so these terms can be

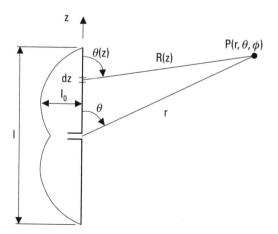

Figure 9.7 Dipole antenna.

assumed to be constant in (9.24). However, small changes in $R(z)$ as a function of z have to be taken into account in the phase term $e^{-jkR(z)}$. The distance from P to the element is

$$R(z) = \sqrt{r^2 + z^2 - 2rz \cos \theta} \approx r - z \cos \theta \qquad (9.26)$$

From (9.24), the field radiated by the dipole is

$$E_\theta = \frac{j\eta I_0}{2\pi r} e^{-jkr} \frac{\cos\left(\frac{1}{2}kl\cos\theta\right) - \cos\left(\frac{1}{2}kl\right)}{\sin\theta} \qquad (9.27)$$

If the dipole is short compared to a wavelength, the current distribution is approximately triangular. Its radiation resistance is a quarter of that of the Hertz dipole having the same length:

$$R_r \approx 20\pi^2 \left(\frac{l}{\lambda}\right)^2 \ \Omega \qquad (9.28)$$

This is valid up to about a length of $l = \lambda/4$.

The half-wave dipole is the most important of dipole antennas. When $l = \lambda/2$, it follows from (9.27) that

$$E_\theta = \frac{j\eta I_0}{2\pi r} e^{-jkr} \frac{\cos\left(\frac{\pi}{2}\cos\theta\right)}{\sin\theta} \qquad (9.29)$$

The maximum of the field is in the plane perpendicular to the wire and the nulls are along the direction of the wire. The half-power beamwidth is $\theta_{3dB} = 78°$. The directivity is $D = 1.64$ (2.15 dB), which is also the gain G for a lossless half-wave dipole. The directional patterns of the half-wave dipole and the Hertz dipole ($\theta_{3dB} = 90°$, $D = 1.5$) are compared in Figure 9.8. The radiation resistance of the half-wave dipole is $R_r = 73.1\Omega$ in a lossless case. The input impedance also includes some inductive reactance. The impedance could be made purely resistive by reducing the length of the wire by a few percent; this will reduce the radiation resistance too. In practice, the properties of the half-wave dipole also depend on the thickness of the wire.

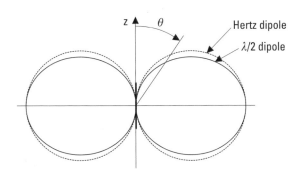

Figure 9.8 Normalized directional patterns of the half-wave and Hertz dipole.

Figure 9.9 shows a folded dipole. Both of the half-wave-long wires have a similar current distribution. Therefore, the folded dipole produces a field twice of that of the half-wave dipole for a given feed current. Thus, the radiated power is four times that of the half-wave dipole and the radiation resistance is about 300Ω. A parallel-wire line having a characteristic impedance of 300Ω is suitable for feeding a folded dipole antenna.

If a dipole antenna has a length of a few half-wavelengths, its directional pattern has several lobes. Figure 9.10 shows the current distribution and directional pattern of a $3\lambda/2$-long dipole. As the length l further increases,

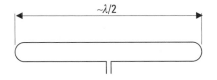

Figure 9.9 Folded dipole antenna.

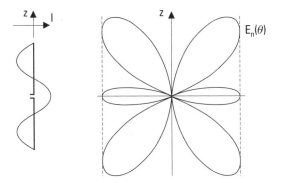

Figure 9.10 A $3\lambda/2$-long dipole antenna: current distribution and directional pattern.

the number of lobes increases. The envelope of the lobes forms a cylinder around the z-axis. The feed point of a dipole antenna is usually in the middle but can be at some other point. The directional pattern and impedance depend on the position of the feed point.

Example 9.2

Let us consider two dipole antennas having lengths of 0.1λ and 0.5λ. Both have a feed current of 1A. What are the radiated powers?

Solution

From (9.28), the radiation resistance is $R_r = 1.97\Omega$ as $l = 0.1\lambda$. The radiated power $P = \frac{1}{2}R_r I^2 = 1.0$W. For the half-wave dipole, $R_r = 73.1\Omega$ and $P = 36.5$W. Thus, a short dipole is ineffective and its small resistance is difficult to match to a transmission line.

The monopole antenna is a straight wire above a ground plane as shown in Figure 9.11(a). In the analysis, the image principle can be applied. The conducting plane can be removed if an image of the current distribution is placed on the other side of the plane, as in Figure 9.11(b). This way the tangential electric field vanishes at the plane where the conducting plane was.

The monopole antenna and the dipole antenna formed according to the image principle have similar fields in the half-space above the ground plane. For a given feed current, the power radiated by the monopole is half of that of the corresponding dipole because the monopole produces no fields below the ground plane. Therefore, the radiation resistance of a quarter-wave monopole is 36.5Ω, which is half of that of a half-wave dipole. The gain of the monopole is twice of that of the dipole.

In practice, the ground plane of a monopole antenna is finite and has a finite conductivity. Therefore, the main lobe is tilted upward and there

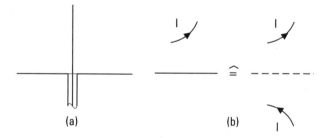

(a)   (b)

Figure 9.11 (a) Monopole antenna; and (b) image principle.

may be a null along the direction of the surface. At low frequencies, a flat ground acts as a ground plane. The conductivity may be improved by introducing metal wires into the ground.

Monopole antennas operating at VLF and LF ranges are short compared to a wavelength and have a low radiation resistance. Their efficiency can be improved by adding a horizontal wire at the top, as shown in Figure 9.12. Due to the top loading, the current in the vertical part is increased. The fields produced by the vertical part and its image add constructively. However, the fields from the horizontal part and its image cancel each other, because their currents flow to opposite directions and their distance is small compared to a wavelength.

Dipole and monopole antennas are omnidirectional in the plane perpendicular to the wire and thus have a low directivity. Figure 9.13 shows a Yagi (or Yagi-Uda) antenna, which is an antenna commonly used for TV reception. It consists of an array of parallel dipoles, which together form a directional antenna. Only one element, the driven element, is fed from the transmission line. There is a reflector behind the driven element and directors in front of it. Currents are induced to these parasitic elements. The fields

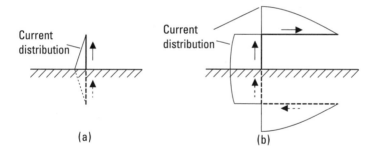

Figure 9.12 (a) Short monopole antenna; and (b) top-loaded monopole antenna.

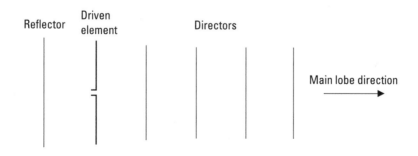

Figure 9.13 Yagi antenna.

produced by the driven and parasitic elements add in phase in the forward direction and cancel in the reverse direction.

The driven element of a Yagi antenna is in a resonance, that is, the input impedance is resistive, when the length of the element is 0.45 to 0.48 wavelength. The driven element is often a folded dipole. The reflector is 0.15 to 0.30 wavelength behind the driven element and it is about 5% longer than the driven element. The directors are about 5% shorter than the driven element and their spacings are 0.15 to 0.30 wavelength. Often the directors have equal lengths and equal spacings, although the optimization of dimensions would give a slightly higher directivity. A larger number of director elements means a higher directivity. Usually there are three to twelve directors. The directivity of a seven-element Yagi is typically 12 dB. The narrow bandwidth is a drawback of the Yagi antenna. In a cold climate snow and ice covering the elements may easily spoil the directional pattern.

A log-periodic antenna is a broadband antenna whose properties repeat at frequencies having a constant ratio of τ. The structure is periodic so that if all the dimensions are multiplied or divided by τ, the original structure, excluding the outermost elements, is obtained. Figure 9.14 shows a log-periodic dipole antenna. The antenna is fed from the high-frequency end, and the feed line goes through all elements, so that the phase is reversed from an element to the next one. Only the element being in resonance radiates effectively. The element behind it acts as a reflector and the element in front of it acts as a director. Thus, the active part of the antenna depends on the frequency. The directivity is typically 8 dB.

9.5 Other Wire Antennas

A loop antenna is a circular or rectangular wire, which may consist of several turns. If the loop is small compared to a wavelength, the current is nearly

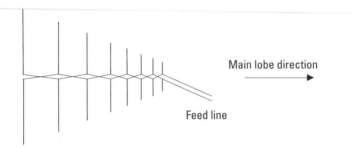

Figure 9.14 Log-periodic dipole antenna.

constant along the loop. The maximum of the directional pattern is in the plane of the loop and the nulls are perpendicular to that plane as in Figure 9.15(a). The pattern is like the pattern of a small dipole having the electric and magnetic fields interchanged. Therefore, a small loop can be considered to be a magnetic dipole. The radiation resistance is

$$R_r = 320\,\pi^4 \left(\frac{NA}{\lambda^2} \right)^2 \Omega \tag{9.30}$$

where A is the area of the loop and N is the number of turns.

The current of a larger loop is not constant. Then the directional pattern differs from that of a small loop. If the length of the circumference is one wavelength, the maximum of the directional pattern is perpendicular to the plane of the loop and the null is in the plane of the loop. Figure 9.15(b) shows a quad antenna, which is made of such loops. Like the Yagi antenna, the quad antenna has a driven element, a reflector, and one or more directors. Quad antennas operating at different frequency ranges can be placed inside each other because the coupling of such loops is small.

A helix antenna, shown in Figure 9.16, is a helical wire having either the left-handed or right-handed sense. If the length of the circumference L is less than $\lambda/2$, the helix antenna radiates in the normal mode; that is, the maximum of the directional pattern is perpendicular to the axis of the helix. This kind of a helix antenna operates as a shortened monopole, except the field is elliptically polarized. If L is from 0.75λ to 1.25λ, the helix antenna operates in the axial mode; that is, the main beam is along the axis of the helix and the field is circularly polarized.

Long-wire and rhombic antennas are traveling-wave antennas, which are used at HF range. The current has constant amplitude but the phase changes linearly along the wire (in a dipole antenna, the amplitude of the current changes but the phase is constant).

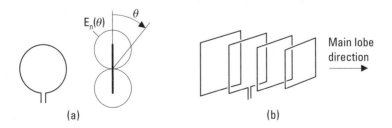

Figure 9.15 (a) Small loop antenna and its directional pattern; and (b) quad antenna.

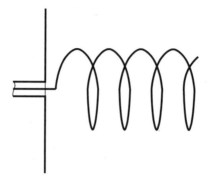

Figure 9.16 Helix antenna fed from a coaxial cable through a conducting plane.

The long-wire antenna is usually a horizontal wire, which is terminated with a matched load, as shown in Figure 9.17. The conical directional pattern is

$$E_n(\alpha) = \frac{\sin \alpha}{1 - \cos \alpha} \sin [\pi L (1 - \cos \alpha)/\lambda] \qquad (9.31)$$

where α is the angle from the direction of the wire and L is the length of the wire. The longer the wire, the smaller the angle α_m is between the directions of the main lobe and the wire. For an antenna having a length of several wavelengths, the main lobe direction is $\alpha_m \approx \sqrt{\lambda/L}$. A V-antenna is made of two long-wire antennas placed in an angle of $2\alpha_m$ to each other. It has a better directional pattern than a single long-wire antenna because the main lobes of the two wires reinforce each other.

A rhombic antenna is made of four horizontal long-wire antennas (or two V-antennas), as shown in Figure 9.18. It is fed from a parallel-wire line and is terminated with a matched load. The fields produced by the long-

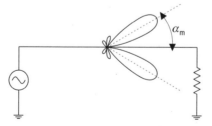

Figure 9.17 Long-wire antenna.

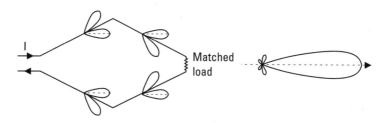

Figure 9.18 Rhombic antenna and its directional pattern.

wire antennas are all in phase in the forward direction. In practice, the main lobe tilts slightly upward, due to the ground.

9.6 Radiation from Apertures

Figure 9.19 shows a surface element $d\mathbf{S}$ at the origin in the xy-plane. The electric field E_x and magnetic field $H_y = E_x/\eta$ are constant over the element. These aperture fields can be replaced with surface currents $\mathbf{M_s} = -E_x\mathbf{u_y}$ and $\mathbf{J_s} = -E_x/\eta\mathbf{u_x}$. The vector potentials at a point $P(r, \theta, \phi)$ are

$$\mathbf{A} = -\frac{\mu E_x}{4\pi r\eta} e^{-jkr} \, dS \, \mathbf{u_x} \tag{9.32}$$

$$\mathbf{F} = -\frac{\epsilon E_x}{4\pi r} e^{-jkr} \, dS \, \mathbf{u_y} \tag{9.33}$$

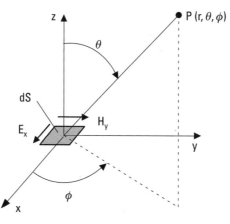

Figure 9.19 Radiating surface element.

These vector potentials are then expressed in the spherical coordinate system. For example, the components of the magnetic vector potential are $A_r = \sin\theta\cos\phi A_x$, $A_\theta = \cos\theta\cos\phi A_x$, and $A_\phi = -\sin\phi A_x$. As the curl of the vector potential is expressed in the spherical coordinate system, it can be noted, that far away from the element the radial component is negligible. Then the curl simplifies to

$$\nabla \times \mathbf{A} = -\frac{\partial A_\phi}{\partial r}\,\mathbf{u}_\theta + \frac{\partial A_\theta}{\partial r}\,\mathbf{u}_\phi \tag{9.34}$$

The θ and ϕ-components of the electric field are solved using (9.9) and (9.13):

$$E_\theta = \frac{jE_x}{2\lambda r}\,e^{-jkr}(1 + \cos\theta)\cos\phi\,dS \tag{9.35}$$

$$E_\phi = \frac{jE_x}{2\lambda r}\,e^{-jkr}(1 + \cos\theta)(-\sin\phi)\,dS \tag{9.36}$$

The power density produced by the surface element is

$$S = \frac{1}{2}\frac{|E_\theta|^2 + |E_\phi|^2}{\eta} = \frac{1}{2\eta}\left(\frac{E_x\,dS}{\lambda r}\right)^2 \cos^4(\theta/2) \tag{9.37}$$

Figure 9.20 shows a rectangular radiating aperture, which is in the xy-plane and whose center is at the origin. The width of the aperture is a in the x-direction and b in the y-direction. The electric field E_x has a constant amplitude and phase over the whole aperture. The magnetic field is $H_y = E_x/\eta$. Thus, the aperture is like a part of a plane wave.

Far away from the aperture the field is obtained by integrating the field of the surface element, (9.35) and (9.36), over the aperture. Because the aperture field is constant, the integration simplifies to an integration of the phase term e^{-jkR}, where the distance from the surface element to the point of observation P varies. Far from the aperture

$$R \approx r - r'\cos\varphi \tag{9.38}$$

where r' is the distance of the surface element from the origin and φ is the angle between the vectors $\mathbf{r}$ and $\mathbf{r}'$. The variable term $r'\cos\varphi$ can be written as

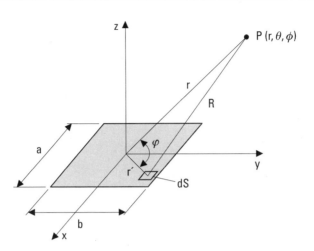

Figure 9.20 Radiating aperture.

$r' \cos \varphi = \mathbf{u_r} \cdot \mathbf{r}'$

$$= (\mathbf{u_x} \sin \theta \cos \phi + \mathbf{u_y} \sin \theta \sin \phi + \mathbf{u_z} \cos \theta) \cdot (\mathbf{u_x} x' + \mathbf{u_y} y')$$

$$= x' \sin \theta \cos \phi + y' \sin \theta \sin \phi \qquad (9.39)$$

where x' and y' are the coordinates of the surface element. Integration gives the θ-component of the electric field:

$$E_\theta = \frac{jE_x}{2\lambda r} e^{-jkr}(1 + \cos \theta) \cos \phi \int_{-b/2}^{b/2} \int_{-a/2}^{a/2} e^{jk(x' \sin \theta \cos \phi + y' \sin \theta \sin \phi)} \, dx' \, dy'$$

$$= \frac{jabE_x}{2\lambda r} e^{-jkr}(1 + \cos \theta) \cos \phi \left[\frac{\sin\left(\frac{1}{2} ka \sin \theta \cos \phi\right)}{\frac{1}{2} ka \sin \theta \cos \phi} \right]$$

$$\cdot \left[\frac{\sin\left(\frac{1}{2} kb \sin \theta \sin \phi\right)}{\frac{1}{2} kb \sin \theta \sin \phi} \right] \qquad (9.40)$$

Correspondingly, the ϕ-component is

$$E_\phi = \frac{jabE_x}{2\lambda r} e^{-jkr}(1 + \cos\theta)(-\sin\phi)\left[\frac{\sin\left(\frac{1}{2}ka\sin\theta\cos\phi\right)}{\frac{1}{2}ka\sin\theta\cos\phi}\right]$$

$$\cdot\left[\frac{\sin\left(\frac{1}{2}kb\sin\theta\sin\phi\right)}{\frac{1}{2}kb\sin\theta\sin\phi}\right] \quad (9.41)$$

In the E- or xz-plane ($\phi = 0°$), the electric field has only the E_θ-component, and in the H- or yz-plane ($\phi = 90°$), only the E_ϕ-component.

If the aperture is large (a and $b \gg \lambda$), the field is significant at small θ angles only. Then $\cos\theta \approx 1$ and $\sin\theta \approx \theta$, and the normalized directional patterns in the E- and H-planes simplify to

$$E_n(\theta, \phi = 0°) = \left|\frac{\sin\left(\frac{1}{2}ka\theta\right)}{\frac{1}{2}ka\theta}\right| \quad (9.42)$$

$$E_n(\theta, \phi = 90°) = \left|\frac{\sin\left(\frac{1}{2}kb\theta\right)}{\frac{1}{2}kb\theta}\right| \quad (9.43)$$

Figure 9.21 shows the directional pattern in the E-plane. It can be solved from (9.42) that the first null in the E-plane is at an angle of

$$\theta_0 = \frac{\lambda}{a} \quad (9.44)$$

and the half-power beamwidth is

$$\theta_{3dB} \approx 0.89\frac{\lambda}{a} \quad (9.45)$$

and the level of the first sidelobe is -13.3 dB.

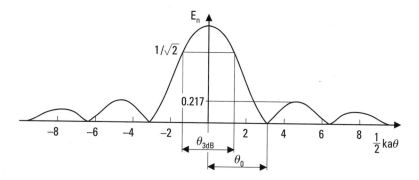

Figure 9.21 Normalized directional pattern of a rectangular aperture.

The maximum power density produced by the rectangular aperture is

$$S_{max} = \frac{1}{2\eta}\left(\frac{E_x ab}{\lambda r}\right)^2 \qquad (9.46)$$

Because $\int_{-\infty}^{\infty} \sin^2 x/x^2\, dx = \pi$, the average power density produced by a large aperture is

$$S_{av} = \frac{1}{4\pi}\int\int_{4\pi} S\,d\Omega \approx \frac{1}{4\pi}S_{max}\frac{2\pi}{ka}\frac{2\pi}{kb} \qquad (9.47)$$

The ratio of these power densities, the directivity, is

$$D = \frac{S_{max}}{S_{av}} = \frac{4\pi}{\lambda^2}ab \qquad (9.48)$$

Assuming a lossless aperture $(D = G)$ and comparing (9.48) to (9.4), we can see that the physical and effective areas are equal, that is, $ab = A_{eff}$.

The radiation pattern of an aperture antenna having an arbitrary shape, amplitude distribution, and phase distribution is calculated using the same principle as above: The fields produced by the surface elements are summed at the point of observation.

If a rectangular aperture has a field distribution of a form $f(x)g(y)$, the normalized patterns in the xz- and yz-planes are those of the line sources (one-dimensional apertures) having aperture distributions of $f(x)$ and $g(y)$, respectively. The normalized pattern is the product of the normalized patterns in the xz- and yz-planes.

Table 9.1 shows properties of line sources having different amplitude distributions. The constant amplitude distribution gives the narrowest beam but the highest level of sidelobes. If the amplitude of the field decreases toward the edge of the aperture, the beamwidth increases, the gain decreases, and the sidelobe level decreases.

Earlier it was assumed that the phase of the aperture was constant. In practice, a quadratic phase distribution is usual. Then constant phase fronts are nearly spherical in the aperture. Figure 9.22 shows directional patterns for line sources having a constant amplitude but quadratic phase distribution. As the parameter Δ (phase difference between the center and edge in wavelengths) increases, gain decreases, sidelobes increase, and nulls get filled.

The properties of circular apertures are listed in Table 9.2 for different amplitude distributions (the phase is constant). If the aperture has a constant amplitude, the normalized directional pattern is

$$E_n(\theta) = 2 \left| \frac{J_1\left(\frac{1}{2} kD \sin \theta\right)}{\frac{1}{2} kD \sin \theta} \right| \qquad (9.49)$$

where D is the diameter of the aperture and J_1 is the Bessel function of the first kind of order one.

Table 9.1
Properties of Line Sources

Amplitude Distribution in Aperture	Half-Power Beamwidth	Level of First Sidelobe	Position of First Null
Constant	$0.89\lambda/a$	−13.3 dB	λ/a
$\cos(\pi x/a)$	$1.19\lambda/a$	−23.1 dB	$1.5\lambda/a$
$\cos^2(\pi x/a)$	$1.44\lambda/a$	−31.5 dB	$2.0\lambda/a$
$1 - 0.5(2x/a)^2$	$0.97\lambda/a$	−17.1 dB	$1.14\lambda/a$
Taylor, $n = 3$, edge −9 dB	$1.07\lambda/a$	−25.0 dB	—

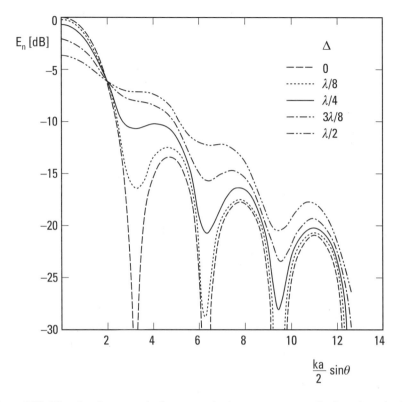

Figure 9.22 Directional pattern of a line source having a constant amplitude and quadratic phase distribution; Δ is the phase difference between the center and edge of the aperture in wavelengths.

Table 9.2
Properties of Circular Apertures

Amplitude Distribution in Aperture	Half-Power Beamwidth	Level of First Sidelobe	Position of First Null
Constant	$1.02\lambda/D$	−17.6 dB	$1.22\lambda/D$
$1 - r^2$	$1.27\lambda/D$	−24.6 dB	$1.63\lambda/D$
$(1 - r^2)^2$	$1.47\lambda/D$	−30.6 dB	$2.03\lambda/D$
$0.5 + 0.5(1 - r^2)^2$	$1.16\lambda/D$	−26.5 dB	$1.51\lambda/D$
Taylor	$1.31\lambda/D$	−40.0 dB	—

9.7 Horn Antennas

An open waveguide end operates as a simple antenna. It has a broad, unsymmetrical beam and a rather large impedance mismatch. A much better antenna, a horn antenna, is obtained by widening the waveguide end, as shown in Figure 9.23.

H-plane, E-plane, and pyramidal horns are fed from a rectangular waveguide. An H-plane horn is widened along the broad side of the waveguide, an E-plane horn along the narrow side. A pyramidal horn is broadened in both directions. The distribution of the aperture field follows the field distribution of the fundamental waveguide mode, TE_{10}. Because the amplitude in the E-plane is constant, the sidelobes are higher in this plane than in the H-plane, which has a cosine amplitude distribution tapering to zero at the edges. However, the phase in the aperture is not constant; rather it is quadratic. The H- and E-plane horns have cylindrical phase fronts, which seem to emanate from the apex. The apex is in the intersection of the slanting side planes. The phase difference between the center and edge of the aperture is in wavelengths

$$\Delta = (1 - \cos \theta_0) \frac{L}{\lambda} \qquad (9.50)$$

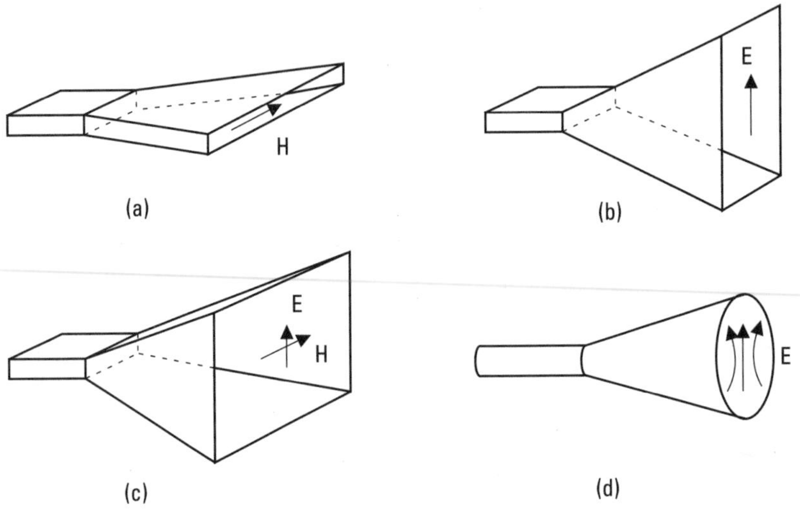

Figure 9.23 Horn antennas: (a) H-plane horn; (b) E-plane horn; (c) pyramidal horn; and (d) conical horn.

where θ_0 is half of the opening angle and L is the distance from the apex to the aperture.

Figure 9.24 gives the directivities D_E and D_H for E- and H-plane horns. Because of the aperture phase error Δ, it is impractical to make a horn, which has a very high directivity. For a fixed length L, the directivity increases as the aperture size increases until it collapses due to the phase error. The directivity of a pyramidal horn is obtained from the directivities of the corresponding E- and H-plane horns:

$$D \approx \frac{\pi D_E D_H \lambda^2}{32ab} \qquad (9.51)$$

where a is the width and b is the height of the input waveguide. Usually, the losses of horn antennas are small, and the gain and directivity are approximately equal.

A conical horn like that shown in Figure 9.23(d) is obtained by widening a circular waveguide. Although the structure is symmetrical, the fields of the fundamental mode TE_{11} are not. Therefore, the E- and H-plane directional patterns are different.

Figure 9.25 shows horn antennas, which produce more symmetrical beams than pyramidal and conical horns. The rectangular waveguide feeding the diagonal horn, shown in Figure 9.25(a), transforms first to a circular waveguide and then to a square waveguide, which is at a 45° angle to the feeding waveguide. The field of the aperture is a combination of the fields of TE_{10} and TE_{01} modes. The beam of a diagonal horn is fairly symmetrical,

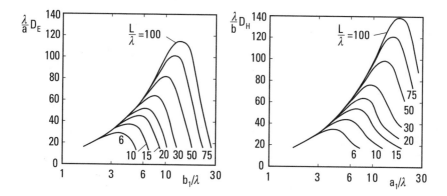

Figure 9.24 Directivities of E-plane horns, D_E, and H-plane horns, D_H. Aperture size in E-plane = b_1, aperture size in H-plane = a_1.

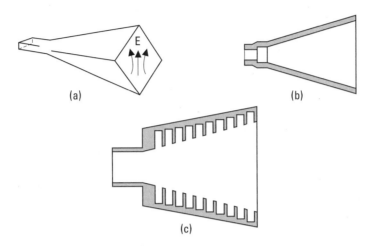

Figure 9.25 (a) Diagonal horn; (b) Potter horn; and (c) corrugated horn.

but the level of cross polarization is high in the 45° and 135° planes between the E- and H-planes.

A Potter horn or a dual-mode horn, shown in Figure 9.25(b), is a conical horn, which has a step in the feeding circular waveguide. The fundamental mode TE_{11} and the TM_{11} mode excited at the step together produce an aperture field having parallel field lines, if the modes have proper amplitudes and a proper phase difference in the aperture. The Potter horn has a symmetrical pattern, low sidelobe level, and low cross-polarization level. However, it has a narrow bandwidth because the phasing of modes depends on the frequency.

A corrugated horn, shown in Figure 9.25(c), is a conical horn having a corrugated inner wall. The number of grooves should be at least two per wavelength. The depth of grooves is about $\lambda/4$. Near the throat the depth changes gradually to $\lambda/2$ to ensure a good impedance match between the input waveguide and the flaring section. The mode propagating in the horn is HE_{11}, a hybrid of TE_{11} and TM_{11} modes. A corrugated horn has many good properties: a symmetrical pattern, low sidelobe level, low cross-polarization level, and broad operating bandwidth.

9.8 Reflector Antennas

Reflector antennas are used as high-gain, narrow-beam antennas in fixed radio links, satellite communication, radars, and radio astronomy.

A parabolic reflector antenna is the most common of reflector antennas. Figure 9.26(a) shows a parabolic antenna fed from the primary focus. The equation of the surface is

$$\rho = \frac{2F}{1 + \cos \theta} \tag{9.52}$$

where F is the focal length. The rays coming from the focal point are converted parallel by the reflector or vice versa. A more physical interpretation is that the fields radiated by the feed antenna induce surface currents, which in turn produce the aperture fields. The feed antenna is often a horn antenna. The phase center of the feed antenna should coincide with the focal point to obtain maximum gain.

The Cassegrainian antenna shown in Figure 9.26(b) is fed from the secondary focus behind the reflector. The subreflector is a hyperbolic reflector. This configuration has several advantages compared to the primary focus-fed antenna: Transmitters and receivers can be placed behind the reflector; transmission lines between the feed and the radio equipment are short; positioning of the feed antenna is less critical; the phase and amplitude distribution of the aperture field can be adjusted with a shaped subreflector; and the feed pattern over the edge of the subreflector is directed toward a cold sky in satellite reception, which leads to a lower antenna noise temperature. A more complicated structure and often a larger blockage of the aperture are the disadvantages of the Cassegrainian antenna.

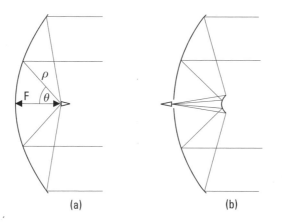

(a)   (b)

Figure 9.26 Parabolic reflector antennas: (a) a primary focus fed antenna; and (b) a Cassegrainian antenna.

The theoretical directional patterns of circular apertures are only rough approximations of real patterns. Aperture field distribution depends on the radiation pattern of the feed antenna and on the ratio of the focal length and diameter of the reflector, F/D. A constant aperture field gives the highest gain but also the highest sidelobe level. A high edge illumination leads also to a high feed radiation over the edge of the reflector. Tapering the aperture illumination toward the edge leads to a lower aperture efficiency and gain but improves the pattern by lowering the sidelobes. Typically, the field at the edge is 10 dB to 12 dB lower than that at the center, and the aperture efficiency is about 0.6.

Many factors have an effect on the pattern of a reflector antenna: amplitude and phase pattern of the feed; positioning of the feed; aperture blockage due to the struts, feed, and subreflector; multiple reflections between the feed and reflector; and errors in the shape of the reflector and subreflector. Small random errors in the surface of the reflector reduce the gain and move energy from the main beam to the sidelobes. If the rms value of the surface errors is ϵ, the aperture efficiency is

$$\eta_{ap} = \eta_0 \exp\left[-(4\pi\epsilon/\lambda)^2\right] \tag{9.53}$$

where η_0 is the aperture efficiency for an ideal surface. The surface error ϵ should not exceed $\lambda/16$.

The struts and the feed or the subreflector block a part of the aperture, which reduces η_{ap} and changes the level of sidelobes. They also scatter and diffract energy over a large solid angle. Also the edge of the reflector diffracts, which often produces a back lobe opposite to the main lobe.

The aperture blockage can be avoided by using offset geometry. Figure 9.27 shows offset-fed reflector antennas. The single-offset antenna has a simpler structure but the offset geometry inherently produces cross polarization. The dual-offset antenna has two distinct advantages compared to the single-offset antenna: The cross-polar field can be compensated and the aperture field distribution can be adjusted by shaping the reflectors. Dual-offset reflectors may have excellent sidelobe properties.

9.9 Other Antennas

In addition to the antennas discussed already, there are a large number of other antenna types. Some of them are briefly described here.

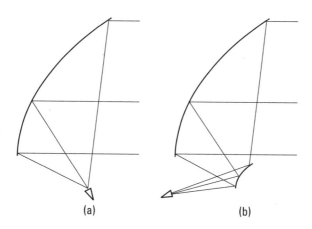

Figure 9.27 Offset-fed reflector antennas: (a) single-offset; and (b) dual-offset.

Microstrip antennas are small, light, and suitable for integration and mass-production [6, 7]. Figure 9.28(a) shows the basic microstrip antenna: a rectangular, half-wave-long patch. It is made on a substrate having a ground plane on the other side. The patch is fed with a microstrip line from the edge and it radiates from both open-ended edges. The linearly polarized main beam is perpendicular to the surface. Because the antenna radiates effectively only at the resonance frequency, it has a narrow bandwidth. Fairly high loss is another disadvantage of microstrip antennas.

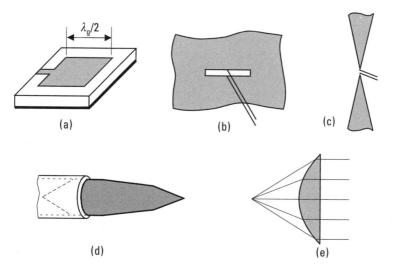

Figure 9.28 (a) Microstrip antenna; (b) slot antenna; (c) bow-tie antenna; (d) dielectric rod antenna; and (e) lens antenna.

There are many variations on the basic microstrip antenna: different shapes of the patch, ways to feed the patch, and possibilities to combine elements to an array. A circularly polarized wave can be produced with a square patch, which is fed from the adjacent sides so that the phase difference of the feeds is 90°. A patch can also be fed with a coaxial cable through the substrate, in which case the input impedance depends on the position of the feed point. Feeding through a slot in the ground plane allows the radiating patches to be separated from the feed lines and other circuits. The directivity of a single element is low. A higher directivity is obtained by combining a large number of elements (see Section 9.10).

A slot antenna is a radiating slot in a metal plane, as shown in Figure 9.28(b). It is dual with a dipole antenna; that is, the radiation pattern is that of a dipole except that the electric and magnetic fields are interchanged. A slot antenna can be fed from a parallel-wire line, coaxial line, microstrip line, or waveguide. A waveguide having an array of slots is a common antenna. A slot in a waveguide wall radiates if it disturbs surface currents; a narrow slot, which is along the current flow, does not radiate.

The bow-tie antenna shown in Figure 9.28(c) is an example of a broadband antenna. The feed point is in the center of two planar conductors. The input impedance and directional pattern may be frequency-independent over a frequency range of one decade or more. In an ideal case, the bow-tie antenna has no dimensions, which can be expressed in wavelengths; the opening angle of the conductors is the only dimension. In practice, the structure of the feed point and the finite length of the conductors set limits for the frequency range. Often bow-tie antennas are placed on a dielectric substrate. Then the main lobe is on the dielectric side. Other frequency-independent shapes used in broadband antennas are spirals and cones.

Antennas made of dielectric materials have some mechanical and electrical advantages [8]. Figure 9.28(d) shows a dielectric rod antenna, which is placed at the open end of a circular waveguide. This kind of an antenna works well as a feed antenna.

Like a parabolic reflector, a lens antenna operates as a phase modifier, which changes a spherical phase front to a planar one. The paths of the rays from the focal point of the lens to a plane in front of the lens have equal electrical lengths. Lenses are usually made of low-loss dielectric materials. The phase velocity of the wave is $c/\sqrt{\epsilon_r}$ in the dielectric material. Figure 9.28(e) shows a simple plano-convex lens. The reflections in the air-dielectric interfaces can be eliminated with quarter-wave matching layers. Lenses are often used to correct the phase error at the aperture of a horn antenna.

9.10 Antenna Arrays

An antenna array is an entity consisting of two or more element antennas. Antenna arrays may have many good properties, which cannot be achieved with a single element, such as high gain, narrow beam, shaped beam, scanning beam, or adaptive beam.

Figure 9.29 shows an array that consists of two elements having a separation of d. Let us assume that the far-field patterns of the antennas are $E_1(\phi)$ and $E_2(\phi)$ and that the phase difference of the feed currents is δ (in this case the lengths of the feed lines are different). The total field produced by the array is

$$E(\phi) = E_1(\phi)\,e^{-j(kd\,\cos\,\phi + \delta)} + E_2(\phi) \tag{9.54}$$

The path length difference of $d\cos\phi$ in free space produces the phase difference of $kd\cos\phi$. The fields of the elements are in the same phase in directions ϕ_{max} that meet the condition of

$$kd\,\cos\,\phi_{max} + \delta = n2\pi \tag{9.55}$$

where n is an integer. The fields have opposite phases in directions ϕ_{min} which meet the condition of

$$kd\,\cos\,\phi_{min} + \delta = n2\pi + \pi \tag{9.56}$$

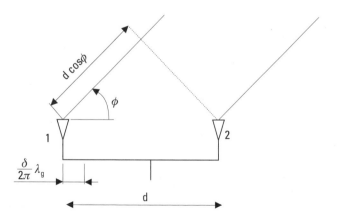

Figure 9.29 An array of two elements.

If the elements of Figure 9.29 are similar, $E_1(\phi) = E_2(\phi)$, and they are fed in phase, $\delta = 0$, (9.54) can be written as

$$E(\phi) = E_1(\phi)(1 + e^{-jkd \cos \phi}) \qquad (9.57)$$

The array pattern is the product of the element pattern and the array factor. If the element pattern maximum and the array factor maximum coincide in the same direction, the maximum field is twice that produced by a single element, $E = 2E_1(\phi_{max})$. However, even if the power density is now four times that produced by a single element, the gain of the array is only twice the gain of an element. The power density produced by an element would be doubled if all the input power of the array were fed to that element alone. The normalized pattern may look like that shown in Figure 9.30. The envelope follows the element pattern, and at minima the fields of the elements cancel each other out. As the separation d increases, the number of maxima and minima in the pattern increases.

Many kinds of directional patterns can be realized by changing the distance (or frequency) and phase difference of the elements. Figure 9.31 shows some patterns when the elements radiate isotropically in the ϕ-plane (for example dipoles which are perpendicular to the ϕ-plane).

Also, the pattern of an array consisting of more than two elements can be expressed as the product of the element pattern and the array factor. The array factor depends on the positions, amplitudes, and phases of the elements. The array may be linear, planar, or conformal (shaped according to the surface). The elements of a linear array are on a line. Figure 9.32 shows a

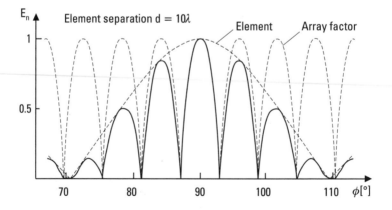

Figure 9.30 Pattern of a two-element array (solid line) equals the element pattern multiplied by the array factor.

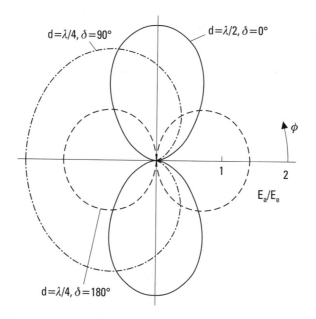

Figure 9.31 Directional patterns of two-element arrays in polar form. The elements are isotropic in the ϕ-plane. E_a/E_e = field of array divided by the field of the element.

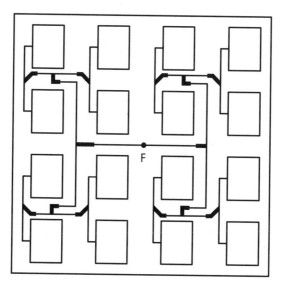

Figure 9.32 Microstrip antenna array (F = feed point).

planar array, which consists of 16 microstrip antenna elements fed in phase and with equal amplitudes. This array is like the rectangular aperture antenna treated in Section 9.6. Many kinds of different patterns can be realized by choosing proper amplitudes and phases for the elements. Besides microstrip elements, an array may consist of many other types of elements such as dipoles, slots, or horns [9].

If there are electronically controlled phase shifters in the feed network of an array, the direction of the beam can be changed rapidly without rotating the antenna. This kind of electronic scanning is much faster than mechanical scanning. A phased array combined with digital signal processing may operate as an adaptive antenna. The pattern of an adaptive antenna changes according to the electromagnetic environment; for example, the beam of a base-station antenna may follow a moving user and a null may be formed in the direction of an interfering signal. An adaptive antenna may also partly correct the deterioration of its pattern, if one or more of its elements breaks down. Adaptive antennas are also called "smart" antennas.

9.11 Matching of Antennas

In principle, an antenna may be matched as any load impedance. However, some wire antennas, such as dipole and loop antennas, need a special attention if they are fed from an unsymmetrical line. For example, if a dipole antenna is connected directly to a coaxial line, currents will flow on the outer surface of the outer conductor. Then the outer conductor will radiate and the directional pattern will be distorted.

The radiation of the outer conductor can be prevented with a balun, a balanced-to-unbalanced transformer. The balun of Figure 9.33(a) has a short-circuited quarter-wave line outside the outer conductor. Thus, the impedance between A and B is large. Now, a symmetric load as a dipole antenna can be connected between A and C so that the outer conductor does not radiate. The balun of Figure 9.33(b) transforms the characteristic impedance of the coaxial line, Z_0, to an impedance of $4Z_0$ between A and B. In the balun of Figure 9.33(c) the coaxial line changes gradually to a parallel-wire line.

9.12 Link Between Two Antennas

Let us assume that a signal is transmitted from one antenna to another. The antennas are in free space and their separation r is large compared to the

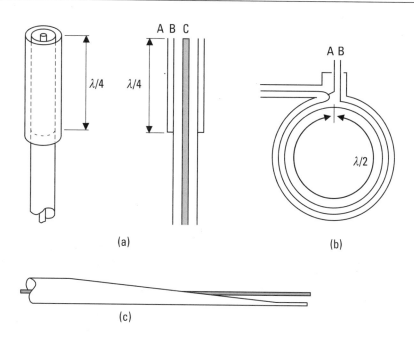

Figure 9.33 Baluns: (a) a short-circuited sleeve of a length $\lambda/4$ over a coaxial cable; (b) a loop of a length $\lambda/2$ of a coaxial line; and (c) the outer conductor of a coaxial line changes gradually to a parallel-wire line.

distances obtained from (9.1). The main beams of the antennas are pointing toward each other and their polarizations are matched.

If the power accepted by the transmitting antenna, P_t, were transmitted isotropically, the power density at a distance of r would be

$$S_{isot} = \frac{P_t}{4\pi r^2} \qquad (9.58)$$

The maximum power density produced by the transmitting antenna having a gain of G_t is

$$S = \frac{G_t P_t}{4\pi r^2} \qquad (9.59)$$

The corresponding electric field amplitude produced by the antenna is

$$E = \sqrt{2\eta S} \qquad (9.60)$$

The power available from the receiving antenna is its effective area A_r times the power density of the incoming wave:

$$P_r = A_r S \tag{9.61}$$

Using (9.4) and (9.59), this can be written as the Friis free-space equation:

$$P_r = G_t G_r \left(\frac{\lambda}{4\pi r} \right)^2 P_t \tag{9.62}$$

where G_r is the gain of the receiving antenna.

In practice, many factors may reduce the power received, such as errors in the pointing of the antennas, polarization mismatch, loss due to the atmosphere, and fading due to multipath propagation. Losses due to impedance mismatches also have to be taken into account; generally, the power accepted by the transmitting antenna is smaller than the available power of the transmitter, and the power accepted by the receiver is smaller than the available power from the receiving antenna.

Example 9.3

What is the loss P_t/P_r at 12 GHz from a geostationary satellite at a distance of 40,000 km? Both the transmitting and receiving antennas have a diameter of $D = 1$m and an aperture efficiency of $\eta_{ap} = 0.6$.

Solution

The antennas have an effective area of $A_{eff} = \eta_{ap} \pi D^2/4 = 0.47$ m^2 and a gain of $G = 4\pi A_{eff}/\lambda^2 = 9\,500$. The loss $P_t/P_r = (4\pi r/G\lambda)^2 = 4.5 \times 10^{12}$, in decibels $10 \log(4.5 \times 10^{12})$ dB $= 126.5$ dB. Here, the attenuation of the atmosphere is not taken into account. During a clear weather, the atmospheric attenuation is about 0.3 dB at 12 GHz.

Example 9.4

How accurately the receiving antenna of the preceding example has to be pointed to the satellite, if the allowed maximum pointing loss is 0.5 dB? The satellite transmits two orthogonal, linearly polarized signals. How accurately must the tilt angle of the linearly polarized receiving antenna be adjusted if (a) the maximum loss due to polarization mismatch is 0.5 dB, and if (b) the maximum power coupled between the orthogonal channels is −30 dB?

Solution

The beamwidth of the receiving antenna is $\theta_{3dB} \approx 1.2\lambda/D = 0.03$ rad = 1.7°. The pattern level depends approximately quadratically on the angle near the main beam maximum. Thus, the maximum allowed pointing error is $(0.5/3)^{1/2} \times 1.7°/2 = 0.35°$. The antenna receives only the component of the incoming wave that has the same polarization as the antenna. (a) From $20 \log (\cos \Delta\tau) = -0.5$ we solve that an error of $\Delta\tau = 19.3°$ in the tilt angle reduces the received power by 0.5 dB. (b) From $20 \log (\sin \Delta\tau) = -30$ we solve that $\Delta\tau = 1.8°$ gives a cross-polar discrimination of 30 dB. Thus, to avoid interference between the orthogonal channels, the error in the tilt angle should not be too large.

References

[1] Kraus, J. D., and R. J. Marhefka, *Antennas for All Applications,* 3rd ed., New York: McGraw-Hill, 2002.

[2] Lo, Y. T., and S. W. Lee, (eds.), *Antenna Handbook: Theory, Applications, and Design,* New York: Van Nostrand Reinhold, 1988.

[3] Rudge, A. W., et al., (eds.), *The Handbook of Antenna Design, Vol. 1,* London, England: Peter Peregrinus, 1982.

[4] Rudge, A. W., et al., (eds.), *The Handbook of Antenna Design, Vol. 2,* London, England: Peter Peregrinus, 1983.

[5] Fujimoto, K., and J. R. James, (eds.), *Mobile Antenna Systems Handbook,* Norwood, MA: Artech House, 1994.

[6] Garg, P., et al., *Microstrip Antenna Design Handbook,* Norwood, MA: Artech House, 2001.

[7] Lee, K. F., and W. Chen, (eds.), *Advances in Microstrip and Printed Antennas,* New York: John Wiley & Sons, 1997.

[8] Chatterjee, R., *Dielectric and Dielectric-Loaded Antennas,* New York: John Wiley & Sons, 1985.

[9] Sehm, T., A. Lehto, and A. Räisänen, "A High-Gain 58-GHz Box-Horn Array Antenna with Suppressed Grating Lobes," *IEEE Trans. on Antennas and Propagation,* Vol. 47, No. 7, 1999, pp. 1125–1130.

10

Propagation of Radio Waves

In the previous chapter we studied a radio link between two antennas. Equation (9.62) applies for the link between two antennas when the wave propagates unhindered and without atmospheric attenuation; only the decrease of power density as $1/r^2$ is taken into account. In practice, many factors, such as troposphere, ionosphere, terrain, and buildings, affect propagation of the radio waves. From a system point of view, the concept of the radio propagation channel or just the radio channel covers the radio wave propagation phenomena between a transmitting and receiving antenna. This channel may be considered as a system element that transforms input signals into output signals. It is analogous to a time-variant linear filter.

10.1 Environment and Propagation Mechanisms

The troposphere is the lowest part of the atmosphere, where all weather phenomena occur. It extends on the poles to about 9 km and on the equator to about 17 km. The troposphere is inhomogeneous and constantly changing. Temperature, pressure, humidity, and precipitation affect the propagation of radio waves. In the troposphere the radio waves attenuate, scatter, refract, and reflect; the amplitude and phase of the received signal may fluctuate randomly due to multipath propagation; the polarization of the wave may change; noise originating from the atmosphere is added to the signal.

The ionosphere extends from about 60 km to 1,000 km. It contains plasma, which is gas ionized by the solar ultraviolet and particle radiation.

The free electrons of the ionosphere form a mirror, which reflects the radio waves at frequencies below about 10 MHz. The upper frequency limit of reflection depends on time of day and season, and on solar activity.

Also terrain and man-made objects diffract, scatter, and reflect radio waves. At low frequencies the attenuation of the ground waves (waves propagating close to the Earth's surface) depends on the electrical properties of the ground.

Radio waves can propagate from one point to another in many ways. The most important mechanisms of propagation used in radio systems are, in order of decreasing frequency, the following:

1. *Propagation along a line-of-sight (LOS) path.* This resembles the propagation in free space. Because of refraction, the radio horizon is farther away than the geometrical horizon. In UHF, SHF, and EHF bands most radio systems require an LOS path. From the millimeter-wave band to infrared, the radio link hops are short because of attenuation due to precipitation and gas molecules. In VHF and UHF bands multipath propagation is common: The LOS path may be complemented or interfered by diffraction and reflection from buildings and ground as well as by propagation through vegetation and building walls.

2. *Scattering from inhomogeneities of the atmosphere.* The applicable frequency range is from 300 MHz to 10 GHz.

3. *Propagation via the ionosphere.* A radio wave may reflect from the ionosphere at frequencies below 30 MHz. A wave may also reflect multiple times between the ionosphere and ground, and thus propagate round the globe.

4. *Ground-wave propagation.* The attenuation of the ground wave increases rapidly versus frequency; this phenomenon is important at frequencies below 10 MHz.

Figure 10.1 illustrates different propagation mechanisms. In a given radio link, the waves may propagate through several different mechanisms. In long hops, a ground wave is dominating up to 150 kHz, and the ionospheric wave in the frequency range of 1.5 MHz to 30 MHz, depending on the state of the ionosphere. At frequencies from 150 kHz to 1,500 kHz both mechanisms are equally important. As it does in VHF and UHF bands, the wave propagates through several paths, but now the reason is diffraction and reflection from buildings and ground. Due to the interference of waves

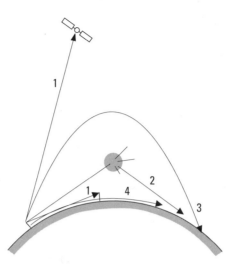

Figure 10.1 Propagation mechanisms of radio waves (numbers refer to different mechanisms described in text).

propagating via different routes, the power level of the received signal may alternate considerably over time and location (fast fading).

Propagation beyond the radio horizon is also possible due to tropospheric reflections at frequencies from 30 MHz to 1,000 MHz, and due to ducting at frequencies above 1 GHz. These propagation mechanisms are, however, so unreliable, that one cannot build a continuous radio path based on them. On the contrary, they cause interference to other radio links in the same frequency band.

In general, the available power received cannot be accurately predicted. The signal power level may alternate several tens of decibels in a given radio path. In order to reach a high reliability in a radio system, one must know the statistical distribution of the link attenuation and design the antenna sizes and power of transmission accordingly.

10.2 Tropospheric Attenuation

At frequencies above a few gigahertz, the attenuation due to atmospheric absorption and scattering must be taken into account. This attenuation can be divided into two parts: attenuation due to clear air and attenuation due to precipitation (raindrops, hail, and snow flakes) and fog. Attenuation of the clear air is mainly due to resonance states of oxygen (O_2) and water vapor (H_2O) molecules. An energy quantum corresponding to the resonance frequency may change the rotational energy state of a gas molecule. When the molecule absorbs an energy quantum, the molecule is excited to a higher energy state. When it returns back to equilibrium—that is, drops back to the ground state—it radiates the energy difference, but not necessarily at the same frequency because returning to equilibrium may happen in smaller energy steps. Under pressure the molecular emission lines have a wide spectrum. Therefore the energy quantum is lost from the propagating wave, and for the same reason the atmosphere is always noisy at all frequencies.

The lowest resonance frequencies of oxygen are 60 GHz and 119 GHz, and those of water vapor are 22, 183, and 325 GHz. The amount of oxygen is always nearly constant, but that of water vapor is highly variable versus time and location. The attenuation constant due to water vapor is directly proportional to the absolute amount of water vapor, which is a function of temperature and humidity. Figure 10.2 presents the clear air attenuation versus frequency. Between the resonance frequencies there are so-called spectral windows centered at frequencies 35, 95, 140, and 220 GHz. At resonance frequencies the attenuation may be tens of decibels per kilometer. These frequencies are, however, suitable for intersatellite links, for short terrestrial links, and for WLANs.

Figure 10.3 presents attenuation due to rain and fog. Attenuation of rain is mainly due to scattering: The electric field of the radio wave polarizes

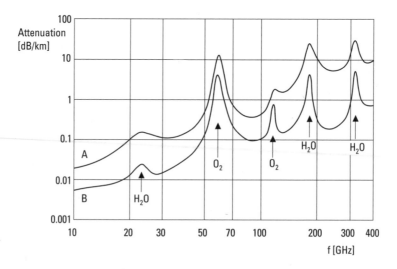

Figure 10.2 Attenuation in clear atmosphere versus frequency. Curve A: at sea level (T = 20°C, water vapor density 7.5 g/m³). Curve B: at altitude of 4 km (T = 0°C, water vapor density 1 g/m³).

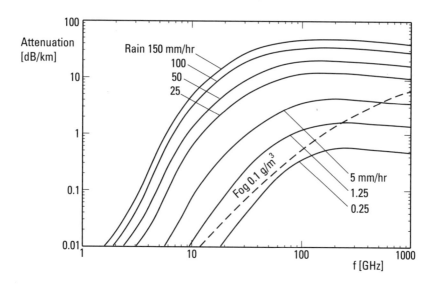

Figure 10.3 Attenuation due to rain and fog.

the water molecules of the raindrop, and then the raindrop acts like a small electric dipole radiating over a large solid angle. A heavy rain makes long radio hops impossible at frequencies above 10 GHz. In a moderate rain (5 mm/hr) attenuation is 0.08 dB/km at 10 GHz and 3 dB/km at 100 GHz. In a pouring rain (150 mm/hr) these values are about tenfold, but on the other hand the time percentage of such strong rains is small. In a heavy rain the drops are large and their shape is ellipsoidal. Then a horizontally polarized wave attenuates more than a vertically polarized wave. This phenomenon, depending on the wind speed, also causes depolarization of the wave, if the electric field is not along either axis of the raindrop. Depolarization results in unwanted coupling between orthogonally polarized channels and an extra loss in reception because the receiving antenna can accept only that polarization for which it is designed. The attenuation constant due to fog and clouds is nearly directly proportional to the amount of water.

Both real and imaginary parts of the dielectric constant of ice are clearly smaller than those of water. Therefore, attenuation due to dry snow is low. Wet snow causes more attenuation, and its attenuation is directly proportional to the amount of water.

Turbulence in the troposphere may cause also scintillation, that is, random changes in amplitude and phase of the wave as it propagates via different routes due to turbulence (refractive index may vary strongly over short distances). Atmospheric propagation phenomena were the subject of many studies at Helsinki University of Technology in the 1990s; some examples of the results are presented in [1–4].

10.3 Bending (Refraction) of Radio Waves in Troposphere

The refraction index $n = \sqrt{\epsilon_r}$ of the troposphere fluctuates over time and location. In normal conditions the refraction index decreases monotonically versus altitude, because the air density decreases. Because a phenomenon of this kind is a weak function of altitude, it causes slow bending of the ray. Fast changes in the refraction index cause scattering and reflections. Turbulence, where temperature or humidity differs strongly from those of the surroundings, gives rise to scattering. Reflections are caused by horizontal boundaries in the atmosphere due to weather phenomena.

Because n is always close to unity, we often use the so-called refractivity N, which is the difference of the refraction index value from unity in parts per million:

$$N = (n - 1) \times 10^6 \tag{10.1}$$

The refractivity for air is obtained from equations

$$N = \frac{77.6}{T}\left(p + 4{,}810\,\frac{e}{T}\right) \tag{10.2}$$

$$e = 6.11R \exp\left[19.7(T - 273)/T\right] \tag{10.3}$$

where T is the absolute temperature, p is the barometric pressure (unit mb = hPa), e is the partial pressure of water vapor (mb), and R is the relative humidity. The error of (10.2) is less than 0.5%, if $f < 30$ GHz, $p = 200\text{--}1{,}100$ mb, $T = 240\text{--}310$K, and $e < 30$ mb. If there is no resonance frequency of oxygen or water vapor molecules in the vicinity, this equation is useful up to 1,000 GHz.

According to an ITU-R specification, the average refractivity of the atmosphere versus altitude follows equation

$$N(h) = N_A e^{-b_A h} \tag{10.4}$$

where $N_A = 315$ and $b_A = 0.136$ km^{-1}. These values are calculated using the standard-atmosphere model: $p = 1{,}013$ mb, its change -12 mb/100m upward, $T = 15°C$, its change $-0.55°C/100m$ upward, $R = 60\%$. A more accurate model may be obtained by using maps published by ITU-R.

Let us now consider a wave that propagates in the troposphere in a direction that makes an angle ϕ with the horizontal plane, as shown in Figure 10.4. Because the refraction index changes with altitude, the angle ϕ changes while the wave propagates. According to Snell's law,

$$n \cos \phi = \text{constant} \tag{10.5}$$

By derivating this equation with altitude h, we get

$$\frac{dn}{dh} \cos \phi - n \sin \phi \frac{d\phi}{dh} = 0 \tag{10.6}$$

Let us mark the traveled distance in propagation direction as s; then we get

$$\frac{d\phi}{dh} = \frac{d\phi}{ds} \frac{ds}{dh} = \frac{d\phi}{ds} \frac{1}{\sin \phi} \tag{10.7}$$

We substitute this into (10.6), from which we solve

$$\frac{d\phi}{ds} = \frac{1}{n} \frac{dn}{dh} \cos \phi \approx \frac{dn}{dh} \tag{10.8}$$

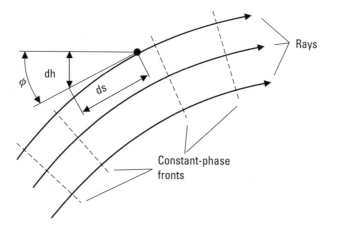

Figure 10.4 Refraction (bending) of a wave in the troposphere.

as $n \approx 1$, and for terrestrial radio paths in general $\phi \approx 0°$, that is, $\cos \phi \approx 1$. In an average atmosphere at sea level, the curvature (= -1/bending radius, i.e., the rate of change of direction with distance) of the ray is

$$\frac{d\phi}{ds} \approx \frac{dn}{dh} = -10^{-6}N_A b_A = -43 \times 10^{-6} \text{ km}^{-1} \qquad (10.9)$$

that is, the ray bends downward.

Also the Earth's surface bends downward, and its curvature is $-1/R$, where the Earth's radius is $R = 6{,}370$ km. Therefore the curvature of the ray in reference to the Earth's surface is

$$\frac{dn}{dh} + \frac{1}{R} = \frac{1}{KR} \qquad (10.10)$$

When analyzing radio paths in the troposphere, we can imagine that the ray is straight, if we use an effective Earth radius KR (see Figure 10.5). In the average atmosphere $KR = 8{,}760$ km or $K = 1.375$. Often we use a value of $K = 4/3$.

Temporarily the distribution of the refraction index versus altitude may differ considerably from that of the average atmosphere. If $dn/dh = -157 \times 10^{-6}$ km^{-1}, the ray bends as fast as the Earth's surface ($K = \infty$). If $dn/dh < -157 \times 10^{-6}$ km^{-1}, the ray bends toward the Earth's surface ($K < 0$). The wave may propagate long distances with successive reflections, as illustrated in Figure 10.6. Propagation with this mechanism is called ducting. Ducting may happen in the so-called inversion layer, where temperature increases rapidly as altitude increases. Such an inversion layer may range in height from a few meters to about 100m and may appear near the ground or at a high altitude.

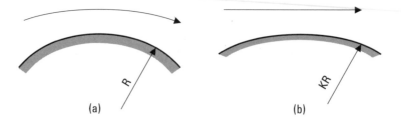

(a)   (b)

Figure 10.5 Propagation in the troposphere: (a) refraction; (b) a model of straight propagation above the surface of an extended globe.

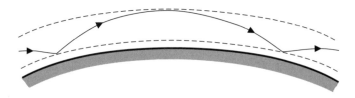

Figure 10.6 Ducting of a radio wave.

10.4 LOS Path

In an LOS path the receiving antenna is above the radio horizon of the transmitting station. Links between two satellites and between an earth station and a satellite are LOS paths, and a path between two terrestrial stations may be such. In the two latter cases the tropospheric effects discussed previously must be taken into account.

According to the ray theory, it is enough that just a ray can propagate unhindered from the transmitting antenna to the receiving antenna. In reality a radio wave requires much more space in order to propagate without extra loss. The free space must be the size of the so-called first Fresnel ellipsoid, shown in Figure 10.7. It is characterized by

$$r_1 + r_2 - r_0 = \lambda/2 \tag{10.11}$$

where r_1 and r_2 are distances of a point on the ellipsoid from the transmitting and receiving points, and r_0 is their direct distance. The radius of the first Fresnel ellipsoid is

$$b_F = \sqrt{\frac{\lambda r_1 r_2}{r_1 + r_2}} \tag{10.12}$$

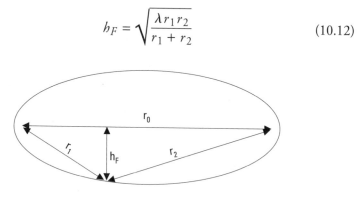

Figure 10.7 The first Fresnel ellipsoid.

We observe that the radius of the ellipsoid in a given path is the smaller the higher the frequency; that is, the ray theory holds better at higher frequencies.

Figure 10.8 shows the extra attenuation due to a knife-edge obstacle in the first Fresnel ellipsoid. According to the ray theory, an obstacle hindering the ray causes an infinite attenuation, and an obstacle just below the ray does not have any effect on the attenuation. However, the result shown in Figure 10.8 is reality and is better explained by Huygens' principle: Every point of the wavefront above the obstacle is a source point of a new spherical wave. This explains diffraction (or bending) of the wave due to an obstacle. Diffraction also helps the wave to propagate behind the obstacle to a space, which is not seen from the original point of transmission. When the knife-edge obstacle is just on the LOS path ($h = 0$), it causes an extra attenuation of 6 dB. When the obstacle reaches just to the lower boundary of the first Fresnel ellipsoid, the wave arriving at the receiving point may be even stronger than that in a fully obstacle-free case. If there is a hill in the propagation path that cannot be considered a knife-edge, extra attenuation is even higher than in case of a knife-edge obstacle.

When terrestrial radio-link hops are designed, bending of the Earth's surface as well as bending of the ray in the troposphere must be taken into

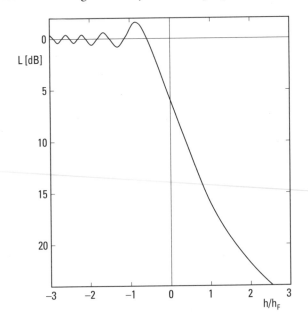

Figure 10.8 Extra attenuation due to the knife-edge diffraction.

account. The radio horizon is at the distance of r_H if the transmitting antenna is at the height of

$$h_H = \frac{r_H^2}{2KR} \qquad (10.13)$$

Example 10.1

Consider a 50-km radio-link hop at 10 GHz, when the antenna heights are the same. What are the required antenna heights?

Solution

Taking $K = 4/3$ we get from (10.13) that the radio horizon of the antennas is in the middle point of the path between the antennas, when $h_H = 36.8$m. By introducing $\lambda = 0.03$m and $r_1 = r_2 = 25$ km into (10.12) we get the radius of the first Fresnel ellipsoid in the middle point as $h_F = 19.4$m. The antenna heights must be then at least $h = h_H + h_F = 56.2$m. In addition, if there are woods in the path, the height of the trees must be taken into account.

At low frequencies, fulfillment of the requirement of leaving the first Fresnel ellipsoid empty is difficult. Often we must compromise. For example, at 100 MHz in the 50-km hop of the example, the maximum radius of the first Fresnel ellipsoid is 194m.

A radio-link hop design is aided by using a profile diagram of the terrain, which takes into account the bending of the radio ray in standard conditions. In the diagram, the height scale is much larger than the horizontal scale, and the terrain along the hop is drawn so that perpendicular directions against the Earth's surface are parallel. The middle point of the hop is placed in the middle of the diagram. After drawing the terrain, the antenna heights are selected so that the first Fresnel ellipsoid is fully in free space, if possible. Figure 10.9 presents a profile diagram between Korppoo and Turku in the Finnish archipelago.

10.5 Reflection from Ground

In an LOS path, the receiving antenna often receives, besides a direct wave, waves that are reflected from the ground or from obstacles such as buildings. This is called multipath propagation.

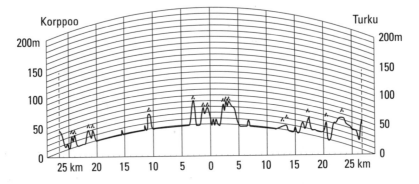

Figure 10.9 Profile diagram for radio-link hop planning.

Let us consider a simple situation, where there is a flat, smooth ground surface between the transmitting and receiving antenna masts, which are located so that their distance is d, and the distance between the transmitting and receiving points is r_0, as presented in Figure 10.10. In practice this situation may be quite typical in VHF and UHF radio broadcasting, where an antenna mast with a height h_1 is at the broadcasting station. Let us further assume that the transmitting antenna radiates isotropically. The electric field strength due to the direct wave at the distance r_0 from the transmitter is E_0. Taking also the reflected wave into account, the total electric field strength at the receiving point is

$$E \approx E_0\left[1 + \rho e^{-j\beta(r_1+r_2-r_0)}\right] \tag{10.14}$$

where ρ is the reflection coefficient of the ground surface, and we have assumed that $r_1 + r_2 \approx r_0$. The reflection coefficient depends on the electric

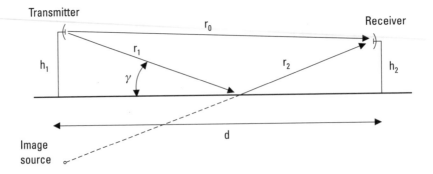

Figure 10.10 A direct and reflected wave.

properties of the surface and on the polarization of the wave. At frequencies above 30 MHz the reflection coefficient can be assumed to be -1 if the polarization is horizontal (or perpendicular) and the antenna heights are much less than the distance d; that is, the grazing angle γ is small. For the vertical or parallel polarization the amplitude and phase angle of the reflection coefficient vary rapidly at small angles γ [5].

In the following we assume a horizontal polarization. In practice the antenna heights h_1 and h_2 are often small compared to the distance d, and therefore the angle γ is small and $r_1 + r_2 - r_0 \approx 2h_1 h_2/d$. Now the field strength is

$$E \approx E_0\left(1 - e^{-j\beta 2h_1 h_2/d}\right) \tag{10.15}$$

The actual radiation pattern corresponds to that of the array formed by the transmitting antenna and its mirror image. The electric field strength E varies as a function of distance between values 0 and $2E_0$, as shown in Figure 10.11(a). Note that E_0 decreases as $1/d$. The nulls of the field strength (maxima for vertical polarization in case of an ideal conducting surface) are at heights $h_2 \approx n\lambda d/(2h_1)$, where $n = 0, 1, 2, \ldots$, as shown in Figure 10.11(b). The receiving antenna height must be selected correctly. In order to reduce the effects of reflections, it is possible to use a transmitting antenna that has radiation nulls at directions of the reflection points. Also, a forest at the theoretical reflection points helps because it effectively eliminates reflections.

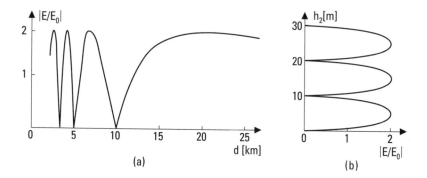

Figure 10.11 Field strength (a) as a function of the distance d when the receiving antenna height is $h_2 = 10$m and (b) as a function of the receiving antenna height h_2 when $d = 10$ km. The situation resembles Figure 10.10: $\rho = -1$, $f = 500$ MHz, $h_1 = 300$m.

Example 10.2

The transmitting antenna is located at a height of 300m. The frequency is 225 MHz, and the polarization is horizontal. What is the best height for a receiving antenna at a distance of 12 km, if the terrain between the antennas is a flat field?

Solution

Reflection from the surface causes a phase shift of 180°. Therefore the electric fields of the direct and reflected wave add up in phase when the path difference $r_1 + r_2 - r_0 \approx 2h_1 h_2/d$ is equal to $\lambda/2$. The optimum height of the receiving antenna mast is $h_2 = \lambda d/(4h_1) = 13.3$m. Other solutions are $(2n + 1) \times 13.3$m.

In the preceding discussion we have assumed that the wave propagates as a ray. However, as we discussed in Section 10.4, the ray requires the volume of the first Fresnel ellipsoid as free space. The surface area, where the reflection may happen, is therefore large. If the distance between the antennas is long, bending of the Earth's surface must also be taken into account in determining the location of reflection.

The surface may be considered smooth, if the rms value of the surface roughness, Δh, fulfils the following condition:

$$\Delta h < \frac{\lambda}{32 \sin \gamma} \tag{10.16}$$

If the surface is rough, a considerable part of power will scatter; that is, it will radiate into a large solid angle.

10.6 Multipath Propagation in Cellular Mobile Radio Systems

Figure 10.11 presents the field strength as a function of distance when a strong reflected wave interferes with an LOS wave. As the receiver moves away from the transmitter, the signal fades wherever the two waves are in opposite phase. In mobile radio systems, the situation is generally much more complex due to the multipath propagation [6, 7].

We can categorize fading phenomena in many ways. Prominent obstacles between the transmitter and receiver cause large-scale fading. Because of this, the path loss increases rapidly over distance and is log-normally distributed about the mean value. Small-scale fading refers to signal amplitude and phase variations due to small changes (order of a wavelength) in position. Interference of several waves—multipath propagation—causes this type of fading. Because of the multipath propagation the signal spreads in time (dispersion) and the channel is time-variant due to the motion of the mobile unit. Both phenomena degrade the performance of the system. Depending on the effect of dispersion, we categorize fading either as frequency-selective or flat. If the radio channel is frequency-selective over the signal bandwidth, *intersymbol interference* (ISI) will degrade the performance. In the case of flat fading all signal components fade equally. According to the rapidity of changes in the time-variant channel, we categorize fading as fast or slow.

When there is a dominant LOS wave in a multipath environment, the amplitude of the signal envelope has a Rician probability distribution. If there is no LOS wave, as in Figure 10.12, the envelope has a Rayleigh probability distribution. There are reflected, diffracted, and scattered waves as well as waves propagating through vegetation and buildings. The Rayleigh distribution is obtained by summing up a large number of independent field components, and its probability distribution is

$$P(r) = \frac{r}{\sigma^2} \exp\left[-r^2/(2\sigma^2)\right] \qquad (10.17)$$

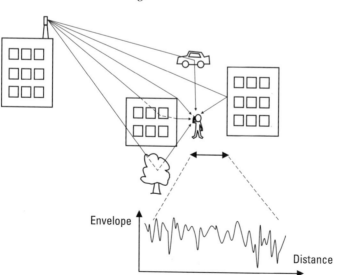

Figure 10.12 Multipath propagation in an urban environment and the signal envelope in a fading radio channel.

where the envelope $r(t)$ of the complex signal $E(t)$ is given as $r(t) = \sqrt{[\text{Re } E(t)]^2 + [\text{Im } E(t)]^2}$, and σ^2 is the mean power, and $r^2(t)/2$ is the short-term signal power.

The effect of small-scale fading may be mitigated by using in receiving or transmitting multiple antennas, time redundancy, several polarizations, or several frequencies (space, time, polarization, and frequency diversity). The diversity increases the probability that at least one of the received signals will be strong enough to be detected. Spread spectrum or multicarrier systems can mitigate the small-scale fading due to their large bandwidth, that is, their frequency diversity. A rake receiver can mitigate it using time diversity by detecting replicas of the transmitted signal with different time delays [7]. A smart antenna system such as *multiple-in-multiple-out* (MIMO) can miti- gate it through space and polarization diversity [8]. Moreover, a MIMO system can increase the spectral efficiency by utilizing different independently fading propagation paths as parallel data channels.

In rural areas the base station antennas are located in high antenna masts so that most of the path is in free space or along the treetops. The final meters or tens of meters of the path to the mobile terminal may cause a lot of attenuation; in a forest the average excess attenuation through vegetation at 2 GHz is about 0.4 dB/m; however, the attenuation of a tree with or without foliage is very different. In urban areas the base station antennas may be located at the roofs or walls of the buildings, while the mobile terminals move along the street canyons or are inside the buildings.

Both deterministic and stochastic propagation models are used in design, optimization, and performance evaluation of cellular mobile radio systems. Deterministic models are based on electromagnetic simulations (utilizing ray tracing together with geometrical optics and uniform theory of diffraction, finite difference time domain method, and so forth) making use of information of the specific physical environment or on measurements. Stochastic models describe the propagation phenomena on average; they are based on defining the fading distributions (log-normal, Rayleigh, Rician). The model parameters are based on measurements or on a deterministic model in a given type of environment [9, 10].

The deterministic propagation models can be divided into simplified semiempirical path loss models and computational site-specific models. An example of the empirical models is the Okumura-Hata model [11]. In the Okumura-Hata model the physical environment can be selected among a large city, a medium to small city, a suburban area, or a rural area, and the model takes into account the antenna heights and frequency. The Walfisch-

Bertoni model [12] allows slightly more detailed characterization of the environment; for example, the average building height and the width and orientation of the streets can be taken into account. It counts the propagation loss as a function of distance (free-space loss), multiscreen diffraction due to rows of houses, and finally the roof-to-street diffraction. Inside the buildings, site-specific computational models are often used, but simplified models such as the Motley-Keenan model [13], which calculates the path loss from the free-space path loss according to the distance added by attenuation of each wall along the path, are also in use.

10.7 Propagation Aided by Scattering: Scatter Link

Inhomogeneities of the atmosphere cause scattering. Scattering means that part of the coherent plane wave is transformed into incoherent form and will radiate into a large solid angle. Normally, scattering will weaken the radio link by attenuating the signal. However, the scattered field may also be useful: A scatter link takes advantage of scattering.

Let us first consider scattering by a single object or particle. The scattering cross section σ of an object to a given direction describes the effective area of the object when it is illuminated by a plane wave. The power intercepted by this area, when scattered equally in all directions, produces the same power density as the object. The scattering cross section also depends on the direction of the incident wave and its polarization. Figure 10.13 shows how the scattering cross section of a conducting (metal) sphere behaves as a function of frequency, when the direction of incidence and the direction of observation are the same. The scattering cross section of a small (in comparison to a wavelength), metallic sphere (or of an object of another shape) is proportional to f^4 (Rayleigh scattering). The scattering cross section σ of a large (in comparison to a wavelength) sphere is equal to its geometric cross section σ_g. This is called the optical region. Between these regions there is a resonance region (Mie scattering). Because the relative permittivity ϵ_r of water is large, the curve in Figure 10.13 also describes the scattering of a raindrop. The total scattering cross section σ_s multiplied by the power density of the incident wave gives the total power scattered by the object into the solid angle of 4π. The total scattering cross section σ_s of a large object is $2\sigma_g$.

If the density of small scattering particles is ρ (particles per cubic meter), the scattering cross-section density is $\sigma_d = \rho\sigma$. In a symmetric radio path utilizing scattering as shown in Figure 10.14, the power received is

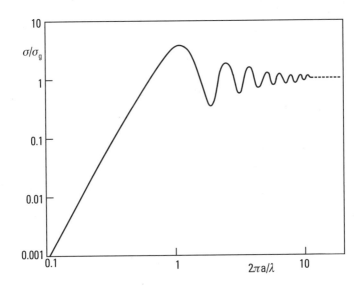

Figure 10.13 Scattering cross section σ versus frequency of a conducting sphere with a radius a.

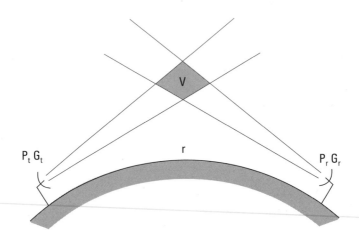

Figure 10.14 A radio path utilizing tropospheric scattering: a scatter link.

$$P_t = G_t G_r \frac{\lambda^2}{4\pi^3 r^4} P_t \int_V \sigma_d \, dV \qquad (10.18)$$

where V is the volume where scattering occurs.

In radio links, three kinds of scattering are utilized: tropospheric, ionospheric, and meteor scattering. The tropospheric scattering is due to turbulence in the troposphere and is the most widely utilized scattering mechanism in communication. This may provide a 500-km hop in the microwave region. The ionospheric scattering is caused by the cloudlike structures of the lowest layers of the ionosphere, and the meteor scattering is caused by the ionized trails of meteors. (The ionized trail is due to the high temperature produced by friction as the meteor enters the atmosphere at high velocity.) These scattering mechanisms may provide radio hops of 2,000 km at frequencies from 30 to 80 MHz. Furthermore, raindrops and snowflakes cause scattering, which may introduce interference between different radio links.

Fading or a random variation of the signal power level is typical for radio systems based on scattering. This phenomenon may be divided into a slow fading, which is due to large changes in the propagation conditions, and into a fast fading, which is due to multipath propagation. Fading can be partially compensated by a feedback, which is used to stabilize the signal power level, or by using diversity, as described in Section 10.6.

10.8 Propagation via Ionosphere

The highest layers of the Earth's atmosphere are called the ionosphere, because they contain plasma, which is ionized gas (free electrons and ions). The ionosphere extends from 60 to 1,000 km. Below 60 km the ionization is insignificant because the solar ionizing radiation is getting weaker due to absorption in the higher layers, and because recombination of plasma is fast due to high density of molecules. Above 1,000 km the density of molecules is too low for a significant phenomenon. It is possible to distinguish different layers in the ionosphere, as shown in Figure 10.15; they are called D, E, F_1, and F_2 layers. The electron density and the height of these layers depend on the solar activity, on the time of day and season, and on the geographical location. During night the D layer nearly disappears, and the F_1 and F_2 layers merge together. The highest electron density is about 10^{12} electrons/m^3, and it can be found at daytime at the altitude of about 250 to 400 km in the F_2 layer.

Let us consider radio wave propagation in plasma. The electric field having a strength E affects (accelerates) a charge q by force qE. If there are N charges in a unit volume, the current density in case of a sinusoidal field is ($F = ma = mdv/dt = mj\omega v$)

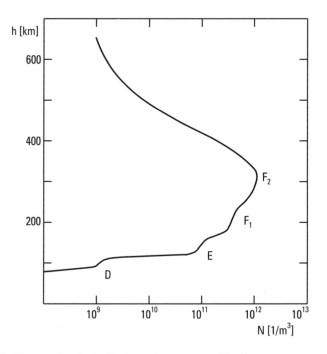

Figure 10.15 Electron density in the ionosphere versus altitude.

$$J = Nq\mathbf{v} = \frac{Nq^2\mathbf{E}}{j\omega m} \qquad (10.19)$$

where $\mathbf{v}$ is the velocity of the charge and m is its mass. Maxwell's IV equation, (2.21), can now be written as

$$\nabla \times \mathbf{H} = \mathbf{J} + j\omega\epsilon\mathbf{E} = j\omega\epsilon_0\left(1 - \frac{Nq^2}{\omega^2 m\epsilon_0}\right)\mathbf{E} \qquad (10.20)$$

The charges cause a decrease of the permittivity of medium. Because the electron rest mass is only 1/1,836 of that of a hydrogen ion, the electrons determine the permittivity. The relative permittivity of plasma is

$$\epsilon_r = 1 - \frac{Ne^2}{\omega^2 m_e \epsilon_0} = 1 - \left(\frac{f_p}{f}\right)^2 \qquad (10.21)$$

where e is the electron charge and m_e is the electron mass, and

$$f_p = \frac{1}{2\pi} \sqrt{\frac{Ne^2}{m_e \epsilon_0}} \qquad (10.22)$$

is the plasma frequency. The plasma frequency in hertz is

$$f_p \approx 9\sqrt{N} \qquad (10.23)$$

where N is the number of electrons in one cubic meter; that is, the plasma frequency is 9 MHz for an electron density of $10^{12}/m^3$.

This treatment does not take into account collisions of electrons with neutral molecules, which causes attenuation. Furthermore, the Earth's magnetic field affects the electron motion, which leads to a direction depending on ϵ_r; that is, plasma is an anisotropic and nonreciprocal medium and ϵ_r is a tensor. The nonreciprocity causes Faraday rotation (see Section 6.2). The electric field of a linearly polarized wave may rotate, causing wrong polarization in reception. Therefore, in radio systems utilizing the ionosphere, a circular polarization is preferred.

A wave can propagate in plasma only if its frequency is higher than the plasma frequency. Otherwise ϵ_r is negative and the wave will be totally reflected. At frequencies well above the plasma frequency, $\epsilon_r \approx 1$, and the effect of plasma on radio wave propagation is negligible. In practice, there is no need to take the ionosphere into account at VHF and higher frequencies.

A wave propagating vertically into the ionosphere will be reflected at altitude where $\epsilon_r = 0$, that is, $f_p = f$. If the wave approaches the ionosphere in an angle ϕ_0, as shown in Figure 10.16, reflection takes place at a height where

$$f_p = f \cos \phi_0 \qquad (10.24)$$

Via the ionosphere it is possible to obtain a radio hop to a distance of 4,000 km just with one reflection. Also, longer hops are possible if the wave reflects from the ground back to the ionosphere. In a given radio link the frequency must be higher than the *lowest usable frequency* (LUF) but lower than the *maximum usable frequency* (MUF). The LUF and MUF depend on the temporary characteristics of the ionosphere.

10.9 Propagation as a Ground (Surface) Wave

If the transmitting and receiving antennas are close (in comparison to a wavelength) to the ground, the wave propagates bound to the ground, as a

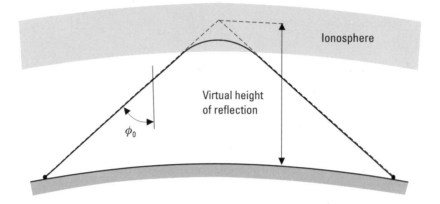

Figure 10.16 Wave propagation via the ionosphere.

surface wave. The electric field strength of the wave decreases rapidly as the distance from the surface increases. At low frequencies the attenuation of such a ground wave is small, and the wave can propagate beyond the horizon thousands of kilometers, especially over seawater. However, the attenuation of a ground wave increases rapidly with frequency. Therefore this propagation mechanism is useful only below 10 MHz.

Attenuation of the wave depends on conductivity and permittivity of the surface (land, lake, or sea). Table 10.1 shows some typical characteristics at frequencies below 30 MHz. At microwave frequencies these characteristics change strongly as a function of frequency. ITU-R publishes field strength graphs for different surface types. Figure 10.17 presents the electric field strength versus distance when the wave propagates along the surface of a medium dry land and sea [14]. The transmitting antenna is a vertical monopole, and the power transmitted is 1 kW. The graphs show that at 10 kHz the electric field strength decreases as $1/r$ (as in free space) up to a distance

Table 10.1
Electrical Properties of Different Ground Surfaces ($f < 30$ MHz)

	ϵ_r'	σ/Sm^{-1}
Seawater	70	5
Fresh water	80	3×10^{-3}
Wet land	30	10^{-2}
Dry land	3	10^{-4}
Ice on a lake	3	$10^{-5}-10^{-4}$

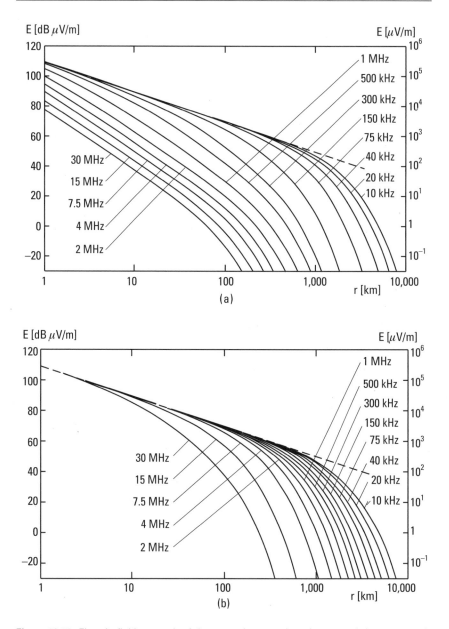

Figure 10.17 Electric field strength of the ground wave when the transmitting antenna is a vertical monopole and the power transmitted is 1 kW: (a) over a medium dry land, $\sigma = 10^{-3}$ S/m, $\epsilon_r = 15$; (b) over sea water, $\sigma = 5$ S/m, $\epsilon_r = 70$. (*After:* [14].)

of 1,000 km. At higher frequencies the attenuation is much higher. Over the sea the wave attenuates much slower than over medium dry land. In practice the electrical characteristics of the surface may vary a lot between the transmitting and receiving stations, and therefore a prediction of the power to be received is difficult.

References

[1]   Salonen, E., et al., "Modeling and Calculation of Atmospheric Attenuation for Low-Fade-Margin Satellite Communications," *ESA Journal*, Vol. 16, 1992, pp. 299–317.

[2]   Zhang, W., S. I. Karhu, and E. T. Salonen, "Predictions of Radiowave Attenuations Due to a Melting Layer of Precipitation," *IEEE Trans. on Antennas and Propagation*, Vol. 42, No. 4, 1994, pp. 492–500.

[3]   Salonen, E. T., J. K. Tervonen, and W. J. Vogel, "Scintillation Effect on Total Fade Distributions for Earth-Satellite Links," *IEEE Trans. on Antennas and Propagation*, Vol. 44, No. 1, 1996, pp. 23–27.

[4]   van de Kamp, M. M. J. L., et al., "Frequency Dependence of Amplitude Scintillation," *IEEE Trans. on Antennas and Propagation*, Vol. 47, No. 1, 1999, pp. 77–85.

[5]   Skolnik, M. I., *Introduction to Radar Systems*, 2nd ed., New York: McGraw-Hill, 1981.

[6]   Rappaport, T. S., *Wireless Communications, Principles, and Practice*, Upper Saddle River, NJ: Prentice Hall, 1996.

[7]   Parsons, J. D., *The Mobile Radio Propagation Channel*, 2nd ed., Chichester, England: John Wiley & Sons, 2000.

[8]   Foschini, G. J., and M. J. Gans, "On Limits of Wireless Communications in a Fading Environment When Using Multiple Antennas," *Wireless Personal Communications*, Vol. 6, No. 3, 1998, pp. 311–335.

[9]   Bach Andersen, J., T. S. Rappaport, and S. Yoshida, "Propagation Measurements and Models for Wireless Communications Channels," *IEEE Communications Magazine*, Vol. 33, No. 1, 1995, pp. 42–49.

[10] Bertoni, H. L., *Radio Propagation for Modern Wireless Systems*, Upper Saddle River, NJ: Prentice Hall, 2000.

[11] Hata, M., "Empirical Formulae for Propagation Loss in Land Mobile Radio Services," *IEEE Trans. on Vehicular Technology*, Vol. VT-29, No. 3, 1980, pp. 317–325.

[12] Walfisch, J., and H. L. Bertoni, "A Theoretical Model of UHF Propagation in Urban Environments," *IEEE Trans. on Antennas and Propagation*, Vol. 36, No. 12, 1988, pp. 1788–1796.

[13] Keenan, J. M., and A. J. Motley, "Radio Coverage in Buildings," *British Telecom Technology Journal*, Vol. 8, No. 1, 1990, pp. 19–24.

[14] International Telecommunication Union, "Ground-Wave Propagation Curves for Frequencies Between 10 kHz and 30 MHz," Recommendation ITU-R P.368-7.

11

Radio System

Performance of a whole radio system, such as a cellular network, navigation system, or radar, depends on the characteristics of the transmitters, receivers, and antennas as well as of propagation of radio waves between the transmitting and receiving antennas. If the transmitted power and the gains and attenuations in different parts of the system are known, the received power can be calculated. However, in addition to the received power, there are other factors affecting the signal detection: modulation of the signal, frequency stability, interference from other radio systems, noise, dispersion due to the radio channel, and so on.

In this chapter we first briefly discuss transmitters and receivers. Then we study noise in more detail as it decreases the performance of any radio system. We also study different modulation techniques, that is, how information can be attached to the carrier. Finally we consider the link budget. In Chapter 12 some radio systems are studied in more detail.

11.1 Transmitters and Receivers

A radio transmitter must produce a signal that has enough power, has generally a very accurate frequency, and has a clean enough spectrum so that the transmitter does not disturb users of other radio systems. Information to be transmitted, the baseband signal, is attached to a sinusoidal carrier signal by modulating the carrier amplitude, frequency, or phase either analogically or digitally (see Section 11.3).

Low-power transmitters are usually based on a semiconductor device, a transistor or diode oscillator. When a transmitter power of hundreds of watts is needed, power is generated with electron tubes or so-called microwave tubes. Tetrodes are used from LF to VHF, and klystrons at UHF and SHF. In radar transmitters, a magnetron oscillator is the most common. In klystrons, magnetrons, and other microwave tubes, microwave oscillation is generated by an electron beam interacting with a resonance cavity or a slow-wave structure [1].

In order to have a sufficiently accurate and clean signal, the oscillator frequency must be stabilized and the signal must be bandpass filtered before transmitting. Oscillators may be stabilized using a resonator with a sufficiently high quality factor. Often the accurate frequency is based on a quartz crystal oscillator at a frequency of 1 to 40 MHz and with a frequency stability of 10^{-9} to 10^{-10} per day. The signal of the quartz oscillator is frequency multiplied to the transmission frequency and then amplified, or it is used to injection lock or phase lock another oscillator to the correct frequency.

Figure 11.1 presents a direct-conversion transmitter. A digital baseband signal modulates the carrier in an IQ-modulator (see Section 11.3.2). The modulated signal is then filtered and amplified. In a superheterodyne transmitter the signal is further upconverted to the final frequency. The carrier frequency is stabilized by phase locking [2]. A basic *phase-locked loop* (PLL) is a feedback system consisting of a VCO, a phase detector (for example, a double-balanced mixer), and a low-pass filter. In the loop of Figure 11.1 there is also in the feedback branch a digital circuit that divides the frequency of the VCO by N. The output of the divider is compared with the signal from the reference oscillator in the phase detector. A possible difference in frequency (in phase) is transformed into a voltage proportional to the phase difference, and after lowpass filtering this voltage is used to control the VCO frequency until the frequency difference is zero. The output frequency of the locked loop is Nf_{ref}. The loop also stabilizes within its bandwidth the random phase variations of the VCO and, thus, the reference oscillator determines the phase-noise characteristics.

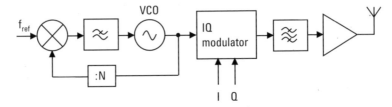

Figure 11.1 Direct-conversion transmitter with a phase-locked oscillator.

If the system must operate at several nearby frequencies (channels), the transmitter and receiver signals are generated in a frequency synthesizer [3]. The synthesis may be based on a PLL, on a direct synthesis, or on a *direct digital synthesis* (DDS). If a programmable divider is employed in Figure 11.1, this PLL can produce several frequencies spaced by f_{ref}. Smaller frequency steps are obtained by combining several PLLs or by using a fractional-N loop, where the division ratio is a fraction and is not limited to integer values. The direct synthesis uses mixers, frequency multipliers, dividers, filters, and switches to produce accurate frequencies. This method may not be practical if a large number of closely spaced frequencies are needed, because the synthesizer would become very complex. In the DDS a *digital-to-analog converter* (DAC) generates the waveform using a look-up table. Accurately modulated signals with very good frequency resolution may be produced using DDS, but the upper frequency is limited by the available DACs to a few hundred megahertz.

The receiver must be sensitive and selective. It must be able to detect even a weak signal among many other, possibly stronger signals. Therefore, a good receiver must have good filters, an accurate local oscillator frequency, and low-noise components. It should have also a large, spurious-free dynamic range.

Receivers are usually superheterodyne receivers (here "super" comes originally from "supersonic," meaning that there is an intermediate frequency higher than the audio frequency, that is, the baseband signal frequency in a voice radio). Figure 11.2 presents such a receiver, where the signal from the antenna is first filtered and then amplified by an LNA by 10 to 20 dB. In front of a mixer an image-rejection filter blocks the image band. A frequency synthesizer generates an accurate *local oscillator* (LO) signal. The mixer downconverts the signal to an IF, where it is again filtered with a narrowband filter (e.g., a SAW filter) and amplified by an IF amplifier (e.g. by 70 to 100 dB) before demodulation. The demodulator recovers the original analog or digital baseband signal. If the signal power level may vary

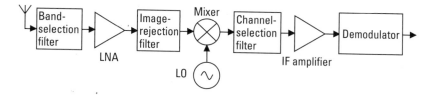

Figure 11.2 Block diagram of a typical superheterodyne receiver used in radio communication.

significantly, the IF gain should be controllable with an *automatic gain control* (AGC) circuit in order to avoid saturation in the back end.

There are many other receiver architectures. Often in a superheterodyne receiver the signal is downconverted twice. In such a dual-conversion receiver the first IF is high and the second IF is low. This facilitates the realization of filters. Distribution of the gain to several frequencies also reduces the tendency of the receiver to oscillate.

Figure 11.3 shows a direct-conversion receiver, which is called also a homodyne or zero-IF receiver. The signal is now downconverted directly to the baseband. There is no IF stage and, thus, this structure is simpler and better suited for integration than the superheterodyne architecture. Lower power consumption and the possibility of making the channel filter at the baseband are other advantages. However, as the LO frequency equals the carrier frequency, leaking of the LO power may cause severe problems. In a dual-conversion receiver the channel selection can be realized with a synthesizer operating at the IF, but in a direct-conversion receiver the synthesizer must operate at the higher carrier frequency.

In a direct IF sampling receiver, which is also called a software radio, the whole band at the IF is sampled with an *analog-to-digital converter* (ADC). Channel filtering and demodulation is then realized with digital signal processing. This architecture is flexible and suited multimode operation, because the system standard may easily be changed. However, the ADC is now a critical component; it has to operate very linearly over a large dynamic range.

A transceiver is a combination of a transmitter and receiver sharing the same antenna. Now the isolation of the transmitter and receiver has to be very large, for example, 120 dB. If the transmitter and receiver operate

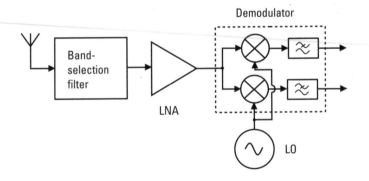

Figure 11.3 Direct-conversion receiver.

at different frequencies, called *frequency division duplexing* (FDD), a duplexing filter separates them from each other. A duplexing filter consists of two bandpass filters. If the transmitter and receiver operate in different time slots, called *time division duplexing* (TDD), a switch can be used to isolate the receiver during transmission. The loss of a switch is usually less than the loss of a duplexing filter.

A high level of integration is essential in the mass production of low-cost transceivers and receivers. The ultimate goal is to integrate all the transceiver electronics on a single chip, because external components increase the cost. High-quality filters and resonators are often too difficult to integrate on a chip. The practical solution is to combine several chips made using different technologies with some external components. Low-cost silicon-based technologies such as bipolar, BiCMOS, and CMOS technology are used to produce chips up to about 3 GHz. When top performance is required or the frequency is higher, chips are made using GaAs and InP technologies.

11.2 Noise

Random fields and voltages, that is, noise, disturb all radio systems. The antenna receives noise from its surroundings, and all receiver components, which are either active or lossy, generate noise. We call the former the antenna noise and the latter the receiver noise; their sum is called the system noise. In a radio system (e.g., a communication link) the system noise power in the receiver bandwidth may be stronger than the signal to be received. The ratio of the signal power to the noise power at the receiver bandwidth, that is, the S/N often determines the quality of a radio link. However, noise signals may also be useful, as is the case in radiometry, for example, in remote sensing and radio astronomy (see Sections 12.7 and 12.8).

In system considerations, a radio channel, where white noise corrupting the signal is the only nonideality, is called the *additive white Gaussian noise* (AWGN) channel. In addition to noise, in practical radio channels there are other nonidealities. When the small-scale fading or Rayleigh fading in multipath propagation conditions is the limiting factor for the channel performance, we call it a Rayleigh fading channel.

11.2.1 Receiver Noise

In a receiver, many kinds of noise are generated, for example, thermal noise, shot noise, $1/f$ noise, and quantum noise.

Thermal noise is generated by the thermal motion of charge carriers. The warmer the material is, the more electrons collide with the crystal lattice of the material. Each collision causes a change in the kinetic energy state of the electron, and the energy difference is radiated as an electromagnetic wave. Similarly, collisions are also the reason for resistivity of a material and, therefore, thermal noise is generated in all materials and circuits absorbing RF power. Thermal noise is directly proportional to the absolute temperature of the medium, but its power density is independent of frequency—it is so-called white noise.

Shot noise is often the most important noise mechanism in semiconductor devices and electron tubes. Shot noise is caused by the fact that charge is not a continuous quantity but always a multiple of an electron charge. For example, a current going through the Schottky interface is not continuous but is a sum of the current impulses of single electrons. The power density of shot noise is directly proportional to the current.

At low frequencies there is $1/f$ noise (flicker noise) in all semiconductor devices. It is caused, for example, by the fluctuating amount of electrons in the conduction band. Its power density is inversely proportional to frequency.

Quantum noise is due to the quantized energy of the radio wave. It is important only in cases of submillimeter and shorter waves, because their energy quantum $W = hf$ is large.

Noise properties of a device are described by the noise factor F or the equivalent noise temperature T_e [4]. The latter is also called the effective input noise temperature, the input noise temperature, or just the noise temperature. The noise factor of a linear two-port is defined [5] by

$$F = \frac{N_{out}}{G_a N_{in}} \tag{11.1}$$

where N_{in} is the available noise power in a bandwidth df from a matched resistive termination (here "matched" means that the termination is matched to the characteristic impedance of the line) at temperature $T_0 = 290K$ connected to the input of the device, and N_{out} is the total noise power available at the output port in a bandwidth df when the input power is N_{in}. G_a is the available power gain of the two-port for incoherent signals from an input bandwidth of df to an output bandwidth of df. The noise factor indicates how many times larger the output noise power of the device is compared to that of a noiseless device, when both have in the input a matched resistive termination at the absolute reference temperature of $T_0 = 290K$.

The equivalent noise temperature is defined by means of the noise factor as follows:

$$T_e = (F - 1) T_0 \tag{11.2}$$

or

$$F = 1 + \frac{T_e}{T_0} \tag{11.3}$$

In other words, the equivalent noise temperature can be defined as the physical temperature, at which the matched resistive input termination of a noiseless device should be in order to have the same available noise power in the output as the noisy device itself produces into its output when its matched resistive input termination is at the absolute zero temperature.

A resistor R at temperature T generates noise, the rms voltage of which in a bandwidth of df is

$$v_n = \sqrt{\frac{4Rhfdf}{e^{hf/kT} - 1}} \approx \sqrt{4kTdfR} \tag{11.4}$$

where $h = 6.626 \times 10^{-34}$ Js is Planck's constant and $k = 1.381 \times 10^{-23}$ J/K is Boltzmann's constant. The approximation of (11.4) is valid when $hf << kT$. The available noise power from this resistor, that is, the noise power from this resistor to another resistor with the same resistance, is

$$P = \left(\frac{v_n}{2R}\right)^2 R = kTdf \tag{11.5}$$

This noise power P is equal to N_{in} in (11.1), and therefore the noise factor is

$$F = \frac{N_{out}}{kT_0 dfG_a} \tag{11.6}$$

In (11.6) N_{out} is sometimes for practical reasons the power delivered (coupled) to the load; then, instead of the available power gain, one must use the transducer power gain G_t (see (5.26)). Because the available noise power in the input is $N_{in} = kT_0\,df$ and the ratio of the signal powers in output and in input is $G_a = S_{out}/S_{in}$, the noise factor can also be presented as a ratio of the signal-to-noise ratios (S/N) in input and in output, as

$$F = \frac{(S/N)_{in}}{(S/N)_{out}} \qquad (11.7)$$

Thus, the noise factor describes the degradation of the S/N in the device, when the matched input termination is at 290K. The noise figure is the noise factor in decibels, that is,

$$F\,(dB) = 10 \log F \qquad (11.8)$$

So far we have assumed that the noise properties of the device are constant over the bandwidth df. An average noise factor is

$$F = \frac{\displaystyle\int_0^\infty F(f)\,G_t(f)\,df}{\displaystyle\int_0^\infty G_t(f)\,df} \qquad (11.9)$$

where $F(f)$ is the noise factor at a point frequency.

An often-useful quantity in noise analysis is the noise bandwidth B_n of the device illustrated in Figure 11.4:

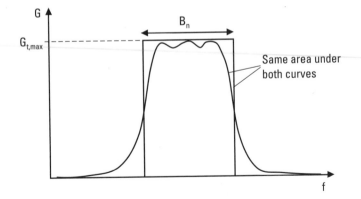

Figure 11.4 Definition of the noise bandwidth B_n.

$$B_n = \frac{1}{G_{t,max}} \int_0^\infty G_t(f) \, df \qquad (11.10)$$

where $G_{t,max}$ is the maximum value of the transducer power gain. In respect to white noise in the input, the device behaves like a device that has a gain of $G_{t,max}$ over the noise bandwidth B_n and a gain of zero at all frequencies outside this band.

Let us next consider the equivalent noise temperature of a resistive attenuator at a physical temperature T. If both the attenuator itself and its matched resistive input termination are at the same physical temperature, the attenuator absorbs and emits the same amount of energy. When we measure the noise power from this attenuator in a bandwidth of df, we get the following result (assuming $hf \ll kT$) as in (11.5)

$$N_{out} = kdfT = N_{in} e^{-\tau} + N_{int} = kdfTe^{-\tau} + kdfT(1 - e^{-\tau}) \qquad (11.11)$$

where τ is the so-called optical depth, which describes the rate of absorption and emission in the attenuator. For a section of a transmission line with a length l and an attenuation constant α, the optical depth is $\tau = \alpha l$, and therefore the attenuation of this attenuator is $L = e^{\alpha l} = e^{\tau}$. Now we know that the intrinsic noise power N_{int} is

$$N_{int} = kdfT(1 - e^{-\tau}) = kdfT\left(1 - \frac{1}{L}\right) \qquad (11.12)$$

By the definition of the equivalent noise temperature, the input noise temperature T_L of a resistive attenuator at a physical temperature T is then

$$T_L = T(L - 1) \qquad (11.13)$$

A receiver is, from the signal and noise point of view, all the way from the antenna terminals to the detector a chain of linear two-ports, as shown in Figure 11.5. The noise factor of such a chain is

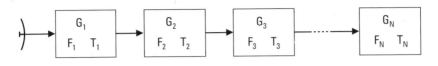

Figure 11.5 Chain of two-ports in series.

$$
\begin{aligned}
F &= \frac{N_{out}}{kT_0 \, df \, G_1 G_2 \ldots G_N} \\
&= \frac{kdf[(T_0 + T_1) G_1 G_2 \ldots G_N + T_2 G_2 \ldots G_N + \ldots + T_N G_N]}{kT_0 \, df \, G_1 G_2 \ldots G_N} \\
&= 1 + \frac{T_1}{T_0} + \frac{T_2}{T_0 G_1} + \frac{T_3}{T_0 G_1 G_2} + \ldots + \frac{T_N}{T_0 G_1 G_2 \ldots G_{N-1}} \\
&= F_1 + \frac{F_2 - 1}{G_1} + \frac{F_3 - 1}{G_1 G_2} + \ldots + \frac{F_N - 1}{G_1 G_2 \ldots G_{N-1}} \quad (11.14)
\end{aligned}
$$

and its equivalent noise temperature is

$$
T_e = T_1 + \frac{T_2}{G_1} + \frac{T_3}{G_1 G_2} + \ldots + \frac{T_N}{G_1 G_2 \ldots G_{N-1}} \quad (11.15)
$$

In (11.14) and (11.15) F_i, T_i, and G_i are the noise factor, noise temperature, and available gain of the ith two-port of the chain. Equations (11.14) and (11.15) are called the Friis noise equations. They are valid only if the two-ports are matched to each other.

According to (11.15), the first stage determines the noise temperature of a receiver, if G_1 is high enough and T_2 low enough. If possible, a good amplifier should be placed as the first stage of the receiver. In a comparison of different amplifiers, a quantity called the noise measure is used. The noise measure is

$$
M = \frac{F - 1}{1 - 1/G_a} \quad (11.16)
$$

which is the noise factor of an infinitely long chain of similar amplifiers minus one. When cascading two amplifiers, it is better to put as the first stage an amplifier, which has the lowest noise measure, and not necessarily the one, which has the lowest noise factor.

Example 11.1

You have two low-noise amplifiers, LNA1 and LNA2, with characteristics $T_1 = 100$K, $G_1 = 13$ dB, and $T_2 = 90$K, $G_2 = 7$ dB, respectively. You want to use these LNAs together in a series connection in the input of a low-noise receiver. Which one should be placed as the first stage in order to obtain the best possible noise performance of the receiver?

Solution

Let us first calculate the corresponding noise factors: $F_1 = 1 + T_1/T_0 = 1 + 100/290 = 1.34$, and $F_2 = 1 + 90/290 = 1.31$. Gains of the amplifiers in absolute values are $G_1 = 20.0$ and $G_2 = 5.0$. Now we can calculate the noise measures: $M_1 = (F_1 - 1)/(1 - 1/G_1) = 0.34/0.95 = 0.36$, and $M_2 = 0.31/0.8 = 0.39$. Therefore, LNA1 should be placed as the first stage.

The noise factor and noise temperature of a mixer are quantities, which continuously cause confusion, especially in the case of millimeter-wave receivers, where a mixer is often the first stage [6]. The reason for the confusion is the presence of an image sideband in the mixer. The most frequent errors in the noise factor and noise temperature usage are made in the following areas:

- The SSB quantities of a DSB mixer (also called a *broadband mixer*) are confused with the respective quantities of an SSB mixer (also called a *narrowband* or *image-rejection mixer*);

- Depending on the situation, the noise generated in the image termination is to be included as a part of either the receiver noise or the source noise;

- Many old rules of thumb, valid for calculating SSB quantities from DSB quantities of a DSB mixer (or vice versa) in a special case, are unfortunately used also in other cases where they are not valid.

In a mixer, power is converted to the intermediate frequency not only from the signal sideband but also from other sidebands, especially from the image sideband. Let us consider a DSB mixer, which has conversion losses L_s and L_i from the signal and image sideband, respectively, to the intermediate frequency band, and the conversion loss values from other (harmonic) sidebands are infinitely large. The DSB noise temperature $T_{M,DSB}$ of this mixer is, according to the definition of the equivalent noise temperature, the temperature of a termination that is connected to the noiseless mixer at both the signal and image sidebands. However, the SSB noise temperature $T_{M,SSB}$ is the temperature of a termination, according to the definition that is connected to the noiseless mixer only at the signal sideband, and at the image sideband there is a termination at the temperature of 0K. Then the DSB and SSB noise temperatures of the DSB mixer are related to each other as

$$T_{M,SSB} = T_{M,DSB}\left(1 + \frac{L_s}{L_i}\right) \qquad (11.17)$$

If the first stage of the receiver is a mixer, the receiver noise temperature is

$$T_R = T_M + L_c T_{IF} \qquad (11.18)$$

where L_c is the conversion loss of the mixer, T_M is the mixer noise temperature, and T_{IF} is the noise temperature of the IF amplifier. The receiver SSB noise temperature is obtained with $T_M = T_{M,SSB}$ and $L_c = L_{M,SSB} = L_s$, and the DSB noise temperature is obtained with $T_M = T_{M,DSB}$ and $L_c = L_{M,DSB} = L_s L_i/(L_s + L_i)$. For diode mixers L_c is larger than unity and, therefore, the noise temperature of the IF amplifier plays a very important role in the receiver noise temperature.

It is worth emphasizing that if an image-rejection filter is placed in front of the DSB mixer, the mixer turns into an SSB mixer, and its conversion loss L_c is no more equal to the original L_s neither is its noise temperature the one obtained from (11.17).

So far we have assumed that when we use a DSB mixer in an SSB mode, there is a termination at 0K at the image sideband. However, this is not the case in practice. For example, a radiometer observing the atmospheric molecular lines often utilizes a DSB mixer as its first stage, and although the useful signal now enters the receiver only at the signal sideband, the same atmospheric background noise enters the receiver at both sidebands, and the termination impedance at both sidebands is nearly the same, that is, the antenna radiation impedance. In this case we have to add a term $(L_s/L_i)\,T_i$ into the receiver noise temperature of (11.18) in order to have a noise quantity, which really describes the receiver's ability to detect the useful signal at the signal sideband. Here T_i is the image sideband termination temperature, which is often nearly equal to the antenna noise temperature (see Section 11.2.2), that is, $T_i \approx T_A$.

Now we are ready to summarize the receiver noise temperatures and noise factors in the case of a DSB mixer used as the first stage [6]:

$$T_{R,DSB} = T_{M,DSB} + L_{M,DSB} T_{IF} \tag{11.19}$$

$$F_{R,DSB} = 1 + \frac{T_{R,DSB}}{T_0} \tag{11.20}$$

$$T_{R,SSB} = \left(1 + \frac{L_s}{L_i}\right) T_{R,DSB} + \frac{L_s}{L_i} T_i = \left(1 + \frac{L_s}{L_i}\right) T_{M,DSB} + \frac{L_s}{L_i} T_i + L_s T_{IF} \tag{11.21}$$

$$F_{R,SSB} = 1 + \frac{T_{R,SSB}}{T_0} = \left(1 + \frac{L_s}{L_i}\right) F_{R,DSB} + \frac{L_s}{L_i}\left(\frac{T_i}{T_0} - 1\right) \tag{11.22}$$

Example 11.2

Calculate the receiver noise temperature and noise figure of a receiver consisting of an LNA, followed by an image-rejection mixer, and an IF amplifier. The characteristics of the components are $T_{LNA} = 50K$ and $G_{LNA} = 10$ dB, $T_M = 500K$ and $L_M = 6$ dB, $T_{IF} = 200K$ and $G_{IF} = 50$ dB. How much worse is the receiver performance if at a room temperature of 295K there is a cable with a loss of 0.2 dB in front of the LNA?

Solution

The component gains in absolute values are $G_{LNA} = 10$, $L_M = 4$, and $G_{IF} = 100,000$, but the latter is not needed in this calculation. $T_R = T_{LNA} + (1/G_{LNA}) T_M + (L_M/G_{LNA}) T_{IF} = 50K + (1/10)500K + (4/10)200K = (50 + 50 + 80)K = 180K$. F_R (dB) $= 10 \log(1 + T_R/T_0) = 10 \log 1.62 = 2.1$ dB. When the cable with loss of $L = 0.2$ dB (in absolute value L is 1.05) is added in front of this receiver, we get a new receiver noise temperature $T_R' = (L - 1) T_{room} + LT_R = (1.05 - 1)295K + 1.05 \times 180 = 15K + 189K = 204K$.

When the aim is to have a very low-noise receiver, the receiver front end is cooled down to, for example, a temperature of 20K. The cooling reduces the noise temperature of an amplifier or a mixer but also the thermal noise from resistive loss in transmission lines and other components. Some amplifier and mixer types are able to operate only at very low temperatures, for example, a maser and a *superconductor-insulator-superconductor* (SIS) quasi-particle mixer. Figure 11.6 presents noise temperatures of different microwave amplifiers and mixers.

11.2.2 Antenna Noise Temperature

Besides the useful signal, an antenna also receives noise power from its surroundings. The antenna noise temperature T_A is defined as the temperature of such a matched resistive termination, which provides the same noise power as the noise power available from the antenna terminals, which is equal to the noise power received by the antenna in case of a lossless antenna. In the following we assume a lossless antenna.

A so-called black surface does not reflect any radiation incident on it. At optical wavelengths such a surface is black in color. In a thermal equilib-

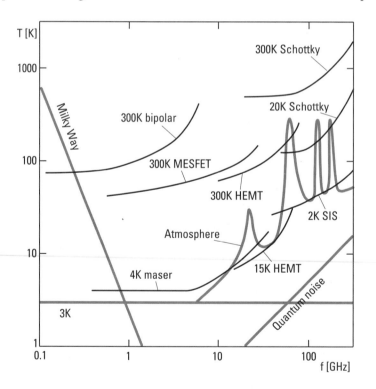

Figure 11.6 Noise temperatures versus frequency of microwave amplifiers and mixers at different physical temperatures. Natural background noise values as a reference.

rium, the black surface must emit the same power as it absorbs. At temperature T its brightness, or the power radiated per square meter, hertz, and steradian, is [7]

$$B = \frac{2hf^3}{c^2} \frac{1}{e^{hf/kT} - 1}$$

(11.23)

At radio frequencies $hf << kT$, and therefore

$$B \approx \frac{2kT}{\lambda^2}$$

(11.24)

Let us consider a situation like that in Figure 11.7, where a black surface fully surrounds a lossless antenna. The noise power received by the antenna in a bandwidth of df is

$$P = \frac{1}{2} A_{ef} \, df \iint\limits_{4\pi} B(\theta, \phi) \frac{G(\theta, \phi)}{G_{max}} \, d\Omega$$

(11.25)

where A_{ef} is the effective aperture area of the antenna, $G(\theta, \phi)$ is the antenna gain in a direction (θ, ϕ), and G_{max} is the maximum antenna gain. The

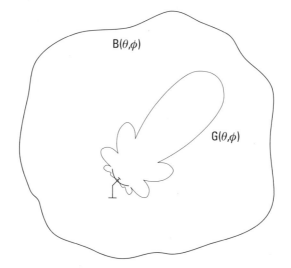

Figure 11.7 A receiving antenna surrounded by a black surface.

factor of 1/2 is due to the fact that an antenna has a certain polarization but the polarization of noise is random. Therefore, one-half of the noise power is in a given polarization. By substituting (11.24) into (11.25) we get

$$P = \frac{1}{2} A_{ef} \, df \, \frac{2kT}{\lambda^2} \frac{4\pi}{G_{max}} = kT \, df \qquad (11.26)$$

Thus, $T_A = T$, and the received noise power is independent of the antenna gain and is directly proportional to the temperature of the black surface and to the bandwidth. If the temperature of the black surface depends on the direction within the radiation pattern of the antenna, the received noise power is calculated by integrating from (11.25).

The antenna receives noise from everywhere, including from space and the atmosphere. For these it is possible to define an equivalent black surface temperature, which depends on frequency and direction, as shown in Figure 11.8.

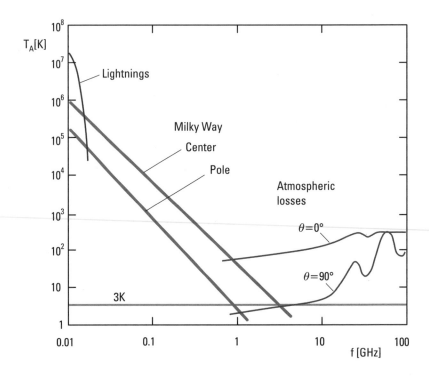

Figure 11.8 Noise temperature of the sky.

At frequencies that do not penetrate the ionosphere, that is, in the HF band and at lower frequencies, noise from electric discharge in the atmosphere (lightning) is dominant. The amount depends on the season and day, location, and frequency.

Noise from space dominates at frequencies from 20 MHz to 1 GHz. The Milky Way produces RF noise, which is at its maximum in the plane of the Milky Way and decreases as the direction goes away from this plane. The Milky Way noise also decreases as frequency increases. At all frequencies there is a 3K cosmic background radiation, which has its origin in the Big Bang, that is, it is a remnant of the birth of the universe.

Thermal noise due to the atmospheric attenuation is the dominating noise source above 1 GHz. It depends on the atmospheric humidity and elevation angle. The atmosphere can be considered as an attenuator at a physical temperature of about 270K.

Noise due to human activity may be considerable, especially near densely populated areas. In the VHF band and at lower frequencies, noise from the spark plugs of cars and power lines may be stronger than that from nature.

11.3 Modulation and Demodulation of Signals

Information to be transmitted in a radio system, such as voice or music, is first transformed to a low frequency, for example, an audio frequency, electric signal. This baseband signal cannot be directly transmitted through a radio channel, or at least that would be very inefficient. The signal is first fed into a modulator, which modulates some property (amplitude, frequency, phase) of a high-frequency carrier according to the baseband signal. The high-frequency signal obtained is then transmitted by a transmitting antenna. A receiving antenna receives the high-frequency signal and feeds it into a receiver. In the receiver the signal is often downconverted to an intermediate frequency and then demodulated, that is, the original baseband signal is detected; for example, in the case of voice radio, the original voice signal is recovered. In other words, with a modulator the information is attached into a carrier, and with a demodulator it is detached.

There are a number of different modulation schemes, which can be divided into analog and digital methods. Modulation is important not only in communication (radio broadcasting, radio links, mobile phone systems) but also in radar, radionavigation, and so on. Modulation is treated in many communication textbooks, for example, [8–10].

11.3.1   Analog Modulation

A sinusoidal waveform can be presented as

$$A(t) = A_0 \cos(\omega_0 t + \psi_0) = A_0 \cos(2\pi f_0 t + \psi_0) \qquad (11.27)$$

Information can be attached into this carrier by modulating one of its basic properties according to the baseband signal. Modulation methods are:

1. *Amplitude modulation* (AM): Information is attached to the carrier amplitude.
2. *Frequency modulation* (FM): Information is attached to the carrier frequency.
3. *Phase modulation* (PM): Information is attached to the carrier phase.

AM is in principle the simplest method, but it has high requirements, especially for the linearity of the transmitter. It is used in radio broadcasting in the LF, MF, and HF bands, and in TV broadcasting. FM is used, for example, in FM radio.

11.3.1.1   AM

Let us consider a signal that is amplitude modulated by a sinusoidal signal at frequency f_m:

$$A(t) = A_0[1 + m \cos(2\pi f_m t)] \cos 2\pi f_0 t \qquad (11.28)$$

Thus, the amplitude varies between values of $A_0(1 - m)$ and $A_0(1 + m)$. Factor m is the modulation index or modulation depth. The signal envelope follows the modulating signal as shown in Figure 11.9(a), if $m < 1$. The carrier frequency should be much higher than the modulating frequency. Equation (11.28) can be presented as

$$A(t) = A_0 \left[\cos \omega_0 t + \frac{m}{2} \cos(\omega_0 + \omega_m)t + \frac{m}{2} \cos(\omega_0 - \omega_m)t \right]$$

$$(11.29)$$

The graphical interpretation of this equation is presented in Figure 11.9(b). A constant voltage phasor A_0 corresponds to the carrier frequency. Two voltage phasors with an amplitude of $(m/2)A_0$ rotate in opposite

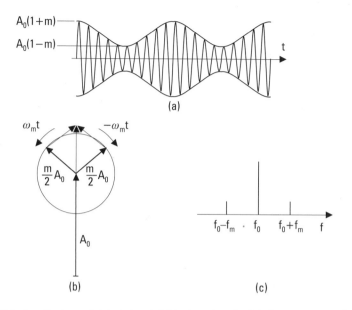

Figure 11.9 Amplitude-modulated signal: (a) in time domain; (b) phasor presentation; and (c) frequency spectrum.

directions at an angular frequency of ω_m. The resultant of these three voltage phasors gives the total voltage. The spectrum contains the components at frequencies f_0, $f_0 + f_m$, and $f_0 - f_m$, as shown in Figure 11.9(c).

If the modulating baseband signal is more complicated, it can be considered as consisting of several sinusoidal components, which have a given amplitude and phase. The modulating signal has a given spectrum and each spectral component modulates the carrier independently.

Figure 11.10 presents the spectrum of an AM signal when the modulating signal is distributed over a given frequency range. The AM is using lavishly both the power and frequency spectrum, because also the carrier not containing information is transmitted and one sideband is only a mirror image of the other. Transmitter power can be saved using DSB modulation, in which the carrier is suppressed, that is, it is not transmitted. This modulation scheme is also called *double-sideband suppressed carrier* (DSBSC) modulation. The frequency spectrum is saved by removing the other sideband, which leads to SSB modulation.

If the modulating signal contains frequency components near the zero frequency, use of SSB modulation becomes complicated, because it is difficult to separate the sidebands. *Vestigial sideband* (VSB) modulation is a compromise between SSB and DSB modulations. In VSB, one sideband is trans-

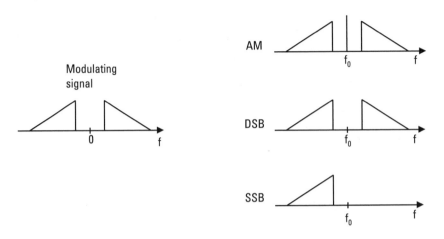

Figure 11.10 Spectra of basic AM, DSB, and SSB modulation.

mitted nearly in full, but only a small part of the other sideband is transmitted, as illustrated in Figure 11.11. VSB can be realized more easily than SSB by filtering from DSB.

11.3.1.2 Amplitude Modulators and Demodulators

A mixer can be used as an amplitude modulator. The modulating waveform is fed into the IF port and the carrier into the LO port, and the modulated signal is obtained from the RF (signal) port, as in Figure 11.12. In a double-balanced mixer there is a good isolation between the LO and RF ports. In that case the carrier is suppressed, and a DSB signal is obtained. The SSB modulation can be realized using the circuit shown in Figure 11.13.

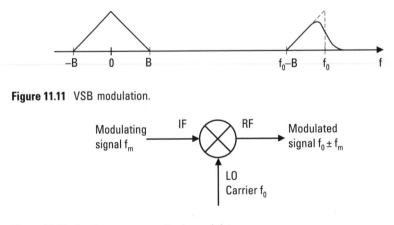

Figure 11.11 VSB modulation.

Figure 11.12 A mixer as an amplitude modulator.

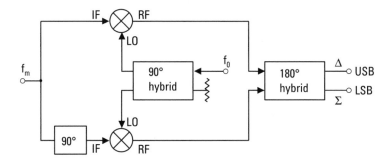

Figure 11.13 An SSB modulator.

An AM signal can be demodulated by an envelope detector. The output of an envelope detector follows the envelope of the input signal, as shown in Figure 11.14. During one half forward cycle the capacitance C is charged rapidly to the peak voltage value of the signal. The time constant $R_S C$ must be much shorter than the cycle length $1/f_0$. In the reverse direction the capacitor C discharges slowly, but it has to be able to follow the modulating signal. This leads to a condition $1/f_0 \ll R_L C \ll 1/B$, where B is the bandwidth of the modulating signal.

In order to demodulate a DSB signal, the carrier must be generated in the receiver. Both the frequency and phase must be correct. The DSB demodulator shown in Figure 11.15 is called the Costas loop, and it resembles the PLL. The input signal is mixed with orthogonal LO signals from a VCO. The difference signals selected by the lowpass filters are proportional to $m(t) \cos \phi$ and $m(t) \sin \phi$, where ϕ is the phase error of the LO. The third mixer produces a signal that adjusts the VCO phase and frequency until the output signal of the upper branch is at maximum and that of the lower branch vanishes. Also, demodulation of an SSB signal requires generation

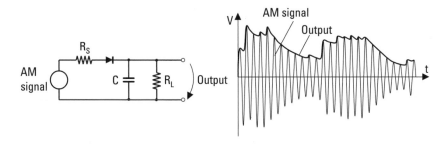

Figure 11.14 An envelope detector as an amplitude demodulator.

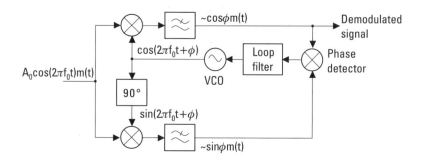

Figure 11.15 A DSB demodulator.

of the carrier. In order to aid this process, a pilot carrier may be transmitted together with the sideband.

11.3.1.3 Quadrature AM (QAM)

QAM is a modulation method that combines two orthogonal DSB signals into the same band. In the transmitter shown in Figure 11.16(a), the phase difference between the two carriers is 90°. In the receiver there is also a 90° phase difference between the two LO signals, and the original baseband signals can be separated. QAM is used in TV broadcasting.

11.3.1.4 FM

The amplitude of a frequency-modulated signal is constant, and the instantaneous frequency varies according to the modulating signal. If the modulating signal is sinusoidal, the instantaneous frequency is

$$f(t) = \frac{1}{2\pi} \frac{d\phi(t)}{dt} = f_0 + \Delta f \cos(2\pi f_m t) \qquad (11.30)$$

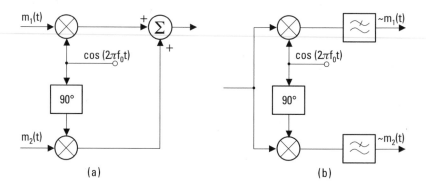

Figure 11.16 QAM: (a) transmitter and (b) receiver.

where Δf is the maximum frequency deviation. The equation for an FM signal waveform is

$$A(t) = A_0 \cos \phi(t) = A_0 \cos\left[2\pi f_0 t + \frac{\Delta f}{f_m} \sin(2\pi f_m t)\right]$$

(11.31)

The spectrum of the FM signal contains, besides the carrier, an infinite number of sidebands with a separation of f_m. The required bandwidth is wider than that in AM, but tolerance to noise and interference is better. The amplitudes of the carrier and sidebands depend on the modulation index $m = \Delta f/f_m$. The amplitude A_{sp} of a sideband p relative to the amplitude A_0 of an unmodulated carrier is obtained from

$$\frac{A_{sp}}{A_0 \ (m = 0)} = J_p(\Delta f/f_m)$$

(11.32)

where J_p is the pth order Bessel function of the first kind. Figure 11.17 presents Bessel functions and Figure 11.18 shows an FM power spectrum when the modulation index is $m = 5.52$. In this case the normalized amplitude J_0 of the carrier component is small.

If m is small—less than unity—there is in the spectrum only one important sideband on both sides of the carrier, and $A_{s1}/A_0 \approx m/2$. The

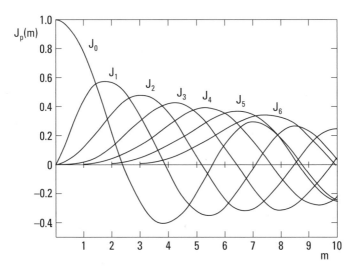

Figure 11.17 Bessel functions (first kind).

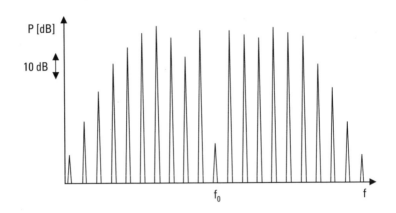

Figure 11.18 Spectrum of a frequency-modulated signal when the modulation index is $m = 5.52$.

spectrum looks like the AM spectrum, but the phases of the sidebands are different.

In theory the FM signal requires an infinite bandwidth. If we allow a given maximum distortion, we can limit the bandwidth. According to Carson's rule the required bandwidth is [10]

$$B \approx 2\Delta f + 2f_m = 2\Delta f(1 + 1/m) = 2f_m(1 + m) \qquad (11.33)$$

11.3.1.5 Frequency Modulators and Demodulators

FM can be realized with a VCO. The output frequency of some oscillators can be controlled directly by changing the operation point of the nonlinear element. In other VCOs the frequency is controlled by voltage tuning the resonance frequency of the high-Q embedding circuit, which contains a voltage-dependent element such as a varactor.

Figure 11.19 shows a Hartley oscillator. The input network contains a varactor. The resonance frequency of the input resonator is

$$f = \frac{1}{2\pi\sqrt{(L_1 + L_2)\,C(t)}} \qquad (11.34)$$

Let us assume that C changes sinusoidally an amount of ΔC around C_0 and that the ratio $\Delta C/C_0$ is small. Then

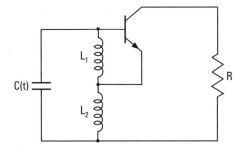

Figure 11.19 A Hartley oscillator.

$$f = \frac{1}{2\pi\sqrt{(L_1 + L_2)(C_0 + \Delta C \cos 2\pi f_m t)}}$$

$$= \frac{1}{2\pi\sqrt{(L_1 + L_2) C_0}} \frac{1}{\sqrt{1 + (\Delta C/C_0) \cos 2\pi f_m t}} \qquad (11.35)$$

$$\approx f_0 \left(1 - \frac{\Delta C}{2C_0} \cos 2\pi f_m t\right)$$

$$= f_0 + \Delta f \cos 2\pi f_m t$$

which shows that we have a frequency modulator.

A frequency demodulator produces a voltage, the instantaneous value of which is proportional to the instantaneous frequency of the signal. Networks capable of doing so include, for example, a frequency discriminator, such as the one shown in Figure 11.20, and a PLL, shown in Figure 11.21. In the frequency discriminator there are two resonance circuits, each followed by an envelope detector. One resonance circuit is tuned to a frequency above the carrier frequency, the other one below. One detector produces a positive output voltage, the other one a negative output voltage. The sum of these voltages is linear in the vicinity of the carrier frequency, if the difference between the resonance frequencies has a proper value. Usually there is an amplitude limiter before the frequency discriminator to eliminate the effects of signal amplitude variations. In the PLL, the control voltage of the VCO contains the demodulated signal, if the frequency depends linearly on the control voltage.

11.3.1.6 PM

PM is closely linked to FM because frequency $f(t)$ is obtained from the derivative of phase $\phi(t) = \omega(t)t + \psi(t)$ and accordingly the phase is obtained as an integral of the frequency:

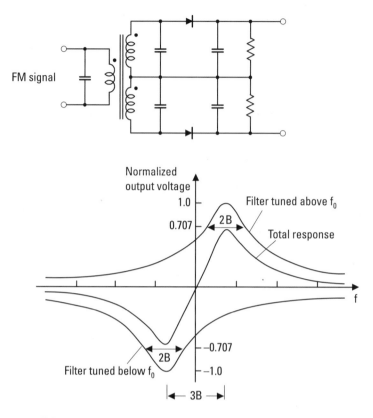

Figure 11.20 FM demodulator based on a frequency discriminator and its normalized output voltage.

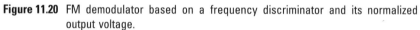

Figure 11.21 A PLL as an FM demodulator.

$$f(t) = \frac{1}{2\pi} \frac{d\phi(t)}{dt} \tag{11.36}$$

$$\phi(t) = 2\pi \int_0^t f(t')\, dt' + \phi(0) \tag{11.37}$$

A PM signal can be presented as

$$A(t) = A_0 \cos [2\pi f_0 t + \psi(t)] \tag{11.38}$$
$$= A_0 [\cos (2\pi f_0 t) \cos \psi(t) - \sin (2\pi f_0 t) \sin \psi(t)]$$

If $\psi(t)$ is small, $\cos \psi(t) \approx 1$ and $\sin \psi(t) \approx \psi(t)$, and (11.38) is simplified into form

$$A(t) \approx A_0 [\cos (2\pi f_0 t) - \sin (2\pi f_0 t) \psi(t)] \tag{11.39}$$

When the modulating signal is sinusoidal $\psi(t) = 2\pi M \cos (2\pi f_m t)$, we obtain

$$A(t) \approx A_0 \{\cos (2\pi f_0 t) - \pi M \sin [2\pi (f_0 + f_m) t] - \pi M \sin [2\pi (f_0 - f_m) t]\} \tag{11.40}$$

Equation (11.40) shows that the spectrum of a PM signal contains frequencies f_0, $f_0 + f_m$, and $f_0 - f_m$, as an AM signal does, but now the phases of these components are different. Figure 11.22 represents a phasor diagram of the PM signal.

11.3.2 Digital Modulation

An analog signal, such as a voice signal in the form of an audio-frequency electric signal, can be transformed into a digital form by sampling it frequently

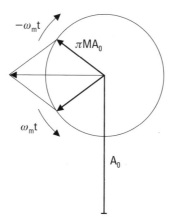

Figure 11.22 Phasor presentation of a PM signal.

enough. A digital signal may be binary, that is, containing only symbols 0 and 1, or *m*-ary, containing *m* different levels or states. The digital modulation has many advantages over the analog modulation; the total use of spectrum is effective, immunity to interference is good, frequency reuse is effective, TDM is easily realized, and it allows the use of encryption for privacy.

The basic digital modulation methods are *amplitude-shift keying* (ASK), *frequency-shift keying* (FSK), and *phase-shift keying* (PSK). Figure 11.23 shows the waveforms of binary ASK, FSK, and PSK signals when a symbol chain 01101001 is transmitted. In ASK, the maximum amplitude corresponds to symbol 1 and a zero amplitude corresponds to symbol 0. In FSK, the symbols are presented by signals with frequencies f_1 and f_2. In PSK, signals corresponding to symbols 1 and 0 have a phase difference of 180°. While analog FM and PM signals closely resemble each other, FSK and PSK signals are easily distinguishable.

In digital modulation, rapid waveform changes occur and thus the power spectrum of a digitally modulated signal is broad. Figure 11.24 shows the spectra of a binary baseband signal consisting of rectangular pulses and a PSK signal modulated with it. The envelopes of the spectra have the shape of a sinc function. The width between the first nulls of the PSK spectrum is twice the bit rate $1/T_b$, where T_b is the symbol period. In practice, the signal is filtered and the spectrum is narrower.

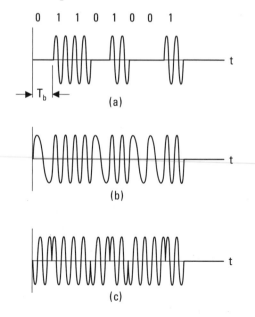

Figure 11.23 Waveforms of digitally modulated signals: (a) ASK, (b) FSK, and (c) PSK.

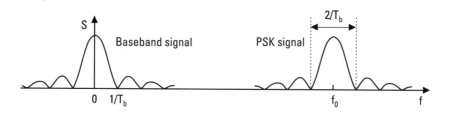

Figure 11.24 Spectra of a digital baseband signal and a PSK signal modulated with it.

In a binary modulation each symbol contains one bit of information. In a modulation scheme having 2^m different states each symbol contains m bits. Then it is possible to transmit more information in a given bandwidth or to use a narrower band to transmit a given signal having a given bit rate. A *four-state FSK* (4FSK), *four-state PSK* (4PSK or QPSK), and *eight-state PSK* (8PSK) are examples of modulation methods that save spectrum compared to the binary methods. In a digital QAM, both the amplitude and phase get several discrete values and the number of states may be 16, 64, or even higher. Therefore QAM is used in high-capacity links requiring effective use of the spectrum.

11.3.2.1 FSK

FSK can be realized by frequency modulating an oscillator or by switching between two oscillators operating at two different frequencies. The receiver may consist of two bandpass filters tuned for the frequencies f_1 and f_2, and followed by envelope detectors. Decision between symbols 1 and 0 is made based on the output voltage of each detector. Such an FSK demodulator, presented in Figure 11.25, is said to be noncoherent.

A coherent demodulator, shown in Figure 11.26, provides a smaller *bit error rate (BER)*. In the receiver, the frequencies f_1 and f_2 are regenerated, and their phases are synchronized with the incoming signal. The output

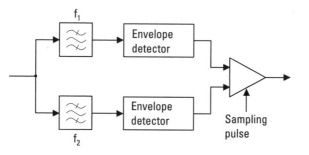

Figure 11.25 A noncoherent FSK demodulator.

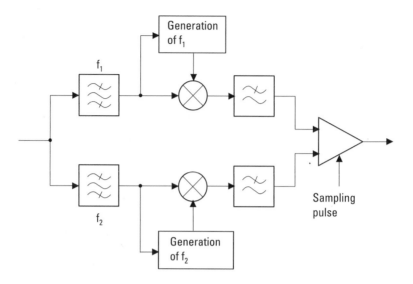

Figure 11.26 A coherent FSK demodulator.

voltage of a phase detector (a double-balanced mixer) is proportional to the phase difference of these two signals. After filtering, the amplitudes are compared at the sampling time, and a decision is made between 1 and 0.

Minimum-shift keying (MSK) is a special case of FSK having the smallest separation of frequencies f_1 and f_2 so that the correlation between the symbols corresponding to 1 and 0 is zero. For MSK, the difference between f_1 and f_2 is half of the bit rate.

11.3.2.2 PSK

PSK can be realized by switching between two oscillators that have the same frequency but opposite phase, or with a double-balanced mixer, as shown in Figure 11.27(a). The double-balanced mixer acts as a polarity-reversing switch: When the sign of the voltage fed into the IF port changes, the phase of the carrier output from the RF port changes 180°. Demodulation takes

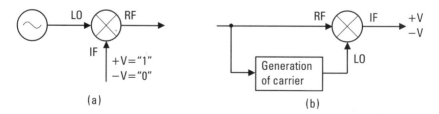

Figure 11.27 PSK: (a) modulation and (b) demodulation with a double-balanced mixer.

place in a reversed order, as in Figure 11.27(b). The carrier is regenerated in the receiver and fed into the LO port. The double-balanced mixer acts as a phase detector, and therefore the voltage from the IF port is either positive ($+V$ = "1") or negative ($-V$ = "0").

It may be difficult to get a phase synchronism between the carrier and the local oscillator during a period of only a few symbols. This difficulty can be avoided, and it is not necessary to generate the carrier in the receiver, if the phase of successive symbols is compared. Figure 11.28 shows such a *differential PSK* (DPSK) demodulator, where the signal is compared in a phase detector with the signal delayed by one symbol period T_b.

In *quadriphase-shift keying* (QPSK), the phase has four possible values, and each symbol corresponds to two bits: phase $\pi/4$ corresponds to 10, $3\pi/4$ corresponds to 00, $5\pi/4$ corresponds to 01, and $7\pi/4$ corresponds to 11. A QPSK signal can be generated using the circuitry shown in Figure 11.29(a). The first bit of the pair is fed to the mixer of the upper branch (I = in-phase), and the second bit of the pair to the mixer of the lower branch (Q = quadrature phase). In the demodulator, shown in Figure 11.29(b), the carrier is regenerated and the phase detectors provide output voltages proportional to the bits.

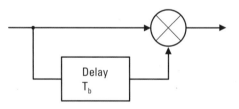

Figure 11.28 A DPSK demodulator.

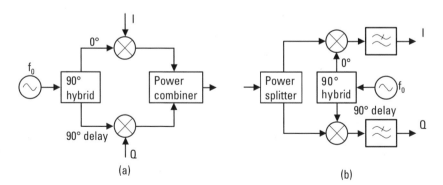

Figure 11.29 QPSK: (a) modulation and (b) demodulation.

11.3.2.3   QAM

The circuits in Figure 11.29 are also called an IQ-modulator and an IQ-demodulator. They may be used to generate and detect digital QAM signals. For example, a 16QAM signal may be produced as a sum of a four-level I-signal and a four-level Q-signal. Figure 11.30 shows the constellation of the 16QAM signal on the IQ-diagram. Each point of the constellation presents one symbol now containing 4 bits. The distance of a point from the origin is proportional to the amplitude of the modulated carrier, and the angle between the positive I-axis and the direction of the point from the origin is analogous to the phase of the signal.

11.3.2.4   Comparison of Digital Modulation Methods

An ideal modulation method uses the radio spectrum efficiently, is robust against noise, interference, and fading, and can be realized with low-cost and power-efficient circuitry. However, these requirements are partly contradictory, and some tradeoffs have to be made to optimize the overall system performance.

Binary ASK, FSK, and PSK signals can be generated with simple circuits. Because ASK and FSK signals can be demodulated incoherently with an envelope detector, these receivers can also be made simple and inexpensive. Coherent detection of ASK and FSK requires more complex circuits but provides a lower *BER*. PSK has the lowest *BER* but requires generation of a synchronized carrier in the receiver.

Figure 11.31 shows how the bit error rate of a PSK system depends on the S/N in an ideal AWGN channel and in a Rayleigh channel. In the AWGN channel, white noise is the only nonideality. An S/N of only about 7 dB is needed to achieve a *BER* of 10^{-3}. Coherent FSK needs 3 dB higher

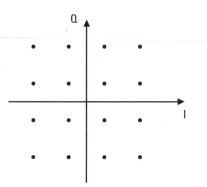

Figure 11.30 Constellation of 16QAM.

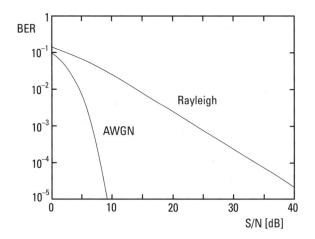

Figure 11.31 The BER of PSK systems in AWGN and Rayleigh channels.

S/N than PSK for a similar performance. In the AWGN channel *BER* decreases exponentially as S/N increases. In the Rayleigh fading channel a much higher average S/N is required for a given *BER*, because during deep fades the error rate is large. ASK has a very poor performance in the Rayleigh channel, because the threshold level between 0 and 1 depends on the signal level; FSK and PSK have no such problem.

The bandwidth efficiency describes how well a modulation method uses a limited bandwidth. The bandwidth efficiency of binary modulation methods is slightly less than 1 bit in 1 second per 1 hertz bandwidth. As noted before, increasing the number of modulation states lowers the symbol rate, making the spectrum narrower. Thus multistate methods have better bandwidth efficiencies than binary methods. However, for a given signal power the states become closer to each other, making the system more susceptible to noise and interference. Also, the equipment requirements of a multistate method are demanding. For example, an imbalance of the branches of an IQ-modulator and IQ-demodulator, and the phase noise of an oscillator may easily increase the *BER*.

In case of multistate QAM, the amplitude variations are large. Therefore transmitters and receivers have to operate linearly; otherwise, the signal will distort and the occupied bandwidth will grow. Modulation methods such as MSK, producing a constant-envelope waveform, allow the use of nonlinear power amplifiers in transmitters. As discussed in Section 8.4, nonlinear amplifiers are more efficient than linear amplifiers. Power efficiency is an important factor in battery-powered transmitters.

In mobile communication, connections have to operate reliably in spite of signal fading and Doppler shifts. Therefore, simple FSK and QPSK modulations or their variations are used in mobile systems. In fixed LOS radio links, good bandwidth efficiency is often required. Size and power consumption are not as critical as they are in mobile units. Multistate QAM can be used in LOS links, because in such links propagation problems are less severe than in mobile systems.

11.4 Radio Link Budget

A radio link between two stations consists of a transmitter, transmission path, and receiver, as presented in Figure 11.32. In a given link it is possible to transmit several channels, which are separated using *frequency division multiplexing* (FDM) or *time division multiplexing* (TDM). The received signal power is

$$P_r = G_t G_r \left(\frac{\lambda}{4\pi r}\right)^2 \frac{1}{L_p} P_t \qquad (11.41)$$

where L_p is the loss of the transmission path in addition to the free space loss, which equals $(4\pi r/\lambda)^2$. Loss L_p contains, among other things, the tropospheric absorption and scattering loss as well as the effects of diffraction and multipath propagation. Thus, it is possible that L_p is less than unity.

The system noise temperature of a receiving system is

$$T_S = T_A + T_R \qquad (11.42)$$

Then the equivalent noise power in the receiver input is

$$P_n = kT_S B_{RF} \qquad (11.43)$$

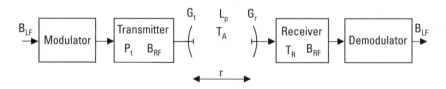

Figure 11.32 Radio link.

where B_{RF} is the noise bandwidth of the receiver (see Figure 11.4). The noise bandwidth is approximately equal to the bandwidth of the modulated RF signal, which, on the other hand, depends on the baseband signal and the modulation method used. For example, the bandwidth of an analog baseband signal required for voice is 3 kHz, and that for a TV picture is 5 MHz.

The S/N in the input of the receiver is

$$S/N = \frac{P_r}{P_n} = \frac{G_t P_t \lambda^2}{(4\pi r)^2 k B_{RF} L_p} \frac{G_r}{T_S} \qquad (11.44)$$

The S/N required for a good transmission depends on the application. For example, a good analog TV picture requires S/N over 40 dB for the video signal. For FM radio, S/N over 10 dB is satisfactory. Often in the receiving end one can affect the ratio G_r/T_S by properly selecting the antenna and receiver. Equation (11.44) in various forms is often called the link-budget formula.

Example 11.3

Let us consider a 12-GHz satellite TV link, where a geostationary satellite is broadcasting to Scandinavia. The distance between the transmitter and receiver is 40,000 km, and the satellite is seen at an elevation angle of about 20°. The transmitted power is 200W, and the transmitting satellite antenna is a 1.5-m paraboloid with an aperture efficiency of 0.6. The required availability of the system is 99.9%. What is the minimum ratio G_r/T_S and the maximum T_R that will result in a good TV reception?

Solution

From long-term statistics it is known that the atmospheric attenuation on the radio path of such a geostationary satellite is during 99.9% of time less than or equal to 3 dB. In order to obtain the required video signal S/N of 40 dB, the received FM signal must have at least $S/N = 14$ dB. By expressing the variables and constants of (11.44) in decibels, we get the link budget in decibels. Now the system properties can be calculated by adding and subtracting the decibel values. Properties of the system in decibels are given in Table 11.1. When the values from Table 11.1 are substituted into (11.44) and it is taken into account that $k = -228.6$ dBWK^{-1}Hz^{-1}, it is obtained that $G_r/T_S = 2.4$ dBK^{-1}. If the receiving antenna is a paraboloidal reflector with a diameter of 0.4m and an aperture efficiency of 0.6, its gain is 31.8 dB. Then T_S may be at maximum 29.4 dBK or 870K. The antenna noise

Table 11.1
Characteristics of a Satellite TV System

Quantity	Absolute Value	Decibel Value
P_t	= 200W	= 23 dBW
G_t	= 21,300	= 43.3 dB
$(4\pi r)^2$	= $(4\pi \times 40,000 \text{ km})^2$	= 174.0 dBm^2
L_p	= 2	= 3.0 dB
λ^2	= $(0.025\text{m})^2$	= −32.0 dBm^2
B_{RF}	= 27 MHz	= 74.3 dBHz
S/N	= 25	= 14 dB

temperature may be assumed to be at maximum 150K, and therefore the receiver noise temperature may be at maximum 720K. At the edges of the satellite antenna beam G_t is smaller than at the center of the beam, and therefore a larger receiving antenna or a more sensitive receiver is needed.

References

[1] Collin, R. E., *Foundations for Microwave Engineering,* 2nd ed., New York: IEEE Press, 2001.

[2] Gardner, F. M., *Phaselock Techniques,* 2nd ed., New York: John Wiley & Sons, 1979.

[3] Manassewitsch, V., *Frequency Synthesizers: Theory and Design,* 3rd ed., New York: John Wiley & Sons, 1987.

[4] Mumford, W. W., and E. H. Scheibe, *Noise Performance Factors in Communication Systems,* Dedham, MA: Horizon House—Microwave, 1968.

[5] "IRE Standards on Methods of Measuring Noise in Linear Twoports, 1959," *IRE Proc.,* Vol. 48, No. 1, 1960, pp. 61–68.

[6] Räisänen, A. V., "Experimental Studies on Cooled Millimeter Wave Mixers," *Acta Polytechnica Scandinavica,* Electrical Engineering Series, No. 46, Helsinki, 1980.

[7] Kraus, J. D., *Radio Astronomy,* 2nd ed., Powell, OH: Cygnus-Quasar Books, 1986.

[8] Bhargava, V. K., et al., *Digital Communications by Satellite,* New York: John Wiley & Sons, 1981.

[9] Carlson, A. B., *Communication Systems,* 3rd ed., New York: McGraw-Hill, 1986.

[10] Haykin, S., *Communication Systems,* 4th ed., New York: John Wiley & Sons, 2001.

12

Applications

Communication is the most important application of radio engineering. Radio communication includes broadcasting, terrestrial and satellite radio link systems, wireless local area networks, and mobile communication. Radionavigation, sensor applications such as locating by radar, remote sensing, and radio astronomy are other important applications. Radio waves are used also in many kinds of other sensors as in industrial sensors, for heating, and in medical applications.

12.1 Broadcasting

Broadcasting means supplying the public with information and entertainment by means of radio and television. Transmitting stations may be either terrestrial or satellite borne. Frequency ranges that are reserved for broadcasting in Region 1 (see Figure 1.2) are listed in Table 12.1. Analog radio transmissions are amplitude modulated in the LF, MF, and HF ranges and frequency modulated in the VHF range. Analog television transmissions use a VSB modulation for picture signal and either an analog FM or a digital QPSK for voice signal. Up to the HF range, waves can propagate long distances, even around the globe, as surface waves or by reflecting from the ionosphere. At VHF and higher frequencies, a nearly free LOS path between the transmitter and receiver is needed.

Broadcasting is currently transitioning from analog transmissions to digitally modulated transmissions. Digital transmission techniques have

Table 12.1
Frequency Ranges for Broadcasting in Region 1

Range	Frequencies	Application	Channel Spacing
LF	148.5–283.5 kHz	AM radio	9 kHz
MF	526.5–1,606.5 kHz	AM radio	9 kHz
HF	Several ranges	AM radio	
VHF I	47–68 MHz	Television	7 MHz
VHF II	87.5–108 MHz	FM radio	100 kHz
VHF III	174–230 MHz	Television	7 MHz
UHF IV	470–582 MHz	Television	8 MHz
UHF V	582–790 MHz	Television	8 MHz
SHF	11.7–12.5 GHz	Satellite TV	27 MHz

several advantages: The radio spectrum is used more effectively than in analog systems, the quality of the sound and picture is excellent even if the receiver is moving, and many kinds of services can be attached to the signal.

Digital Audio Broadcasting (DAB) is a European standard for digital radio transmissions. DAB uses a *coded orthogonal frequency division multiplex* (COFDM), in which information is coded effectively to reduce the number of errors. Bits are then distributed to several orthogonal carriers, which are modulated using a differential QPSK. A signal with 1,536 carriers has a bandwidth of about 1.5 MHz and can carry, for example, 6 stereo programs or 18 speech programs. *Digital Video Broadcasting* (DVB) is a standard for broadcasting digital TV. It is also based on COFDM. The maximum number of carriers is 6,817, and alternative modulation methods are QPSK, 16QAM, and 64QAM. Four or five TV programs fit to an 8 MHz wide channel. Because there are many carriers in COFDM, in each carrier the symbol rate is low and the symbol duration long. This makes COFDM insensitive to the adverse effects of multipath propagation and allows a use of single-frequency networks where all synchronized transmitters use the same frequency.

12.1.1   Broadcasting in Finland

In Finland, radio and television programs are delivered by the Finnish Broadcasting Company, *Yleisradio* (YLE) and some commercial companies. The network includes about 40 large transmission stations, 160 substations, and link stations. There are also two MF stations and one HF station. DAB test transmissions were started in 1994 and regular transmissions in the

VHF III range (174–240 MHz) began in 1998. Test transmissions of digital TV were started in 1998 and regular transmissions in the UHF range began in 2001.

The antenna masts for FM, DAB, and TV broadcasting are usually 100m to 300m high. Several antennas are placed on a mast so that the antennas of the highest frequency range are placed on the top. The directional pattern should usually be omnidirectional in the horizontal plane, whereas in the vertical plane the beam should be narrow and shaped to give equal field strength at different distances. The mast disturbs antennas, except the one on the top. The antennas lower in the mast have to be made of several elements. There are usually three or four elements in the horizontal plane and several elements in the vertical plane. The vertical pattern is realized by adjusting the phase and amplitude of the elements. The antenna elements are often dipoles with a reflector. Slot antennas are also used at UHF. Tetrodes and parallel-connected transistor amplifiers are used as the output stages of the VHF transmitters. At UHF, klystrons work as output stages.

Because frequencies used for the FM, DAB, and TV need an almost free LOS path, one transmitter can cover typically an area with a radius of about 70 km. Therefore, about 40 stations are needed to cover all of Finland, which has a land area of 338,000 km^2 as well as scattered islands. Figure 12.1 shows the locations of FM stations and their coverage areas. At the outer limit of the coverage area, the field strength is 0.5 mV/m (54 dBμV/m). Reception is often possible at distances 20 km to 30 km greater than these limits. The *equivalent isotropic radiated power* (EIRP), or the transmitted power that would be needed in the case of an isotropic antenna to give the same field strength as the actual antenna, is usually a few tens of kilowatts for FM transmissions. Total real radiated power is much less than *EIRP*. The polarization of FM signals is horizontal. In Lapland, circular polarization is also used. DAB transmissions are vertically polarized.

EIRP of TV transmissions can be as high as 1,000 kW. The polarization of TV signals is mainly horizontal; in the VHF I range vertical polarization is also used. In addition to the main transmission stations, many substations are needed to cover the whole country. A substation receives the signal from a main station, converts the frequency of the signal, and transmits it to those viewers who are unable to receive the signal from any main station. The coverage of the TV-1 and TV-2 networks is more than 99.9% of the population.

MF stations are in Helsinki (558 kHz) and Pori (963 kHz). The antennas are short (compared to wavelength) monopoles and the output stages are tetrodes. The HF station in Pori operates in several bands. The

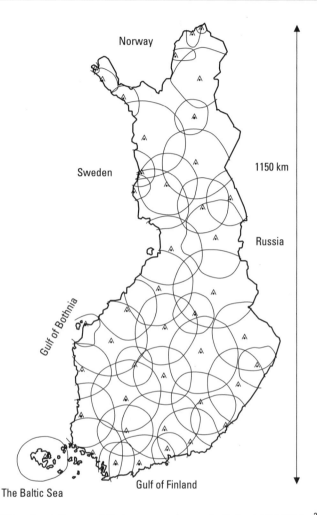

Figure 12.1 FM radio stations and their coverage areas in Finland (338,000 km^2).

antennas are horizontal dipole arrays. Reception of these HF signals is possible even in Australia.

In addition to YLE, many local FM radio stations operate in Finland. They use vertical polarization. In urban areas cable network companies distribute TV programs received from satellites.

12.1.2 Broadcasting Satellites

A satellite can be used as a platform for a broadcasting station. One single transmitter onboard a satellite can cover a whole country or continent.

Broadcasting and most other communication satellites are placed on *geosynchronous Earth orbit* (GEO) at the height of 35,800 km above the equator. At that height the orbiting time is equal to the rotation time of the Earth, 23 hours and 56 minutes. Then the satellites seem to be stationary and the antennas on Earth can be fixed. Positions of the satellites have to be corrected every now and then due to disturbances in the gravitational field. The amount of the steering gas limits the lifetime of satellites to about 10 years.

Broadcasting satellite service (BSS) satellites transmit (downlink) at frequencies from 11.7 GHz to 12.5 GHz into Europe. *Fixed satellite service* (FSS) satellites transmitting in the bands 10.7 to 11.7 GHz and 12.5 to 12.75 GHz also send radio and TV programs. The band 11.7 to 12.5 GHz is divided into 40 channels having a separation of 19.18 MHz. The width of the channels is 27 MHz and they are interleaved in orthogonal polarizations. BBS satellites send circularly polarized waves and FSS satellites linearly polarized waves. Analog TV programs are frequency modulated. Several digitally modulated TV programs fit in one 27-MHz band. The programs are sent to broadcasting satellites (uplink) in the band 17.3 to 18.1 GHz and to FSS satellites in the band 14.0 to 14.5 GHz. Due to crowding of the 12-GHz band, 20-GHz (downlink) and 30-GHz (uplink) bands will be introduced for the broadcasting service.

The microwave unit of a broadcasting satellite includes antennas and transponders. A transponder consists of a low-noise receiver, mixers and oscillators for frequency conversion, and power amplifiers. To improve reliability, transponders often have parallel units; for example, a broken power amplifier can be replaced with another unit. The power transmitted is typically about 100W so that an antenna having a diameter of 0.5m can be used for reception. The beam of the satellite antenna is shaped according to the service area. Figure 12.2 shows a typical footprint of a TV satellite.

In Finland, TV programs can be received from more than 20 satellites. The maximum elevation angle of geostationary satellites is only 21° in the most southern part of Finland. Because transmissions are usually directed to Central Europe, especially in the northern Finland, a large receiving antenna may be necessary.

Example 12.1

A geostationary satellite transmits with a power of $P_t = 100$W. The width of the circular antenna beam is 3°. The beam can be assumed ideal so that the normalized pattern level is 1 within the beam and 0 outside the beam. Find the power density at a distance of $r = 40,000$ km. What is the power received with a 0.5-m dish?

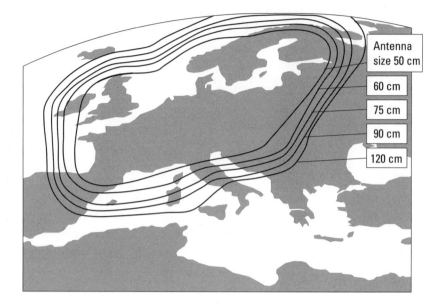

Figure 12.2 Typical footprint of a GEO TV satellite beam directed at Central Europe.

Solution

The beam area is approximately $\Omega_A = (\pi/4)(3\pi/180)^2 = 2.15 \times 10^{-3}$ steradians (see Section 9.1). The directivity is $D = 4\pi/\Omega_A = 5,840$. The power density at a distance of r is $S = (DP_t)/(4\pi r^2)$. Thus, $S = (5,840 \times 100)/[4\pi \times (4 \times 10^7)^2]W/m^2 = 2.90 \times 10^{-11}$W/m^2, that is, -105.4 dBW/m^2. The atmosphere is assumed to be lossless. The effective area of a 0.5-m antenna having an aperture efficiency of 0.6 is $A_{ef} = 0.6\pi \times 0.25^2$ m$^2 = 0.118$ m^2. The power received is $P_r = A_{ef} S = 3.42 \times 10^{-12}$W, that is, -114.7 dBW or -84.7 dBm.

12.2 Radio Link Systems

Radio link systems convey telephone and data traffic, TV and radio signals to broadcasting stations, and so on. Stations may be terrestrial or space borne. In this section, only fixed links are considered. Short communication links allowing user mobility are the topic of Section 12.3.

12.2.1 Terrestrial Radio Links

A radio link system typically consists of terminal stations and repeater stations, as shown in Figure 12.3. There are several frequency bands reserved for

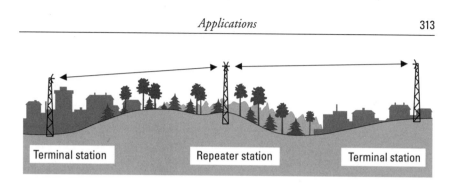

Figure 12.3 A point-to-point radio link system (horizontal distances not in scale).

fixed terrestrial point-to-point radio links, including 7/8, 13, 15, 18, 23, 38, and 58 GHz. Bands below about 2 GHz are nowadays reserved for other applications, such as mobile communication. Below 10 GHz the curved surface of the Earth or the height of masts (60m to 80m) limits the length of a hop to about 50 km. At frequencies higher than 10 GHz, the atmospheric attenuation and especially the attenuation due to rain limits the hop length. For example, at 23 GHz the maximum hop length is about 10 km and at 58 GHz (near the oxygen resonance) about 1 km.

The reliability of a radio link system is important. Between two stations, the first Fresnel ellipsoid should be free from obstacles to avoid excessive propagation loss. The curved surface of the Earth, the ground profile between the stations, and the bending of rays have to be taken into account when planning the heights of antennas. The statistical nature of the bending of rays and rain attenuation must be considered in the link budget. Diversity techniques can reduce the adverse effects of multipath propagation; space diversity in which two antennas are at different heights is a common technique.

Radio link antennas are usually parabolic reflectors. At millimeter-wave range, low-profile array antennas are also used [1]. The half-power beamwidth is typically 1° to 3°. Often antennas are protected against weather with a radome. Repeater stations have transponders, which change the frequency so that successive hops do not interfere with each other.

Radio links are either analog or digital. Analog links use FDM; digital links use TDM. Standard capacities of digital links are 2, 8, 34, 140, and 155 Mbit/s, or multiples of these bit rates. A 2-Mbit/s signal is composed of the content of 32 channels with 64 kbit/s. Low- and medium-capacity (34 Mbit/s or less) long-haul links below 10 GHz often use the QPSK modulation. In high-capacity links more complicated modulation methods such as 16QAM and 64QAM are needed. The modulation method of short-haul links above 10 GHz is often 4FSK.

Point-to-multipoint radio links are used in *wireless local loops* (WLLs) and *local multipoint distribution systems* (LMDSs), which offer a wireless access to fixed telecommunication networks. Point-to-multipoint links are often a good alternative to cable.

12.2.2 Satellite Radio Links

When the link stations on satellites are placed in geostationary orbit, three satellites can cover the whole globe, excluding the polar regions.

The *International Telecommunications Satellite Organization* (INTEL-SAT) was founded in 1964. In 2000, its 144 member states approved the privatization of INTELSAT. The geostationary satellites of INTELSAT are placed over the Atlantic, Indian, and Pacific Ocean. They convey voice, data, Internet, and video traffic. The first geostationary communication satellite was INTELSAT-1, Early Bird, which was placed in orbit in 1965. Its capacity was 240 voice channels or one TV channel. Satellites from fifth to ninth generation were in operation in 2002. Figure 12.4 illustrates INTELSAT-6, which has a capacity of 36,000 voice channels and three TV channels. It has 48 transponders having a total bandwidth of 3.3 GHz. The antenna system includes 4- and 6-GHz zonal reflector antennas, 4- and 6-GHz horn antennas that cover the whole globe seen from the satellite, two steerable 14/11-GHz (uplink/downlink) spot antennas, and two omnidirectional antennas for telemetry and command signals. Figure 12.5 shows the beams of an Atlantic satellite. The transmitting power of the 4-GHz beam is 5W to 15W; the 11-GHz spot beams have transmitting powers of 20W and 40W. Due to the vast service area, the ground stations have large 30-m antennas.

Many countries, including the United States, Canada, Australia, Indonesia, and Japan, as well as regional organizations have their own communication satellites. European countries have formed the *European Telecommunications Satellite Organization* (EUTELSAT). INTERSPUTNIK is a satellite organization of the eastern European countries.

12.3 Wireless Local Area Networks

A *wireless local area network* (WLAN) is a data communication system that can be used as an alternative to or as an extension of a wired LAN. A WLAN can cover a building or campus. A wireless network covering a larger area

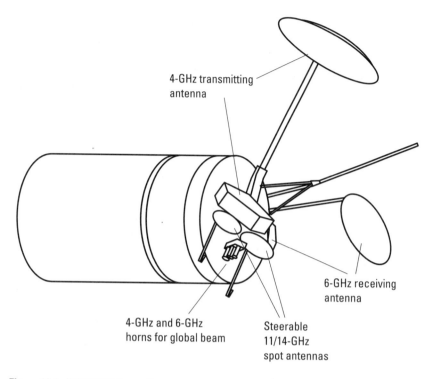

4-GHz transmitting antenna

6-GHz receiving antenna

4-GHz and 6-GHz horns for global beam

Steerable 11/14-GHz spot antennas

Figure 12.4 INTELSAT-6 satellite.

is called a *wireless wide area network* (WWAN) or a *wireless metropolitan area network* (WMAN). A network covering only a small range is called a *wireless personal area network* (WPAN).

Computers, printers, robots, and so on can be connected to a wireless network by infrared or radio links. Most WLANs use radio waves and are also called *radio local area networks* (RLANs). Radio waves can penetrate most walls and floor surfaces, whereas these solid objects block infrared. WLANs offer many advantages over traditional wired networks, for example, user mobility, installation speed, and flexibility.

Many standards are available for WLANs. IEEE 802.11, Bluetooth, and HomeRF operate in the unlicensed *industrial, scientific, and medical* (ISM) band, 2,400 to 2,483.5 MHz. Bluetooth and HomeRF are more like WPANs than WLANs. HiperLAN/2 is a high-performance standard operating in the 5-GHz band that was developed by the *European Telecommunications Standards Institute* (ETSI). DECT is a standard for cordless phones that can also be used for WLANs.

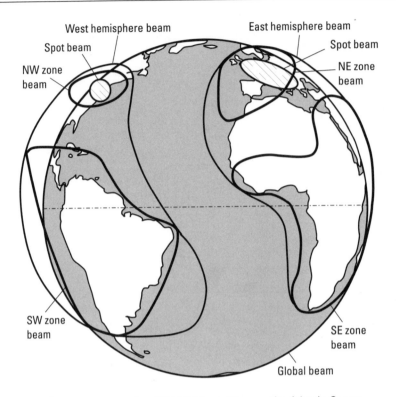

Figure 12.5 Coverage areas of an INTELSAT satellite over the Atlantic Ocean.

No license is required for low-power transmitters operating in the 2.45-GHz band. In addition to WLANs, several other applications, including microwave ovens and *radio frequency identification* (RFID) systems, use this band. To reduce interference between different users, spread spectrum techniques can be used. There are two types of spread spectrum techniques: *direct sequence spread spectrum* (DSSS) and *frequency hopping spread spectrum* (FHSS) [2].

In DSSS, a digital bit stream representing the source data is multiplied by a pseudorandom (PN) code with a bit or chip rate much higher than that of the data. Thus this product has a much higher symbol rate than the original data, causing the spectrum to spread. In the receiver, the original data can be recovered by multiplying the received signal with the same PN code. Only the signal with the same PN code despreads. To an unintended receiver, a DSSS signal appears as wideband noise.

In FHSS, the transmitter changes carrier frequency in a pattern known to the receiver. To an unintended receiver, an FHSS signal appears to be short-duration impulse noise.

12.4 Mobile Communication

Mobile communication [3–5] has grown faster during the last decade than any other application of radio engineering. Optical fibers and copper cables cannot compete with freely propagating radio waves in this application. In addition to cellular mobile systems, which are the main topic of this section, a moving person can use satellite systems or pager systems for voice or data transfer. The geostationary satellites of *International Mobile* (earlier Maritime) *Satellite Organization* (INMARSAT) offer communication services for ships, airplanes, and trucks. The operating frequencies between the satellites and mobile users are 1.6/1.5 GHz (uplink/downlink). Several other systems based on satellites on *low Earth orbit* (LEO) have been launched since 1998. Compared to the GEO systems, many more satellites are needed in the LEO systems, but shorter path lengths allow the use of handheld terminals.

In a cellular network, the coverage areas of the base stations form a "cellular" structure. To offer a good availability both in densely and sparsely populated areas, cells of different sizes are needed. To avoid interference, adjacent cells use different frequencies. The same frequencies can be reused in cells, which are far enough from each other. Also, the power levels of transmitters should be controlled to reduce interference. When a mobile phone moves from one cell to another, the network has to take care of this handover without interruption. (Cellular systems can be used also for rough locating because the cell, in which the mobile unit locates, is known. The accuracy may be enhanced by using measurements performed by more than one base station.)

In the development of cellular mobile systems, three generations can be distinguished: first generation analog systems, second generation digital systems, and third generation wideband systems. In addition to voice transfer, the second generation systems are usable also for low bit rate data services. Third generation systems support wideband multimedia services. The following introduces an example of each generation.

Nordic Mobile Telephone (NMT) represents the first generation. It was developed by the Nordic countries: Denmark, Finland, Norway, and Sweden. The NMT 450 network, operating in the 450-MHz band, was launched in 1981. In response to congestion, the upgraded NMT 900 network, which had a larger capacity, started in 1986. NMT networks are still in operation in many countries outside Scandinavia. Several other analog systems have been in use around the world, including AMPS in the United States and TACS in the United Kingdom. However, due to emerging digital systems, many first generation networks have been closed down.

In NMT 450, the transmitting frequencies of mobile phones (receiving frequencies of base stations) are 453 to 457.5 MHz, and the transmitting frequencies of base stations (receiving frequencies of mobile phones) are 463 to 467.5 MHz. Thus, the duplex frequency is 10 MHz. In NMT 900, the transmitting and receiving frequencies are 890 to 915 MHz and 935 to 960 MHz, and the duplex frequency is 45 MHz. A frequency channel is assigned for each user in a cell, that is, the access method is the *frequency division multiple access* (FDMA). The channel spacing is 25 kHz. Thus, NMT 450 has 180 channels and NMT 900 has 1,000 channels. The modulation method is FM. The *mobile telephone exchange* (MTX) is a central component of the NMT network. Each MTX is responsible for a group of base stations. The MTX determines the frequencies and transmitting powers of mobile phones, and takes care of the handovers from one base station to another. One base station covers an area with a radius of 0.5 km to 20 km.

Global System for Mobile Communications (GSM) represents the second generation. It is a digital cellular standard developed at first by CEPT and later by ETSI. Originally, the acronym GSM came from the name of the study group Groupe Spécial Mobile, which was formed to develop a common European standard. The first GSM networks were launched in 1991. GSM was rapidly accepted worldwide. Other second generation standards include *Personal Digital Cellular* (PDC) operating in Japan, American standards IS-95 and IS-136, and *Trans-European Trunked Radio* (TETRA), which is a standard for private mobile networks.

GSM (or GSM 900) operates in the same frequency range as NMT 900 (i.e., 890–915 MHz and 935–960 MHz). The access method is a combination of the FDMA and TDMA. There are 124 carrier frequencies, which are spaced 200 kHz apart. Each frequency channel is divided into eight time slots for different users. Mobile phones and base stations transmit short bursts of data. The bit rate during a burst is 270.833 kbit/s. The length of a burst is 0.577 ms or 156.25 bit periods. Consequently, a TDMA frame of eight bursts lasts 4.615 ms. Effects of multipath fading are alleviated by using slow frequency hopping, that is, the carrier frequency changes from one frame to another. The modulation method of the carrier is a *Gaussian minimum shift keying* (GMSK). To reduce the number of bit errors, channel coding and interleaving is used. In channel coding, redundancy bits are added in order to detect and correct errors. Interleaving disperses a series of consecutive bit errors to several blocks, making error correction easier.

Figure 12.6 shows the architecture of a GSM network. The mobile station is connected to a *base transceiver station* (BTS) via a radio link. The *base station controller* (BSC) controls a group of BTSs and manages their

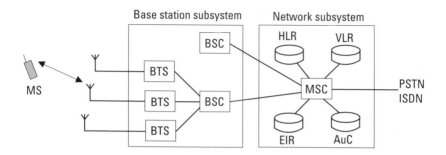

Figure 12.6 Architecture of GSM network. (MS = mobile station; HLR = home location register; VLR = visitor location register; EIR = equipment identity register; AuC = authentication center; PSTN = public switched telephone network; ISDN = integrated services digital network.)

radio resources. The *mobile-services switching center* (MSC) performs the switching functions of the network and provides a connection to other networks. MSCs also take care of the registration, authentication, and location updating of subscribers. Received power levels are continuously monitored. MSCs and BSCs make decisions about handovers using these received signal strengths. Transmitter power levels are also controlled according to the signal strengths; the maximum transmitter power of a handheld phone is 2W, and thus the maximum average power is (2W)/8 = 0.25W.

Digital Cellular System, DCS 1800 or GSM 1800, is an upgraded version of GSM 900. Mobile units transmit at frequencies from 1,710 to 1,785 MHz and base stations at 1,805 to 1,880 MHz. The number of frequency channels is 374. GSM 1800 is especially useful in metropolitan areas where the cells are small.

GSM supports data transfer at the speed of 9.6 or 14.4 kbit/s. An extension to the GSM standard, *High-Speed Circuit Switched Data* (HSCSD), permits using three time slots per frame, allowing a data speed of 43.2 kbit/s. *General Packet Radio Service* (GPRS) and *Enhanced Data Rates for GSM Evolution* (EDGE) are further extensions of GSM, which may operate in the existing GSM networks. GPRS is better suited for data transfer than GSM or HSCSD, which are circuit-switched systems. In GPRS, data is transmitted in packets and more than one timeslot per TDMA frame may be allocated for a user. In EDGE, the eight-level phase modulation, 8PSK, is used. One 8PSK symbol contains 3 bits of data, allowing a higher transfer rate than the GMSK modulation of GSM.

The standardization work for the third generation systems is ongoing. Within ITU these systems are called *International Mobile Telecommunications*

2000 (IMT-2000), whereas *Universal Mobile Telecommunications System* (UMTS) is used in Europe [6]. Third generation systems will operate in the 2-GHz band and will provide data rates up to 2 Mbit/s. A *wideband code division multiple access* (WCDMA) will be one of the access methods of the third generation systems.

12.5 Radionavigation

Radionavigation means determining position, speed, or some other quantity using radio waves for navigation, such as for steering a vehicle. Radionavigation is used in aviation, in shipping, and on land [7]. Radionavigation systems can be divided into two groups:

1. *Base station systems.* The positions of stations on the ground or on satellites are known. The position of a vehicle can be determined by measuring distances, differences in distances (hyperbolic systems), or directions to the base stations.

2. *Autonomous systems.* Doppler navigation is an example of autonomous navigation: Antenna beams are directed from an airplane to ground. The speed of the plane is obtained from the measured Doppler shifts. The position of the plane is calculated by integrating the velocity vector.

Hyperbolic systems, satellite systems, and systems used in aviation are treated in this section. In addition to these systems, radio beacons, broadcasting stations, and base stations of mobile phone systems are used for navigation. By taking a bearing to two beacons, the position of the vehicle can be solved. The null in the radiation pattern of a loop or Adcock antenna can be used for bearing.

12.5.1 Hyperbolic Radionavigation Systems

In a hyperbolic system, differences in distances to the base stations are measured. The difference in distance for a pair of stations corresponds on a plane surface to a hyperbola, on which the vehicle is located. The position is obtained from the intersection of two such hyperbolas.

Both pulsed and continuous signals are usable: The difference of the arrival times of pulses, Δt, or the phase difference of continuous waves, $\Delta \phi$, from two stations determine a hyperbola. The transmitted signals from different stations have to be time- or phase-synchronized to each other. On the line between two stations, a time difference of 1 ms corresponds to 150 km and a phase difference of 360° corresponds to $\lambda/2$.

In the example in Figure 12.7, stations A, B, and C transmit pulses simultaneously. (In practice, this would cause interference.) The pulse from station A arrives at the receiver on the vehicle 2 ms earlier than the pulse from station B and 1 ms earlier than the pulse from station C.

Decca, Loran-C, and Omega are hyperbolic radionavigation systems used in shipping and aviation. Only Loran-C is in use at present. Decca was closed down in 2000 after having been in operation more than 50 years. Decca consisted of chains having fours stations, which transmitted in the 100-kHz range. Navigation was based on the measurement of phase differences. The operating range of a Decca chain was a few hundred kilometers and it had an accuracy range of 5m to 50m. The worldwide Omega system was closed down in 1997. It consisted of eight stations, which operated at about 10 kHz. The determination of position was based on the measurement of phase differences, and it had an accuracy range of from 2 to 4 km.

Loran-C (for long-range navigation) is a hyperbolic system that is based on the differences in arrival times of pulses transmitted by the base stations.

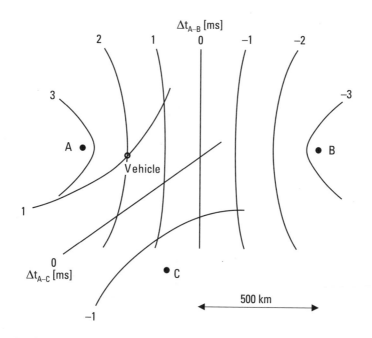

Figure 12.7 Hyperbolic navigation system.

Loran-C consists of chains, which have one master station and two to five slave stations. The stations are located about 1,000 km apart. There are about 30 chains around the world.

The carrier frequency of Loran-C pulses is 100 kHz. Transmitted pulse power is typically 400 kW. The shape of the pulse is well defined, as shown in Figure 12.8. Both the envelope of the pulses and the phase of the carrier are used to determine time differences. The transmission sequence of a chain starts with nine pulses from the master station. The pulses are 1 ms apart, except the ninth pulse, which is 2 ms apart from the eighth pulse. Then, after a given delay, each slave station transmits eight pulses. Because of the delay, signals are always received from the stations in the same order in spite of the location of the receiver. The length of the pulse pattern is 30 to 100 ms. Figure 12.8 shows an example of a received pulse pattern. Adjacent chains have different repetition frequencies, which helps in the identification of the chain.

The signals of Loran-C system propagate to a distance of about 2,000 km as surface waves. Reflections from the ionosphere come at least 30 μs later than the surface waves and do not disturb if only the beginning of the pulse is used for timing. Navigation accuracy is about 250m at a distance

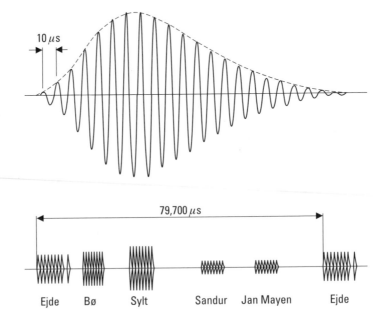

Figure 12.8   Pulse of Loran-C, and pulse pattern of the Norwegian Sea chain received in Helsinki.

of 1,000 km. Reflections from the ionosphere can be used for navigation at distances greater than 2,000 km but with inferior accuracy.

12.5.2 Satellite Navigation Systems

A global navigation system is realized best by positioning the stations on satellites. Satellite navigation has several advantages:

- Vast areas can be covered with a few satellites, which makes the maintenance of the system economical.
- Navigation accuracy is better because the radio frequency used can be higher than in terrestrial systems.
- Three-dimensional navigation is possible.

In addition to navigation, satellite systems are used for locating, surveying, and transferring time signals.

Transit and GPS are briefly described below. Many other satellite-based navigation and location determination systems are in operation. The *Global Navigation Satellite System* (GLONASS) and Tsikada are the Russian counterparts of GPS and Transit. Cospas-Sarsat is a worldwide rescue system, which can locate rescue transmitters.

Transit was the first satellite navigation system and was operating between 1964 and 1997. It was initially maintained by the U.S. Navy. Six satellites in polar orbits at the altitude of 1,075 km transmitted at frequencies of about 150 and 400 MHz. The use of two frequencies made it possible to correct the effect of the ionospheric delay. Transit navigation was based on the Doppler effect. The position of a receiver was determined from the measured Doppler shift, f_D, as illustrated in Figure 12.9. The longitude was obtained from the rate of change in f_D, and the latitude from time of passage when $f_D = 0$. The location accuracy for an immobile vehicle was 50m.

The *Global Positioning System* (GPS) is maintained by the U.S. Department of Defense. Full operational status was reached in 1995. GPS includes 24 satellites, of which three are spare. Satellites are placed on six orbits at the height of about 20,000 km (orbiting time: 12 hours), as shown in Figure 12.10. At least five satellites are high enough above the horizon for any location on the globe.

GPS satellites transmit at two carrier frequencies, L1 = 1,575.42 MHz and L2 = 1,227.60 MHz. Using both frequencies, the ionospheric delay can be taken into account. The signal contains information about the orbit and

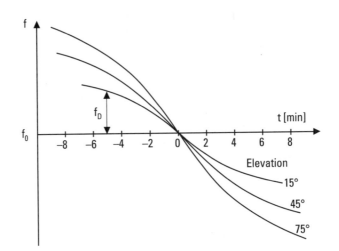

Figure 12.9 Principle of Transit satellite navigation. The elevation is the maximum angle from the horizon during a passage.

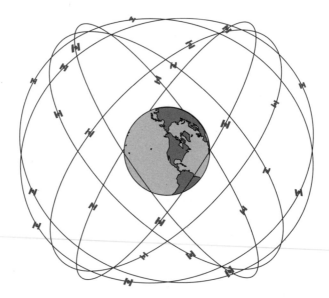

Figure 12.10 Orbits of GPS satellites.

clock correction, and general notices. Timing of signals is based on accurate atomic clocks.

GPS is based on the measurement of the distances between the user and satellites. The distance is determined from the time of propagation from the satellite to the receiver. The coordinates of the receiver can be calculated from distances to three satellites and from the coordinates of the satellites. The clock error of the receiver can be eliminated by using four satellites.

The GPS signal is PSK modulated with two pseudorandom codes, precise, or P, code and coarse/acquisition, or C/A, code, which have rates of 10.23 and 1.023 Mbit/s, respectively. The received code is compared to a similar code generated in the receiver, as illustrated in Figure 12.11. The delay of the generated code is adjusted until the correlation is at maximum. The transit time from the satellite to the receiver is the sum of the delay and a multiple of the length of the code. Figure 12.11 also shows the autocorrelation function of a pseudorandom code. Correlation is near zero if the phase difference is more than one bit. An error of one-hundredth bit period in the peak of the autocorrelation function corresponds to errors of 30 cm and 3m in the distance to the satellite with P and C/A codes, respectively.

The uncertainties of the clocks on the satellites and in the receiver, the uncertainties in orbital parameters, the propagation delays in the atmosphere and receiver, and multipath propagation are sources of error that impair navigation accuracy. The absolute accuracy of position is typically some tens of meters. The relative accuracy, that is, the difference in position for two receivers, is better, about 2m to 5m, because most of the errors are the same for both receivers. This is utilized in the *differential GPS* (DGPS), in which fixed stations monitor their positions and send correction signals to nearby GPS receivers. In surveying, the accuracy can be further improved by using the phase of the carrier and a long measurement time. The accuracy may be as good as about 1 cm.

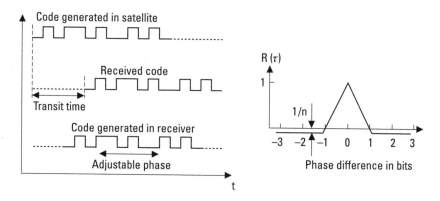

Figure 12.11 Determination of the transit time from a satellite to the receiver, and the autocorrelation function of a pseudorandom code. The code length is *n* bits.

The European Union has a definite plan to deploy a new satellite navigation system called Galileo starting in 2005. The Galileo system should be ready for full operation in 2008 when all 30 satellites are orbiting at the altitude of 24,000 km.

12.5.3 Navigation Systems in Aviation

In addition to hyperbolic and satellite navigation systems, many other radio-navigation systems are in use in aviation.

VHF Omnidirectional Range (VOR) is based on omnidirectional beacons operating in the range of 108 to 118 MHz. The carrier is amplitude or frequency modulated at 30 Hz so that the phase of modulation depends on the azimuth angle. Two subcarriers 9,960 Hz apart from the carrier are frequency modulated at 30 Hz and are angle-independent reference signals. The receiver on an aircraft measures the phase difference of the 30-Hz signals and thus reveals the direction of the beacon.

Distance Measuring Equipment (DME) operates in the range of 962 to 1,213 MHz and is usually located with a VOR beacon. Its frequency can be "paired" with VOR or ILS. The distance between an interrogator on an aircraft and a transponder at a ground station is obtained from the time it takes for the signal to propagate from the aircraft to the ground station and back, as shown in Figure 12.12. The interrogator sends a pair of pulses. The transponder delays its response by 50 μs and changes the frequency by 63 MHz.

The *Instrument Landing System* (ILS) and *Microwave Landing System* (MLS) are landing systems that give guidance for airplanes approaching a runway. ILS was introduced in the 1940s. It consists of three radio systems, as indicated in Figure 12.13: localizer, glide slope, and marker signals. The localizer signal (108–112 MHz) provides lateral guidance. The right side of the antenna pattern, as seen by an approaching aircraft, is modulated at

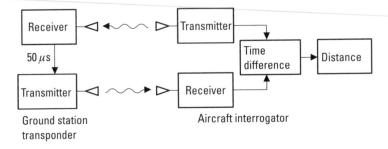

Figure 12.12 Operating principle of DME.

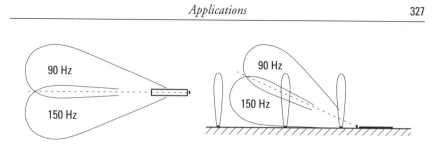

Figure 12.13 ILS localizer, glide slope, and marker beams.

150 Hz, and the left side at 90 Hz. On the correct track, the 90 and 150 Hz signals are of equal intensity. The glide slope signal (329–335 MHz) provides vertical guidance. The upper part of the pattern is modulated at 90 Hz and the lower part at 150 Hz. The intensities of the modulating signals are equal in the optimum glide angle, which is typically 2.5° to 3°. Marker beacons at 75 MHz provide information on the distance from the runway.

MLS is a precision landing system that will replace ILS. MLS allows different glide angles and curved approach paths, and has many other advantages over ILS. Navigation is based on five signals: (1) the scanning azimuth signal, ±40° or ±60°; (2) the scanning elevation signal, maximum scan 0.9° to 30°; (3) the back-azimuth signal for missed approaches; (4) *precision DME* (DME/P); and (5) data signals. With the exception of DME/P, all MLS signals are transmitted on a single frequency through time-sharing. The operating range, 5,031 to 5,091 MHz, contains 200 channels. Figure 12.14 shows how the azimuth angle of an approaching plane is measured. The narrow beam produced by a phased antenna array sweeps at a fixed scan rate, and the receiver on the plane measures the time interval between sweeps,

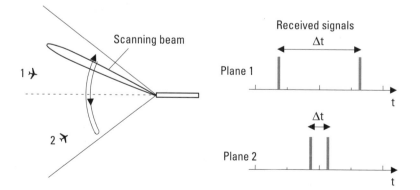

Figure 12.14 Azimuth signal of MLS.

Δt. The position of the plane is obtained from the measured azimuth, elevation, and distance.

Traffic-alert and collision-avoidance systems (TCAS) are based on transponders, which warn pilots about potential midair collisions. There are three versions of the system: TCAS I indicates potential threats, TCAS II gives simple advice such as "climb" or "descend," and TCAS III gives more detailed advice.

12.6 Radar

The technique to detect and locate reflecting objects—targets—by using radio waves was first called *radio detection and ranging* [8]. Eventually, this expression was reduced to the acronym *radar*. The serious development of radar began in the mid-1930s and progressed rapidly during World War II.

The applications of radar are numerous: Surveillance radar is used in air-traffic control; tracking radar continuously tracks aircraft or missiles; weather radar reveals rain clouds and their movements; police speedometers are used in traffic control; collision-avoidance radar may be installed on all kinds of vehicles; surface-penetrating radar can locate buried objects or interfaces beneath the Earth's surface or within visually opaque objects; and so on. Radar is applied in navigation (Section 12.5), in remote sensing of the environment (Section 12.7), in radio astronomy (Section 12.8), and in various sensors (Section 12.9).

Radar is either monostatic or bistatic. In monostatic radar the same antenna transmits and receives; in bistatic radar these are at separate locations. According to the waveforms used, radar can be divided into pulse radar, Doppler radar, and frequency-modulated radar. The basic principles of these different types of radar and the surveillance and tracking radar are treated in this section.

12.6.1 Pulse Radar

Pulse radar transmits a repetitive train of short-duration pulses, which reflect from the target back to the receiver. The distance to the target can be calculated from the speed of radio waves in the medium, which in most cases is with a good approximation of the speed of light in vacuum and the time Δt it takes for the pulses to propagate back and forth:

$$R = \frac{c\Delta t}{2} \tag{12.1}$$

The resolution of the pulse radar is

$$\Delta R = \frac{c\tau}{2} \tag{12.2}$$

where τ is the length of the pulse. Typically τ is in microseconds. Echoes from two objects, which are in radial direction closer than ΔR to each other, merge in the receiver. To avoid ambiguities in the measurement of distance, the pulse repetition rate, $f_p = 1/T$, should be so low that all the echoes produced by a given pulse have traveled back to the receiver before the next pulse is sent.

Figure 12.15 shows the block diagram of a monostatic pulse radar (the transmitter and receiver of a bistatic radar are located at different sites). The transmitter is often based on a magnetron oscillator, whose peak power may be one megawatt. Usually, the same antenna is used both in transmitting and receiving. A duplexer isolates the sensitive receiver during the high-power pulses transmitted and directs the echoes to the receiver. The direction of the target is obtained from the direction of the narrow main beam of the antenna. The antenna may be a reflector antenna, which is rotated mechanically, or a phased array, whose main beam direction is scanned electronically. The output voltage of the superheterodyne receiver is compared

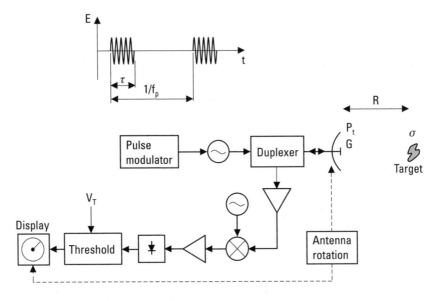

Figure 12.15 Block diagram of pulse radar.

to an adjustable threshold voltage, V_T. An output voltage higher than V_T is interpreted as a target. A too-low V_T increases the probability that noise is interpreted as a target; a too-high V_T reduces the probability of observing a weak target. The display may be a *plan position indicator* (PPI), in which the echo signal modulates an electron beam rotating synchronously with the antenna. Thus, the display shows the surroundings of the radar in polar form.

The power density produced by the radar at a distance of R is

$$S = \frac{P_t G}{4\pi R^2} \qquad (12.3)$$

where P_t is the transmitted power (during a pulse) and G is the gain of the antenna. The radar cross section of a target, σ, is the fictional area intercepting that amount of power that, when scattered equally in all directions, produces an echo at the radar equal to that from the target. In other words,

$$\sigma = \frac{\text{power reflected towards radar/unit solid angle}}{\text{incident power density}/4\pi}$$

The radar cross section of a target depends on the frequency and polarization, as well as on the direction of observation. In case of monostatic radar, the power density produced by the target at the radar is (same R in both directions)

$$S_r = \frac{P_t G}{4\pi R^2} \times \frac{\sigma}{4\pi R^2} \qquad (12.4)$$

and the power received is (same G both in transmitting and receiving mode)

$$P_r = S_r A_{ef} = S_r \frac{G\lambda^2}{4\pi} = \frac{P_t G^2 \lambda^2 \sigma}{(4\pi)^3 R^4} \qquad (12.5)$$

If $P_{r,min}$ is the minimum received power, which is reliably interpreted as a target, the maximum operating range of the radar is

$$R_{max} = \left[\frac{P_t G^2 \lambda^2 \sigma}{P_{r,min} (4\pi)^3} \right]^{1/4} \qquad (12.6)$$

This equation is called the radar equation. Because of the two-way propagation loss, doubling the transmitted power increases the maximum range only by 19%.

The minimum power $P_{r,min}$ or the sensitivity of the radar is

$$P_{r,min} = kT_s B_n \frac{S}{N} \tag{12.7}$$

where T_S is the system noise temperature, B_n is the noise bandwidth of the receiver, and S/N is the signal-to-noise ratio corresponding to the threshold voltage. Usually the IF filter determines the noise bandwidth, which should be about $1/\tau$. If the bandwidth were narrower, the received pulses would distort. If it were broader, the sensitivity would be reduced.

The radar equation (12.6) is based on many idealizations. The atmospheric attenuation reduces the maximum operating range, especially at high microwave and millimeter-wave frequencies. The radar cross section of the target often changes rapidly, fluctuates, and thus has a statistical nature. Also noise and other interfering signals are statistical. Therefore, instead of exact figures, only probabilities can be estimated for a given radar measuring a target of a given type. The maximum operating range for radar may be calculated by assuming a certain probability of detection and a certain probability of false alarms.

The performance of pulse radar may be improved considerably by pulse integration, pulse compression, and moving target indication. Even if the beam of the antenna is scanning rapidly, several pulses are received from a target during each scan. The sensitivity of the radar can be improved by summing these pulses. The summing, or integration, is performed either coherently at IF or noncoherently after detection. An ideal coherent integration of n pulses having equal amplitudes improves the S/N by a factor of n. A noncoherent integration is not as effective as the coherent integration but it is much simpler to realize.

In pulse compression, the transmitted pulse is long and its carrier frequency or phase is modulated. In the receiver, the pulse is then compressed to a short impulse, for example, by using a filter whose delay is frequency dependent. Pulse compression combines the advantages of high-energy pulses and short pulses, that is, a large operating range and a good resolution.

The echoes originating from fixed objects in the radar's surroundings, clutter, may mask the detection of more interesting weak targets. The effect of clutter may be reduced by the use of a *moving target indicator* (MTI). Figure 12.16 shows the principle of a simple MTI in which echoes of

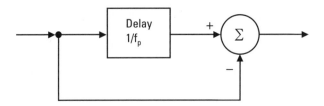

Figure 12.16 MTI based on a delay line.

successive pulses are compared. For a fixed target, the echoes are similar, giving no output. Moving targets can be detected because the distance of a moving target changes from one pulse to the next and there is a phase difference between successive received pulses. However, if the distance of a target changes by a multiple of the wavelength during the delay $1/f_p$, the phase difference is zero and the target cannot be detected. Such blind speeds can be avoided by using two or more different pulse repetition frequencies. The delay circuit may be an analog filter or a digital shift register.

Example 12.2

The properties of an air surveillance radar are: transmitted power $P_t = 250$ kW, antenna gain $G = 40$ dB, pulse length $\tau = 1$ μs, system noise temperature $T_S = 500$K, wavelength $\lambda = 0.1$m. The radar cross section of the target is $\sigma = 1$ m^2 and the S/N required for detection is $S/N = 13$ dB $= 20$. Find the maximum operating range.

Solution

The noise bandwidth is about $1/\tau = 1$ MHz. From (12.7) we obtain the minimum power $P_{r,min} = 1.38 \times 10^{-23} \times 500 \times 10^6 \times 20$W $= 1.38 \times 10^{-13}$W. Substituting this in (12.6) gives $R_{max} = [250 \times 10^3 \times 10^8 \times 0.1^2 \times 1/(1.38 \times 10^{-13} \times 4^3 \pi^3)]^{1/4}$m $= 174$ km.

12.6.2 Doppler Radar

The block diagram of a simple Doppler radar, called *continuous wave* (CW) radar, is shown in Figure 12.17. The radar transmits a continuous and unmodulated wave at a frequency of f_0. If the radial velocity of the target is v_r, the frequency of the reflected wave is $f_0 + f_D$ where the Doppler frequency is

$$f_D = \pm \frac{2v_r}{\lambda} \tag{12.8}$$

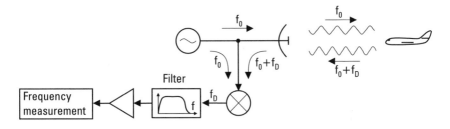

Figure 12.17 Simple Doppler radar.

Doppler frequency is positive for an approaching target and negative for a receding target. Mixing the transmitted and received signals produces an output frequency of $|f_D|$. Thus, the sign of f_D is lost in mixing. The filter removes the dc component due to fixed targets. To obtain a good resolution in velocity measurement, the signal should be produced with an oscillator having low phase noise.

Figure 12.18 shows a more sophisticated Doppler radar. It has two antennas, one for transmission and one for reception, which reduces the leakage of power from the transmitter to the receiver. The local oscillator

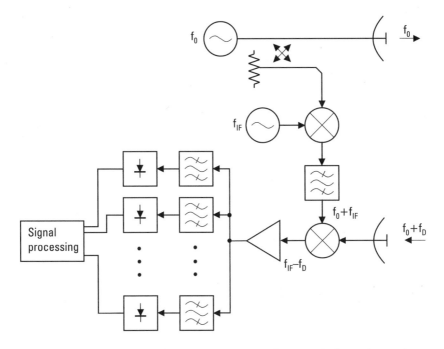

Figure 12.18 Doppler radar having separate antennas for transmission and reception.

frequency is shifted from f_0 to $f_0 + f_{IF}$. Now the output frequency $f_{IF} - f_D$ reveals the sign of Doppler frequency. The higher output frequency also reduces the effect of low-frequency noise. The use of a filter bank consisting of narrow-band filters improves the signal-to-noise ratio compared to the simple radar of Figure 12.17.

Doppler radar is used for many kinds of velocity measurements: in traffic control, to measure ascent speeds of aircrafts, and so on. They are also used to detect intruders.

Doppler radar is not able to measure the distance to a target. However, pulsed Doppler radar may measure both the distance and the radial velocity. The pulse repetition rate is so high that the velocity of the target can be extracted from the phase shifts of the pulses, but at the expense of ambiguity in distance measurement.

12.6.3 Frequency-Modulated Radar

Conventional pulse radar is not suitable for measuring short distances because for that the pulses should be extremely short. FM radar, or FM-CW radar, is better suited for such measurements. FM-CW radar can be used as airplane altimeters, to measure liquid surface heights in containers and the thickness of different layers, and so on.

FM-CW radar transmits a continuous wave whose frequency is modulated. The distances of reflecting objects are obtained from the frequency difference, f_d, of the transmitted and received signals. If the frequency is modulated with a triangular wave, as shown in Figure 12.19, the absolute value of the frequency difference is, except near the turning points, directly proportional to the distance R:

$$f_d = \frac{2R|df/dt|}{c} = \frac{4R\Delta f f_m}{c} \tag{12.9}$$

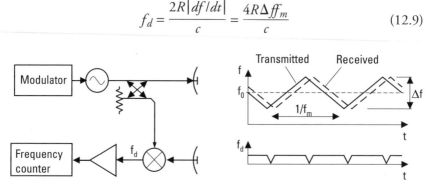

Figure 12.19 Block diagram and frequency waveforms of FM-CW radar.

where Δf is the maximum change of the transmitted frequency and f_m is the modulation frequency. Equation (12.9) is valid only if the reflecting object is stationary. Other modulating waveforms can also be used.

Example 12.3

The frequency of FM-CW radar, as shown in Figure 12.19, is modulated with a triangular wave between 3.0 and 3.2 GHz. The modulation frequency is 50 Hz. The output frequency is 1,200 Hz. Find the distance of the target.

Solution

Now $\Delta f = 3.2$ GHz $- 3.0$ GHz $= 200$ MHz, $f_m = 50$ Hz, and $f_d = 1,200$ Hz. From (12.9) we solve $R = cf_d/(4\Delta f f_m) = 3 \times 10^8 \times 1,200/(4 \times 200 \times 10^6 \times 50)$m $= 9$m. This distance is too short to be measured with pulse radar.

12.6.4 Surveillance and Tracking Radars

Surveillance radar covers for example an air space surrounding an airport, whereas tracking radar follows a target continuously. Surveillance and tracking radar are usually pulse radar, and they differ from each other mainly by their beam shape and scanning techniques.

The beam of surveillance radar is usually scanned in the horizontal plane mechanically by rotating the antenna or electronically by using a phased array. In the circular scanning shown in Figure 12.20(a) the beam is fan-shaped, that is, narrow in the horizontal plane and broader in the vertical plane. If the beam is cosec^2-shaped in the vertical plane, a target flying at a constant height produces an echo having a constant strength. A simple conical scanning reveals only the azimuth angle of the target. Stepped circular scanning [Figure 12.20(b)], and nodding circular scanning [Figure 12.20(c)], also give information on the elevation angle. Now the antenna may have a symmetrical pencil beam.

Tracking radar is used to track the paths of airplanes, missiles, rockets, and so on. Often tracking radar has a surveillance mode in which the radar seeks targets for tracking. As the target moves, the direction of the antenna has to be changed. In a conical scanning [Figure 12.20(d)], the axis of the beam makes a cone. If the target is not on the axis of the cone, the amplitude of the received pulses is modulated at the scanning rate. An error signal is generated from this modulation to correct the direction of the cone axis.

Monopulse radar has four beams, as shown in Figure 12.20(e). Now an error signal can be derived from a single pulse by comparing the amplitudes

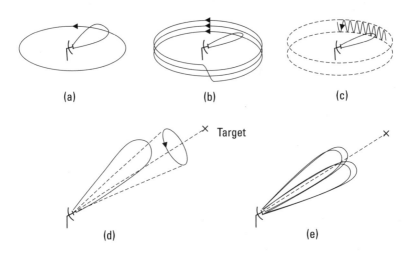

Figure 12.20 Scanning techniques: (a) circular scanning; (b) stepped circular scanning; (c) nodding circular scanning; (d) conical scanning; and (e) monopulse.

from all four beams. Therefore, the fluctuation of the radar cross section causing amplitude modulation does not impair the tracking accuracy. A multibeam antenna can be realized by placing an array of feed antennas on the focal plane of a reflector antenna.

12.7 Remote Sensing

Remote sensing means measuring or observing of atmosphere or surface of the Earth by using electromagnetic waves without any physical contact with the object and the analysis of these measurements. Radio astronomy investigating other celestial bodies is a separate field and is treated in Section 12.8.

Aerial photography has been carried out for more than one hundred years. Optical pictures taken from satellites have good resolution, at its best about 1m. Radio waves have been used for remote sensing since the 1960s. Radio waves have some advantages over visible light and infrared waves: Darkness and clouds do not prevent measurements; radio waves penetrate deeper in the vegetation and soil; and higher radio frequencies give information on the upper layers and lower radio frequencies on the deeper layers. However, the resolution of radio images is poorer than that of optical images.

Remote-sensing methods may be divided into passive and active methods. Passive remote sensing is called radiometry, in which thermal emission from the ground or atmosphere is measured with a sensitive receiver, a radiometer. In active remote sensing, radar techniques are used: objects are at first illuminated with the radar signal and then the reflected or scattered signal is measured.

Remote sensing using radio waves may reveal many properties of our environment [9–11]. Subjects that can be studied are numerous: ground profile, vegetation, moisture content of soil, water content of snow, oil leakages from ships, wind speed and direction, temperature and water vapor profiles of atmosphere, abundance of ozone and other molecules in the upper atmosphere, and so on.

Measurements can be carried out with instruments on the ground, on aircraft, or on satellites. The American Seasat (launched in 1978), Nimbus-7 (1978), and TOPEX/Poseidon (1992), the Canadian Radarsat (1995), and the European ERS-1 (1991), ERS-2 (1995), and ENVISAT (2002) are examples of remote-sensing satellites carrying radiometers or radar onboard. Several sounders for the measurement of the temperature profile and the contents profiles of water vapor, ozone, and many pollutants are planned.

12.7.1 Radiometry

All matter emits electromagnetic energy. A body in a thermodynamic equilibrium emits energy at the same rate as it absorbs energy. A blackbody is an object that absorbs all the energy that is incident on it, that is, the reflection coefficient is zero at all frequencies. If an antenna is pointing toward the surface of a blackbody at a temperature of T, the power coupled to the antenna in a bandwidth of B is (see Section 11.2.2)

$$P = kTB \qquad (12.10)$$

Most natural bodies are "gray." The power coupled to the antenna from a gray body is obtained by replacing the physical temperature T in (12.10) by the brightness temperature

$$T_B = eT \qquad (12.11)$$

where e is the emissivity, or the power transmission coefficient, of the surface. The emissivity is related to the voltage (electric field) reflection coefficient of the surface as

$$e = 1 - |\rho|^2 \qquad (12.12)$$

The emissivity depends on the electrical properties of the object (ϵ_r, σ), on the roughness of its surface, and on the angle, frequency, and polarization of the measurement. For a blackbody the emissivity is 1, for an ideal conductor it is 0, and for other objects it is between these limits. Thus, T_B is always smaller than or equal to the physical temperature. If the temperature of the object is not constant as a function of depth from the surface, T_B depends on the temperature distribution within a few skin depths. Radiometry is based on the fact that different objects have different temperatures and emissivities, and thus the measured brightness temperature may give a lot of information on the object.

Figure 12.21 shows a radiometer measuring the brightness temperature of the ground surface. In an ideal case, the noise signal is not attenuated by the atmosphere ($L = 0$ dB), the brightness temperature of the sky is $T_i = 0$K, and the thermal noise from the ground having a brightness temperature of T_B fills the whole antenna beam and is independent of direction. Then the antenna noise temperature is $T_A = T_B$. In practice, the atmosphere attenuates the signal and itself produces thermal noise, the surface reflects noise from the sky ($T_i \neq 0$K), and a part of the antenna pattern is not pointing toward the surface. The noise coming to the antenna can be characterized by a direction-dependent antenna noise temperature $T_{AP}(\theta, \phi)$. The measured antenna noise temperature is obtained by weighing $T_{AP}(\theta, \phi)$ by the normalized radiation pattern $P_n(\theta, \phi)$:

$$T_A = \frac{\iint\limits_{4\pi} T_{AP}(\theta, \phi) P_n(\theta, \phi)\, d\Omega}{\iint\limits_{4\pi} P_n(\theta, \phi)\, d\Omega} \tag{12.13}$$

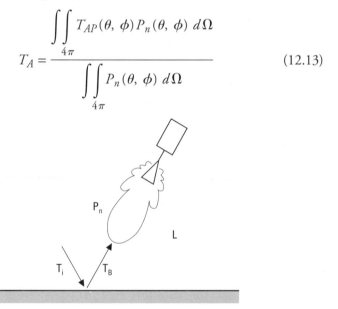

Figure 12.21 Radiometer measuring the brightness temperature of ground.

The brightness temperature T_B can be best figured out from the measured T_A, if T_i and L are small. This situation realizes well in the frequency range of 1 to 10 GHz, because at these frequencies the sky looks very "cold" and the attenuation of the atmosphere is small enough.

A microwave image of a terrain is acquired by placing a radiometer on an airplane or a satellite and by scanning the beam of the antenna. The emissivity of a rough ground surface is usually close to 1, whereas water has much lower emissivity, about 0.4. Therefore, the brightness temperature of a sea surface is $T_B = e T_{water} + (1 - e) T_{sky} \approx 100K$ to $150K$. Metallic objects reflecting the cold sky are also easily distinguished. At longer wavelengths the emissivity is sensitive to the soil moisture content, but the effects due to the surface roughness and vegetation may reduce the accuracy. Combining radiometric measurements at many frequencies and at both polarizations with infrared measurements may enhance the accuracy.

Radiometry can also be applied for the measurement of thicknesses of different layers. For example, a layer of ice or oil on the sea surface can be detected because the layer works as a matching element between the wave impedances of air and water. The reflection coefficient has a minimum and the brightness temperature a maximum when the thickness of the layer is a quarter (or an odd number of quarters) of wavelength.

Thermal emission of atmospheric gases can be used to study both the lower and upper atmosphere. The oxygen resonance at 60 GHz reveals the height profile of the temperature. The height profiles of the contents of water vapor, ozone (O_3), and many other molecules can be retrieved from the measured spectral lines, which these molecules have at microwave and millimeter-wave ranges. The emission or absorption spectrum of a molecule that is not interacting with its surroundings is composed of a set of narrow spectral lines. The collisions of molecules broaden these lines. Therefore, molecules at lower altitudes and higher pressures emit broader spectral lines than those at higher altitudes and lower pressures. Because the pressure versus altitude is well known, the content profile of a molecule may be obtained from the shape of its spectral line. A spectral line and the corresponding height distribution of stratospheric ozone are shown in Figure 12.22.

The depletion of the ozone layer first observed in the 1980s is alarming and requires constant monitoring. Global monitoring of the atmosphere can best be carried out with radiometers onboard satellites. A proper geometry for the measurement of upper atmosphere is achieved with a limb sounder, a satellite instrument that has a narrow-beam antenna directed toward the horizon. Height profiles can be measured by scanning the antenna.

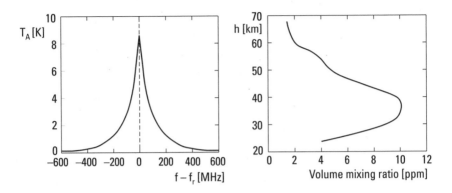

Figure 12.22 Spectral line of ozone centered at 110.836 GHz (background noise of atmosphere removed) and height profile corresponding to this line.

Example 12.4

A ground surface having a temperature of 295K and an emissivity of 1 is covered with a quarter-wave layer of lossless material having a relative permittivity of 5. Find the antenna temperature measured with a radiometer pointing perpendicularly to the surface. Assume that the brightness temperature of sky is 0K.

Solution

The wave impedance of the layer is $Z_{layer} = \sqrt{\mu/\epsilon} = \sqrt{\mu_0/\epsilon_0}/\sqrt{\epsilon_r} = 376.7/\sqrt{5}\,\Omega = 168.5\Omega$. Because now the ground is like a blackbody (emissivity $e = 1$), its wave impedance $Z_{ground} = 376.7\Omega$ equals the wave impedance of free space, η_0. The layer operates as a quarter-wave transformer (see Section 4.3.3) that transforms Z_{ground} to a value of $Z_t = Z_{layer}^2/Z_{ground} = 75.4\Omega$. The reflection coefficient between the free space and this impedance is $\rho = (\eta_0 - Z_t)/(\eta_0 + Z_t) = 0.666$. The brightness temperature of the ground is $T_B = eT = \left(1 - |\rho|^2\right)T = 164K$. This is also the antenna temperature seen by the radiometer, because the lossless layer itself does not emit thermal radiation and the sky is cold. Without the layer, the antenna noise temperature would be 295K.

12.7.2 Total Power Radiometer and Dicke Radiometer

A radiometer is a sensitive receiver that measures absolute noise power levels accurately and that is calibrated to display the brightness temperature.

Figure 12.23 shows a block diagram of a total power radiometer. It is a superheterodyne receiver, whose IF signal is fed to a detector. The mixer

and the theoretical cross-range resolution is

$$\Delta R_{cr} = R\theta_s = \frac{D}{2} \tag{12.21}$$

It is not practical to improve the resolution by using a smaller antenna because echoes would get weaker and various sources of error over a long section s would limit the resolution to a value higher than given by (12.21).

The reflectivity of the ground or sea surface depends on frequency, polarization, and the angle of incidence. At higher frequencies, echoes depend on the roughness of surface, whereas at lower frequencies, waves penetrate into ground and echoes are sensitive to the humidity of soil. By combining dual-polarization measurements made at different frequencies and angles of incidence, SLAR and SAR measurements provide multifaceted information for agriculture, forestry, geography, oceanography, and so on.

Scatterometers and altimeters are remote-sensing radar that do not produce images. A scatterometer is radar calibrated for the measurement of scattering. Scatterometers on satellites are used for the measurement of winds over the oceans. Sea waves correlate with the wind, and scattering in turn is sensitive to the height and shapes of the waves. Thus, by measuring scattering from different angles, the speed and direction of wind may be retrieved.

An altimeter is based on the measurement of the two-way propagation time of an echo. Altimeters provide information of the shape of the globe, ocean currents, ice coverage of glaciers, and so on.

12.8 Radio Astronomy

For a long time, only the optical window of the atmosphere covering visible light and the shortest infrared and longest ultraviolet waves was available for astronomers. In 1932, the American engineer Karl Jansky observed noise coming from the Milky Way as he was studying interference in communication produced by thunderstorms. In the late 1930s, the American amateur astronomer Grote Reber built a parabolic reflector and made the first rough map of the radio sky. After World War II, microwave technology became available to astronomers, and eventually radio astronomy developed into an important part of astronomy. A very important milestone was the observation of the interstellar neutral hydrogen at 1,420 MHz in 1953.

The atmosphere is nearly transparent (to zenith) from about 10 MHz to tens of GHz. Thus, the radio window covers about four decades of spectrum, whereas the width of the optical window is less than one decade. The reflection from the ionosphere sets the lower frequency limit. At millimeter and submillimeter waves the attenuation of gases becomes prohibitive, and telescopes must be placed on satellites.

The Sun, planets, gas and dust clouds of the Milky Way, pulsars, radio galaxies, quasars, and cosmic background radiation are subjects studied in radio astronomy [12]. Radio telescopes are also used for *searching extraterrestrial intelligence* (SETI).

12.8.1 Radio Telescopes and Receivers

Signals from radio astronomical sources are very weak. Thus, a large radio telescope and a sensitive receiver are crucial. A large telescope gathers waves from a large area and has a good angular resolution. The telescope should be situated at a high altitude and in a dry climate, especially if it is used at submillimeter wavelengths. The location should also be selected so that the level of man-made interference is low. The accuracy of the reflector surfaces should be better than $\lambda/10$, which is a formidable requirement for a large telescope operating at high frequencies. Surface errors reduce the gain and deteriorate the radiation pattern of the antenna.

Radio telescopes are typically parabolic reflector antennas. The telescope of the *National Radio Astronomy Observatory* (NRAO) in Green Bank, West Virginia, which started its operation in 2000, is the largest fully steerable telescope. The size of this offset-fed reflector, shown in Figure 12.27, is 100m × 110m. It is usable even at millimeter wavelengths. Other large parabolic reflectors are the 100-m telescope of the Max Planck Institute in Effelsberg, Germany, the 76-m telescope of the University of Manchester in Jodrell Bank, England, the 64-m telescope of CSIRO near Parkes, Australia, and the 45-m telescope of the Nobeyama Radio Observatory, Japan, which operates up to 100 GHz. The 30-m telescope of the Institut de Radioastronomie Millimétrique at Pico Veleta, Spain, and the 15-m James Clerk Maxwell telescope at Mauna Kea, Hawaii, are so accurate that they can be used even at submillimeter wavelengths.

Due to gravitation, construction of steerable parabolic reflectors much larger than 100m is not practical on Earth. However, even fixed telescopes can cover large parts of the sky. The 305-m spherical reflector at Arecibo, Puerto Rico, is situated in a mountain valley. Moving the feed antenna allows observations up to 20° from the zenith. A large telescope can also be

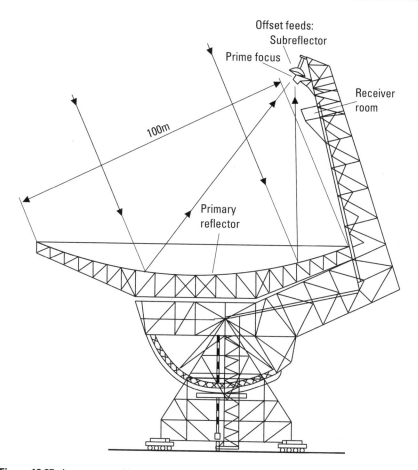

Figure 12.27 Large steerable radio telescope of NRAO in Green Bank. (*After:* [13].)

made of a tilting flat reflector, which directs the waves to a fixed segment of a parabola.

Even the largest radio telescopes, as measured in wavelengths, are very small compared to optical telescopes and have correspondingly an inferior resolution. The angle resolution may be improved by an aperture synthesis, in which signals from several telescopes are combined. The *Very Large Array* (VLA) of the NRAO in New Mexico consists of 27 parabolic reflectors, each 25m in diameter. The antennas can be moved on three tracks 21 km long, so that a Y-shaped configuration is formed on the plain. By taking advantage of the Earth's rotation and combining measurements made in 8 hours, an angle resolution equal to that of a continuous 40-km telescope may be obtained.

In *very long baseline interferometry* (VLBI) radio telescopes are separated by intercontinental distances or may even be in space. Signals cannot be compared in real time but are recorded with accurate time signals from atomic standards for later processing. The achievable resolution is far better than that of optical telescopes. The Japanese satellite HALCA was launched in 1997 and makes VLBI measurements with its 8-m telescope at 1.6 GHz, 5 GHz, and 22 GHz. It is in an elliptical orbit with an apogee height of 21,000 km.

The sensitivity of the receiver is very important in radio astronomical measurements. Doubling of the system noise temperature increases the time needed for a measurement by a factor of four. At microwave frequencies, cooled transistor amplifiers (HEMT) are used as the front ends of the receivers. At millimeter and submillimeter wavelengths, receivers are based on Schottky mixers, SIS mixers, cooled bolometric mixers, or bolometers. Often an array of receivers is placed on the focal plane of the reflector.

Figure 12.28 shows a block diagram of a cooled Schottky-mixer receiver operating in the 100-GHz frequency range. Signal from the reflector first enters a quasioptical calibration and beam-switching system. Calibration is based on two absorbing loads at known temperatures, one at the ambient temperature (T_H), the other inside a cooled dewar (T_C). Beam switching produces two adjacent beams in the sky by using a segmented, rotating mirror and two fixed mirrors. The radio source to be observed is in one of the beams while the other beam looks at the cold sky. The purpose of beam switching is to reduce the influence of the fluctuations caused by the atmosphere. The front-end components, feed horn, filter for LO injection, mixer, and the first IF amplifier are cooled to 20K with a closed-cycle helium refrigerator. The local oscillator is a phase-locked Gunn oscillator. The IF

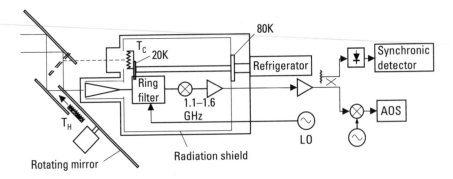

Figure 12.28 Cooled 100-GHz Schottky-mixer receiver.

signal is fed both to a detector operating synchronously with the beam switching and to an *acousto-optical spectrometer* (AOS) for spectrum analysis.

12.8.2 Antenna Temperature of Radio Sources

The flux S of a radio source is calculated by integrating the brightness B_S over the solid angle Ω_S covered by the source:

$$S = \iint_{\Omega_S} B_S(\theta, \phi) \, d\Omega \qquad (12.22)$$

The unit of flux is jansky (Jy); one jansky is $10^{-26} \, \mathrm{Wm^{-2} Hz^{-1}}$.

Some radio sources are like points in the sky, and some sources are extended. If the radio source is a point source and in the middle of the antenna beam, the received power in the frequency band Δf is

$$P_r = \frac{1}{2} A_{ef} S \Delta f \qquad (12.23)$$

For an extended source, the flux S has to be replaced with the flux S_o observed by the antenna. S_o is obtained by weighing the right side of (12.22) with the normalized directional pattern $P_n(\theta, \phi)$. If the brightness of the radio source is constant over the whole antenna beam, the received power is

$$P_r = \frac{1}{2} A_{ef} B_S \Omega_A \Delta f \qquad (12.24)$$

where $\Omega_A = \iint_{4\pi} P_n(\theta, \phi) \, d\Omega$ is the solid angle of the beam. Now the observed flux is $S_o = B_S \Omega_A$.

The received power may be written using the antenna noise temperature T_A as

$$P_r = k T_A \Delta f \qquad (12.25)$$

Combining this with (12.23) gives

$$T_A = \frac{A_{ef} S_o}{2k} \qquad (12.26)$$

If the brightness temperature of the source, T_B, is constant over the whole beam, then $T_A = T_B$. For a small source ($P_n \approx 1$ over the whole source), the antenna noise temperature is

$$T_A = \frac{\Omega_S}{\Omega_A} T_B \qquad (12.27)$$

Above, the influence of the atmospheric loss was not taken into account. Because the fluxes of radio sources are values defined outside the atmosphere, the measured results have to be corrected with the attenuation of the atmosphere.

Example 12.6

A point source having a flux of 2 Jy is measured with a 13.7-m radio telescope. Find the antenna noise temperature produced by the source and the required integration time τ. The attenuation of the atmosphere is $L = 0.8$ dB, the aperture efficiency is $\eta_{ap} = 0.6$, the noise temperature of the Dicke receiver is $T_R = 100$K, and the bandwidth is $\Delta f = 300$ MHz.

Solution

The physical area of the aperture is $A = \pi D^2/4 = 147.4$ m^2. The effective area $A_{ef} = \eta_{ap} A = 0.6 \times 147.4$ m^2 = 88.4 m^2. The flux at the antenna is $S = 2 \times 10^{-0.08}$ Jy = 1.66 Jy. From (12.26), the antenna noise temperature produced by the source is $T_{A,source} = 88.4 \times 1.66 \times 10^{-26}/(2 \times 1.38 \times 10^{-23})$K = 53 mK. The sensitivity of a Dicke radiometer is $\Delta T = 2T_s/\sqrt{\tau \Delta f}$. The antenna noise temperature produced by the atmosphere is $T_{A,atm} = (1 - 1/L) T_{phys} = (1 - 10^{-0.08}) \times 290$K = 49K, assuming that the physical temperature of the atmosphere, T_{phys}, is 290K. Thus, the system noise temperature is $T_S = T_{A,atm} + T_R = 49$K + 100K = 149K. The integration time depends on the required S/N (note that now signal is also noise). $S/N = 1$ or $T_A = \Delta T$ is achieved if $\tau = (2T_S/T_A)^2/\Delta f = 0.11$ second. The integration time needed for $S/N = 10$ is 100 times longer, nearly 11 seconds.

12.8.3   Radio Sources in the Sky

The radio sky is very different from the sky we see at optical wavelengths. Point sources, radio "stars," are not ordinary stars, which are relatively weak emitters of radio waves. The most significant similarities are the plane and the center of the Milky Way, which can be seen clearly in both optical and radio pictures.

Radio sources have different frequency dependencies. The radiation produced by thermal sources obeys Planck's radiation law. Nonthermal sources often emit synchrotron radiation, which is produced by electrons spiraling in a magnetic field. The intensity of synchrotron radiation decreases as frequency increases. Both thermal and synchrotron radiation have a broad, continuous spectrum and are called continuum radiation. Some sources emit only at discrete frequencies and have a line spectrum. Atoms and molecules emit spectral lines as their energy levels change, that is, when the atom or molecule after excitation returns to equilibrium.

There are many radio sources in our solar system, in our galaxy, and outside it. Moreover, from all directions comes a weak background radiation, which corresponds to the radiation from a blackbody at a temperature of 2.7K; see Figure 12.29. The intensity of the cosmic background radiation is at maximum at millimeter wavelengths, but on Earth it can best be observed in microwave range, where the noise level is the lowest. The discovery of background radiation in 1964 was proof in favor of the Big Bang theory, which assumes that the universe was born in a huge explosion. After its birth, the universe is believed to have expanded and cooled, and now we can observe the remnant of this explosion. The background radiation obeys extremely accurately Planck's law and is very isotropic. However, some anisotropy had to be in the young universe because galaxies have formed. In 1992, the *Cosmic Background Explorer* (COBE) satellite launched by NASA observed these anisotropies: The brightness of background radiation had tiny fluctuations whose relative amplitude was one part in one hundred thousand (1:100,000). The aim of successive space missions, such as the

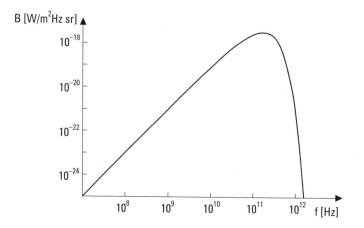

Figure 12.29 Spectrum of the cosmic background radiation.

Microwave Anisotropy Probe (MAP), launched in 2001, and Planck Surveyor, scheduled for launch in 2007, is to measure these fluctuations with a much better angle resolution and with a better receiver sensitivity.

Although stars are weak radio sources, the Sun is an exception because of its vicinity. The radiation from the Sun at frequencies higher than 30 GHz resembles the radiation of a blackbody at a temperature of about 6,000K. At lower frequencies the brightness temperature may be as high as 10^{10} K and depends on the activity of the Sun. When the Sun is active and there are plenty of sunspots, there are variations in the intensity of radiation. The sunspots are a source of slow variations and the flares are a source of rapid variations.

The planets and the Moon radiate almost as a blackbody. Jupiter is an exception: Below microwave frequencies it radiates more than a blackbody at the same temperature. The intensity of Jupiter's radiation varies in a complicated manner and is related to the position of its moon Io. Before the time of spacecraft, planets were studied using radar techniques. For example, the rotation times of Mercury and cloud-covered Venus were determined with radar in the 1960s. The surface of Venus was mapped more accurately in the beginning of the 1990s with SAR on the Magellan spacecraft. The rings of Saturn, its moon Titan, and asteroids have also been studied with radar.

Gas and molecular clouds, remnants of supernovas, and pulsars are radio sources in our galaxy. The continuum radiation of the Milky Way consists of synchrotron radiation and thermal radiation from ionized hydrogen. The synchrotron radiation dominates at frequencies lower than about 1 GHz and the thermal radiation at higher frequencies.

At 1,420 MHz (λ = 21 cm) interstellar neutral hydrogen emits a spectral line, which has been used to map the structure of the Milky Way. By measuring radial velocities of hydrogen clouds in different directions using the Doppler shift, it has been concluded that we live in a spiral galaxy. Even the center of the Milky Way can be studied using radio waves, which penetrate through dust clouds.

In addition to hydrogen, many different molecules, both inorganic and organic, have been observed in interstellar clouds, in which new stars are born. More than 80 different molecules have been found, the most complicated of which has 13 atoms [14]. The line spectra of molecules are produced by changes in the rotational energy states and occur at millimeter and submillimeter wavelengths. Lines may be either emission or absorption lines. An absorption line is produced when a cloud absorbs a narrow band of frequencies from continuum radiation coming from background. The measurement of the spectral lines reveals the distribution of molecules and dynamics of clouds. Figure 12.30 shows a measured spectrum of a molecular cloud in Orion [15].

Pulsars, originally called pulsating stars, are swiftly rotating neutron stars. They emit radiation in two narrow beams that sweep space like the beams from a lighthouse. The periods of short pulses received from pulsars range from one-thousandth of a second to a few seconds. The periods are very stable but are in some cases increasing as the neutron star slows down.

Radio galaxies and quasars (quasistellar objects) are radio sources outside our galaxy. The nearest normal galaxies have been mapped using radio waves. The radio emission of an ordinary galaxy is only a small fraction of its optical emission. In radio galaxies, the intensities of radio and optical emissions are of the same order. Quasars look like point sources. Their optical spectra show such large red shifts or recession velocities that the most distant quasars must be located near the edge of the known universe, or they are seen as they looked in the early universe. The intensities of both optical and radio emissions change with periods as small as one day, indicating that the quasars are small. The huge radiation of such a small object can be explained only by assuming that matter is falling down a black hole.

12.9 Sensors for Industrial Applications

Microwaves can be used for many kinds of measurements in industry [16–19]. The electrical properties of matter determine how radio waves propagate in it and reflect from interfaces. Electrical properties in turn depend on physical properties such as moisture, density, composition, and temperature. The

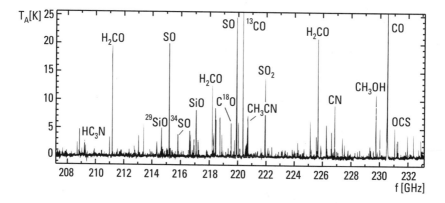

Figure 12.30 Spectral lines of an interstellar molecular cloud. (*After:* [15].)

advantages of microwave sensors are that measurements can be carried out without touching the object and that microwaves penetrate into the material. Different types of sensors and their applicability are treated here.

12.9.1 Transmission Sensors

A typical transmission sensor has two horn antennas, a transmitter, and a receiver. Waves pass through the object placed between the antennas. The phase shift due to the change in propagation velocity and the attenuation due to loss in the material are measured. Transmission sensors are simple and can be used for the measurement of materials moving on a conveyor belt, for example, or in a large tube. They are used to measure the moisture content of grain, coal, sand, and so on.

12.9.2 Resonators

A microwave resonator may be a cavity, strip-line, slot-line, parallel-wire line, or coaxial-line resonator. Resonators based on a slot or parallel-wire line may be used to measure liquid, granular, or pasty materials. Strip-line resonators are suitable for measuring sheets and material layers. Cavity resonators may be used as gas analyzers and to measure bars and materials flowing in tubes. Resonators may be used for many kinds of measurements: the moisture content of paper (see Figure 12.31), veneer, and air, the thickness of paper mass, the fiber orientation in paper, the thickness of plastic bars

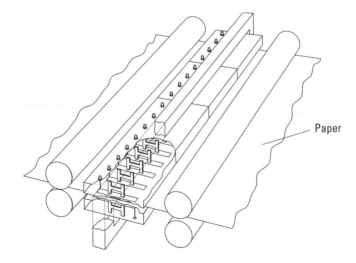

Figure 12.31 Strip-line resonator array for measuring paper moisture profile. (*After:* [17].)

and metal sheets, the burning energy value of peat, the water content of snow, and so on.

12.9.3 Reflection Sensors

The complex reflection coefficient of an object depends on the relative permittivity ϵ_r and its distribution within a few skin depths from the surface. If the object is layered, the thickness and permittivity of the layers may be solved from the frequency response of the reflection coefficient. An open end of a coaxial cable or waveguide, which is pressed on the surface of the object, is a simple reflection sensor. The reflection coefficient depends on the end capacitance and conductance, which in turn are functions of ϵ_r. Measurement of ground moisture and testing of materials are applications of reflection sensors.

12.9.4 Radar Sensors

Radar sensors can measure the amplitude of reflection, propagation time, or Doppler shift. Applications of radar sensors are numerous: door openers, movement detectors in burglar alarms, surface height detectors in vessels (applicable also when there is danger of explosion or foam on the surface), measuring power line vibrations, detecting rot in trees (see Figure 12.32), detecting pipes, cables, ancient relics, and mines in the ground, measuring marsh depth, and more.

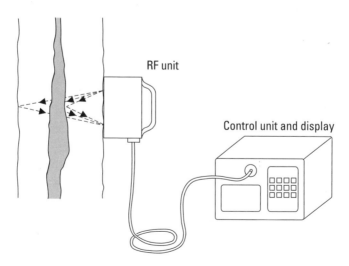

Figure 12.32 Impulse radar used to measure rot in trees.

12.9.5 Radiometer Sensors

Radiometer sensors provide information on the physical temperature and emissivity of an object. If one is known, the other may be found from the measured brightness temperature. A radiometer can make measurements through steam and smoke. By measuring also the reflection coefficient, the accuracy can be improved. The depth profile of temperature may be obtained by using several frequencies.

12.9.6 Imaging Sensors

In microwave tomography, the changes in amplitude and phase distribution caused by the object are measured as shown in Figure 12.33. The three-dimensional distribution of the permittivity may then be determined. In microwave holography, the shape of the object is resolved by measuring the scattered field. Imaging sensors can be used to search for objects in the ground, inside ceilings, or in security inspections.

12.10 Power Applications

Radio waves can be used for heating lossy materials. Often losses are caused by polar molecules such as water molecules, which the electric field turns back and forth. In many dielectric materials $\mu'' = 0$ and $\sigma = 0$, and according to (2.99) the power absorbed is

$$P = \frac{\omega}{2} \int_V \epsilon'' \mathbf{E} \cdot \mathbf{E}^* \, dV = \frac{\omega}{2} \int_V \epsilon'' |E|^2 \, dV \qquad (12.28)$$

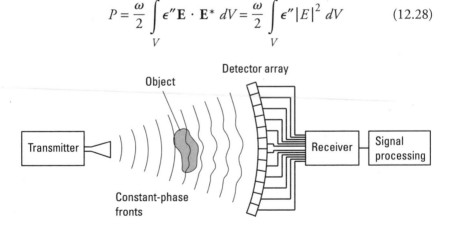

Figure 12.33 Measurement of permittivity distribution using microwave tomography. (*After:* [16].)

where E is the electric field within the material. Figure 12.34 shows how the electric field E inside bodies of different shapes is related to the field E_0 in the surrounding air.

Frequencies of 27 MHz and 2.45 GHz are allocated for power applications in Europe. Microwave ovens in the 2.45-GHz range are the most common power application. The oven shown in Figure 12.35 is a large cavity resonator within which many resonance modes are excited to realize a field that is as even as possible. The household ovens have a magnetron oscillator and their power is typically 600W to 1,000W. In industry, radio-frequency power is used to dry lumber, bake bread, vulcanize rubber, seam plastic, dry concrete, and so on.

12.11 Medical Applications

Radio waves are used in thermography, diathermy, and hyperthermia. Diathermy and hyperthermia are based on the absorption of radio-frequency

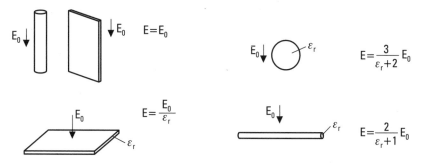

Figure 12.34 Electric field E inside bodies of different shapes. E_0 is electric field in the surrounding air.

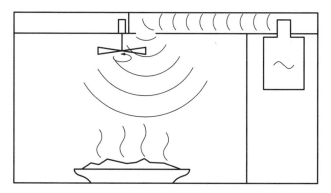

Figure 12.35 Microwave oven.

energy by a tissue, whereas in thermography, the thermal emission of the tissue is measured.

12.11.1 Thermography

According to Planck's law, the maximum intensity of thermal radiation is at infrared wavelengths if the temperature of a blackbody is 310K, the temperature of a human being. However, a human being can easily be detected with a microwave radiometer also. At microwaves, the human body is a gray object: at 3 GHz the emissivity of skin is about 0.5 and at 30 GHz over 0.9 [20].

The skin depth δ_s given in (2.69) is a measure of how deep the waves penetrate into the material. At a depth of δ_s from the surface, the field has attenuated by a factor of e from its original value at the surface. Correspondingly, the skin depth determines from how deep the thermal radiation of the tissue can be detected. The skin depth depends on the frequency and electric properties of the material. In bone and fatty tissue, water content is low and, thus, the skin depth is large. Muscles and skin have much higher water content and smaller skin depth, as shown in Figure 12.36 [21].

Thermography offers a noninvasive technique for early detection of cancer. A tumor having a temperature 1°C to 5°C higher than its surround-

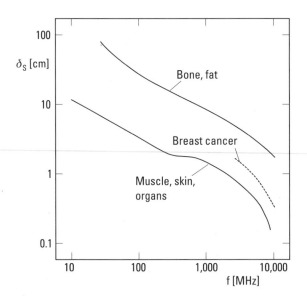

Figure 12.36 Skin depth for different tissues. (*After:* [21].)

ings can be detected with a microwave radiometer if the tumor is close enough to the surface. At RF a tumor can be detected from a depth of a few centimeters; at microwave frequencies a tumor can be detected only if it is on the skin or just below it. The antenna of the radiometer may be a large focusing antenna or a contact antenna pressed on the skin.

12.11.2 Diathermy

In diathermy, the temperature of a tissue or body is elevated by radio-frequency energy. Frequencies for diathermy are 27 MHz and 2.45 GHz. The temperature of the tissue is raised to between 39°C and 45°C. Higher temperatures, which kill cells, must be avoided. The power density may be 100 to 1,000 mW/cm^2. The power is focused to a restricted area and sensitive parts of body, such as eyes, are protected. Raising the temperature has many positive effects: Blood vessels become distended and circulation quickens, muscles relax, the threshold of pain gets higher, the stretching ability of a connective tissue increases, the penetration ability of cell membranes increases, and metabolism and enzyme reactions speed up. Diathermy is used for relieving muscle tension and as a pretreatment for physical therapy.

12.11.3 Hyperthermia

Microwave hyperthermia is used to treat cancer. A tissue containing a tumor is heated without destroying the healthy cells surrounding the tumor. This is possible because at 41°C to 45°C the cancer cells are destroyed more readily than the healthy cells [22]. Because the power density is high (1 W/cm^2) and the skin absorbs well, a burn may arise in the skin on top of the tumor. To be able to focus the energy into the tumor, microwave frequencies have to be used.

12.12 Electronic Warfare

Radar and wireless communication have many important military applications. There are also many other ways to utilize radio engineering techniques or knowledge for military purposes: jamming enemy communication and radar, stealth technology, signal intelligence, and so on. These applications go under the name *electronic warfare* (EW). Electronic warfare can be defined as military action involving the use of electromagnetic energy to determine, exploit, reduce, or prevent the use of the electromagnetic spectrum by the enemy, and as action that retains effective use of this spectrum, but sometimes also as military action where an electromagnetic weapon is used against personnel. EW is divided into three categories:

- *Electronic support* (ES), formerly *EW support measures* (ESM);
- *Electronic attack* (EA), formerly *electronic countermeasures* (ECM);
- *Electronic protection* (EP), formerly *electronic counter-countermeasures* (ECCM).

12.12.1   ES

ES is defined as actions taken to search for, intercept, locate, record, and analyze radiated electromagnetic energy for the purpose of exploiting it in support of military operations, especially for the purpose of immediate threat recognition. ES involves *signal intelligence* (SIGINT), which is divided into *electronics intelligence* (ELINT) and *communications intelligence* (COMINT). Detection, identification, evaluation, and location of foreign electromagnetic radiation from radar, communication radios, and so on are called electronic reconnaissance.

In ELINT wideband monitoring receivers covering, typically, frequency ranges from 20 to 500 MHz and from 0.5 to 40 GHz, as well as omnidirectional or rotating antennas are used to detect the presence of a radar signal. A high-gain steerable antenna is used to find the rough direction of the signal source. The signal is then analyzed and characterized using a sophisticated channelized receiver and analyzer, and compared to known radar signals in a signal library. Direction-finding antenna systems consisting of an array of antenna elements and utilizing, for example, interferometric or *time difference of arrival* (TDOA) techniques, are used at several receiving sites in order to locate the transmitting radar. Similarly, in COMINT communication signals in the HF, VHF, and UHF ranges are characterized and their sources located.

12.12.2   EA

EA is a division of EW involving actions taken to prevent or reduce an enemy's effective use of the electromagnetic spectrum by either passive or active means. EA involves, for example, radar or communication link jamming, high-power *electromagnetic pulse* (EMP), stealth technology, and the use of chaff to make fake radar targets.

Active EA involves jamming, high-power microwave weapons, and EMP. Jamming is deliberate radiation of wideband RF noise for the purpose of preventing or reducing an enemy's effective use of radar or communication link. The high-power microwave weapon or electromagnetic weapon is a class of *directed energy weapons* (DEW), and it is any device that can produce a directed microwave field of such intensity that targeted items of electronic equipment experience damage. EMP is often related to the electromagnetic radiation from a nuclear explosion, but it may also be caused by non-nuclear means, such as radio equipment; the resulting strong electric and magnetic fields may damage electronic systems.

Passive EA includes the use of chaff or decoys and stealth technology. Chaff is highly microwave-reflective material, such as sections of thin metallic stripes or wires with a resonant length, dispensed over a large volume to present a false radar target in order to protect a battleship or aircraft. A decoy is a passive dummy target or a radio repeater that appears as a false radar target. Stealth technology is used to reduce the radar cross section of an aircraft, ship, or ground facility by shaping the object and covering its surfaces with layers of absorbing composite materials.

12.12.3 EP

This division of EW involves actions taken to ensure effective use of the electromagnetic spectrum despite the enemy's use of electronic warfare by protecting equipment and facilities. EP involves technologies, such as shielding, that make electronic equipment robust against jamming, electromagnetic weapons, and EMP.

References

[1] Sehm, T., A. Lehto, and A. Räisänen, "A High-Gain 58-GHz Box-Horn Array Antenna with Suppressed Grating Lobes," *IEEE Trans. on Antennas and Propagation*, Vol. 47, No. 7, 1999, pp. 1125–1130.

[2] Prasad, R., *CDMA for Wireless Personal Communications*, Norwood, MA: Artech House, 1996.

[3] Gibson, J. D., (ed.), *The Mobile Communications Handbook*, New York: IEEE Press, 1996.

[4] Lee, W. C. Y., *Mobile Communications Engineering: Theory and Applications*, 2nd ed., New York: McGraw-Hill, 1998.

[5] Rappaport, T. S., *Wireless Communications, Principles, and Practice*, Upper Saddle River, NJ: Prentice Hall, 1996.

[6] Holma, H., and A. Toskala, (eds.), *WCDMA for UMTS, Radio Access for Third Generation Mobile Communications*, Chichester, England: John Wiley & Sons, 2000.

[7]   Kayton, M., (ed.), *Navigation: Land, Sea, Air, & Space,* New York: IEEE Press, 1990.

[8]   Skolnik, M. I., *Introduction to Radar Systems,* 2nd ed., New York: McGraw-Hill, 1981.

[9]   Ulaby, F. T., R. K. Moore, and A. K. Fung, *Microwave Remote Sensing, Vol. I, Microwave Remote Sensing Fundamentals and Radiometry,* Reading, MA: Addison-Wesley, 1981.

[10] Ulaby, F. T., R. K. Moore, and A. K. Fung, *Microwave Remote Sensing, Vol. II, Radar Remote Sensing and Surface Scattering and Emission Theory,* Reading, MA: Addison-Wesley, 1982.

[11] Ulaby, F. T., R. K. Moore, and A. K. Fung, *Microwave Remote Sensing, Vol. III, From Theory to Applications,* Dedham, MA: Artech House, 1986.

[12] Kraus, J. D., *Radio Astronomy,* 2nd ed., Powell, OH: Cygnus-Quasar Books, 1986.

[13] Kraus, J. D., and R. J. Marhefka, *Antennas for All Applications,* 3rd ed., New York: McGraw-Hill, 2002.

[14] Payne, J. M., "Millimeter and Submillimeter Wavelength Radio Astronomy," *Proc. of the IEEE,* Vol. 77, No. 7, 1989, pp. 993–1017.

[15] Phillips, T. G., and J. Keene, "Submillimeter Astronomy," *Proc. of the IEEE,* Vol. 80, No. 11, 1992, pp. 1662–1678.

[16] Nyfors, E., and P. Vainikainen, *Industrial Microwave Sensors,* Norwood, MA: Artech House, 1989.

[17] Fischer, M., P. Vainikainen, and E. Nyfors, "Dual-Mode Stripline Resonator Array for Fast Error Compensated Moisture Mapping of Paper Web," *1990 IEEE MTT-S International Microwave Symposium Digest,* 1990, pp. 1133–1136.

[18] Fischer, M., P. Vainikainen, and E. Nyfors, "Design Aspects of Stripline Resonator Sensors for Industrial Applications," *Journal of Microwave Power and Electromagnetic Energy,* Vol. 30, No. 4, 1995, pp. 246–257.

[19] Toropainen, A. P., "New Method for Measuring Properties of Nonhomogeneous Materials by a Two-Polarization Forward-Scattering Measurement," *IEEE Trans. on Microwave Theory and Techniques,* Vol. 41, No. 12, 1993, pp. 2081–2086.

[20] Edrich, J., "Centimeter- and Millimeter-Wave Thermography—A Survey on Tumor Detection," *The Journal of Microwave Power,* Vol. 14, No. 2, 1979, pp. 95–103.

[21] Myers, P. C., N. L. Sadowsky, and A. H. Barrett, "Microwave Thermography: Principles, Methods and Clinical Applications," *The Journal of Microwave Power,* Vol. 14, No. 2, 1979, pp. 105–113.

[22] Storm, F., "Hyperthermia," *Proc. of the IEEE MTT-S International Microwave Symposium,* 1981, pp. 474–475.

13

Biological Effects and Safety Standards

RF radiation does not ionize molecules in biological tissue, because the energy quantum hf is only 4 meV at 1 THz, while the minimum energy to ionize those molecules is about 12 eV. Therefore, according to the information and understanding of today, RF radiation cannot cause mutations leading to, for example, cancer. However, RF radiation may have other hazards: So-called thermal hazards are known for sure.

The biological effects of RF radiation have been studied through experiments with animals and models, and through epidemiological research. Effects may be divided into two classes: thermal effects and nonthermal effects [1]. Firmly observed thermal effects are the following:

- Cataracts;

- Increase of tissue temperature (see diathermy and hyperthermia in Section 12.11);

- Burns.

In addition, heat is known to weaken sperm, so this is also a possible side effect of strong RF radiation. Furthermore, RF radiation is suspected of causing instability in blood pressure and pulse rate, and changes in breathing due to thermal effects.

Nonthermal effects are subjective (like sensitivity to electricity) and include headache, tiredness, insomnia, irritation, weak appetite, loss of memory, and so on. The origin of these effects is not known, neither are they unambiguously proven.

Dosimetry is a field of research studying how radiation is absorbed into a tissue. The absorption of RF radiation depends on the skin depth δ_s of the tissue, on the size of the object in wavelengths, and on the polarization of radiation [2, 3]. Depending on whether the electric field, the magnetic field, or the propagation vector of the incident wave is parallel to the longitudinal axis of the object, the polarization is said to be E-, H-, or k-polarization.

To measure absorption we use the specific absorption rate (*SAR*), which has a unit of watts per kilogram. The *SAR* depends strongly on the size of the object. According to model measurements, the *SAR* on E-polarization of an average-sized person is as shown in Figure 13.1 [4]. At 70 MHz there is a strong resonance. Various parts of the body have their own resonance frequencies; the human head has a resonance at about 400 MHz. Because of resonance and depending on the tissue type, hot spots may appear in the human body exposed to RF radiation; however, these hot spots are not very pronounced due to high losses in the human body.

In practice, nearly all human beings are exposed to RF radiation from, for example, mobile phones [5]. A person in a certain profession may be exposed to a considerably higher power density. The industrial personnel working with RF heaters or dryers is a good example of this. A faulty

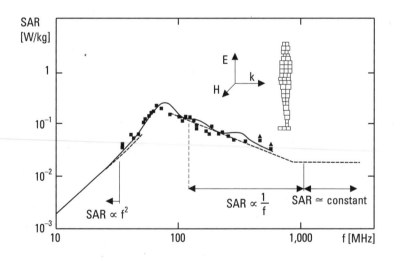

Figure 13.1 Average *SAR* in plane wave conditions with power density of 10 W/m² calculated using a block model of size of an average human being. Measurement points are obtained with experimental models with human shape but artificial tissues. (*After:* [4].)

microwave oven may expose its user to a high RF radiation dose. However, we do not know any incidence where a person has been permanently harmed by leakage radiation from a microwave oven. When an oven is mechanically damaged, however, its leakage radiation should be checked before the oven is used.

We consider harmless all the appliances that have maximum power below 100 mW. Table 13.1 lists typical sources of RF radiation.

Most countries use both national and international safety standards. The standards set limits on RF radiation power density or field strengths to which people in the general public and specific personnel dealing with strong RF radiation sources may be exposed.

In 1998 the *International Commission on Non-Ionizing Radiation Protection* (ICNIRP) developed new guidelines for limiting exposure to time-varying electric, magnetic, and electromagnetic fields [6], based on which

Table 13.1
Sources of RF Radiation in Finland

Source	Frequency (MHz)	Max. Average Power	Application
RF heater/dryer	13.56	250 kW	Drying glue
	27.12	25 kW	
Diathermy equipment	27.12	500W	Diathermy
MRI equipment	1–100	100W	MR imaging, diagnostics
MF broadcasting station	0.525–1.605	600 kW	Radio broadcasting
HF broadcasting station	5.95–26.1	500 kW	Radio broadcasting
FM broadcasting station	87.5–108	50 kW	Radio broadcasting
VHF broadcasting station	174–230	8 kW	TV broadcasting
UHF broadcasting station	470–790	16 kW	TV broadcasting
Mobile base station	450	320W	Mobile communications
	900	80W	
	1,800	50W	
Radar	1,200	2 kW	Air and sea surveillance, military applications, meteorology
	3,000		
	9,000		
Microwave oven	2,450	1,500W	Cooking
Microwave dryer	2,450	5 kW	For example, drying of concrete
Microwave heater	2,450	50 kW	Drying of materials

the Commission of the European Union in 1999 issued a directive concerning limiting acceptable exposure to electromagnetic fields to between 0 Hz and 300 GHz. Table 13.2 provides these limits. It is worth noticing that, because of the human body's resonance, the frequency range from 10 to 400 MHz is considered more harmful than other frequency ranges. In Finland, the Radiation and Nuclear Safety Authority supervises the safety of RF equipment.

Table 13.2
Limits of Exposure to RF Radiation as Electric and Magnetic Field Strengths and as Equivalent Power Densities (Frequency f Must Be Introduced in Megahertz)

Frequency Range	Electric Field [V/m]	Magnetic Field [A/m]	Equivalent Power Density [W/m²]
3–150 kHz	87	5	—
0.15–1 MHz	87	$0.73/f$	—
1–10 MHz	$87/f^{1/2}$	$0.73/f$	—
10–400 MHz	28	0.073	2
400–2,000 MHz	$1.375f^{1/2}$	$0.0037f^{1/2}$	$f/200$
2–300 GHz	61	0.16	10

Source: [6].

References

[1] Johnson, C., and A. Guy, "Nonionizing Electromagnetic Wave Effects in Biological Materials and Systems," *Proc. of the IEEE,* Vol. 60, No. 6, 1972, pp. 692–718.

[2] Durney, C., "Electromagnetic Dosimetry for Models of Humans and Animals: A Review of Theoretical and Numerical Techniques," *Proc. of the IEEE,* Vol. 68, No. 1, 1980, pp. 33–39.

[3] Gandhi, O., "State of the Knowledge for Electromagnetic Absorbed Dose in Man and Animals," *Proc. of the IEEE,* Vol. 68, No. 1, 1980, pp. 24–32.

[4] Hagmann, M. J., O. P. Gandhi, and C. H. Durney, "Numerical Calculation of Electromagnetic Energy Deposition for a Realistic Model of Man," *IEEE Trans. on Microwave Theory and Techniques,* Vol. MTT-27, No. 9, 1979, pp. 804–809.

[5] Jokela, K., et al., "Radiation Safety of Handheld Mobile Phones and Base Stations," Radiation and Nuclear Safety Authority of Finland, STUK-A161, 1999.

[6] International Commission on Non-Ionizing Radiation Protection (ICNIRP), "Guidelines for Limiting Exposure to Time-Varying Electric, Magnetic, and Electromagnetic Fields (Up to 300 GHz)," *Health Physics,* Vol. 74, No. 4, 1998, pp. 494–522.

Appendix A:
Vector Operations

$$\nabla (fg) = f\nabla g + g\nabla f$$

$$\nabla \cdot (f\mathbf{A}) = \mathbf{A} \cdot \nabla f + f\nabla \cdot \mathbf{A}$$

$$\nabla \cdot (\mathbf{A} \times \mathbf{B}) = \mathbf{B} \cdot (\nabla \times \mathbf{A}) - \mathbf{A} \cdot (\nabla \times \mathbf{B})$$

$$\nabla \times (f\mathbf{A}) = (\nabla f) \times \mathbf{A} + f\nabla \times \mathbf{A}$$

$$\nabla \times (\mathbf{A} \times \mathbf{B}) = \mathbf{A}\nabla \cdot \mathbf{B} - \mathbf{B}\nabla \cdot \mathbf{A} + (\mathbf{B} \cdot \nabla)\mathbf{A} - (\mathbf{A} \cdot \nabla)\mathbf{B}$$

$$\nabla (\mathbf{A} \cdot \mathbf{B}) = (\mathbf{A} \cdot \nabla)\mathbf{B} + (\mathbf{B} \cdot \nabla)\mathbf{A} + \mathbf{A} \times (\nabla \times \mathbf{B}) + \mathbf{B} \times (\nabla \times \mathbf{A})$$

$$\nabla \cdot \nabla f = \nabla^2 f$$

$$\nabla \cdot \nabla \times \mathbf{A} = 0$$

$$\nabla \times \nabla f = 0$$

$$\nabla \times \nabla \times \mathbf{A} = \nabla (\nabla \cdot \mathbf{A}) - \nabla^2 \mathbf{A}$$

Gauss' theorem $$\oint_S \mathbf{A} \cdot d\mathbf{S} = \int_V \nabla \cdot \mathbf{A} \, dV$$

Stokes' theorem $$\oint_\Gamma \mathbf{A} \cdot d\mathbf{l} = \int_S (\nabla \times \mathbf{A}) \cdot d\mathbf{S}$$

In rectangular coordinate system

$$\nabla f = \mathbf{u_x} \frac{\partial f}{\partial x} + \mathbf{u_y} \frac{\partial f}{\partial y} + \mathbf{u_z} \frac{\partial f}{\partial z}$$

$$\nabla^2 f = \frac{\partial^2 f}{\partial x^2} + \frac{\partial^2 f}{\partial y^2} + \frac{\partial^2 f}{\partial z^2}$$

$$\nabla \cdot \mathbf{A} = \frac{\partial A_x}{\partial x} + \frac{\partial A_y}{\partial y} + \frac{\partial A_z}{\partial z}$$

$$\nabla \times \mathbf{A} = \mathbf{u_x} \left(\frac{\partial A_z}{\partial y} - \frac{\partial A_y}{\partial z} \right) + \mathbf{u_y} \left(\frac{\partial A_x}{\partial z} - \frac{\partial A_z}{\partial x} \right) + \mathbf{u_z} \left(\frac{\partial A_y}{\partial x} - \frac{\partial A_x}{\partial y} \right)$$

$$\nabla^2 \mathbf{A} = \mathbf{u_x} \nabla^2 A_x + \mathbf{u_y} \nabla^2 A_y + \mathbf{u_z} \nabla^2 A_z$$

In cylindrical coordinate system

$$\nabla f = \mathbf{u_\rho} \frac{\partial f}{\partial \rho} + \mathbf{u_\phi} \frac{1}{\rho} \frac{\partial f}{\partial \phi} + \mathbf{u_z} \frac{\partial f}{\partial z}$$

$$\nabla^2 f = \frac{1}{\rho} \frac{\partial}{\partial \rho} \left(\rho \frac{\partial f}{\partial \rho} \right) + \frac{1}{\rho^2} \frac{\partial^2 f}{\partial \phi^2} + \frac{\partial^2 f}{\partial z^2}$$

$$\nabla \cdot \mathbf{A} = \frac{1}{\rho} \frac{\partial}{\partial \rho} (\rho A_\rho) + \frac{1}{\rho} \frac{\partial A_\phi}{\partial \phi} + \frac{\partial A_z}{\partial z}$$

$$\nabla \times \mathbf{A} = \mathbf{u_\rho} \left(\frac{1}{\rho} \frac{\partial A_z}{\partial \phi} - \frac{\partial A_\phi}{\partial z} \right) + \mathbf{u_\phi} \left(\frac{\partial A_\rho}{\partial z} - \frac{\partial A_z}{\partial \rho} \right) + \mathbf{u_z} \frac{1}{\rho} \left[\frac{\partial (\rho A_\phi)}{\partial \rho} - \frac{\partial A_\rho}{\partial \phi} \right]$$

In spherical coordinate system

$$\nabla f = \mathbf{u_r} \frac{\partial f}{\partial r} + \mathbf{u_\theta} \frac{1}{r} \frac{\partial f}{\partial \theta} + \mathbf{u_\phi} \frac{1}{r \sin \theta} \frac{\partial f}{\partial \phi}$$

$$\nabla^2 f = \frac{1}{r^2} \frac{\partial}{\partial r} \left(r^2 \frac{\partial f}{\partial r} \right) + \frac{1}{r^2 \sin \theta} \frac{\partial}{\partial \theta} \left(\sin \theta \frac{\partial f}{\partial \theta} \right) + \frac{1}{r^2 \sin^2 \theta} \frac{\partial^2 f}{\partial \phi^2}$$

$$\nabla \cdot \mathbf{A} = \frac{1}{r^2} \frac{\partial}{\partial r} (r^2 A_r) + \frac{1}{r \sin \theta} \frac{\partial}{\partial \theta} (\sin \theta A_\theta) + \frac{1}{r \sin \theta} \frac{\partial A_\phi}{\partial \phi}$$

$$\nabla \times \mathbf{A} = \frac{\mathbf{u_r}}{r \sin \theta} \left[\frac{\partial}{\partial \theta} (\sin \theta A_\phi) - \frac{\partial A_\theta}{\partial \phi} \right] + \frac{\mathbf{u_\theta}}{r} \left[\frac{1}{\sin \theta} \frac{\partial A_r}{\partial \phi} - \frac{\partial}{\partial r} (rA_\phi) \right]$$

$$+ \frac{\mathbf{u_\phi}}{r} \left[\frac{\partial}{\partial r} (rA_\theta) - \frac{\partial A_r}{\partial \theta} \right]$$

Appendix B:
Physical Constants and Material Parameters

Physical Constants

Name	Symbol	Value
Speed of light in vacuum	c	299,792,458 m/s
Permittivity of vacuum	ϵ_0	8.854×10^{-12} As/Vm
Permeability of vacuum	μ_0	$4\pi \times 10^{-7}$ Vs/Am
Wave impedance in vacuum	η	$376.7\,\Omega$
Boltzmann's constant	k	1.381×10^{-23} J/K
Planck's constant	h	6.626×10^{-34} Js
Charge of electron (magnitude)	e	1.602×10^{-19} As
Mass of electron	m_e	9.109×10^{-31} kg

Conductivity of Some Materials at 20°C

Material	σ [S/m]
Aluminum	3.8×10^7
Brass (66% Cu, 34% Zn)	2.6×10^7
Copper	5.8×10^7
Germanium	2.2
Glass	10^{-12}
Gold	4.1×10^7
Iron	1.0×10^7
Nickel	1.4×10^7
Porcelain	2×10^{-13}
Quartz	1.3×10^{-18}
Seawater	4
Silicon	1.2×10^3
Silver	6.2×10^7
Tin	8.8×10^6
Water, distilled	2×10^{-4}

Dielectric Constant (Relative Permittivity) of Some Materials (at 10 GHz If Not Otherwise Stated)

Material	ϵ_r	$\tan \delta$
Alumina (Al$_2$O$_3$)	9.7	2×10^{-4}
RT/duroid®5880	2.20	9×10^{-4}
RT/duroid®6010LM	10.2	2.3×10^{-3}
Gallium arsenide	13.0	6×10^{-4}
Glass	4–10	2×10^{-3}–2×10^{-2}
Ice (fresh water)	3–4	10^{-3}
Polyethylene	2.3	10^{-3}
Polystyrene	2.54	5×10^{-4}
Porcelain	5.5	1.5×10^{-2}
Quartz (fused)	3.78	10^{-4}
Sapphire	$\epsilon_\rho = 9.4$, $\epsilon_z = 11.6$	10^{-4}
Seawater (20°C)	54	0.7
Seawater (1 GHz, 20°C)	69	1.4
Silicon	11.9	10^{-3}–10^{-2}
Styrox	1.05	
Teflon	2.06	3×10^{-4}
Water, distilled (20°C)	60	0.5
Water, distilled (1 GHz, 20°C)	80	0.06

RFID	radio frequency identification
RLAN	radio local area network
SAR	specific absorption rate
SAR	synthetic-aperture radar
SAW	surface acoustic wave
SETI	search for extraterrestrial intelligence
SHF	super high frequency
SIGINT	signal intelligence
SIS	superconductor-insulator-superconductor
SLAR	side-looking airborne radar
SSB	single sideband
TACS	Total Access Communications System
TCAS	Traffic-Alert and Collision-Avoidance System
TDD	time division duplexing
TDM	time division multiplexing
TDMA	time division multiple access
TDOA	time difference of arrival
TE	transverse electric
TED	transferred electron device
TEM	transverse electric and magnetic
TETRA	Trans-European Trunked Radio
TM	transverse magnetic
UHF	ultra high frequency
UMTS	Universal Mobile Telecommunications System
VCO	voltage-controlled oscillator
VHF	very high frequency
VLA	Very Large Array
VLBI	very long baseline interferometry
VLF	very low frequency
VLR	visitor location register
VOR	VHF omnidirectional range
VSB	vestigial sideband
VSWR	voltage standing wave ratio
WARC	World Administrative Radio Conference
WCDMA	wideband code division multiple access
WLAN	wireless local area network
WLL	wireless local loop
WMAN	wireless metropolitan area network
WPAN	wireless personal area network

WRC	World Radiocommunication Conference
WWAN	wireless wide area network
YIG	yttrium iron garnet

About the Authors

Antti V. Räisänen received a Diploma Engineer (M.Sc.), a Licentiate of Science (Tech), and a Doctor of Science (Tech) in electrical engineering from Helsinki University of Technology (HUT), Finland, in 1973, 1976, and 1981, respectively. Dr. Räisänen was appointed to the professor chair of radio engineering at HUT in 1989, after previously having held the same position as an acting professor. He has held visiting scientist and professor positions at the Five College Radio Astronomy Observatory (FCRAO), the University of Massachusetts, Amherst, the Chalmers University of Technology, Göteborg, Sweden, at the Department of Physics, University of California, Berkeley, the Jet Propulsion Laboratory and California Institute of Technology, Pasadena, and the Paris Observatory and University of Paris 6.

Currently, Dr. Räisänen is supervising research in millimeter-wave components, antennas, receivers, and microwave measurements at HUT Radio Laboratory and MilliLab. He has authored or coauthored about 400 scientific or technical papers and five books: *Microwave Measurement Techniques, Radio Engineering, RF and Microwave Techniques, Millimeter-Wave Techniques,* and *Fundamentals of Radio Engineering* (with A. Lehto, published by Otatieto, in 1991, 1992, 1994, 1997, and 2001, respectively, all in Finnish). He also coauthored a chapter, "Radio-Telescope Receivers" with M. E. Tiuri, in J. D. Kraus, *Radio Astronomy, Second Edition* (Cygnus-Quasar Books, 1986). In 1994 he was elected to the grade of Fellow of the Institute of Electrical and Electronics Engineers (IEEE) with the citation "for contribution to and leadership in millimeter-wave receiver technology." In 1998 he received the EIS Award with a citation "for raising education and research of radio engineering in Finland to the top international level." The Smart and Novel Radios Research Unit (SMARAD), led by Dr. Räisänen at HUT, obtained in 2001 the national status of Center of Excellence in Research from The Academy of Finland after competition and international review. Dr. Räisänen was the secretary general of the Twelfth European Microwave Conference in 1982. He was the chairman of the IEEE MTT/AP chapter in Finland from 1987 to 1992. He was the conference chairman for the Twenty-Second European Microwave Conference in 1992, and for the ESA Workshop on Millimetre Wave Technology and Applications in 1998. From 1997 to 2000 he served as vice-rector for research and international relations of HUT. Currently he serves as an associate editor of the *IEEE Transactions on Microwave Theory and Techniques.*

Arto Lehto received a Diploma Engineer (M.Sc.), a Licentiate of Science (Tech), and a Doctor of Science (Tech) in electrical engineering from HUT, in 1981, 1986, and 1990, respectively. Since 1981 he has held different teaching and research positions at HUT. Currently he is the docent of radio engineering at HUT. Dr. Lehto has authored and coauthored more than 80 scientific or technical papers about antenna measurement techniques, low-profile antennas, and millimeter-wave components. He has also authored or coauthored eight books (all in Finnish and published by Otatieto): *Microwave Measurement Techniques* (1991 with A. V. Räisänen), *Radio Engineering* (1992 with A. V. Räisänen), *RF and Microwave Techniques* (1994 with A. V. Räisänen), *Exercises for Radio Engineering* (1996 with J. Louhi), *Millimeter-Wave Techniques* (1997 with A. V. Räisänen), *Radar Engineering* (1998 with O. Klemola), *Fundamentals of Radio Engineering* (2001 with A. V. Räisänen), and *Exercises for RF and Microwave Techniques* (2002 with V. Möttönen). He also coauthored a chapter, "Antenna Measurements" with P. Vainikainen, in J. D. Kraus and R. J. Marhefka, *Antennas for All Applications, Third Edition* (McGraw-Hill, 2002).

Index

For further information on these and other Artech House titles, including previously considered out-of-print books now available through our In-Print-Forever® (IPF®) program, contact:

Artech House
685 Canton Street
Norwood, MA 02062
Phone: 781-769-9750
Fax: 781-769-6334
e-mail: artech@artechhouse.com

Artech House
46 Gillingham Street
London SW1V 1AH UK
Phone: +44 (0)20 7596-8750
Fax: +44 (0)20 7630-0166
e-mail: artech-uk@artechhouse.com

Find us on the World Wide Web at:
www.artechhouse.com

The Artech House Universal Personal Communications Series

Ramjee Prasad, Series Editor